Early U.S. Blackball Teams
in Cuba

Early U.S. Blackball Teams in Cuba

*Box Scores, Rosters
and Statistics from the
Files of Cuba's Foremost
Baseball Researcher*

SEVERO NIETO

Foreword by PETER C. BJARKMAN

McFarland & Company, Inc., Publishers
Jefferson, North Carolina, and London

LIBRARY OF CONGRESS CATALOGUING-IN-PUBLICATION DATA

Nieto, Severo, 1923–[2005]
Early U.S. blackball teams in Cuba : box scores, rosters and statistics
from the files of Cuba's foremost baseball researcher / Severo Nieto ;
foreword by Peter C. Bjarkman.
p.   cm.
Includes bibliographical references and index.

ISBN 978-0-7864-1928-9
softcover : 50# alkaline paper

1. Baseball — Cuba — History.   2. Baseball — Statistics.   3. African
American baseball players — History — 20th century.   I. Title.
GV863.25.A1N54   2008   796.357097291 — dc22   2007052587

British Library cataloguing data are available

On the cover: John Henry "Pop" Lloyd; background
©2008 Index Stock

Manufactured in the United States of America

McFarland & Company, Inc., Publishers
Box 611, Jefferson, North Carolina 28640
www.mcfarlandpub.com

Table of Contents

Foreword

Peter C. Bjarkman

This deceptively thin yet data-rich and groundbreaking volume provides a potential treasure trove for baseball scholars. It should be especially welcomed by those whose interests cluster primarily around early professional Cuban baseball, or whose Holy Grails are the long-buried details surrounding North America's blackball stars who populated the disgraceful decades separating an infamous "gentlemen's agreement" from post-war integration of our U.S. big league game. These pages contain a large dose of hard facts—game dates, historic match-ups, batting and pitching stats, and other such treasured ephemera—certain to fill in many missing corners and also to fuel numerous new scholarly debates. But this work is also just as much a fitting monument to a legendary researcher as it is a long-awaited new window on Cuba's vaunted and veiled baseball past. These pages are the legacy of a tenacious scholar who long struggled alone against large odds to adequately document the horribly jumbled records of the sport that was both his professional passion and his life-long recreational obsession. When Havana-native Severo Nieto succumbed at age 82, on October 11 of 2005, a remarkable chapter was regrettably closed on the too-long-mysterious realm of old-time Cuban baseball.

For those few of us American researchers who traveled the unsanctioned byways of Cuba during the past decade, Severo (Say-VER-oh) Nieto was a cherished friend as well as a remarkable gnome-like character and constant professional inspiration. No visit to Havana was complete for any serious student of the island's national game without a visit to Severo's haunts and a peak into his always growing archives. Milton Jamail wrote lovingly of his own first visit with Señor Nieto in the pages of *Full Count: Inside Cuban Baseball* (1999). Journalist Matt Welch penned a remarkable tribute (2002) which poignantly captured much of Nieto's career mission, even if it somewhat distorted the purported "sad plight" of a researcher living in Cuba in order to illustrate Welch's rather obvious anti–Castro political agenda. My own indebtedness to Severo Nieto and his dedicated work has already been carefully laid out in several places in my own recent McFarland volume surveying the lengthy span of Cuban baseball history.

Jamail's portrait of Nieto and his quaint, cluttered Havana residence (*Full Count*, 17–18) is as concise and accurate as anything ever written about the beloved Cuban journalist-turned-historian. Jamail was understandably quite shocked when first discovering the extensiveness of the aged researcher's hidden Cuban archives. But he was even more impressed by Severo's passion for sharing his treasured materials—in Jamail's case, details of the life of Nemesio Guilló who reportedly first brought "the American game" to the island in December 1864. Jamail would discover that Nieto not only had been a personal friend of the pioneer ballplayer's nephew (they worked together in the Ministry of Public Works during the Second World War) but had maintained detailed computer files on Guilló's significant though largely undocumented career ("after fifty-five years of working on a typewriter, Nieto began transferring more than half a century of research onto floppy disks when he was already seventy years old").

Of course part of that passion for sharing his discoveries was driven by a self-serving motive endemic to all of us who devote endless hours to uncovering and then retelling the hidden moments of the game's cherished past. Severo desperately wanted an appreciative audience for his work. He was always proposing to those of us who visited with him that perhaps his newest American comrade of the moment could find him a contract with an American publisher. Perhaps there could someday be an English-language version of one of his many works-in-progress that would be co-written with an understanding and well-connected American friend. In this way readers in the land of the big leagues would know something more of both Cuban baseball and the extensive labors that he himself had expended in documenting its glories. It was a reasonable enough wish and one that is ironically now being at least partially fulfilled, less than two years after his own most unwelcome death.

Nieto was also an anomaly in his own land. While no corner of the world is more passionate about the bat and ball sport, it is also a fact that most Cubans have been focused in recent decades almost exclusively on the amateur league spectacle that overnight replaced professional baseball in Havana in 1962. But Severo's unrivaled passions for his country's national pastime ran in a slightly different direction. His narrow fascination lay with the players, teams and games of his distant youth — a time when oversized blackball legends of both American and Cuban birthright pranced on the local diamonds and when he personally watched nonpareils like Martin Dihigo, Adolfo Luque and Miguel Angel González performing in the living flesh. During a post-revolution era that largely ignored the moribund professional game, Nieto savored most of his ballpark thrills in the dusty archives of the National Library and not in the dimly lit press box at stately if deteriorating Latin American Stadium.

Nieto was not entirely unique in his passions for the detailed records of Cuba's bygone baseball days. Over the years Milton Jamail and I, and others privileged to roam Havana frequently, discovered a small battalion of like-spirits who shared a similar avocation-turned-obsession. One is Alberto Pestana, seventy-something veteran journalist who spends his "retirement years" maintaining detailed statistics for the island's current high-quality national league. Pestana, like Nieto, has also long labored to carefully glean the archives of old newspapers and to painstakingly correct and amend the many inaccuracies of early-century pro Cuban league records. Pestana's particular specialties, however, were the earliest years of Cuban national team triumphs (pre-revolution) in international amateur venues like the Amateur World Series (today's IBAF World Cup) and Central American Games. While well past the age of comfortable retirement, Pestana is still hard at work as both a Cuban League servant (still doing much of his painstaking data-keeping by hand and not on a new-fangled computer) and tenacious recreational researcher; in both capacities he has been of immense help over the years to this particular author during my own efforts to document the full scope of Cuba's remarkable baseball history.

Another such legendary figure was the recently deceased Edel Casas, also portrayed by Jamail in *Full Count* and once memorialized by Thomas Boswell in the pages of *How Life Imitates the World Series* (1982); for years Casas amazed American visitors, who came to know him as "The Walking and Talking Cuban Baseball Encyclopedia" because he was virtually impossible to stump with even the most arcane factoid from big league records and lore. (The remarkable man could recite verbatim line-ups from any big league team of the 20s or 30s even if he had trouble pronouncing the Anglo names.) Casas also differed from Nieto, mainly in the fact that his own expertise fell heavily on the major league game up north which he had never seen in person. One of the genuine surprises for any American visitor to Havana who tries to tap the island's baseball culture is indeed the number of Cubans who are generally better informed about the distant majors—without any regular radio or press contact—than most American fans.

Yet if Nieto was not entirely unique in either his historical expertise or his often stunning mastery of baseball trivia, he was indeed unrivalled in the single-mindedness of his life-long obsessions. Nieto's whole existence seemed to be devoted to writing about and documenting the game which across the twentieth century became one of the primary signposts of Cuban culture. Born in the age of Babe Ruth (1923 to be precise), Severo witnessed the final three dwindling decades of the Cuban professional league firsthand as a working journalist. When the revolution came he did not flee the island (as did many professional class veterans of the Old Guard) but continued to practice his trade at home with undiminished enthusiasms. As a senior writer at the newly minted *Prensa Latina* government news agency in the early years of the revolution, he not only recorded the Havana sports scene but also trained and inspired many young journalists in the craft of sports journalism.

One who benefited from this tutelage was destined to become a living legend in his own right. Eddy Martin over the final third of the twentieth century would immerge as the most recognizable voice of Cuban radio and television baseball. Martin's own premature passing at age 77 (he was still a nightly presence as number one league and national team television play-by-play man) has now left the Cuban baseball world with a huge void that may never adequately be filled. But shortly before his demise Eddy Martin himself would fondly remember Nieto in his own recent volume of memoirs, published in Havana shortly before the tragic automobile crash which snuffed out his own career in July 2006. Within the preface to *Memorias a los setenta y ...* (2004) Martin generously credited Nieto's immense baseball archives as playing a vital role in the writing of his own memoirs. And still another notable contemporary Cuban journalist trained by Nieto was Martin Hacthoun, a fluent English speaker as well verse in world politics as in baseball. Before his recent posting to the Far East as *Prensa Latina*'s representative in Hanoi, Hacthoun was one Cuban journalist that most American baseball researchers setting foot in Havana crossed paths with and quickly befriended, usually sooner rather than later.

This extent of Severo Nieto's personal influence and matchless reputation both in Havana and elsewhere across his native island was altogether apparent at the time of his untimely death. An internet version of the periodical *Juventud Rebelde* (an official communist party publication) understatedly called him "one of the nation's most prestigious journalists." *Prensa Latina* colleague and one-time apprentice Faustino Triana wrote that "The death of Severo Nieto—our dear Severo—is a lamentable fact that only reminds us painfully of the inevitable course of life." Triana also offered that "Nieto was in every sense an example of a true teacher of journalists." Nieto's extensive practical service to his nation and his colleagues was also fondly remembered and recorded in numerous posthumous tributes. Readers were reminded that he had long served as vice president of the National Commission of Cuban Sports Historians. He had won numerous national writing awards that were fully listed in dozens of published obituaries. And he had even taken out memberships during the final decade of his life in such prestigious external fraternities as The Baseball Writers of America (BBWA) and The Society for American Baseball Research (SABR). Former apprentice Martin Hacthoun (writing to this author from Hanoi) expressed the sentiments of many who followed in Nieto's footsteps by remarking that he himself had seemingly now lost a spiritual grandfather, since it had been Nieto who had first taken him under his wing and trained him as a young journalist way back the early eighties.

But for all his mentoring of fellow journalists and nurturing of cub reporters—and all his own practice of his journalistic craft with *Prensa Libre* before the revolution, and with the communist government news agency *Prensa Latina* after the sweeping events of 1959 and until his "official" retirement in 1987—it was a dedicated researcher into the Cuban game's earliest days that Severo Nieto left his true legacy. It is a legacy at least partially but not entirely revealed in this present volume. As the new amateur-controlled game fostered by the retooled socialist society swept the country, and as the glorious days of professional winter leagues faded into the distant past, Nieto became one of the shrinking cadre of island *aficionados* who remained adamant in his passions for the details and minutia of the first half-century of the island's national pastime. In the process he himself became something of a ballpark relic. As social priorities and athletic tastes shifted, Severo Nieto was over the years increasingly isolated in his crusade to document, update, preserve and correct his laboriously reconstructed statistical records of eight decades of Cuban professional contests.

Writing for an on-line magazine entitled *Reason-online*, free-lance journalist Matt Welch brought Nieto and his work to the attention of North American readers in June 2002 by documenting the aging writer's struggle as a singular exemplar of evils surrounding an ongoing political stalemate between the Castro and Washington governments. For Welch, who had visited with the then-79-year-old researcher during his own self-announced "illegal" visit to the island earlier that same year, Nieto was a fitting octogenarian "poster boy" for the follies of U.S.-Cuba political wrangling — perhaps "the most peculiar and unsung victim" of Fidel's tyranny and an equal pernicious U.S. economic embargo.

From Welch's viewpoint, there could not be a more poignant example of the standoff which "starves both sides of meaningful and important communication." Nieto had told his visitor of the difficulties of finding publishing outlets for his research projects in a nation faced with severe shortages of printing paper — shortages which Welch then claims Fidel Castro himself exacerbated by "reserving precious pulp for odes to Cuba's famed amateur athletic accomplishments while rejecting books that glorify anything about the pre-revolution era." And if Nieto's potential books about Cuba's pro-baseball glory days were repeatedly blocked by a communist government unwilling to acknowledge much less celebrate its history with the professional sport, there were also no avenues available to search for a publisher north of the Straits of Florida. Few American researchers could visit or communicate, and contact with colleagues and publishing houses up north were altogether sabotaged by the Helms-Burton policies which made travel and telephone or email contacts virtually impossible. It was seemingly a sad tale indeed. But Welch didn't quite get the story right, and the picture he painted was certainly not the best service that Nieto's work and his long struggles to publish his research might have received.

Nieto had most certainly not "basically invented Cuban baseball research in 1955" with his one pre-revolution published book (*Béisbol Cubano*, coauthored with Gabino Delgado) as Welch over-enthusiastically contends in his internet hagiography. Valuable as that thin 186-page volume is for its lists of records and statistical leaders from the Cuban Professional League (then only a half-dozen years short of its demise), it was definitely not the island's "first-ever baseball encyclopedia" (Welch's description) but instead drew rather heavily from an earlier volume by Raúl Díez Muro (*Historia del base ball profesional de Cuba*, 1949), itself crammed with line scores, rosters, yearly standings and even turn-of-the-century photographs. Delgado and Nieto provided much amplified statistical data not offered by Díez Muro (especially their lists of individual batting and pitching leaders, drawn from painstaking perusal of old newspaper records); without question they brought Cuban baseball research to a new level of semi-completeness and dedicated professionalism. Thereafter Nieto continued to fine tune his accumulation of dusty archives throughout the long years following the island sport's rapid transition to strictly amateur play and its tumble off the U.S. baseball radar screen.

It is true enough that the type of research Nieto was doing was not particularly easy, as Welch makes quite abundantly clear. A third world country devoid of easy access to computers, Xerox copiers, expendable income for book-purchasing (which in turn drives a publishing industry), and at times even pencils and paper, is assuredly not a hospitable environment for the academic researcher in any field. In my early years of regular Cuba travel (1997–2001) I found myself regularly carrying pencils and notepads to my friend Marcelo Sánchez, as well as antique carbon ribbons for an ancient Underwood manual typewriter, so that Marcelo could carry on his own passion of expanding lists of Cuban big leaguers and their wintertime island stats. But Nieto's work was difficult mostly for reasons that were not at all driven merely by the supposed sordidness of the Castro government or the admitted economic deprivation fostered in large part by the U.S. embargo of the island.

Certainly book publishing was increasingly difficult in Havana in the 1980s and 1990s, but that was already decades into Nieto's career as a dedicated baseball researcher and investigator of old newspaper archives. The doors to publishers in Havana were never altogether closed to a scholar with Nieto's considerable hometown reputation, and he did indeed publish some of his best work, both early and late in his career. (Welch's bald statement that none of his major research projects were published as of June 2002 was blatantly false.) There was his already-mentioned book with Delgado in 1955. And then after years of tinkering, his massive collections of data began to see further light in Havana during the most recent decade. There was a book on the Pan American Games released in 1995 by Cuba's leading sports publisher, Editorial Científico-Técnica. And in the last couple years of his life there were his immensely helpful even if regrettably sketchy published biographies of pre-revolution diamond icons Conrado Marrero (Cuba's greatest amateur pitching star of the 1930s and 1940s) and José Méndez (the island's most over-sized Negro leagues legend and a most-recent Cooperstown inductee).

Despite these few efforts, however, much of Nieto's work indeed never saw the light of day beyond its obscure existence in his dust-covered archives that nearly overwhelmed his cramped four-room Havana apartment. My own office files today contain a long inventory of important projects in various stages of partial completion that Nieto urged me to carry back to the States (usually on faded and almost illegible blue mimeograph paper, but also occasionally also on 1980s-vintage plastic three-by-five floppy disks). My own office file folder on Nieto contains more than 40 pages of typed outlines for "works-in-progress"— proposed books on Negro league barnstormers in Cuba; biographies of Cristóbal Torriente, José de la Caridad Méndez, Lázaro Salazar, Cocaina García, Ramón Bragaña, and Miguel Angel González; an encyclopedia of Cuban professional baseball; tomes on Cubans in the North American Negro leagues and Cubans in the Mexican League; and much, much more. There may indeed have been some few among these projects that were finished if not polished books, as the article by Welch suggests when he states "[Nieto] has spent a half-century documenting Cuba's tremendously rich professional past in more than a dozen books, but not a single one has been published in any country." What Severo's occasional American visitors saw, however, were always bare-bones outlines and sketches and sometimes reams of box scores and statistics, but nothing that would constitute organized books ready for an editor or printer. Most of this treasure trove seemed to lie in various scattered states of still-ongoing compilation.

Why did Nieto publish so little of this massive collection of work? The answer in the end was most likely not either countrywide paper shortages or an uncooperative and perhaps hostile Castro government. It is indisputably true that for a long time in the seventies, eighties and early nineties there was not all that much interest in the pre–1959 game to be found anywhere in the streets and libraries of baseball-crazy Havana. The professional version of the sport— either the distant contemporary big leagues, or Cuba's own rich history before 1961— was never mentioned on popular Havana sports talk shows like Radio Rebelde's *Deportivamente* hosted by Roberto Pacheco. Winter league action of the pre-sixties was an armchair passion of ex-patriots in Miami, who seemingly refused to let go of the idea that Cuban baseball had peaked decades before the revolution and was now the proper realm of sad nostalgia. (For an alternative view—one that suggests that Cuba's true diamond glories lie largely in the most recent four post-revolution decades—readers are directed to my own treatments of the pre- and post–1959 game in *A History of Cuban Baseball, 1864–2006*). In Havana during the sixties, seventies, eighties and nineties it is true enough that fans and book publishers together were almost exclusively focused on a new brand of Cuban baseball and Nieto's work was thus very much out of synch with the sporting interests of most potential readers.

But by the 1990s the Cuban government and thus the Cuban print and broadcast media was no longer branding open discussions of the early-epochs professional game as strictly taboo. Several years before the end of the millennium, veteran sports journalist Jorge Alfonso was already publishing quality articles about early twentieth-century stars in the pages of the glossy government magazine *Bohemia*. Alfonso wrote loving and highly informative tribute pieces (complete with archive photos) about a full range of pre-revolution baseball icons, including Martín Dihigo, José Méndez, Iron Mike González and big-league pioneers Rafael Almeida and Armando Marsans. When Mark Rucker and I brought copies of our 1999 coffee table volume (*Smoke: The Romance and Lore of Cuban Baseball*) onto the island in 2000 to distribute to friends and to government and baseball officials who had facilitated our 1997–1999 research, the book was widely hailed both formally and informally. I appeared on Cuban television where the book was mentioned (a photo of the cover was shown); there were official presentations of the work to officials in the Cuban sports ministry (INDER), and we were saluted with an award for "advancing knowledge of Cuban baseball" by the government-sanctioned Peña Deportiva in Matanzas (a club of baseball enthusiasts largely equivalent to the Society for American Baseball Research). I mention all this to suggest that Nieto was not blocked by either politics of a sagging economy. Such events (as the honoring of my own book *Smoke*) demonstrate that any de facto ban on talk of an earlier baseball tradition in Cuba had almost entirely evaporated by the late 1990s, and even Nieto himself gained a public face during these changing times. His books on Conrado Marrero (2000) and José Méndez (2004) were published by a government press (Editorial Científico-Técnica) and officially celebrated at the annual Havana Book Fair. When Welch's internet article appeared in June 2002, Nieto's Marrero biography (never mentioned in the Welch article) had already been in Havana bookstores for two years, and his volume on José Méndez was also already in the hands of his Havana publisher (again Editorial Científico-Técnica).

If Severo Nieto had indeed ever received an official cold shoulder from government printing houses in Havana, this was definitely no longer the case by the time that Welch was penning his bleak portrait of Nieto's plight. What really held back the intrepid researcher was demonstrably not any Castro-inspired closed door policy on baseball history. The same Havana publishing house that would release Nieto's books in 2000 and 2004 had already printed a carefully crafted if somewhat sketchy biography of native Cooperstown hall of famer Martín Dihigo (penned by Matanzas resident Alfredo Santana Alonso) as far back as 1997, and that book was also officially welcomed into print at the prestigious Havana Book Fair. And to underscore the distortions in Welch's portrait of the contemporary Havana publishing scene, the same government editorial house in 2003 (the year between Welch's article and Nieto's book on Méndez) released a book entitled *Béisbol Términos y Anécdotas* (*Baseball Teams and Anecdotes*) filled with a strange mixture of tales about the amateur Cuban league, the U.S. Negro leagues and even the American big leagues. This latter book remarkably carried photos of Babe Ruth, Satchel Paige, Nolan Ryan, Casey Stengel and Mickey Mantle, among others. If ancient Cuban baseball history was not a hot topic in the latter years of the Castro reign it was definitely not forbidden. There was, then, something else behind Nieto's strange silence. It was more likely that it was the very nature of the venerable author's obsessions with his painstaking research that was always getting in the way, the very obsession which had made Severo Nieto such a fascinating icon to all of us who knew him in the first place.

The truth was that Nieto himself was a dedicated and even fanatical researcher and not very much of an enthusiastic writer. This may seem a strange set of circumstances for a man whose career was spent in journalism. Yet even as a professional writer Nieto was very much the laconic, fact-oriented newspaper man. He was not a born storyteller and the thrill was always in ferreting out lost box scores and compiling accurate baseball stats, not in weaving a finely crafted tale that might bring historic personages and lost events back to life. His joy was in searching through dusty archives and not in pounding away at his electric typewriter or computer keys. He had difficulty turning all those crusty box scores into gripping narratives that would translate the games and the athletes of a half-century ago into vibrant verbal images. And he even had difficulty in compiling his mountains of collected data in some kind of architectural structure that would provide a marketable or even readable book. If publishing opportunities were rare in Havana in the first several decades following Fidel Castro's seizure of power (especially if the subject was baseball's halcyon professional league days), a finished Nieto manuscript, ready for the editors desk and prepared to entice a potential publisher, was a rarer commodity still. Severo Nieto was always very much of an unparalleled painstaking researcher and thus also very much in need of a deadline sensitive and craft-conscious storytelling collaborator. That he wrote and spoke only Spanish didn't enhance his chances with U.S.-based publishing houses much either.

Those of us who carried back the reams of printed materials and soiled computer discs Severo often gave us from his archives— hopefully to hand over to perspective North American publishers— knew this fact all too well. There were endless lists of league standings and player statistics to be poured over and attached to a coherent story line. There were photocopies of countless lost box scores to be sorted through and given some cogent meaning. There were old photos by the batches that often sorely lacked a context. But there were almost never any contextual explanations to guide and entice the potential publisher. This is to say that there were few insights behind the raw facts and thus Nieto's valuable records of Cuban history often appeared to reveal little to someone not already fairly well versed in the island's baseball lore. Nieto uncovered skeletons and not highlight reels. When pouring over the outlines for books that he frequently handed me in Havana I frequently found myself recalling the cogent words of author and publisher John Thorn, once delivered at a SABR Convention workshop on baseball publishing in the late 1980s. Speaking to potential authors of baseball history manuscripts, Thorn asked his listeners (as best as I can recall his precise words) "What can you show me that convinces me as an editor that you can do something more than simply anchor yourself in an uncomfortable wooden library carrel for eight hours at a stretch and pour over eye-weakening microfilm?"

Nieto's two recent published biographies of Marrero and Méndez are the best illustrations of the challenges his otherwise valuable work always faced. Severo was a collector of dry records and not of lively anecdotes. He searched newspaper sports pages (those from an era when those pages were filled with line-scores and not editorials or interviews); he did not interview Marrero personally to ferret out the still-living ballplayer's own accounts of his fascinating or unique experiences. Well over half the text of this volume is devoted to retyped newspaper box scores. Such books as Nieto's "statistical biographies" of Marrero and Méndez do serve a valued purpose, of course. I have turned repeatedly in the last three years to these two books for details not found elsewhere — records of nearly every game pitched by either Marrero and Méndez on Cuban soil. There is nowhere else where I can put my hands on day-by-day results of every amateur league game Marrero ever hurled, or find the box scores (should I ever wish them) for games in which "The Black Diamond" Méndez once mesmerized barnstorming big leaguers in 1911, 1913 or 1914. But I do not ever read those books cover-to-cover to capture a flavor of either legendary athlete's diamond career, or to revisit the 98 percent of their fascinating lives not recounted in line scores of games pitched or yearly summaries of strikeout or base-on-balls totals. Roberto González Echevarría (*The Pride of Havana*) tells us more of the life and impact on Cuban baseball of both these Cuban hall-of-famers in a few well-crafted paragraphs than Nieto does in either 200-page book taken as a whole.

This is meant of course to be a much-needed explanation and not an unkind or untimely condemnation of Severo Nieto—either the gentle and generous man or the compulsive historian. He undeniably played a vital role that few if any others could ever match. He has left us a legacy of facts and figures that those of us treasuring Cuban baseball would all be poorer without. At least those of us largely interested in the facts and legends of professional baseball as it was once played in Havana in a far different bygone age. What Nieto needed to complete that legacy, however, was an understanding editor that would provide the formats and contexts for his work. That was something he rarely found. And it is also the beauty and the value of the current volume now in the hands of the present reader.

The editorial staff of McFarland (especially Gary Mitchem on baseball matters and Virginia Tobiassen conducting a voluminous correspondence in Spanish with Severo Nieto and his son Eduardo Severo Nieto Misas) have here given a forum and a life to Nieto's newly unearthed and richly rewarding data from one of the most vital corners of Cuban baseball history. Here are the detailed records of the numerous visits of North American blackball teams to Havana in the first half of the last century. This historically significant ballgames known as Cuba's "American season" have earlier been set in larger context by González Echevarría in *The Pride of Havana* (1999) and by this author in *A History of Cuban Baseball, 1864–2006* (2007). The nature and scope of the early twentieth-century Havana "American season" is explained quite well by González Echevarría, who more than likely provides sufficient accounting for the casual reader of Cuban baseball history. But for the Negro leagues researcher or Cuban league enthusiast craving precise data and hoping to trace particular seasons or the careers of individual ballplayers, here are the tons of details not accessible through other previous sources. What some of us have tried to explain in more context-sensitive narratives, Nieto's research recreates in fine-hewed isolated detail. For devotees of the Cuban or blackball games it is here possible to pour over corrected records of games long forgotten, and to fill in details about ballplayers and events that have long been lost in a mist of inaccurate or incomplete reports. I know the perusal of these rare archives will prove highly rewarding.

Peter C. Bjarkman
Lafayette, Indiana
January 2008

Preface

This book is about the series of games played between the best of the early black teams from the United States and clubs, professional and amateur, of Cuba. The information —composed mainly of rosters, box scores and statistics— is of interest to historians of those black teams and their players, early international contests, and early interracial baseball.

But the emphasis is squarely on U.S. blackball teams that made the voyage to Cuba. The motivation for such trips was clearly financial; Cuba was a country as infatuated with baseball as the United States, and the hope was for large crowds and a fair cut of the gate. Such a trip was solidly within the black baseball tradition of barnstorming, which stretches back to at least the 1880s. As Michael Lomax writes, the early black clubs remained solvent for as long as they did not by relying on local support and extended homestands (most of these clubs had no permanent home park) but by taking their game abroad. So when the Cuban X-Giants made that first trip to Cuba in 1900, the idea was not so radical as it might now appear; they were merely "expanding into an international market with promising economic potential" (*Black Baseball Entrepreneurs, 1860–1901*, 167–169).

But the reader will find no substantial discussion of this or any other topic. Nieto's intention was not to explain the American Series, or even to describe it closely. He was, as Peter Bjarkman points out in the foreword, a recorder of history. What fascinated him were the details— players, teams, games, and series that add up to a foundation in fact that others might build on. And the book certainly succeeds in filling holes in the available research. No one has previously written at length on the series, in large part because most of the primary sources— published game accounts, scorecards, records— still lie in Cuba. Newspaper coverage in the States was isolated and unpredictable, even for the traveling team's hometown black papers. One or two games out of fifteen or twenty might receive brief mention. Games were often reported secondhand and might be published weeks after the fact.

When Severo Nieto died in 2005, it became clear just how scarce reliable information is. The manuscript had just entered the editing stage, and it was quickly apparent that the author's help was needed. Items seemed to be omitted, as some chapters included brief introductory paragraphs while others launched directly into the records; biographical information for some of the players was repeated verbatim in chapter after chapter; box scores didn't add up; sentences that began in English would continue in Spanish, sometimes for multiple paragraphs. Two of the chapters in the original manuscript covered trips by black teams who competed in the Cuban League. (They have been removed from the main sequence of chapters and run as appendices C and D.)

After several months of mostly fruitless research and discussion, it was decided that the manuscript should be published more or less as it was submitted. Most of the information Nieto had hoped to include was in place, and it was impractical to think that someone else could satisfactorily address its omissions and peculiarities. In general, then, the published chapters differ in minor ways from the manuscript versions. A handful of game reports (most translated by Peter Bjarkman) have been added, the biographical and team information is in places enhanced by new information, and a few names have been corrected. One or two plainly extraneous sections (on, for instance, games played in the United States by teams that later traveled to Cuba) have been cut. Two series registers, one for batting and one for pitching, have been compiled from statistics Nieto provided at the end of each chapter (except 1900, for which even he was unable to dig up detailed records).

We thank Peter Bjarkman, who knew Severo Nieto, for his lengthy foreword about the Cuban writer's life and career.

The Editors at McFarland

♦ 1 ♦

1900
Cuban X-Giants

In 1900, the Cuban X-Giants became the first black team from the United States to visit Cuba. It would be the first of a handful of trips the team made to the island.

Among the eleven players manager E.B. Lamar took with him in 1900, the standouts were veteran catcher Clarence Williams, second baseman Charles Grant, shortstop and power hitter Grant Johnson, and rookie pitcher Andrew "Rube" Foster.

Roster

Player	Position	Regular Season Club, 1900
Charles "Kid" Carter	p	Independent
Charles Grant	2b	Chicago Columbia Giants
Andrew Jackson	3b	X-Giants (1899)
William Jackson	cf	X-Giants
Robert Jordan	cf	X-Giants
John Nelson	p,rf	X-Giants
Parker	cf	Genuine Cuban Giants
James Robinson	p	X-Giants
Sol White	ss	Chicago Columbia Giants
Clarence Williams	c	Independent
Ed Wilson	1b	X-Giants

The Havana newspapers took note of the games planned for the Cuban X-Giants. The January 27, 1900, issue of *El Nuevo País* announced the team's imminent arrival, noting that they had compiled a record of 110 wins and only 21 losses.* On February 10, *El Nuevo Pais* published another report:

> Ayer tarde ha embarcado en New York en el vapor Mexico de la Linea Ward, debiendo llegar el miercoles a esta ciudad la celebre novena de jugadores de color que con el nombre de Cuban Giants (Gigantes Cubanos), existe organizada en Estados Unidos hace mas de 20 años.
>
> Según carta que tenemos a la vista el notable club profesional viene completo, sin que le falte un solo player, figurando entre estos los afamados pitchers Robinson, Nelson y Carter; Williams y Parker, catchers; Grant, notable segunda base; Wilson, primera base; White, short-stop; A. Jackson, tercera base; y sus tres notables outfielders Nelson, R. Jordan y Jackson.
>
> [Departing yesterday afternoon from New York, on the Ward line's ship *Mexico*, were the cele-

---

*Here and in other reports the "X" was dropped from the club's name. The "Cuban Giants," one of the earliest — and perhaps the first — all-professional black team, had formed in 1885, several years before. Just as Charles Comiskey would a few years later adopt "White Stockings," tweaking the nose of the cross-town rival long known by that name, X-Giants owner E.B. Lamar seized a name well established in baseball circles, capitalizing on the earlier club's popularity and renown. And as Roberto González Echeverría adds in *The Pride of Havana*, the name functioned as a pun; a number of the original payers were formerly Cuban Giants, or ex–Giants.

brated colored nine called the Cuban Giants, a team that has existed in the United States for more than 20 years. They are expected to arrive in this city on Wednesday.

According to a letter we have in hand, this notable professional club will arrive complete, without a single player missing. Among their ranks are the famous pitchers Robinson, Nelson, and Carter; Williams and Parker, catchers; Grant, the noted second baseman; Wilson, first base; White, short-stop; A. Jackson, third base; and the three notable outfielders Nelson, R. Jordan, and Jackson.]

An eight-game schedule, later expanded, had been arranged against local competition:

Sunday, Feb.18: vs. Cuba	Thursday, Mar. 8: vs. Cuba
Thursday, Feb. 22: vs. Havana	Thursday, Mar. 15: vs. Almendares
Sunday, Feb. 25: vs. Almendares	Sunday, Mar. 18: vs. All-Cubans
Sunday, Mar. 4: vs. Havana	Thursday, Mar. 22: Picked nine of Colón

The Scores

GAME ONE: THURSDAY, FEBRUARY 15

X-Giants	13
Almendares	6

Playing for Almendares were Valentín González, Alfredo Arcaño, Bernardo P. Carrillo, Ramón P. Carrillo, José María Baeza, Pedro Pablo Baeza, Esteban Prats, Juan M. Magriñat, José Zubillaga, Armando Molina, de Miguel, Vidal, Penichet, Silva and others.

GAME TWO: SUNDAY, FEBRUARY 18

The game was called for rain.

GAME THREE: THURSDAY, FEBRUARY 22

X-Giants	000	012	400	7
Cuba	300	000	002	5

On February 27, *El Nuevo País* assessed the U.S. club this way: "A la excepción del catcher Williams, la primera base Wilson y la segunda base Grant, los demas son ni mas ni menos que los nuestros y hasta inferiores." ["With the exception of catcher Williams, first baseman Wilson and second baseman Grant, the rest seem no better than ours, and might be inferior."]

GAME FOUR: SUNDAY, FEBRUARY 25

X-Giants	004	000	002	6
Havana	003	001	010	5

James Robinson doubled against Havana starting pitcher José Romero. Standouts on the Cuban team were Bernardo Carrillo and Sirique, who made a barehanded catch of a strong line drive by Grant. A costly error by José Zubillaga might have been the difference in the game.

GAME FIVE: SUNDAY, MARCH 4

X-Giants	13
Almendares	6

Playing for Almandares were Valentín González, Alfredo Arcaño, Bernardo Carrillo, Ramón Carrillo, José María Baeza, Pedro Pablo Baeza, Esteban Prats, Juan M. Magriñat, José Zubillaga, Armando Molina, de Miguel, Vidal, Penichet, Silva and others. The press spoke highly of Clarence Williams.

GAME SIX: THURSDAY, MARCH 8

Criollos	003	003	000	6	12	3
Cuban X-Giants	030	000	100	4	4	3

Triples: Juan Magriñat and V. González
Double: Carlos Royer

GAME SEVEN: SUNDAY, MARCH 11

Cuba	010	020	120	6
X-Giants	010	601	00x	8

Multiple accounts of the game indicate that a brawl erupted among the players.

GAME EIGHT: SUNDAY, MARCH 18, IN REGLA

X-Giants	304	611	000	15
Libertad	005	203	001	11

GAME NINE: SUNDAY, MARCH 25 (FIRST GAME)

Cuba	101	000	000	2
X-Giants	000	020	13x	6

GAME TEN: SUNDAY, MARCH 25 (SECOND GAME)

X-Giants	101	002	000	4
Cuba	000	100	000	1

GAME ELEVEN: MONDAY, MARCH 26

10 de Octubre	000	000	000	0
X-Giants	105	143	00x	14

GAME TWELVE: THURSDAY, MARCH 30

Invencible	000	100	001	2
X-Giants	001	030	00x	4

Playing for Invencible were Carlos Royer (c), Armando Molina (p), Esteban Prats (1b), Valentín González (2b), Carlos Morán (3b), Juan M. Magriñat (ss), Alfredo Arcaño (lf), Manuel Martínez (cf) and Rafael "Felo" Rodríguez (rf).

GAME THIRTEEN: SATURDAY, APRIL 1

Criollos	102	300	000	6
X-Giants	001	002	100	4

Playing for Criollos were Armando Molina (p), Carlos Royer (c), Esteban Prats (1b), Felo Rodríguez (2b), A. Silva (3b), Juan M. Magriñat (ss), Florentino González (1f), José María Baeza (cf) and Julio Vidal (rf).

Game Fourteen: Monday, April 3

Independencia	102	200	010	6
X-Giants	200	401	13x	10

Game Fifteen: Saturday, April 8

X-Giants	200	011	003	7
Havana	104	000	23x	10

Game Sixteen: Sunday, April 9

X-Giants	000	040	000	4
Criollos	000	201	000	3

A final table, which carried the title "Individual Pitching Statistics," has been omitted. The table included no data for the three pitchers listed — Kid Carter, John Nelson, and James Robinson — but did indicate that the Giants played a total of 17 games in Cuba, winning 14 and losing 3 for a winning percentage of .825. This despite the inclusion of information for only 15 games.* The table below shows the club standings according to the information presented in this chapter:

Position	Club	G	W	L	T	Pct
1.	X-Giants	15	12	3	0	.800
2.	Criollos	3	2	1	0	.666
3.	Havana	2	1	1	0	.500
t4.	Libertad	1	0	1	0	.000
t4.	10 de Octubre	1	0	1	0	.000
t4.	Indepencia	2	0	2	0	.000
t4.	Almendares	2	0	2	0	.000
t4.	Cuba	3	0	3	0	.000

*At least one other source claims that the number of games played was higher than 17. According to the June 11, 1902, issue of the *Wellsboro, PA, Agitator*, "In 1900 the Cuban X Giants played nineteen games in Cuba, winning sixteen. The Habana was the only club which defeated them, winning three out of five from the Giants."

◆ 2 ◆
1903
Cuban X-Giants

After a two-year absence from Cuba, the X-Giants returned to the island for a series of games against local clubs, some of them picked nines. Fresh off of their defeat of the Philadelphia Giants for the U.S. blackball championship, the X-Giants arrived in Havana in late November 1903, the X-Giants played their first match on December 1. They remained in Cuba a little more than three weeks, playing ten games. Despite a roster full of stars, the X-Giants enjoyed little success against the Cuban teams, winning only two games while losing seven and tying one.

Roster

Player	Position	Regular Season Club, 1903
Andrew "Rube" Foster	p,rf	X-Giants
Charles Grant	2b	X-Giants
J. Preston "Pete" Hill	cf	Philadelphia Giants
John A. Hill	3b	X-Giants
Grant Johnson	ss,lf	X-Giants
Robert Jordan	ss,lf	X-Giants
Daniel McClellan	lf,p	X-Giants
Clarence Williams	c	X-Giants
Ed Wilson	p,lf	X-Giants
George Wilson	rf	Independent Team
Ray Wilson	1b	X-Giants

Andrew "Rube" Foster, a pitcher, started with the Chicago Union Giants in 1902 before moving to the Cuban X-Giants in 1903. In the just-concluded championship series against the Philadelphia Giants, Foster had dominated the competition, winning four games for the X-Giants, who claimed five victories in seven contests.

Charles "Tokohoma" Grant, second base, began his career in 1896 with the Page Fence Giants (Adrian, Michigan) and played for the Columbia Giants before joining the Cuban X-Giants. The story behind Grant's nickname will be familiar to many who have read about this great 19th-century player. According to Sol White and others, John McGraw saw Grant play for a black club while the Baltimore Orioles were in Hot Springs, Arkansas, for spring training in 1901. Impressed with the second baseman's talent and always eager to seize an advantage, McGraw tried to sign Grant and pass him off as a "full-blooded Cherokee" named Tokohoma (sometimes spelled, incorrectly, as "Tokahoma"). McGraw had apparently gotten the name from a creek near Hot Springs. Back in Baltimore, the well-known Grant was quickly recognized, his identity made public, and McGraw was forced to release the player from the Orioles roster.

J. Preston "Pete" Hill, an outfielder, started his career in 1903 with the Philadelphia Giants.

Hill, who began his Hall of Fame career in 1899, was 23 when he traveled with the X-Giants to Cuba in 1903. His biography at the National Baseball Hall of Fame indicates that Hill was an exceptional center fielder with a strong throwing arm. A left-handed batter, he was credited by Cum Posey (Peterson, *Only the Ball Was White*, p. 244) as "the most consistent hitter of his time."

John Hill, the third baseman, started with the Genuine Cuban Giants in 1900 and also played for the Philadelphia Giants before joining the Cuban X-Giants. He would go on to play for the Brooklyn Royal Giants in 1908, though according to Nieto it was John Preston "Pete" Hill, the Hall of Famer, who accompanied that club to Cuba for the American Series.

Grant Johnson, deadball-era shortstop, earned the nickname "Home Run" with his powerful right-handed swing. In 1895 he began a career that would take him to the best clubs in the early years of the twentieth century. Before joining the Cuban X-Giants, he played with the Page Fence Giants (Adrian, Michigan), the Columbia Giants, and the Brooklyn Royal Giants. Johnson's career in black baseball was well established by the time he joined Lamar and the X-Giants in Cuba. Having started his career in 1895, Johnson was already 29 at the time of the trip. He would later return to Cuba, playing for the Havana Reds against the 1910 Detroit Tigers and batting .412 against big-league pitching (Peterson, *Only the Ball Was White*, p. 72).

Robert Jordan, an outfielder, began with the Cuban Giants in 1896. He played both catcher and first base before joining the Cuban X-Giants.

Daniel McClellan, pitcher and outfielder, started his career with the Cuban X-Giants and would go on to play for several big-name teams, including the Philadelphia and the Lincoln Giants, in a career that stretched until 1930.

Clarence Williams, catcher, began his career with the Cuban Giants in 1886. He also played for the New York Gorhams and the Cuban X-Giants. Williams was described, in an article in the May 10, 1886, *Trenton, NJ, Times* as a "heavy batsman, fine base runner and good catcher (White, *History of Colored Baseball*, p. 131).

Ed Wilson, a pitcher and outfielder, started with the Cuban X-Giants in 1896. According to Robert Peterson's *Only the Ball Was White*, Ed Wilson's career did begin in 1896, and with the X-Giants; but he was a first baseman. A pitcher named Edward Wilson began his career two years later, in 1898, playing in the Iron and Oil League for the Celeron Acme Colored Giants (p. 397). It should be noted, however, that players who made the trip to Cuba often played out of position.

F. "George" Wilson, an outfielder, started with the Page Fence Giants in 1896 and also played for the Columbia Giants and the Chicago Union Giants. Wilson was better known as a pitcher. Sol White wrote of him that he had "pitched some wonderful games against the strongest teams of the West. Wilson is one of the most difficult men to hit among the colored pitchers. He is a 'bronzed Waddell' when right" (*History of Colored Baseball*, pp. 63–65).

Ray Wilson, first baseman, began with the Cuban X-Giants in 1902. His career stretched at least until 1909, when he played with the Philadelphia Giants.

Games Played

Date	Winning Club		Losing Club		Winning Pitcher	Losing Pitcher
Dec. 1	Colombia	6	Cuban X-Gs	3	G. Cárdenas 1–0	E. Wilson 0–1
Dec. 3	Nuevo Azul	4	Cuban X-Gs	3	J. Romero 1–0	G. Johnson 0–1
Dec. 6	Colombia	2	Cuban X-Gs	1	G. Cárdenas 2–0	A. Foster 0–1
Dec. 8	Cuban X-Gs	4	Nuevo Azul	0	E. Wilson 1–1	J. Romero 1–1
Dec. 10	San Francisco	10	Cuban X-Gs	3	B.P. Carrillo 1–0	D. McClellan 0–1
Dec. 13	Cuban X-Gs	3	Nuevo Azul	1	A. Foster 1–1	J. Romero 1–2
Dec. 14	Clío	2	Cuban X-Gs	1	J. Violá 1–0	E.Wilson 1–2
Dec. 17	Criollo	4	Cuban X-Gs	0	B.P. Carrillo 2–0	D. McClellan 0–2
Dec. 20	Criollo	3	Cuban X-Gs	2	B.P. Carrillo 3–0	A. Foster 1–2

Date	Winning Club		Losing Club		Winning Pitcher	Losing Pitcher
Dec. 21 (10)	Criollo	2	Cuban X-Gs	2	(Tied)	

Club Standings

Pos	Club	G	W	L	T	Pct
1–2	Colombia	2	2	0	0	1.000
1–2	Criollo	3	2	0	1	1.000
T3	San Francisco	1	1	0	0	1.000
T3	Clío	1	1	0	0	1.000
5	Nuevo Azul	3	1	2	0	.333
6	Cuban X-Giants	10	2	7	1	.222

The Games

GAME ONE: TUESDAY, DECEMBER 1

Colombia	Pos	AB	R	H	O	A	E	Cuban X-Giants	Pos	AB	R	H	O	A	E
R. Valdés	lf	4	1	0	2	0	0	C. Grant	2b	5	0	0	2	4	2
A. Cabañas	cf	3	1	1	4	0	0	R. Jordan	lf,ss	5	0	0	1	0	3
V. González	2b	5	2	1	0	1	3	G. Johnson	ss,p	5	1	0	0	2	0
J. Castillo	1b	5	1	1	9	0	0	J.P. Hill	cf	5	0	0	3	0	0
G. González	c	5	0	1	11	0	0	C. Williams	c	2	0	0	8	1	1
R. Almeida	ss	4	0	1	2	4	2	R. Wilson	1b	3	0	0	14	0	0
A. Zaldivar	3b	4	0	0	1	0	1	J. Hill	3b	4	1	2	1	3	1
G. Cárdenas	p	4	0	0	0	3	0	F. Wilson	rf	4	1	0	1	0	0
L. Urrutia	rf	3	0	0	0	0	0	E. Wilson	p,lf	4	0	0	0	0	0
Totals		37	6	5	30	8	6	Totals		37	3	2	30	10	7

```
Colombia        000   100   020   3   6 (10 innings)
Cuban X-Giants  002   001   000   0   3
```

Bases on balls: Off E. Wilson 4, G. Johnson 0, G. Cárdenas 3
Strikeouts: By E. Wilson 8, G. Johnson 0, G. Cárdenas 10
Hits: Off E. Wilson 5 in 9 innings; G. Cárdenas, 2 in 10 innings
Winning pitcher: G. Cárdenas
Losing pitcher: E. Wilson

GAME TWO: THURSDAY, DECEMBER 3

Cuban X-Giants	Pos	AB	R	H	O	A	E	Nuevo Azul	Pos	AB	R	H	O	A	E
C. Grant	2b	3	0	0	2	3	1	A. Cabrera	2b	4	0	0	2	4	0
R. Jordan	ss	4	1	0	2	2	0	B.P. Carrillo	ss	4	1	2	1	4	1
G. Johnson	p	3	1	0	0	3	0	H. Hidalgo	cf	3	1	1	0	0	2
D. McClellan	lf	4	1	1	1	1	0	J. Violá	3b	4	1	3	1	5	0
C. Williams	c	3	0	0	4	1	1	J. Romero	p	3	1	0	0	6	0
R. Wilson	1b	3	0	0	10	0	0	A. Molina	1b	4	0	1	17	0	0
J. Hill	3b	4	0	1	1	3	0	J. Santacruz	rf	4	0	1	1	0	0
J.P. Hill	cf	3	0	0	2	0	0	G. Sánchez	c	3	0	0	4	3	0
F. Wilson	rf	3	0	0	2	0	1	M. Jacques	lf	2	0	0	1	0	0
Totals		30	3	2	24	13	3	Totals		31	4	8	27	22	3

```
Cuban X-Giants  000   000   300   3
Nuevo Azul      300   000   01x   4
```

Sacrifice hits: Cuban X-Giants 1
Double plays: Nuevo Azul 1

Bases on balls: Off Johnson 3, Romero 4
Strikeouts: By Johnson 4, Romero 5
Winning pitcher: J. Romero
Losing pitcher: G. Johnson
Time: 1 hour 30 minutes
Umpires: F. Poyo (home) and Antonio Maria García (bases)

GAME THREE: SUNDAY, DECEMBER 6

Colombia	Pos	AB	R	H	O	A	E		Cuban X-Giants	Pos	AB	R	H	O	A	E
A. Cabañas	cf	3	1	0	1	0	0		C. Grant	2b	5	0	0	2	4	0
A. Acano	lf	4	0	1	1	0	0		R. Jordan	lf	5	0	0	2	0	0
V. González	2b	4	0	0	4	5	1		G. Johnson	ss	5	0	1	3	2	1
J. Castillo	1b	5	0	1	13	0	0		F. Wilson	rf	1	0	0	0	0	0
G. González	c	5	0	1	4	0	0		D. McClellan	rf	4	0	1	0	0	0
R. Almeida	ss	5	0	2	2	1	2		C. Williams	c	4	1	1	16	0	0
A. Mesa	3b	2	0	0	2	5	1		A. Foster	p	4	0	0	0	1	1
G. Cárdenas	p	4	0	0	0	2	2		R. Wilson	1b	4	0	1	6	0	1
L. Urrutia	rf	3	1	0	3	0	0		J. Hill	3b	4	0	2	1	0	2
Totals		35	2	4	30	13	6		Totals		40	1	6	30	7	5

Colombia	000	100	000	1	2 (10 innings)
Cuban X-Giants	000	100	000	0	1

Stolen bases: Cuban X-Giants 1, Colombia 4
Double plays: Cuban X-Giants 1, Colombia 1
Bases on balls: Off Foster 6, Cárdenas 0
Strikeouts: By Foster 14, Cárdenas 3
Passed balls: Williams 1
Winning pitcher: G. Cárdenas
Losing pitcher: A. Foster
Time: 2 hours
Umpires: Bernardo P. Carrillo (home) and Francisco Poyo (bases)

GAME FOUR: TUESDAY, DECEMBER 8

Cuban X-Giants	Pos	AB	R	H	O	A	E		Nuevo Azul	Pos	AB	R	H	O	A	E
C. Grant	2b	5	0	0	6	0	1		A. Cabrera	2b	4	0	0	0	4	0
R. Jordan	lf	5	0	0	2	0	0		B.P. Carrillo	ss	4	0	1	3	2	2
G. Johnson	ss	4	2	2	0	5	1		J. Violá	3b	3	0	2	0	0	2
E. Wilson	p,rf	4	1	2	0	4	0		H. Hidalgo	cf	4	0	0	5	0	0
C. Williams	c	4	1	1	6	1	0		A. Molina	1b	4	0	0	17	0	1
A. Foster	rf,p	4	0	0	1	0	0		J. Santacruz	lf	4	0	1	0	0	1
R. Wilson	1b	3	0	1	11	0	0		J. Romero	p	4	0	1	0	4	0
J.A. Hill	3b	3	0	0	0	5	0		G. Sánchez	c	4	0	0	7	0	0
J.P. Hill	cf	0	0	0	0	0	0		Carratala	lf	1	0	0	0	0	0
G. Wilson	cf,rf,p	4	0	1	1	0	0		Totals		32	0	5	27	15	6
Totals		36	4	7	27	15	2									

Cuban X-Giants	000	220	000	4
Nuevo Azul	000	000	000	0

Stolen bases: Cuban X-Giants 2
Double plays: Nuevo Azul 1
Bases on balls: Off J. Romero 1, E. Wilson 1, A. Foster 1, G. Johnson 1
Strikeouts: By J. Romero 5, E. Wilson 2, A. Foster 3, G. Wilson 0
Hits: Off E. Wilson 4 in 6 innings
Winning pitcher: E. Wilson
Losing pitcher: J. Romero

Time: 2 hours
Umpires: Antonio Maria García (home) and Francisco Poyo (bases)

GAME FIVE: THURSDAY, DECEMBER 10

Cuban X-Giants	Pos	AB	R	H	O	A	E	San Francisco	Pos	AB	R	H	O	A	E
C. Grant	2b	3	0	0	8	2	0	Laguardia	2b	1	0	0	0	0	2
R. Jordan	lf	4	1	1	2	0	2	J. Santacruz	rf	4	2	2	2	0	0
G. Johnson	ss	4	1	1	1	3	2	C. Morán	cf,3b	3	1	0	0	0	0
D. McClellan	p	4	1	0	0	2	0	M. Prats	lf	3	2	1	1	0	1
C. Williams	c	3	0	0	4	1	0	J. Violá	3b,2b	3	1	0	1	0	1
A. Foster	rf	4	0	0	0	0	0	R. Almeida	1b	4	2	0	6	3	0
R. Wilson	1b	2	0	1	7	0	0	A. Cabrera	ss	3	1	3	8	1	1
J. Hill	3b	3	0	0	1	0	1	B.P. Carrillo	p	4	0	0	1	2	0
J.P. Hill	cf	3	0	0	1	0	1	G. Sánchez	c	4	1	2	8	0	0
Totals		31	3	3	24	11	6	Totals		33	10	9	27	6	5

Cuban X-Giants	300	000	000	**3**
San Francisco	004	020	04x	**10**

Earned runs: Cuban X-Giants 1, San Francisco 1 (R. Almeida)
Doubles: R. Almeida
Double plays: San Francisco 1, Cuban X-Giants 1
Bases on balls: Off D. McClellan 3, B.P. Carrillo 2
Strikeouts: By D. McClellan 2, B.P. Carrillo 7
Wild pitches: D. McClellan 1
Winning pitcher: B.P. Carrillo
Losing pitcher: D. McClellan
Time: 1 hour 20 minutes
Umpires: Francisco Poyo (home) and Antonio Maria García (bases)

GAME SIX: SUNDAY, DECEMBER 13

Cuban X-Giants	Pos	AB	R	H	O	A	E	Nuevo Azul	Pos	AB	R	H	O	A	E
C. Grant	2b	4	0	1	4	2	1	C. Morán	cf	3	0	2	3	0	0
R. Jordan	lf	4	1	2	1	0	0	M. Prats	rf	4	0	0	1	0	0
G. Johnson	ss	4	1	0	4	2	2	J. Violá	2b	4	0	0	4	3	0
D. McClellan	rf	5	0	1	2	0	0	A. Cabrera	1b	4	0	0	11	0	3
C. Williams	c	3	1	0	8	2	0	R. Almeida	ss	4	0	0	1	5	0
A. Foster	p	4	0	0	0	1	0	H. Hidalgo	lf	3	1	0	1	0	0
R. Wilson	1b	4	0	1	9	0	2	J. Romero	p	4	0	1	1	0	2
J. Hill	3b	4	0	1	2	0	0	B.P. Carrillo	3b	3	0	0	0	1	2
E. Wilson	cf	4	0	0	0	0	0	G. Sánchez	c	4	0	0	5	1	0
Totals		36	3	6	27	9	5	Totals		33	1	3	27	10	7

Cuban X-Giants	200	000	010	**3**
Nuevo Azul	000	000	001	**1**

Stolen bases: Nuevo Azul 3
Double plays: Nuevo Azul 1, Cuban X-Giants 1
Bases on balls: Off J. Romero 1, A. Foster 2
Strikeouts: By J. Romero 4, A. Foster 8
Wild pitches: A. Foster
Winning pitcher: A. Foster
Losing pitcher: J. Romero
Time: 1 hour 45 minutes
Umpires: Francisco Poyo (home) and Antonio Maria García (bases)

GAME SEVEN: MONDAY, DECEMBER 14

Cuban X-Giants	Pos	AB	R	H	O	A	E
C. Grant	2b	3	1	0	3	3	0
R. Jordan	lf	4	0	0	2	0	0
G. Johnson	ss	3	0	1	0	5	2
D. McClellan	cf,p	4	0	0	3	1	1
C. Williams	c	4	0	1	3	2	0
A. Foster	rf,cf	4	0	0	0	0	0
R. Wilson	1b	3	0	1	11	0	0
J. Hill	3b	3	0	0	2	3	0
E. Wilson	p	2	0	0	0	0	0
Totals		30	1	3	24	14	3

Clío	Pos	AB	R	H	O	A	E
A. Mesa	3b	4	0	0	1	1	0
M. Prats	rf	3	0	0	1	0	0
A. Cabrera	2b	4	0	0	1	4	1
M. Alfonso	1b	4	0	0	10	0	0
J. Violá	p	4	1	0	0	2	0
R. Almeida	ss	1	0	0	0	0	0
B.P. Carrillo	ss	2	0	1	0	2	0
D. De Miguel	lf	3	1	0	0	0	2
J. Romero	cf	2	0	1	1	0	0
G. Sánchez	c	2	0	1	13	1	0
Totals:		30	2	2	27	10	3

Cuban X-Giants	100	000	000	**1**	
Clío	001	000	10x	**2**	

Earned runs: Clío 1 (J. Violá)
Home runs: J. Violá
Three-base hits: D. De Miguel
Two-base hits: J. Romero
Stolen bases: J. Romero, E. Wilson
Double plays: Cabrera, Carrillo, Alfonso
Bases on balls: Off J. Violá 2, E. Wilson 2, D. McClellan 0
Strikeouts: By J. Violá 9 (C. Grant 2, R. Jordan, G. Johnson 3, D. McClellan, A. Foster and R. Wilson), E. Wilson 2, D. McClellan 1
Hits: Off E. Wilson 2 in 7 innings
Winning pitcher: J. Violá
Losing pitcher: E. Wilson
Time: 1 hour 30 minutes
Umpires: Francisco Poyo (home) and Antonio Maria García (bases)

GAME EIGHT: THURSDAY, DECEMBER 17

Criollo	Pos	AB	R	H	O	A	E
A. Cabañas	cf	3	1	1	0	0	0
J. Violá	3b	5	0	0	2	3	0
V. González	2b	5	1	2	3	0	0
J. Castillo	1b	5	1	0	8	0	0
A. Arcano	lf	4	1	0	2	0	0
R. Almeida	ss	4	0	2	3	3	0
G. Sánchez	c	4	0	0	7	0	0
B.P. Carrillo	p	4	0	3	0	2	2
M. Prats	rf	4	0	1	2	1	0
Totals:		38	4	10	27	9	2

Cuban X-Giants	Pos	AB	R	H	O	A	E
C. Grant	2b	4	0	2	4	6	0
R. Jordan	lf	4	0	0	2	1	0
G. Johnson	ss	2	0	0	0	2	2
D. McClellan	p	4	0	0	1	4	1
C. Williams	c	4	0	0	4	0	0
A. Foster	cf	4	0	0	1	0	1
R. Wilson	1b	4	0	2	13	1	1
J. Hill	3b	4	0	0	2	2	0
E. Wilson	rf	3	0	1	0	0	0
Totals		33	0	5	27	16	5

Criollo	000	100	021	**4**
Cuban X-Giants	000	000	000	**0**

Earned runs: Criollo 3
Three-Base hits: A. Arcano, J. Castillo
Sacrifice hits: A. Cabañas 2, G. Johnson
Stolen bases: J. Castillo
Bases on balls: Off D. McClellan 2, B.P. Carrillo 1
Strikeouts: By D. McClellan 3, B.P. Carrillo 6
Wild pitches: D. McClellan, 1
Winning pitcher: B.P. Carrillo

Losing pitcher: D. McClellan
Time: 1 hour 30 minutes
Umpires: Francisco Poyo (home) and Antonio Maria García (bases)

GAME NINE: SUNDAY, DECEMBER 20

Criollo	*Pos*	*AB*	*R*	*H*	*O*	*A*	*E*
A.Cabañas	cf	2	1	0	3	0	0
J.Violá	3b	4	0	1	1	1	0
V.González	2b	4	0	1	4	3	2
J.Castillo	1b	4	0	0	10	0	0
A.Arcano	lf	3	1	1	0	0	1
R.Almeida	ss	4	0	1	2	2	3
G.Sánchez	c	3	1	0	4	1	0
B.P.Carrillo	p	3	1	0	1	3	0
M.Prats	rf	4	0	1	2	1	0
Totals		32	3	6	27	11	6

Cuban X-Giants	*Pos*	*AB*	*R*	*H*	*O*	*A*	*E*
C.Grant	2b	5	1	3	5	4	1
R.Jordan	lf	4	0	1	0	0	0
G.Johnson	ss	4	0	0	1	4	2
D.McClellan	cf	4	0	0	1	0	1
C.Williams	c	4	0	0	5	2	0
A.Foster	p	4	0	1	0	2	0
R.Wilson	1b	3	0	0	11	0	0
J.Hill	3b	4	0	0	3	3	0
E.Wilson	rf	4	0	1	1	0	0
Totals		34	2	6	27	15	4

Criollo	010	110	000	3
Cuban X-Giants	001	010	000	2

Earned runs: Criollo 1 (V.González), Cuban X-Giants 1 (G. Johnson)
Home run: V. González, G. Johnson
Double plays: Criollo 2, Cuban X-Giants 1
Bases on balls: Off B.P. Carrillo 3, A. Foster 1
Strikeouts: By B.P. Carrillo 2, A. Foster 6
Wild pitches: A. Foster 2
Passed balls: C. Williams
Winning pitcher: B.P. Carrillo
Losing pitcher: A. Foster
Time: 1 hour 30 minutes
Umpires: Antonio Maria García (home) and Francisco Poyo (bases)

GAME TEN: MONDAY, DECEMBER 21

Criollo	2 (11 innings)
Cuban X-Giants	2

Final Statistics

CUBAN X-GIANTS

Individual Pitching

Pitcher	*G*	*SG*	*CG*	*W*	*L*	*Pct*	*IP*	*R*	*H*	*W*	*K*
Andrew Foster	4	3	3	1	2	.333	31.0	6	14	10	31
Grant Johnson	2	1	1	0	1	.000	9.0	4	8	3	4
Daniel McClellan	3	2	2	0	2	.000	18.0	14	19	3	7
Ed Wilson	3	3	2	1	2	.333	22.0	8	11	7	12
Totals	12	9	8	2	7	.222	80.0	32	52	23	54

Individual Batting

Player	*Pos*	*G*	*AB*	*R*	*H*	*2B*	*3B*	*HR*	*SH*	*SB*	*Pct*
Andrew Foster	p,rf	7	28	0	1	0	0	0	0	0	.036
Charles Grant	2b	9	37	2	6	0	0	0	0	0	.108
John A. Hill	3b	9	34	1	6	0	0	0	0	0	.176

Player	Pos	G	AB	R	H	2B	3B	HR	SH	SB	Pct
J. Preston Hill	cf	5	15	0	0	0	0	0	0	0	.000
Grant Johnson	ss,lf	9	33	7	5	0	0	1	1	0	.152
Robert Jordan	ss,lf	9	39	3	4	0	0	0	0	0	.103
Daniel McClellan	lf,p	6	24	2	2	0	0	0	0	0	.083
Clarence Williams	c	9	31	3	4	0	0	0	0	0	.129
Ed Wilson	p,lf	6	21	1	4	0	0	0	0	1	.190
George Wilson	rf	3	11	1	1	0	0	0	0	0	.091
Ray Wilson	1b	9	29	0	7	0	0	0	0	0	.241
Totals		9	307	20	40	0	0	1	1	0	.130

Individual Fielding

Player	Pos	G	O	A	E	Pct
Andrew Foster	p,rf	7	2	4	2	.075
Charles Grant	2b	9	33	28	6	.910
John A. Hill	3b	9	18	17	5	.875
J. Preston Hill	cf	5	6	0	1	.857
Grant Johnson	ss,lf	9	9	28	12	.755
Robert Jordan	ss,lf	9	14	3	5	.773
Daniel McClellan	lf,p	6	6	8	3	.824
Clarence Williams	c	9	58	10	2	.971
Ed Wilson	p,lf	6	1	4	0	1000
George Wilson	rf	3	4	0	1	.800
Ray Wilson	1b	9	92	1	4	.990
Totals		9	240	110	41	.895

CRIOLLO

Individual Pitching

Pitcher	G	CG	W	L	T	Pct	IP	R	H	W	K	ERA
B.P. Carillo	3	3	2	0	1	1.000	29	4	11	4	8	1.24

Individual Batting

Player	Pos	G	AB	R	H	2B	3B	HR	SH	SB	Pct
A. Cabañas	cf	2	5	2	1	0	0	0	2	0	.200
J. Violá	3b	2	9	0	1	0	0	0	0	0	.111
V. González	2b	2	9	1	4	0	0	1	0	0	.444
J. Castillo	1b	2	9	1	2	0	1	0	0	1	.222
A. Arcano	lf	2	7	2	2	0	1	0	0	0	.286
R. Almeida	ss	2	8	0	3	0	0	0	0	0	.375
G. Sánchez	c	2	7	1	0	0	0	0	0	0	.000
B.P. Carrillo	p	2	7	1	3	0	0	0	0	0	.429
M. Prats	rf	2	8	0	2	0	0	0	0	0	.250
Totals		2	70	7	20	0	2	1	2	1	.286

Individual Fielding

Player	Pos	G	O	A	E	Pct
A.Cabañas	cf	2	3	0	0	1.000
J. Violá	3b	2	3	4	0	1.000
V. González	2b	2	7	3	2	.833
J. Castillo	1b	2	18	0	0	1.000
A. Arcano	lf	2	2	0	1	.667
R. Almeida	ss	2	5	5	3	.769
G. Sánchez	c	2	11	1	0	1.000
B.P. Carrillo	p	2	1	5	2	.750

Player	Pos	G	O	A	E	Pct
M. Prats	rf	2	4	2	0	1.000
Totals		2	54	20	8	.902

COLOMBIA

Individual Pitching

Pitcher	G	CG	W	L	Pct	IP	R	H	W	K	ERA
G. Cárdenas	2	2	2	0	1.000	20.0	4	8	3	13	1.80

Individual Batting

Player	Pos	G	AB	R	H	Pct
R. Valdés	lf	1	4	1	0	.000
A. Cabañas	cf	2	6	2	1	.167
V. González	2b	2	9	2	1	.111
J. Castillo	1b	2	10	1	2	.200
G. González	c	2	10	0	2	.200
R. Almeida	ss	2	9	0	3	.333
A. Zaldivar	3b	1	4	0	0	.000
G. Cárdenas	p	1	4	0	0	.000
A. Acano	lf	1	4	0	1	.250
A. Mesa	3b	1	2	0	0	.000
G. Cárdenas	p	1	4	0	0	.000
L. Urrutia	rf	2	6	1	0	.000
Totals			72	8	10	.139

Stolen bases: Colombia 4

Individual Fielding

Player	Pos	G	O	A	E	Pct
R. Valdés	lf	1	2	0	0	1.000
A. Cabañas	cf	2	5	0	2	.714
V. González	2b	2	4	6	4	.714
J. Castillo	1b	2	22	0	0	1.000
G. González	c	2	15	0	0	1.000
R. Almeida	ss	2	4	5	4	.692
A. Zaldivar	3b	1	1	0	1	.500
G. Cárdenas	p	2	0	3	0	1.000
A. Acano	lf	1	1	0	0	1.000
A. Mesa	3b	1	2	5	1	.875
G. Cárdenas	p	1	0	2	2	.500
L. Urrutia	rf	2	3	0	0	1.000
Totals			60	21	12	.871

NUEVO AZUL

Individual Pitching

Pitcher	G	CG	W	L	Pct	IP	R	H	W	K	ERA
J. Romero	3	3	1	2	.333	27	10	15	6	14	3.33

Individual Batting

Player	Pos	G	AB	R	H	Pct
A. Cabrera	2b(2),1b(1)	3	12	0	0	.000
B.P. Carrillo	ss	3	11	1	3	.272
H. Hidalgo	cf(2),lf(1)	3	10	2	1	.100

Player	Pos	G	AB	R	H	Pct
J. Violá	3b(2),2b(1)	3	11	1	5	.454
J. Romero	p	3	11	1	2	.191
A. Molina	1b	2	8	0	1	.125
J. Santacruz	rf(1),lf(1)	2	8	0	2	.250
G. Sánchez	c	3	11	0	0	.000
M. Jacques	lf	1	2	0	0	.000
Carratala	lf	1	1	0	0	.000
C. Morán	cf	1	3	0	2	.667
M. Prats	rf	1	4	0	0	.000
R. Almeida	ss	1	4	0	0	.000
Totals		3	96	5	16	.167

Stolen bases: Nuevo Azul 3

Individual Fielding

Player	Pos	G	O	A	E	Pct
A. Cabrera	2b(2),1b(1)	3	13	8	3	.875
B.P. Carrillo	ss	3	4	7	5	.688
H. Hidalgo	cf(2),lf(1)	3	6	0	0	1.000
J. Violá	3b(2),2b(1)	3	5	8	2	.867
J. Romero	p	3	1	10	2	.846
A. Molina	1b	2	34	0	1	.971
J. Santacruz	rf(1),lf(1)	2	1	0	1	.500
G. Sánchez	c	3	16	4	0	1.000
M. Jacques	lf	1	1	0	0	1.000
Carratala	lf	1	0	0	0	.000
C. Morán	cf	1	3	0	0	1.000
M. Prats	rf	1	1	0	0	1.000
R. Almeida	ss	1	1	5	0	1.000
Totals		3	81	47	16	.889

SAN FRANCISCO BASE BALL CLUB

Individual Pitching

Pitcher	G	CG	W	L	Pct	IP	R	H	W	K	ERA
B.P. Carrillo	1	1	1	0	1.000	9.0	3	3	2	7	3.00

Individual Batting

Player	Pos	G	AB	R	H	2B	3B	HR	SH	SB	Pct
Laguardia	2b	1	1	0	0	0	0	0	0	0	.000
J. Santacruz	rf	1	4	2	2	0	0	0	0	0	.500
C. Morán	cf,3b	1	3	1	0	0	0	0	0	0	.000
M. Prats	lf	1	3	2	1	0	0	0	0	0	.333
J. Violá	3b,2b	1	3	1	0	0	0	0	0	0	.000
R. Almeida	1b	1	4	2	1	1	0	0	0	0	.250
A. Cabrera	ss	1	3	1	3	0	0	0	0	0	1.000
B.P. Carrillo	p	1	4	0	0	0	0	0	0	0	.000
G. Sánchez	c	1	4	1	2	0	0	0	0	0	.500
Totals		1	33	10	10	1	0	0	0	0	.303

Individual Fielding

Player	Pos	G	O	A	E	Pct
Laguardia	2b	1	0	0	2	.000
J. Santacruz	rf	1	2	0	0	1.000
C. Morán	cf,3b	1	0	0	0	.000
M. Prats	lf	1	1	0	1	.500

Player	Pos	G	O	A	E	Pct
J. Violá	3b,2b	1	1	0	1	.500
R. Almeida	1b	1	6	3	0	1.000
A. Cabrera	ss	1	8	1	1	.900
B.P. Carrillo	p	1	1	2	0	1.000
G. Sánchez	c	1	8	0	0	1.000
Totals		1	27	6	5	.868

Clío

Individual Pitching

Pitcher	G	CG	W	L	Pct	IP	R	H	W	K	ERA
J. Violá	1	1	1	0	1.000	9.0	1	3	2	9	1.00

Individual Batting

Player	Pos	G	AB	R	H	2B	3B	HR	SH	SB	Pct
A. Mesa	3b	1	4	0	0	0	0	0	0	0	.000
M. Prats	rf	1	3	0	0	0	0	0	0	0	.000
A. Cabrera	2b	1	4	0	0	0	0	0	0	0	.000
M. Alfonso	1b	1	4	0	0	0	0	0	0	0	.000
J. Violá	p	1	4	1	1	0	0	1	0	0	.250
R. Almeida	ss	1	1	0	0	0	0	0	0	0	.000
B.P. Carrillo	ss	1	2	0	1	0	0	0	0	0	.500
D. De Miguel	lf	1	3	1	1	0	1	0	0	0	.333
J. Romero	cf	1	2	0	2	1	0	0	0	1	1.000
G. Sánchez	c	1	2	0	1	0	0	0	0	0	.500
Totals		1	30	2	6	1	1	1	0	1	.200

Individual Fielding

Player	Pos	G	O	A	E	Pct
A. Mesa	3b	1	1	1	0	1.000
M. Prats	rf	1	1	0	0	1.000
A. Cabrera	2b	1	1	4	1	.833
M. Alfonso	1b	1	10	0	0	1.000
J. Violá	p	1	0	2	0	1.000
R. Almeida	ss	1	0	0	0	.000
B.P. Carrillo	ss	1	0	2	0	1.000
D. De Miguel	lf	1	0	0	2	.000
J. Romero	cf	1	1	0	0	1.000
G. Sánchez	c	1	13	1	0	1.000
Totals		1	27	10	3	.925

Though Rube Foster would win only one of the three games that he started for the X-Giants, his pitching line is nevertheless impressive. In an era of few strikeouts, he averaged one per inning pitched, giving up only six runs along the way. The box scores presented by Nieto don't allow for the calculation of earned runs with any certainty, but at worst Foster had a 1.74 ERA over 31 innings. In the end, however, poor hitting proved the ruin of good pitching, as the X-Giants batted a mere .130 as a team.

♦ 3 ♦

1904
Cuban X-Giants

After another strong season in the States, which ended with their loss in a three-game series to arch-rivals the Philadelphia Giants, the Cuban X-Giants returned to Havana in October of 1904 for a series of matches opposite Cuban teams. The X-Giants were introduced in Cuba with the following players:

Roster

Player	Position	Regular Season Club, 1904
Bill Bowman	p,rf	X-Giants
Emmett Bowman	p	X-Giants
Harry Buckner	p,lf,rf,3b	X-Giants
Luis Bustamente	ss	All-Cubans
Grant Johnson	ss	X-Giants
Robert Jordan	cf	X-Giants
Daniel McClellan	p,lf	X-Giants
Harry Moore	lf	X-Giants
John B. Patterson	2b	X-Giants
James Smith	3b	X-Giants
Clarence Williams	c	X-Giants
Ray Wilson	1b	X-Giants

William "Bill" Bowman, pitcher and outfielder, a versatile independent. Little is known about Bowman, except that he and Rube Foster played together for the Philadelphia Giants and that, in 1907, Bowman followed Foster to the Leland Giants (Cottrell, *The Best Pitcher in Baseball*, p. 34).

Emmett Bowman, pitcher, was a rookie in 1904, though with what team he played is open to question. While Nieto indicates that "Scotty" Bowman was with the X-Giants, Sol White indicates that this "star" pitcher was a member of the Philadelphia Giants that year (*A History of Colored Baseball*, pp. 65, 192). He would play until 1912, for the Leland Giants and Brooklyn Royal Giants as well as Philadelphia and the X-Giants, and spend time at third base, shortstop, and catcher when he wasn't pitching (Peterson, *Only the Ball Was White*, p. 318).

Harry Buckner, pitcher and outfielder for the X-Giants in Cuba, started with the Chicago Unions in 1896 and also played for the Columbia Giants and the Philadelphia Giants before joining the X-Giants. Sol White writes that Buckner played for the Philadelphia Giants too, from 1903 to 1907, and for the Brooklyn Royal Giants, also in 1907. Robert Peterson adds the Quaker Giants, Lincoln Giants, the Smart Set, and the Chicago Giants.

Luis Bustamente was a Cuban shortstop who began his career with Abel Linares' All-Cubans, batting .333 against the Philadelphia Giants and Cuban X-Giants during a tour of the States in 1903 (Holway, *The Complete Book of Baseball's Negro Leagues*, p. 46). He eventually played with the Brooklyn Royal Giants and the Cuban Stars. Sol White wrote in 1907 that Bustamente was "the leading Cuban player in the estimation of the American public ... although this player is not as fast as he was three seasons back." So it might be that Bustamente was in top form when he took the field in Cuba for the X-Giants (*History of Colored Baseball*, p. 91). Interestingly, Nieto's box scores and statistics indicate that Bustamente played both for the X-Giants, in two games, and for the Cubans, appearing in one game for Azul and two games for Carmelita.

Grant "Home Run" Johnson, shortstop, had played in Cuba for the X-Giants in 1903. Both trips saw Johnson, an all-time great hitter, struggle at the plate. Along with nearly all of his teammates, Johnson failed twice to hit .200.

Robert Jordan, outfielder, was the only player on the X-Giants roster who had played in both of the two previous trips to Cuba.

Dan McClellan, pitcher and outfielder, improved on his 1903 American Series performance by hitting .241 (compared with .083 the year before), and reversing his record on the mound, this time going 2–0.

Harry "Mike" Moore, an outfielder, began his career with the Chicago Unions in 1896 and also played with the Algona (Iowa) Brownies before joining the Cuban X-Giants in 1904.

John W. "Pat" Patterson played second base for the barnstorming X-Giants. He began with the Lincoln Giants of Nebraska in 1890 and played with the Page Fence Giants of Adrian, Michigan (1895), the Columbia Giants of Chicago [1899–1900], the Philadelphia Giants (1903), before joining the Cuban X-Giants in 1904. He went on to play for the Brooklyn Royal Giants in 1906.

James Smith, third base, was a rookie in 1904. There is no record that he played with a major black baseball club in the years that followed.

Clarence Williams caught every American Series game for the X-Giants, both in 1903 and in 1904. On the second trip to Cuba, he led all regulars on the club in batting.

Ray Wilson, first base, was another returning player, having made the trip to Cuba in 1903, when his modest .241 batting average led the team.

Members of the regular-season X-Giants who didn't travel to Cuba: George Ball, pitcher; William Jackson, left field; James Robinson, pitcher and right fielder; William "Big Bill" Smith, right field; L. Wilson, pitcher (Clark and Lester, *The Negro Leagues Book*, p. 57).

Games Played

Date	Winning Club		Losing Club		Winning Pitcher	Losing Pitcher
Oct 13	X-Giants	8	Azul	1	H. Buckner 1–0	A. D'Meza 0–1
Oct 20	X-Giants	2	Carmelita	0	D. McClellan 1–0	J. Muñoz 0–1
Oct 21	X-Giants	11	Azul	7	E. Bowman 1–0	E. Palomino 0–1
Oct 24	Habana	9	X-Giants	3	J. Muñoz 1–1	H. Buckner 1–1
Oct 24	X-Giants	2	Carmelita	0	H. Buckner 2–1	A. Acosta 0–1
Oct 26	X-Giants	8	Habana	7	D. McClellan 2–1	J. Muñoz 1–2
Oct 30	Habana	12	X-Giants	0	J. Muñoz 2–2	E. Bowman 1–1

Club Standings

Pos	Club	G	W	L	Pct
1.	Cuban X-Giants	7	5	2	.714
2.	Habana	3	2	1	.667
t3.	Azul	2	0	2	.000
t3.	Carmelita	2	0	2	.000

Box and Line Scores

GAME ONE: THURSDAY, OCTOBER 13

Azul	Pos	AB	R	H	O	A	E
M. Valdés	cf	3	0	0	4	0	1
A. Cabañas	2b	4	0	1	5	3	3
M. Prats	rf	4	0	0	2	0	0
A. Cabrera	ss	4	0	0	1	1	0
H. Hidalgo	3b	4	0	0	2	2	0
A. Marsans	lf,1b	4	0	1	2	0	1
M. Alfonso	1b,lf	3	1	0	3	0	2
A. Molina	c	1	0	0	1	0	0
A. Ortega	c	2	0	0	3	1	0
A.D'Meza	p	3	0	0	1	2	0
Totals		34	8	8	27	10	5

Cuban X-Giants	Pos	AB	R	H	O	A	E
G. Johnson	ss	3	1	1	2	1	0
W. Patterson	2b	3	2	1	1	2	1
R. Jordan	cf	5	0	0	1	0	0
D. McClellan	rf	5	1	1	1	0	0
H. Moore	lf	3	1	1	4	0	0
R. Wilson	1b	5	1	1	11	0	1
J. Smith	3b	5	2	2	1	1	3
C. Williams	c	2	0	1	6	0	0
H. Buckner	p	3	0	0	0	6	0
Totals		32	1	2	27	9	6

Cuban X-Giants	100	401	020	8
Azul	000	010	000	1

Sacrifice Hits: W. Patterson, H. Buckner
Stolen bases: A. Marsans, W. Patterson, G. Johnson
Bases on balls: A. D'Meza 5, H. Buckner 1
Strikeouts: A. D'Meza 2, H. Buckner 6
Dead balls: A. D'Meza (H. Moore)
Winning pitcher: H. Buckner
Losing pitcher: A. D'Meza

The *Chicago Daily Tribune* of October 20 reported an account of the game, "taken from a Havana exchange of October 14," that differed in a number of details, including the score:

The first of the series of games to be played between the American team, the Cuban X-Giants, and the various Cuban teams, took place yesterday, and resulted in a victory for the Americans over the blues, the champions of last season, by a score of 3 to 1.

A large crowd greeted the initial affair and the game was sufficiently interesting to keep enthusiasm up to a high pitch. The Betting was in favor of the American team, bettors giving them one run.

Buckner was in the box for the Giants, and pitched a wonderful game.

The next game will take place next Sunday afternoon at Almendares park, the opposing team being the All Cubans, the crack Cuban baseball team which has been making such a great success in a tour through the United States.

The score yesterday was as follows:

Cuban X-Giants	R	B	P	A	E
Johnson, ss	1	1	3	1	0
Patterson, 2b	0	1	1	0	1
Jordan, cf	0	0	1	0	0
McClellan, rf	0	2	1	0	0
Moore, lf	0	1	3	0	0
Wilson, 1b	2	2	10	0	1
Smith, 3b	0	2	1	4	3
Williams, c	0	1	6	1	0
Buckner, p	0	0	1	4	0
Totals	3	10	27	10	5

Almendares	R	B	P	A	E
Valdés, cf	0	0	4	0	1
Cabañas, 2b	0	1	5	2	2
Prats, rf	0	0	2	0	0
Cabrera, ss	0	0	1	2	0
Hidalgo, 3b	0	0	1	1	0
Alfonso, lf	0	0	0	1	0
Marsan, 1b	1	1	6	1	0
Ortega, c	0	0	6	1	0
Mesa, p	0	0	0	2	0
Totals	1	2	27	10	4

X-Giants	010	100	001–3
Almendares	000	000	010–1

Earned runs: Giants, 1
Left on bases: Giants, 13; Almendares, 6
Base on balls: off Buckner, 1; off Mesa, 5
Struck out: by Buckner, 6; by Mesa, 2
Umpires: Castaner and Marrero
Time of game: 1:30

GAME TWO: THURSDAY, OCTOBER 20

Cuban X-Giants	Pos	AB	R	H	O	A	E
G. Johnson	ss	5	1	1	5	0	0
W. Patterson	2b	4	0	1	3	0	1
R. Jordan	cf	3	1	1	3	0	0
H. Moore	lf	4	0	0	2	0	0
H. Buckner	rf	4	0	1	1	0	1
R. Wilson	1b	2	0	0	7	0	0
J. Smith	3b	4	0	0	0	6	0
C. Williams	c	4	0	0	8	0	0
D. McClellan	p	3	0	0	1	3	0
Totals		33	2	4	27	9	2

Carmelita	Pos	AB	R	H	O	A	E
L. Bustamante	ss	4	0	2	4	6	1
J. Muñoz	p	4	0	2	1	3	0
E. Palomino	rf	2	0	0	0	0	1
J.M. Magrinat	rf	2	0	0	0	1	0
R. Almeida	3b	4	0	0	1	3	3
J. Borges	2b	4	0	0	2	1	0
S. García	lf	3	0	0	1	0	1
G. Sánchez	c	4	0	1	2	2	1
A. Acosta	1b	3	0	1	15	1	0
M. Martinez	cf	3	0	0	1	0	1
Totals		33	0	6	27	17	8

Cuban X-Giants	200	000	000	2
Carmelita	000	000	000	0

Sacrifice hits: R. Jordan, R. Wilson
Bases on balls: D. McClellan 1, J. Muñoz 2
Strikeouts: D. McClellan 6, J. Muñoz 1
Passed balls: G. Sánchez 1
Winning pitcher: D. McClellan
Losing pitcher: J. Muñoz
Umpires: Francisco Poyo (home) and Antonio Maria García (bases)

GAME THREE: FRIDAY, OCTOBER 21

Cuban X-Giants	Pos	AB	R	H	O	A	E
G. Johnson	ss	6	0	2	0	6	1
W. Patterson	2b	6	1	1	2	2	2
D. McClellan	cf	6	1	1	2	0	0
H. Moore	lf	6	1	6	2	1	0
H. Buckner	rf	6	1	2	0	0	0
R. Wilson	1b	6	1	1	15	0	1
J. Smith	3b	3	1	0	1	3	1
C. Williams	c	4	2	1	2	1	0
E. Bowman	p	3	3	0	3	3	0
Totals		46	11	14	27	16	5

Azul	Pos	AB	R	H	O	A	E
L. Bustamante	ss	4	1	0	2	6	1
J. Muñoz	lf	5	0	0	4	3	1
M. Prats	rf	4	3	2	2	0	0
A. Cabañas	2b	3	2	1	3	1	0
A. Cabrera	1b	4	1	1	11	3	3
H. Hidalgo	3b	4	0	2	1	1	1
E. Palomino	p	4	0	1	0	0	2
G. Sánchez	c	4	0	0	3	2	0
R. Almeida	cf	4	0	1	1	1	0
Totals		36	7	8	27	9	8

Cuban X-Giants	002	101	700	11
Azul	303	000	100	7

Sacrifice hits: A. Cabañas, J.Smith, E. Bowman 2
Bases on balls: E. Palomino 3, E. Bowman 1
Strikeouts: E. Palomino 3, E. Bowman 2
Winning pitcher: E. Bowman
Losing pitcher: E. Palomino
Umpires: Francisco Poyo (home) and Antonio Maria García (bases)

GAME FOUR: MONDAY, OCTOBER 24 (FIRST GAME OF A DOUBLEHEADER)

Habana	Pos	AB	R	H	O	A	E
R. Valdés	ss	4	1	1	2	2	2
V. González	cf	5	1	1	0	0	1
J. Violá	3b	5	0	0	2	3	0
J. Castillo	1b	4	1	3	13	1	1
L. Padrón	rf	5	2	1	0	0	0
J. Muñoz	p	4	0	1	2	4	1
G. González	c	4	1	0	5	3	0
S. Valdés	2b	4	1	2	3	2	1
A. Arcano	lf	3	1	2	0	0	2
Totals		38	9	10	27	15	8

Cuban X-Giants	Pos	AB	R	H	O	A	E
G. Johnson	ss	4	0	0	1	4	1
W. Patterson	2b	4	0	0	1	1	1
R. Jordan	cf	4	0	0	3	0	0
H. Moore	lf	3	0	0	2	1	0
D. McClellan	rf	4	1	3	0	1	0
R. Wilson	1b	4	1	1	7	0	0
J. Smith	3b	2	1	0	2	3	5
C. Williams	c	4	0	1	2	2	0
H. Buckner	p	4	0	0	3	3	0
Totals		33	3	5	27	15	7

Habana	100	210	040	9
Cuban X-Giants	000	300	000	3

Earned runs: Habana 3 (J. Muñoz, V. González, L. Padrón), Cuban X-Giants 0
Two-Base hits: J. Castillo
Sacrifice hits: G. Johnson, J. Muñoz
Stolen bases: R. Valdés
Bases on balls: H. Buckner 3, J. Muñoz 3
Strikeouts: H. Buckner 2, J. Muñoz 5
Wild pitches: J. Muñoz
Winning pitcher: J. Muñoz
Losing pitcher: H. Buckner
Umpires: Francisco Poyo (home) and Antonio Maria García (bases)

GAME FIVE: MONDAY, OCTOBER 24 (SECOND GAME OF A DOUBLEHEADER)

Cuban X-Giants	Pos	AB	R	H	O	A	E
G. Johnson	ss	5	0	1	3	5	1
W. Patterson	2b	5	0	2	5	3	0
D. McClellan	cf	4	0	1	4	0	0
H. Moore	lf	5	0	0	1	0	0
R. Wilson	1b	3	1	0	9	0	0
J. Smith	3b	4	1	0	0	3	1
C. Williams	c	4	0	3	5	2	0
H. Buckner	p	4	0	0	0	2	0
B. Bowman	rf	4	0	1	0	0	0
Totals		38	2	8	27	15	2

Carmelita	Pos	AB	R	H	O	A	E
L. Bustamante	ss	4	0	2	2	4	0
E. Palomino	cf	3	0	0	1	3	0
S. García	lf	4	0	1	2	0	0
J. Borges	2b	3	0	0	2	0	0
G. Sánchez	c	4	0	2	6	0	1
J.M. Magrinat	rf	3	0	1	2	0	0
M. Martinez	1b	3	0	0	6	0	2
J. Romero	3b	3	0	0	5	0	0
A. Acosta	p	3	0	0	0	0	2
Totals		30	0	6	27	7	5

Cuban X-Giants	020	000	000	2
Carmelita	000	000	000	0

Two-base hits: W.Patterson
Stolen bases: J.Smith, C.Williams, J.Borges
Double plays: G.Johnson, J.Patterson, R.Wilson (2)
Bases on balls: H.Buckner 2, A.Acosta 1
Strikeouts: H.Buckner 5, A.Acosta 3
Hit Batsmen: A.Acosta 1 (R.Wilson)
Passed balls: C.Williams
Winning pitcher: H.Buckner
Losing pitcher: A.Acosta
Umpires: Francisco Poyo (home) and Antonio Maria García (bases)

GAME SIX: WEDNESDAY, OCTOBER 26

Habana	Pos	AB	R	H	O	A	E
R. Valdés	ss	5	1	2	3	3	4

Cuban X-Giants	Pos	AB	R	H	O	A	E
G. Johnson	ss	5	2	1	3	2	1

Habana	Pos	AB	R	H	O	A	E
V. González	cf	5	2	2	3	0	0
L. Padrón	3b	5	2	1	1	3	1
J. Castillo	1b	5	0	2	11	0	0
J. Violá	p,rf	4	0	1	0	2	1
J. Muñoz	rf,p	3	0	1	2	1	1
G. González	c	4	0	0	5	0	0
S. Valdés	2b	4	0	1	1	1	0
A. Arcano	lf	3	2	1	0	0	1
Totals		30	7	10	25	10	8

Cuban X-Giants	Pos	AB	R	H	O	A	E
W. Patterson	2b	5	0	1	4	3	1
L. Bustamante	ss	5	2	3	1	1	1
H. Moore	lf	4	1	0	2	1	0
H. Buckner	3b	4	0	1	0	0	o
R. Wilson	1b	4	0	0	11	0	0
J. Smith	3b	4	1	1	0	0	1
C. Williams	c	2	1	0	6	1	0
D. McClellan	p	5	1	1	0	2	1
Totals		38	8	8	27	10	5

```
Habana           002    020    300 : 7
Cuban X-Giants   100    100    204 : 8
```

The winning run was scored with one out in the inning
Earned runs: Habana 2 (V.González, L.Padrón), Cuban X-Giants 1
Two-Base hits: L.Bustamante, L.Padrón, J.Smith
Sacrifice hits: J.Muñoz, W.Patterson, J.Smith, C.Williams
Stolen bases: R.Valdés, V.González, W.Patterson, L.Bustamante 3, H.Buckner, R.Wilson
Bases on balls: J.Violá 4, J.Muñoz 3, D.McClellan 2
Strikeouts: J.Violá 2, J.Muñoz 1, D.McClellan 6
Hits: J.Violá 6 in 8 innings
Passed balls: G.González
Winning pitcher: D.McClellan
Losing pitcher: J.Muñoz
Umpires: Francisco Poyo (home) and Antonio Maria García (bases)

GAME SEVEN: SUNDAY, OCTOBER 30, 1904.

Cuban X-Giants	Pos	AB	R	H	O	A	E
G. Johnson	ss	4	0	0	1	3	0
W. Patterson	2b	4	0	0	4	2	2
L. Bustamante	3b	3	0	0	3	4	3
H. Moore	lf	2	0	0	1	0	0
D. McClellan	cf	2	0	0	0	1	0
R. Wilson	1b	3	0	0	10	0	0
H. Buckner	rf	3	0	0	0	0	0
C. Williams	c	3	0	0	4	2	0
B. Bowman	p	3	0	0	1	1	1
Totals		27	0	0	24	13	6

Habana	Pos	AB	R	H	O	A	E
R. Valdés	ss	3	1	1	0	5	0
V. González	cf	3	3	1	2	0	0
L. Padrón	3b	4	0	1	1	4	0
J. Castillo	1b	3	1	0	14	0	0
J. Violá	rf	2	2	0	1	0	0
G. González	c	4	2	1	2	1	0
J. Muñoz	p	3	0	1	2	1	1
S. Valdés	2b	3	1	1	4	2	0
A. Arcano	lf	3	2	1	1	0	0
Totals		38	12	7	27	13	1

```
Cuban X-Giants   000    000    000    0
Habana           200    620    02x    12
```

Earned runs: Habana 3 (V. González 3), Cuban X Giants 0
Three-Base hits: L. Padrón, J. Muñoz
Sacrifice hits: V. González, G. González. Stolen bases: V. González 2, J. Castillo
Bases on balls: J. Muñoz 3 (L. Bustamante, H. Moore and D. McClellan), B. Bowman 6
Strikeouts: J. Muñoz 2 (G. Johnson and H. Buckner), B. Bowman 4
Hit Batsmen: B. Bowman 4 (R. Valdés 2, J. Castillo and J. Violá)
Wild pitches: E. Bowman
Winning pitcher: J. Muñoz
Losing pitcher: B. Bowman
Umpires: Francisco Poyo (home) and Antonio Maria García (bases)

A no-hit, no-run for the Cuban X-Giants

Final Statistics

CUBAN X-GIANTS

Individual Pitching

Pitcher	G	GS	G	W	L	Pct	IP	R	H	W	K	ERA
Bill Bowman	2	2	2	1	1	.500	17.0	19	15	7	6	ND
Harry Buckner	3	3	3	2	1	.667	27.0	10	18	6	13	ND
Daniel McClellan	2	2	2	2	0	1.000	18.0	7	16	3	12	ND
Totals	7	7	7	5	2	.714	62.0	36	49	16	31	ND

Individual Batting

Player	Pos	G	AB	R	H	2B	3B	HR	SH	SB	Pct
Bill Bowman	p,f	3	10	3	1	0	0	0	2	0	.100
Harry Buckner	p,f,rf,3b	7	28	1	4	0	0	0	1	1	.143
Grant Johnson	ss	7	32	4	6	0	0	0	1	1	.188
Robert Jordan	cf	3	12	1	1	0	0	0	1	0	.083
Daniel McClellan	p,lf	7	29	4	7	0	0	0	0	0	.241
Harry Moore	lf	7	27	3	7	0	0	0	0	0	.259
John B. Patterson	2b	7	31	3	6	1	0	0	2	2	.194
James Smith	3b	6	22	6	4	0	0	0	2	1	.182
Clarence Williams	c	7	23	3	6	0	0	0	1	1	.261
Ray Wilson	1b	7	27	4	3	1	0	0	0	2	.111
Luis Bustamante	ss	2	8	2	3	0	0	0	0	3	.375
Totals		7	249	34	47	2	2	0	10	11	.189

Individual Fielding

Player	Pos	G	O	A	E	Pct
Bill Bowman	p,rf	3	4	4	1	.889
Harry Buckner	p,lf,rf,3b	7	4	11	1	.938
Grant Johnson	ss	7	15	21	4	.900
Robert Jordan	cf	3	4	0	0	1.000
Daniel McClellan	p,lf	7	8	7	1	.938
Harry Moore	lf	7	14	3	0	1.000
John B. Patterson	2b	7	25	13	8	.826
James Smith	3b	6	4	15	11	.633
Clarence Williams	c	7	27	7	0	1.000
Ray Wilson	1b	7	70	0	2	.972
Luis Bustamante	ss	2	4	5	4	.692
Totals		7	179	86	32	.895

AZUL

Individual Pitching

Pitcher	G	CG	W	L	Pct	IP	AB	R	H	W	K	ERA
A. D'Meza	1	1	0	1	.000	9.0	34	8	8	5	2	8.00
E. Palomino	1	1	0	1	.000	9.0	46	11	14	3	3	11.00
Totals	2	2	0	2	.000	18.0	80	19	22	8	5	9.50

Individual Batting

Player	Pos	G	AB	R	H	2B	3B	HR	SH	SB	Pct
A. Cabañas	2b	2	7	2	2	0	0	0	1	0	.286
M. Prats	rf	2	8	3	2	0	0	0	0	0	.250
A. Cabrera	ss(1),1b(1)	2	8	1	1	0	0	0	0	0	.125
M. Hidalgo	3b	2	8	0	2	0	0	0	0	0	.250

Player	Pos	G	AB	R	H	2B	3B	HR	SH	SB	Pct
A. Marsans	lf(1),1b(1)	1	4	0	1	0	0	0	0	1	.250
M. Alfonso	1b(1),lf(1)	1	3	1	0	0	0	0	0	0	.000
A. Molina	c	1	1	0	0	0	0	0	0	0	.000
A. Ortega	c	1	2	0	0	0	0	0	0	0	.000
A. D'Meza	p	1	3	0	0	0	0	0	0	0	.000
L. Bustamante	ss	1	4	1	0	0	0	0	0	0	.000
J. Muñoz	lf(1)	1	5	0	0	0	0	0	0	0	.000
E. Palomino	p	1	4	0	1	0	0	0	0	0	.250
G. Sánchez	c	1	4	0	0	0	0	0	0	0	.000
R. Almeida	cf	1	4	0	1	0	0	0	0	0	.250
Totals		2	68	8	10	0	0	0	1	1	.147

Individual Fielding

Player	Pos	G	O	A	E	Pct
A. Cabañas	2b	2	8	4	3	.800
M. Prats	rf	2	4	0	0	1.000
A. Cabrera	ss(1),1b(1)	2	12	4	3	.842
M. Hidalgo	3b	2	3	3	1	.853
A. Marsans	lf(1),1b(1)	1	2	0	1	.667
M. Alfonso	1b(1),lf(1)	1	3	0	2	.600
A. Molina	c	1	1	0	0	1.000
A. Ortega	c	1	3	1	0	1.000
A. D'Meza	p	1	1	2	0	1.000
L. Bustamante	ss	1	2	6	1	.889
J. Muñoz	lf	1	4	3	1	.875
E. Palomino	p	1	0	0	2	.000
G. Sánchez	c	1	3	2	0	1.000
R. Almeida	cf	1	1	1	0	1.000
Totals		2	54	18	14	.837

HABANA

Individual Pitching

Pitcher	G	CG	W	L	Pct	IP	R	H	W	K	ERA
J.Muñoz	3	2	2	1	.667	18.1	5	7	6	7	2.45
J.Violá	1	0	0	0	.000	8.0	6	6	4	2	6.75
Totals	4	2	2	1	.667	26.1	11	13	10	9	3.76

Individual Batting

Player	Pos	G	AB	R	H	2B	3B	HR	SH	SB	Pct
R. Valdés	ss	3	12	3	4	0	0	0	0	2	.333
V. González	cf	3	13	6	4	0	0	0	1	3	.308
J. Violá	p(1),rf(2),3b(1)	3	11	2	1	0	0	0	0	0	.091
J. Castillo	1b	3	12	2	5	1	0	0	0	1	.417
L. Padrón	3b(2),rf(1)	3	14	4	3	0	1	0	0	0	.214
J. Muñoz	p(3),rf(1)	3	10	0	3	0	1	0	2	0	.300
G. Gonalez	c	3	12	3	1	0	0	0	1	0	.083
S. Valdés	2b	3	11	2	4	0	0	0	0	0	.364
A. Arcano	lf	3	9	5	4	0	0	0	0	0	.444
Totals		3	106	28	27	1	2	0	4	6	.255

Individual Fielding

Player	Pos	G	O	A	E	Pct
R. Valdés	ss	3	5	10	6	.714
V. Gonxalez	cf	3	5	0	1	.833

Player	Pos	G	O	A	E	Pct
J. Violá	p(1),rf(2),3b(1)	3	3	5	1	.889
J. Castillo	1b	3	38	1	1	.975
L. Padrón	3b(2),rf(1)	3	2	7	1	.900
J. Muñoz	p(3),rf(1)	3	6	6	3	.800
G. Gonalez	c	3	12	4	0	1.000
S. Valdés	2b	3	8	5	1	.929
A. Arcano	lf	3	1	0	3	.250
Totals		3	79	38	17	.873

CARMELITA

Individual Pitching

Pitcher	G	CG	W	L	Pct	IP	R	H	W	K	ERA
J. Muñoz	1	1	0	1	.000	9.0	2	4	2	1	2.00
A. Acosta	1	1	0	1	.000	9.0	2	8	1	3	2.00
Totals	2	2	0	2	.000	18.0	4	12	3	4	2.00

Individual Batting

Player	Pos	G	AB	R	H	2B	3B	HR	SH	SB	Pct
L. Bustamante	ss	2	8	0	4	0	0	0	0	0	.500
J. Muñoz	p	1	4	0	2	0	0	0	0	0	.500
E. Palomino	rf(1),3b(1)	2	5	0	0	0	0	0	0	0	.000
J.M. Magrinat	rf	2	5	0	1	0	0	0	0	0	.200
R. Almeida	3b	1	4	0	0	0	0	0	0	0	.000
J. Borges	2b	2	7	0	0	0	0	0	0	1	.000
S. García	lf	2	7	0	1	0	0	0	0	0	.143
G. Sánchez	c	2	8	0	3	0	0	0	0	0	.375
A. Acosta	p(1),1b(1)	2	6	0	1	0	0	0	0	0	.167
M. Martinez	cf(1),1b(1)	2	6	0	0	0	0	0	0	0	.000
J. Romero	cf	1	3	0	0	0	0	0	0	0	.000
Totals		2	63	0	12	0	0	0	0	1	.190

Individual Fielding

Player	Pos	G	O	A	E	Pct
L. Bustamante	ss	2	6	10	1	.941
J. Muñoz	p	1	1	3	0	1.000
E. Palomino	rf(1),3b(1)	2	1	3	1	.800
J. M.Magrinat	rf	2	2	1	0	1.000
R. Almeida	3b	1	1	3	3	.571
J. Borges	2b	2	4	1	0	1.000
S. García	lf	2	3	0	1	.750
G. Sánchez	c	2	8	2	2	.833
A. Acosta	p(1),1b(1)	2	15	1	2	.889
M. Martinez	cf(1),1b(1)	2	7	0	3	.700
J. Romero	cf	1	5	0	0	1.000
Totals		2	54	24	13	.857

According to Jorge Figueredo, the X-Giants also played one game against another visiting U.S. club, the independent Lynn, Massachusetts, club. Lynn, which would in two years be home to a New England League team (Chadwick, *Spalding's Official Baseball Guide, 1906*, p. 239), won the contest by a slim, 2–1 margin. Harry Buckner took the loss, while Lynn's Jerry Nops got the win.

The Lynn roster included E. McAuliffe, catcher; W. Clancy, first baseman; W. Taylor, second baseman; R.E. Rock, Providence; Phil Lewis, shortstop; J.F. Hayden, outfield; C.A. Weeden, outfield; Jerry Nops, pitcher, outfielder; J. Donovan, pitcher, outfielder; J.J. Nugent, pitcher, oufielder (*Cuban Baseball: A Statistical History, 1878–1961*, p. 54).]

◆ 4 ◆

1905
Cuban X-Giants

In 1905 the Cuban X-Giants traveled to Cuba for the fourth time. While it was a team made up of more Philadelphia Giants than X-Giants, the roster this year did not include the most feared hitter on either club, Grant "Home Run" Johnson. The Giants and X-Giants were again the dominant black teams in the East, but no championship series was played against Western competition, as "the teams could not come to any agreement, and no championship series was played" (White, *History of Colored Base Ball*, 46). Despite a formidable line-up and the return of Rube Foster, the Americans faced stiff competition and won only one more game than they lost.

Roster

Player	Position	Regular Season Club, 1905
Harry Buckner	p	Cuban X-Giants
Andrew "Rube" Foster	p	Philadephia Giants
J. Preston Hill	lf	Philadelphia Giants
John A. Hill	ss	Cuban X-Giants
Daniel McClellan	p,cf	Philadelphia Giants
Harry Moore	3b	Philadelphia Giants
Dangerfield Talbot	2b	Cuban X-Giants
Clarence Williams	c	Famous Cuban Giants
Ray Wilson	1b	Cuban X-Giants
Clarence Winston	cf	Philadelphia Giants

Harry Buckner, the X-Giants' star pitcher, had played an important role in the X-Giants successful 1904 trip, winning two of his three starts, including a shutout of Carmelita and an 8–1 win over Azul.

Andrew "Rube" Foster had been dominant in the 1903 American Series— and in the U.S. championship series that preceded it, which pitted the X-Giants against the Philadelphia Giants. After Foster won all four of his starts against the Philadelphia club, they plucked him from the X-Giants roster, and in the 1904 rematch between the two teams, it was again Foster who pitched his team to victory.

J. Preston "Pete" Hill, like Foster, had made his first visit to Cuba as a member of the X-Giants before leaving the New York club in favor of Philadelphia. In the 1903 American Series, the great hitter saw limited action, getting only 15 at-bats. This time Hill would prove the driving force behind the X-Giants offense.

John A. Hill, shortstop, began with the Genuine Cuban Giants in 1900 and also played for the Philadelphia Giants and Cuban X-Giants. The 1905 American Series was his second, as he was the starting third baseman for the X-Giants in 1903.

Dan McClellan, a pitcher and outfielder, started in 1903 with the Cuban X-Giants. McClellan had made the trip twice before, having pitched poorly in 1903 and then both steadily and well in 1904.

Harry "Mike" Moore had been the X-Giants third baseman in the 1904 American Series, when he was one of the more reliable contributors at the plate.

Dangerfield Talbot, second base, started with the Leland Giants in 1900. He later played with the Chicago Union Giants and with the Cuban X-Giants in 1905.

Clarence Williams, catcher, made his fourth appearance in the American Series and would once again find himself starting every game for the X-Giants.

Ray Wilson, first base, returned for his third American Series.

Clarence "Bobby" Winston, outfield, was a fast runner. Though he had started with the Cuban X-Giants in 1903, this was his first trip to Cuba with the club.

Other Members of the 1905 X-Giants Who Didn't Play in Cuba: Aubury, first baseman; George Ball, pitcher, center fielder; William Jackson, center fielder; Robert Jordan, catcher; John W. Patterson, left fielder; Rogello Valdés, shortstop; T. Williams, catcher; Ed Wilson, right fielder.

Games Played

Date	Winning Club		Losing Club		Winning Pitcher	Losing Pitcher
Oct 22	X-Giants	8	All-Cubans	6	A. Foster 1-0	A. D'Meza 0-1
Oct 24	X-Giants	4	Habana	0	H. Buckner 1-0	P. Olave 0-1
Oct 27	Fe	2	X-Giants	1	J. Muñoz 1-0	A. Foster 1-1
Oct 29	X-Giants	5	Habana	3	H. Buckner 2-0	L. Padrón 0-1
Oct 30	X-Giants	8	Fe	1	A. Foster 2-1	J. Muñoz 1-1
Nov 2	All-Cubans	7	X-Giants	0	I. Pérez 1-0	H. Buckner 2-1
Nov 5	X-Giants	8	Fe	5	D. McClellan	J. Muñoz 1-2
Nov 7	All-Cubans	4	X-Giants	1	I. Pérez 2-0	A. Foster 2-2
Nov 9	Habana	6	X-Giants	1	L. Padrón 1-1	H. Buckner 2-2
(9)						

Club Standings

Pos	Club	G	W	L	Pct
1.	All-Cubans	3	2	1	.667
2.	Cuban X-Giants	9	5	4	.556
3-4	Fe	3	1	2	.333
3-4	Habana	3	1	2	.333

The Games

SUNDAY, OCTOBER 22, AT ALMENDARES PARK

Cuban X-Giants	Pos	AB	R	H	O	A	E
D. Talbot	2b	4	1	1	2	5	2
J.P. Hill	lf	6	0	3	1	0	0
C. Winston	cf	4	1	1	0	0	0
D. McClellan	rf	5	1	0	0	0	0
H. Moore	3b	5	2	2	3	4	0
R. Wilson	1b	5	1	2	15	0	0
A. Foster	p	5	1	3	0	3	1
C. Williams	c	3	1	1	3	1	0
J. Hill	ss	3	0	0	3	3	0
Totals		40	8	13	27	16	3

All-Cubans	Pos	AB	R	H	O	A	E
L. Bustamante	ss	4	0	0	3	3	0
S. Valdés	2b	4	1	1	1	4	3
R. Almeida	3b	4	1	1	3	1	0
E. Palomino	rf	3	2	2	1	0	0
R. García	c	4	1	1	4	3	1
H. Hidalgo	cf	3	0	0	0	1	0
A. Cabañas	cf	1	1	1	0	0	0
A. Marsans	lf	4	0	2	2	0	1
A. Cabrera	1b	4	0	0	13	0	2
A. D'Meza	p	3	0	0	0	5	0
J. Muñoz	p	1	0	0	0	0	0
Totals		34	6	8	27	17	7

| Cuban X-Giants | 010 | 007 | 000 : 8 |
| All-Cubans | 100 | 003 | 002 : 6 |

Earned runs: Cuban X-Giants (1), All-Cubans (3)
Two-Base hits: R. Wilson
Sacrifice hits: C. Winston, J. Hill (2)
Stolen bases: Talbot, J.P. Hill, H. Moore, R. García and A. D'Meza
Double-plays: H. Moore, Talbot and R. Wilson
Bases on balls: A. D'Meza 3, J. Muñoz 0, A. Foster 2
Strikeouts: A. D'Meza 3, J. Muñoz 0, A. Foster 2
Passed balls: R. García 2
Hits: A. D'Meza 11 in 5.1 innings
Winning pitcher: A. Foster
Losing pitcher: A. D'Meza
Time: 2 hours 5 minutes
Umpires: Poyo and García
Secretary: Fernando Rodríguez

GAME ONE: TUESDAY, OCTOBER 24, AT ALMENDARES PARK

Cuban X-Giants	Pos	AB	R	H	O	A	E
D. Talbot	2b	4	0	1	1	5	0
J.P. Hill	lf	3	1	1	3	0	0
C. Winston	cf	4	0	0	0	0	0
D. McClellan	rf	3	1	0	1	0	0
H. Moore	3b	4	0	0	4	2	0
R. Wilson	1b	4	0	0	8	0	0
H. Buckner	p	4	0	0	1	0	0
C. Williams	c	2	1	0	7	2	0
J. Hill	ss	2	1	0	2	1	1
Totals		30	4	2	27	10	1

Habana	Pos	AB	R	H	O	A	E
E. Prats	1b	4	0	0	12	0	1
A. Arcano	lf	4	0	0	2	0	0
J. Violá	cf	3	0	0	0	0	0
R. Valdés	ss	3	0	0	1	4	0
V. González	2b	3	0	0	1	2	2
L. Padrón	rf	3	0	2	0	0	0
B.P. Carrillo	3b	3	0	0	3	1	1
A. Molina	c	2	0	0	8	3	0
P. Olave	p	2	0	0	0	2	0
M. Prats	p	1	0	1	0	0	0
Totals		28	0	3	27	12	4

| Cuban X-Giants | 000 | 220 | 000 : 4 |
| Habana | 000 | 000 | 000 : 0 |

Earned runs: Cuban X-Giants (1), Habana (0)
Three-base hits: J.P. Hill
Stolen-bases: J.P. Hill (2), C. Winston
Double-plays: Talbot, J. Hill and R. Wilson
Bases on balls: H. Buckner 1, P. Olave 3, M. Prats 0
Strikeouts: H. Buckner 6, P. Olave 6, M. Prats 1
Passed balls: A. Molina 1
Hits: P. Olave 2 in 6.0 innings
Winning pitcher: H. Buckner
Losing pitcher: P. Olave
Umpires: Antonio Maria García (home) and Antonio Pérez Utrera (bases)
Secretary: Mendoza and F. García

GAME TWO: THURSDAY, OCTOBER 26, CUBAN X-GIANTS VS. CARMELITA

Suspended for rain in the fourth inning.

GAME THREE: FRIDAY, OCTOBER 27, AT ALMENDARES PARK

Cuban X-Giants	Pos	AB	R	H	O	A	E
D. Talbot	2b	3	0	0	2	2	0

Fe	Pos	AB	R	H	O	A	E
C. Morán	3b	4	0	1	0	3	1

Cuban X-Giants	Pos	AB	R	H	O	A	E
J.P. Hill	lf	3	1	1	4	0	0
C. Winston	cf	4	0	1	0	0	0
D. McClellan	rf	4	0	0	0	0	0
H. Moore	3b	3	0	0	1	2	0
R. Wilson	1b	4	0	1	8	0	1
A. Foster	p	4	0	0	0	3	0
C. Williams	c	2	0	0	9	1	0
J. Hill	ss	3	0	0	0	2	1
Totals		30	1	3	24	10	2

Fe	Pos	AB	R	H	O	A	E
S. Valdés	2b	5	0	1	0	8	0
R. Govantes	rf	3	1	0	0	0	0
J. Castillo	1b	3	0	1	15	0	0
G. González	c	2	1	0	5	1	0
F. Morán	lf	2	0	1	0	1	1
J. Muñoz	p	4	0	1	0	1	0
P. Benavides	cf	4	0	2	5	0	0
R. Figarola	ss	3	0	0	2	2	0
Totals		30	2	7	27	16	2

Cuban X-Giants	000	001	000 : 1
Fe	000	110	00x : 2

Two-Base hits: J.Castillo
Sacrifice hits: F.Morán, R.Figarola
Bases on balls: A.Foster 7, J.Muñoz 6
Strikeouts: A.Foster 7, J.Muñoz 4
Winning pitcher: J.Muñoz
Losing pitcher: A.Foster
Umpires: Antonio Maria García (home) and Pérez Utrera (bases)

GAME FOUR: SUNDAY, OCTOBER 29, AT ALMENDARES PARK

Cuban X-Giants	Pos	AB	R	H	O	A	E
D. Talbot	2b	5	0	0	3	1	1
J.P. Hill	lf	5	2	1	1	0	1
C. Winston	cf	5	1	2	1	0	0
D. McClellan	rf	4	1	3	0	0	0
H. Moore	3b	4	0	0	2	4	1
R. Wilson	1b	4	0	0	12	0	0
H. Buckner	p	4	1	1	1	4	0
C. Williams	c	3	0	0	5	1	0
J. Hill	ss	4	0	1	2	3	1
Totals		Y38	5	8	27	13	4

Habana	Pos	AB	R	H	O	A	E
R. Valdés	ss	3	1	0	2	3	1
M. Prats	rf	2	1	0	0	0	0
E. Prats	1b	3	1	1	7	0	2
L. Padrón	p	4	0	1	0	1	1
V. González	2b	3	0	0	3	0	2
J. Violá	cf	4	0	1	1	0	0
A. Arcano	lf	4	0	1	2	0	1
B.P. Carrillo	3b	4	0	0	4	4	0
A. Molina	c	3	0	0	8	3	0
Totals		30	3	4	27	11	7

Cuban X-Giants	021	020	000 : 5
Habana	200	000	010 : 3

Sacrifice hits: D. McClellan, E. Prats, M. Prats
Stolen bases: J.P. Hill, R. Valdés
Double-plays: C. Williams, H. Buckner and R. Wilson; D. Talbot, H. Moore and R. Wilson
Bases on balls: L. Padrón 0, H. Buckner 3
Strikeouts: L. Padrón 8, H. Buckner 4
Hit Batsmen: L. Padrón 1 (by C. Williams)
Winning pitcher: H. Buckner
Losing pitcher: L. Padrón
Time: 1 hour 40 minutes
Umpires: Francisco Poyo (home) and Antonio Maria García (bases)
Secretary: Francisco Rodríguez

GAME FIVE: MONDAY, OCTOBER 30, AT ALMENDARES PARK

Cuban X-Giants	Pos	AB	R	H	O	A	E
D. Talbot	2b	5	1	2	5	3	1
J.P. Hill	lf	4	1	0	2	0	0
C. Winston	cf	5	0	1	1	0	1
D. McClellan	rf	5	1	1	0	0	0

Fe	Pos	AB	R	H	O	A	E
C. Morán	3b	4	0	2	4	0	1
S. Valdés	2b	4	0	0	2	5	0
R. Govantes	rf	3	0	0	0	1	2
J. Castillo	1b	3	1	0	14	0	0

Cuban X-Giants	Pos	AB	R	H	O	A	E
H. Moore	3b	5	1	1	0	2	1
R. Wilson	1b	5	1	1	9	0	0
A. Foster	p	5	0	2	0	4	0
C. Williams	c	4	1	2	5	1	1
J. Hill	ss	4	2	2	5	5	0
Totals		42	8	12	27	15	4

Fe	Pos	AB	R	H	O	A	E
G. González	c	4	0	1	3	0	0
F. Morán	lf	3	0	1	2	0	0
P. Benavides	cf	3	0	0	0	0	0
J. Muñoz	p	3	0	0	1	2	0
R. Figarola	ss	3	0	0	1	4	1
Totals		30	1	5	27	12	4

Cuban X-Giants	000	020	600 : 8
Fe	000	100	000 : 1

Earned runs: Cuban X-Giants (1), Fe (0)
Two-Base hits: Talbot, A.Foster
Sacrifice hits: J.P.Hill, R.Govantes
Bases on balls: A.Foster 1, J.Muñoz 0
Strikeouts: A.Foster 4, J.Muñoz 2
Winning pitcher: A.Foster
Losing pitcher: J.Muñoz

GAME SIX: THURSDAY, NOVEMBER 2, AT ALMENDARES PARK

Cuban X-Giants	Pos	AB	R	H	O	A	E
D. Talbot	2b	4	0	0	0	3	0
J.P. Hill	lf	3	0	0	4	1	1
C. Winston	cf	3	0	0	3	0	1
D. McClellan	cf	1	0	0	0	0	0
A. Foster	rf	4	0	0	0	0	0
H. Moore	3b	3	0	1	0	2	0
R. Wilson	1b	3	0	0	6	0	2
H. Buckner	p	2	0	1	0	3	0
C. Williams	c	3	0	0	6	2	0
J. Hill	ss	3	0	0	5	2	1
Totals		31	7	8	27	12	3

All-Cubans	Pos	AB	R	H	O	A	E
L. Bustamante	ss	4	0	1	3	3	1
A. Cabañas	2b	3	1	1	1	2	1
R. Almeida	3b	3	2	1	0	1	0
E. Palomino	rf	4	2	3	0	0	0
R. García	c	3	0	1	9	3	0
H. Hidalgo	cf	3	0	0	3	0	0
A. Marsans	lf	3	1	1	3	0	0
A. Cabrera	1b	4	1	0	8	1	1
I. Pérez	p	4	0	0	0	2	0
Totals		29	0	2	24	13	5

Cuban X-Giants	000	000	000 : 0
All-Cubans	300	000	04x : 7

Earned runs: All-Cubans 2 (R.Almeida and E.Palomino), Cuban X-Giants.
Sacrifice hits: L.Bustamante.
Stolen bases: C.Winston, A.Cabañas.
Double-plays: J.Hill (s.a).
Bases on balls: I.Pérez 2, H.Buckner.
Strikeouts: I.Pérez 9, H.Buckner 6.
Winning pitcher: I.Pérez.
Losing pitcher: H.Buckner.

GAME SEVEN: SUNDAY, NOVEMBER 5, AT ALMENDARES PARK

Cuban X-Giants	Pos	AB	R	H	O	A	E
J.P. Hill	lf	5	1	2	0	0	2
D. McClellan	p,rf	4	1	1	0	2	0
H. Buckner	rf,p	5	1	1	1	1	0
H. Moore	3b	5	2	3	3	2	1
R. Wilson	1b	4	0	2	11	1	0
D. Talbot	2b	5	0	1	1	2	1
C. Winston	cf	5	2	3	4	0	0
C. Williams	c	5	0	1	6	3	1
J. Hill	ss	2	1	1	1	2	0
Totals		40	8	15	27	13	5

Fe	Pos	AB	R	H	O	A	E
C. Morán	3b	5	1	3	2	5	0
S. Valdés	2b	5	1	3	0	2	1
R. Govantes	ss	4	1	0	1	4	1
J. Castillo	1b	5	1	2	12	1	2
G. González	c	3	0	0	5	1	0
F. Morán	lf	4	0	2	2	0	1
P. Benavides	cf	5	0	2	4	0	0
P. Medina	rf,p	4	0	0	0	1	1
J. Muñoz	p,rf	4	1	1	1	2	0
Totals		39	5	13	27	16	6

Cuban X-Giants	220	200	200 : 8
Fe	000	140	000 : 5

Earned runs: Cuban X-Giants (5), Fe (0)
Two-base hits: P. Benavides
Sacrifice hits: D. McClellan, R. Wilson, J. Hill, G. González
Stolen bases: H. Buckner, C. Williams, R. Govantes
Bases on balls: D. McClellan 1, H. Buckner 1, J. Muñoz 0, P. Medina 0
Strikeouts: D. McClellan 4, H. Buckner 2, J. Muñoz 3, P. Medina 2
Hit Batsmen: D. McClellan 1
Hits: D. McClellan 8 in 5.0; J. Muñoz 9 in 4.0
Winning pitcher: D. McClellan
Losing pitcher: J. Muñoz
Time: 2 hours 10 minutes
Umpires: Francisco Poyo (home) and Antonio Maria García (bases)
Secretary: Francisco Rodríguez

GAME EIGHT: TUESDAY, OCTOBER 7, AT ALMENDARES PARK

Cuban X-Giants	Pos	AB	R	H	O	A	E
J.P. Hill	lf	4	0	3	2	1	1
D. McClellan	cf	4	0	0	1	0	0
H. Buckner	rf	4	0	0	0	0	0
H. Mooke	3b	4	0	0	2	1	1
R. Wilson	1b	4	0	1	10	0	1
D. Talbot	2b	4	0	0	2	2	1
A. Foster	p	3	1	0	0	4	1
C. Williams	c	2	0	0	5	1	0
J. Hill	ss	3	0	0	2	2	1
Totals		32	1	4	24	11	6

All-Cubans	Pos	AB	R	H	O	A	E
L. Bustamante	ss	3	1	1	2	3	1
A. Cabañas	2b	4	0	1	1	0	0
R. Almeida	3b	4	0	0	1	4	0
E. Palomino	rf	4	0	1	1	0	0
R. García	c	3	2	1	3	0	0
H. Hidalgo	cf	4	1	1	6	0	0
A. Marsans	lf	2	0	0	3	0	0
A. Cabrera	1b	3	0	0	10	0	0
I. Pérez	p	3	0	0	0	1	0
Totals		30	4	5	27	8	1

Cuban X-Giants	001	000	000 : 1
All-Cubans	100	201	00x : 4

Stolen bases: L. Bustamante, R. Almeida, R. García (2), H. Hidalgo
Bases on balls: I. Pérez 1, A. Foster 1
Strikeouts: I. Pérez 3, A. Foster 3
Hit Batsmen: A. Foster 2 (R. García and A. Marsans)
Winning pitcher: I. Pérez
Losing pitcher: A. Foster
Time: 2 hours
Umpires: Antonio Pérez Utrera (home) and Antonio Maria García (bases)
Secretary: Francisco Rodríguez

GAME NINE: THURSDAY, NOVEMBER 9, AT ALMENDARES PARK

Cuban X-Giants	Pos	AB	R	H	O	A	E
J.P. Hill	lf	4	1	2	4	0	0
D. McClellan	cf	3	0	1	0	0	0
H. Buckner	p	4	0	0	0	7	0
H. Moore	3b	3	0	0	1	2	1
R. Wilson	1b	4	0	0	5	0	1
D. Talbot	2b	2	0	0	0	1	1
A. Foster	rf,1b	4	0	0	9	1	1
C. Williams	c	4	0	0	4	1	2
J. Hill	ss	1	0	0	1	0	0
C. Winston	rf	2	0	0	0	0	0
Totals		31	1	3	24	12	6

Habana	Pos	AB	R	H	O	A	E
R. Valdés	ss	4	1	2	2	4	1
M. Prats	rf	2	2	0	2	0	0
E. Prats	1b	4	0	1	11	0	0
L. Padrón	p	4	1	1	1	3	0
J. Violá	cf	4	1	1	3	1	1
V. González	2b	4	0	1	5	4	0
A. Arcano	lf	4	0	1	0	0	0
B.P. Carrillo	3b	3	0	1	0	0	1
A. Molina	c	3	1	1	3	0	0
Totals		32	6	9	27	12	3

Cuban X-Giants	000	000	001 : 1
Habana	102	001	20x : 6

Earned runs: Cuban X-Giants (1), Habana (2)
Two-base hits: D. McClellan
Sacrifice hits: M. Prats and B.P. Carrillo
Stolen bases: D. McClellan and J. Violá
Bases on balls: H. Buckner 0, L. Padrón 5
Strikeouts: H. Buckner 4, L. Padrón 2
Winning pitcher: L. Padrón
Losing pitcher: H. Buckner
Umpires: Antonio Pérez Utrera (Home) and Antonio Maria García (bases)

Final Statistics

CUBAN X-GIANTS

Individual Pitching

Pitcher	G	GS	GC	W	L	Pct	IP	R	H	W	K	HP	ERA
Andrew Foster	4	4	4	2	2	.500	34.0	13	25	6	12	2	ND
Harry Buckner	5	4	4	2	2	.500	37.0	16	4	10	23	0	ND
Daniel McClellan	1	1	0	1	0	.000	5.0	5	9	1	3	0	ND
Totals	10	9	8	[5	4	.555]	76.0	34	38	17	38	2	ND

Individual Batting

Player	Pos	G	AB	R	H	2B	3B	HR	SH	SB	Pct
Harry Buckner	p	6	23	2	3	0	0	0	0	1	.130
Andrew Foster	p	6	25	2	5	1	0	0	0	0	.200
John A. Hill	ss	9	25	4	4	0	0	0	3	0	.160
J. Preston Hill	lf	9	37	7	13	0	1	0	1	4	.351
Daniel McClellan	cf-p	9	33	5	6	1	0	0	2	1	.182
Harry Moore	3b	9	36	5	7	0	0	0	0	1	.194
Dangerfield Talbot	2b	9	36	2	5	1	0	0	0	1	.139
Clarence Williams	c	9	29	3	4	0	0	0	0	1	.138
Ray Wilson	1b	9	37	2	7	1	0	0	1	0	.189
Clarence Winston	cf	8	32	4	8	0	0	0	1	2	.250
Totals		9	312	38	62	4	1	0	8	11	.167

Individual Fielding

Player	Pos	G	O	A	E	Pct
Harry Buckner	p	6	3	15	0	1.000
Andrew Foster	p	6	9	15	3	.889
John A. Hill	ss	9	21	20	5	.891
J. Preston Hill	lf	9	21	2	5	.821
Daniel McClellan	cf,p	9	2	2	0	1.000
Harry Moore	3b	9	16	21	5	.881
Dangerfield Talbot	2b	9	16	24	7	.851
Clarence Williams	c	9	50	13	4	.940
Ray Wilson	1b	9	84	1	5	.950
Clarence Winston	cf	8	9	0	2	.818
Totals		9	231	113	36	.905

ALL-CUBANS

Individual Pitching

Pitcher	G	CG	W	L	Pct	IP	R	H	W	K	ERA
A. D'Meza	1	0	0	1	.000	5.1	6	11	3	3	10.13
J. Muñoz	1	0	0	0	.000	3.2	2	2	0	0	4.90
I. Pérez	2	2	2	0	1.000	18.0	1	6	3	12	0.50
Totals	4	2	2	1	.667	27.0	9	19	6	15	3.00

Individual Batting

All-Cubans	Pos	G	AB	R	H	2B	3B	HR	SH	SB	Pct
L. Bustamante	ss(3)	3	11	1	2	0	0	0	1	1	.191
S. Valdés	2b(1)	1	4	1	1	0	0	0	0	0	.250
R. Almeida	3b(3)	3	11	3	2	0	0	0	0	1	.191
E. Palomino	rf(3)	3	11	4	6	0	0	0	0	0	.545
R. García	c(3)	3	10	3	3	0	0	0	0	3	.300
H. Hidalgo	cf(3)	3	10	1	1	0	0	0	0	1	.100
A. Cabañas	2b(2),cf(1)	3	8	2	3	0	0	0	0	1	.375
A. Marsans	lf()	3	9	1	3	0	0	0	0	0	.333
A. Cabrera	1b(3)	3	11	1	0	0	0	0	0	1	.000
A. D'Meza	p(1)	1	3	0	0	0	0	0	0	1	.000
J. Muñoz	p(1)	1	1	0	0	0	0	0	0	0	.000
I. Pérez	p(2)	2	7	0	0	0	0	0	0	0	.000
Totals		3	95	17	21	0	0	0	1	9	.221

Individual Fielding

All-Cubans	Pos	G	O	A	E	Pct
L. Bustamante	ss(3)	3	8	9	2	.895
S. Valdés	2b(1)	1	1	4	3	.625
R. Almeida	3b(3)	3	4	6	0	1.000
E. Palomino	rf(3)	3	2	0	0	1.000
R. García	c(3)	3	16	6	1	.957
H. Hidalgo	cf(3)	3	9	1	0	1.000
A. Cabañas	2b(2),cf(1)	3	2	2	1	.800
A. Marsans	lf()	3	8	0	1	.889
A. Cabrera	1b(3)	3	31	1	3	.914
A. D'Meza	p(1)	1	0	5	0	1.000
J. Muñoz	p(1)	1	0	0	0	.000
I. Pérez	p(2)	2	0	3	0	1.000
Totals		3	81	37	11	.915

HABANA

Individual Pitching

Pitcher	G	CG	W	L	Pct	IP	R	H	W	K	ERA
P. Olave	1	0	0	1	.000	6.0	4	2	3	6	6.00
M. Prats	1	0	0	0	.000	3.0	0	0	0	1	0.00
L. Padrón	2	2	1	1	.500	18.0	6	11	5	10	3.00
Totals	4	2	1	2	.333	27.0	10	13	8	17	3.33

Individual Batting

Habana	Pos	G	AB	R	H	2B	3B	HR	SH	SB	Pct
E. Prats	1b(3)	3	11	1	2	0	0	0	1	0	.191
A. Arcano	lf(3)	3	12	0	2	0	0	0	0	0	.167
J. Violá	cf(3)	3	11	1	2	0	0	0	0	0	.191

Habana	Pos	G	AB	R	H	2B	3B	HR	SH	SB	Pct
R. Valdés	ss(3)	3	10	2	2	0	0	0	0	1	.200
V. Gonalez	2b(3)	3	10	0	1	0	0	0	0	0	.100
L. Padrón	p(2),rf(1)	3	11	1	4	0	0	0	0	0	.373
B.P. Carrillo	3b(3)	3	10	0	1	0	0	0	1	0	.100
A. Molina	c(3)	3	8	1	1	0	0	0	0	0	.125
P. Olave	p(1)	1	2	0	0	0	0	0	0	0	.000
M. Prats	p(1),rf(2)	3	5	3	1	0	0	0	2	0	.200
Totals		3	90	9	16	0	0	0	4	1	.178

Individual Fielding

Habana	Pos	G	O	A	E	Pct
E. Prats	1b(3)	3	30	0	3	.909
A. Arcano	lf(3)	3	4	0	1	.800
J. Violá	cf(3)	3	4	1	1	.833
R. Valdés	ss(3)	3	5	11	2	.889
V. Gonalez	2b(3)	3	9	6	4	.789
L. Padrón	p(2),rf(1)	3	1	4	1	.833
B.P. Carrillo	3b(3)	3	7	5	2	.857
A. Molina	c(3)	3	19	6	0	1.000
P. Olave	p(1)	1	0	2	0	1.000
M. Prats	p(1),rf(2)	3	2	0	0	1.000
Totals		3	81	35	14	.891

Fe

Individual Pitching

Pitcher	G	CG	W	L	Pct	IP	R	H	W	K	ERA
J.Muñoz	3	2	1	2	.333	22.0	15	24	6	9	6.14
P.Medina	1	0	0	0	.000	5.0	2	6	0	2	3.60
Totals	4	2	1	2	.333	27.0	17	30	6	11	5.67

Individual Batting

Fe	Pos	G	AB	R	H	2B	3B	HR	SH	SB	Pct
C. Morán	3b(3)	3	13	1	5	0	0	0	0	0	.385
S. Valdés	2b(3)	3	14	1	4	0	0	0	0	0	.286
R. Govantes	rf(2),ss(1)	3	10	2	0	0	0	0	1	1	.000
J. Castillo	1b(3)	3	11	2	3	1	0	0	0	0	.273
G. González	c(3)	3	9	1	1	0	0	0	1	0	.111
F. Morán	lf(3)	3	9	0	4	0	0	0	1	0	.444
J. Muñoz	p(3),rf(1)	3	11	1	2	0	0	0	0	0	.191
P. Beanvides	cf(3)	3	12	0	4	1	0	0	0	0	.333
P. Medina	rf(1),p(1)	1	4	0	0	0	0	0	0	0	.000
R. Figarola	ss(2)	2	6	0	0	0	0	0	1	0	.000
Totals		3	99	8	25	2	0	0	4	1	.253

Individual Fielding

Fe	Pos	G	O	A	E	Pct
C. Morán	3b(3)	3	2	9	1	.917
S. Valdés	2b(3)	3	2	15	1	.944
R. Govantes	rf(2),ss(1)	3	1	5	3	.667
J. Castillo	1b(3)	3	41	1	2	.955
G. González	c(3)	3	13	2	0	1.000
F. Morán	lf(3)	3	4	1	2	.714
J. Muñoz	p(3),rf(1)	3	2	5	0	1.000

Fe	Pos	G	O	A	E	Pct
P. Benavides	cf(3)	3	9	0	0	1.000
P. Medina	rf(1),p(1)	1	0	1	1	.500
R. Figarola	ss(2)	2	3	6	1	.900
Totals		3	81	44	12	.912

♦ 5 ♦

1906
Cuban X-Giants

Before making their fifth post-season appearance in Cuba, the X-Giants once again squared off against the Philadelphia Giants for the championship of U.S. blackball clubs. And once again the team that sailed for Cuba was made up of X-Giants from the regular season roster and selected players from the champion Philadelphia club.

Roster

Player	Position	Regular Season Club, 1906
Emmett Bowman	p,2b	Philadelphia Giants
Harry Buckner	p,cf	X-Giants
Luis Bustamente	ss	Cuban Stars
Regino García	c	X-Giants
Bill Gatewood	p,rf	X-Giants
Pete Hill	cf	Philadelphia Giants
John A. Hill	ss	X-Giants
George Johnson	1b	Philadelphia Giants
Harry Moore	3b	Philadelphia Giants
Bruce Petway	c	X-Giants
Clarence Williams	c	X-Giants
Clarence Winston	lf	X-Giants

Emmett "Scotty" Bowman made his second American Series appearance, having played in 1904, then as a member of the X-Giants.

Harry Buckner started with the Chicago Unions in 1896. He also played for the Columbia Giants and Philadelphia Giants before joining the Cuban X-Giants. This was his third trip to Cuba with the X-Giants, and his performance on the mound was marked by the same steadiness he had shown on previous trips.

William "Big Bill" Gatewood made his first appearance in the American Series in 1906, at the age of 25. His career had begun in 1905, with the Leland Giants, and would go on to play for at least 15 different teams before retiring after the 1928 season. He was a good hitter, and when pitching didn't hesitate to knock down other good hitters. His career included the firsr no-hitter pitched in the Negro National League (Heaphy, *Black Baseball and Chicago*, pp. 79–80.)

J. Preston "Pete" Hill appeared in two previous American Series, in 1903 and 1905. After a poor showing on the first trip, he hit .351 against the Cuban clubs in 1905. He would put up nearly identical numbers in the 1906 series, again leading the regulars in batting and stolen bases.

John A. Hill began his career with the Genuine Cuban Giants in 1900. He also played for the Philadelphia Giants and Cuban X-Giants. Like Pete Hill, John Hill had joined the X-Giants in Cuba on two other occasions, in 1903 and in 1905. In 1906 he would lead the barnstormers in sacrifice hits but bat a mere .100.

George "Chappie" Johnson started in 1899 with the Columbia Giants. He also played with the Chicago Union Giants and Brooklyn Royal Giants before his trip to Cuba. Playing out of position for an X-Giants team that already included two superb catchers, Clarence Williams and Bruce Petway, Johnson held his own at first base and enjoyed a strong series at the plate.

Harry "Mike" Moore started with the Chicago Unions in 1896 and also played with the Algona Brownies and Cuban X-Giants. Playing in his third American Series in 1906, Moore was among the leading base stealers but also committed 12 errors at third base.

Bruce Petway appeared in his first American Series in 1906. Petway, among the all-time great defensive catchers of any league, possessed a legendary throwing arm. His performance in Cuba against the 1910 Detroit Tigers contributed heavily to that legend, as Petway is said to have thrown out Ty Cobb three times on consecutive steal attempts (Heaphy, *Black Baseball and Chicago*, pp. 110–111). Bill James ranks Petway fifth among all Negro League catchers and notes that he "could rank higher" (*New Bill James Historical Abstract*, p. 181).

Clarence Williams, the X-Giants' mainstay at catcher for all previous American Series, this time shared the duties with 20-year-old Bruce Petway. Neither player did very much at the plate, but Williams was again steady behind it.

Clarence "Bobby" Winston a fast runner who joined the team on this trip, had previously gained fame as a skilful player. [According to Robert Peterson, Winston would go on to play for the Philadelphia Giants, the Leland Giants, and the Chicago Giants in a career that stretched until 1923 (*Only the Ball Was White*, p. 398).]

Games Played

Date	Winning Club		Losing Club		Winning Pitcher	Losing Pitcher
Nov 4	Habana	8	X-Giants	7	L. González 1–0	W. Gatewood 0–1
Nov 6	X-Giants	10	Habana	1	H. Buckner 1–0	L. González 1–1
Nov 9	X-Giants	8	Almendares	4	W. Gatewood 1–1	A. D'Meza 0–1
Nov 10	Almendares	7	X-Giants	4	E. Palomino 1–0	E. Bowman 0–1
Nov 11	X-Giants	4	Habana	3	H. Buckner 2–0	P. Olave 0–1
Nov 13	Almendares	6	X-Giants	0	J. Muñoz 1–0	H. Buckner 2–1
Nov 16	X-Giants	7	Habana	4	E. Bowman 1–1	L. González 1–2
Nov 17	Almendares	6	X-Giants	0	R. Figarola 1–0	W. Gatewood 1–2
Nov 22	X-Giants	2	Habana	1	E. Bowman 2–1	L. González 1–3
Nov 29	Almendares	4	X-Giants	3	J. Muñoz 2–0	H. Buckner 2–2
Nov 30	X-Giants	10	Almendares	1	W. Gatewood 2–2	A. D'Meza 0–2
(11)						

Club Standings

Clubs	G		W	L	Pct
1.	Almendares	6	4	2	.667
2.	Cuban X-Giants	11	6	5	.545
3.	Habana	5	1	4	.200

Box and Line Scores

SUNDAY, NOVEMBER 2, 1906, AT ALMENDARES PARK

Cuban X-Giants	Pos	AB	R	H	O	A	E		Habana	Pos	AB	R	H	O	A	E
C. Winston	lf	3	1	1	1	1	1		L. Bustamante	ss	4	2	2	2	5	0
J.P. Hill	cf	5	1	2	2	0	0		B. Carrillo	3b	3	0	1	0	3	1

Cuban X-Giants	Pos	AB	R	H	O	A	E
H. Buckner	rf	4	1	1	0	1	1
H. Moore	3b	5	1	2	1	6	4
W. Gatewood	p	4	1	1	1	4	0
E. Bowman	2b	4	1	0	2	1	0
G. Johnson	1b	4	0	1	10	1	1
C. Williams	c	4	0	1	8	3	1
J. Hill	ss	4	1	0	1	1	0
Totals		37	7	9	26	18	8

Habana	Pos	AB	R	H	O	A	E
J. Violá	cf	4	1	0	1	0	1
E. Prats	1b	4	1	2	14	0	2
G. Sánchez	c	4	2	1	4	1	0
V. González	2b	2	1	0	2	3	0
A. Arcano	lf	4	0	1	1	0	0
P. Olave	p	2	1	1	0	6	0
L. González	p	1	0	0	0	0	0
M. Prats	rf	3	0	0	3	0	0
Totals		31	8	8	27	18	4

```
Cuban X-Giants    300    003    010 : 7
Habana            002    003    021 : 8
```

Earned runs: Cuban X-Giants (2), Habana (0)
Sacrifice hits: B. Carrillo, M. Prats
Stolen bases: J. Violá, H. Buckner
Double-plays: L. Bustamante to E. Prats; V. González to L. Bustamante to E. Prats
Bases on balls: P. Olave 4 (C. Winston, H. Buckner, G. Johnson and C. Williams), L.González 1 (H. Buckner), W. Gatewood 5 (L. Bustamante, B.P. Carrillo, P. Olave, V. González 2)
Strikeouts: P. Olave 2 (J.P. Hill and H. Moore), L. González 2 (W. Gatewood, C. Williams), W. Gatewood 6 (L. Bustamante 2, J. Violá, A. Arcano, P. Olave, M. Prats)
Hit Batsmen: P. Olave 1 (W. Gatewood), L. González 1 (a C. Winston)
Passed balls: C. Williams 1
Hits: P. Olave 6 in 7.0 innings
Winning pitcher: L. González
Losing pitcher: W. Gatewood
Time: 2 hours, 26 minutes
Umpires: Antonio Maria García (home) and Eustaquio Gutiérrez (bases)

GAME ONE: THURSDAY, NOVEMBER 6, 1906, AT ALMENDARES PARK

Habana	Pos	AB	C	H	O	A	E
L. Bustamante	ss	4	0	0	2	2	3
B. Carrillo	3b	4	0	0	0	2	1
J. Violá	cf	4	1	1	2	0	0
E. Prats	1b	4	0	0	8	0	0
A. Arcano	lf	4	0	1	2	0	0
V. González	2b	2	0	0	1	1	0
R. Govantes	2b	2	0	1	0	1	0
L. González	p	4	0	1	0	3	0
G. Sánchez	c	3	0	0	6	0	1
M. Prats	rf	2	0	0	3	0	2
Totals		33	1	4	24	9	7

Cuban X-Giants	Pos	AB	R	H	O	A	E
C. Winston	lf	4	2	2	2	0	0
J.P. Hill	cf	5	3	2	3	0	1
H. Buckner	p	5	1	1	1	1	0
H. Moore	3b	4	2	2	1	5	1
W. Gatewood	rf	4	1	1	0	0	0
E. Bowman	2b	4	0	2	0	2	1
G. Johnson	1b	5	0	1	10	0	0
J. Hill	ss	4	0	1	2	1	2
B. Petway	c	4	1	1	8	0	0
Totals		39	10	13	27	10	4

```
Habana           000    000    001 : 1
Cuban X-Giants   102    002    32x : 10
```

Earned runs: Cuban X-Giants (2), Habana (0)
Three-base hits: R. Govantes
Two-base hits: J.P. Hill
Stolen bases: C. Winston, H. Buckner, H. Moore 2, W. Gatewood, B. Petway, E. Prats
Double-plays: L. Bustamante and E. Prats
Bases on balls: L. González 4 (C. Winston, H. Moore, W. Gatewood, E. Bowman), H. Buckner 1 (M. Prats)
Strikeouts: L. González 3 (C. Winston, H. Buckner, W. Gatewood), H. Buckner 7 (B. Carrillo, J. Violá 2, A. Arcano, L. González, M. Prats)
Passed balls: G. Sánchez 1, B. Petway 1
Winning pitcher: H. Buckner

Losing pitcher: L. González
Umpires: Antonio Maria García (home) and Antonio Pérez Utrera (bases)
Scorers: Ramon Mendoza and Francisco Rodríguez

GAME TWO: SUNDAY, NOVEMBER 9, 1906, AT ALMENDARES PARK

Cuban X-Giants	Pos	AB	R	H	O	A	E
C. Winston	lf	4	2	1	2	0	0
J.P. Hill	cf	4	2	1	4	1	0
H. Buckner	rf	5	0	2	0	0	0
H. Moore	3b	3	0	1	4	3	1
W. Gatewood	p	4	0	0	1	4	1
E. Bowman	2b	4	0	0	3	2	1
G.Johnson	1b	4	2	2	9	1	1
C. Williams	c	1	2	0	3	0	0
J. Hill	ss	2	0	0	2	3	1
Totals		31	8	7	27	17	5

Almendares	Pos	AB	R	H	O	A	E
A. Marsans	lf	5	0	0	2	1	0
A. Cabañas	2b	5	1	0	1	0	0
E. Palomino	lf	4	0	2	0	0	0
J. Castillo	1b	4	0	2	12	0	1
G. González	c	4	1	2	8	2	0
H. Hidalgo	cf	3	1	0	3	0	0
R. Valdés	3b	4	1	1	0	1	0
A. Cabrera	ss	3	0	1	1	7	1
A. D'Meza	p	1	0	0	0	0	2
J. Muñoz	p	2	0	0	0	1	0
Totals		35	4	8	27	12	4

Cuban X-Giants	003	400	010 : 8
Almendares	120	000	010 : 4

Earned runs: Cuban X-Giants (1), Almendares (0)
Sacrifice hits: W. Gatewood, C. Williams, J. Hill (2), H. Hidalgo, J. Muñoz
Stolen bases: J.P. Hill 2, H. Buckner, A. Cabañas, H. Hidalgo, A. Cabrera
Double-plays: Cuban X Giants (1), Almendares (1)
Bases on balls: A. D'Meza 3 (P. Hill, H. Moore, G. Johnson), J. Muñoz 2 (H. Moore, C. Winston)
Strikeouts: A. D'Meza 2 (H. Buckner, G. Johnson), J. Muñoz 2 (H. Moore and G. Johnson),
    W. Gatewood 1 (G. González)
Passed balls: G. González
Hits: A. D'Meza 6 in 4.0 innings
Winning pitcher: W. Gatewood
Losing pitcher: A. D'Meza
Time: 2 hours 17 minutes
Umpires: Bobadilla (home) and Antonio Maria García (bases)
Scorers: Ramon Mendoza and Francisco Rodríguez

GAME THREE: MONDAY, NOVEMBER 10, 1906, AT ALMENDARES PARK

Almendares	Pos	AB	R	H	O	A	E
A. Marsans	lf	4	1	1	3	0	1
A. Cabañas	2b	2	1	0	1	0	0
E. Palomino	p	4	1	1	1	3	0
J. Castillo	1b	4	2	1	6	0	0
G. González	c	2	0	0	6	1	0
H. Hidalgo	cf	5	2	3	4	2	0
R. Valdés	ss	4	0	0	2	0	0
R. Almeida	rf	3	0	1	2	0	0
A. Cabrera	ss	4	0	1	2	3	0
Totals		31	7	8	27	9	1

Cuban X-Giants	Pos	AB	R	H	O	A	E
C. Winston	lf	3	0	2	0	0	1
J.P. Hill	cf	4	0	1	5	0	1
H. Buckner	rf	4	0	0	3	0	1
H. Moore	3b	4	1	0	1	1	0
W. Gatewood	2b	4	1	1	2	1	0
E. Bowman	p	3	1	2	0	6	1
G. Johnson	1b	2	1	2	7	0	0
J. Hill	ss	2	0	0	3	1	0
B. Petway	c	2	0	0	6	2	1
C. Williams	c	1	0	0	0	0	0
Totals		31	4	9	27	11	4

Almendares	010	102	111 : 7
Cuban X-Giants	001	000	102 : 4

Earned runs: Cuban X-Giants (1), Almendares (2)
Three-base hits: W. Gatewood, G. Johnson
Two-base hits: E. Palomino

Sacrifice hits: G. Johnson, B. Petway, A. Masans, A. Cabañas, G. González
Stolen bases: C. Winston, E. Palomino, G. González, H. Hidalgo (3)
Double-plays: A. Cabrera (sin asistencia)
Bases on balls: E. Palomino 3 (C. Winston, E. Bowman, G. Johnson), E. Bowman 5
    (E. Palomino, A. Cabañas, G. González 2, R. Almeida)
Strikeouts: E. Palomino 4 (C. Winston, H. Moore, W. Gatewood, C. Williams), E. Bowman 3
    (A. Cabañas, R. Valdés 2)
Wild pitches: E. Bowman
Hit by pitcher: E. Bowman (A. Cabañas, J. Castillo)
Passed balls: B. Petway
Winning pitcher: E. Palomino
Losing pitcher: E. Bowman
Time: 2 hours
Umpires: Bobadilla (home) and Antonio Maria García (bases)
Scorers: Ramon Mendoza and Francisco Rodríguez

GAME FOUR: TUESDAY, NOVEMBER 11, 1906, AT ALMENDARES PARK

Cuban X-Giants	Pos	AB	R	H	O	A	E
C. Winston	lf	5	1	2	5	0	0
J.P. Hill	cf	2	0	0	2	0	0
B. Petway	c-cf	3	2	1	2	0	0
H. Buckner	p	5	1	3	1	7	0
H. Moore	3b	5	0	1	2	1	0
W. Gatewood	rf	4	0	0	0	0	0
E. Bowman	2b	3	0	0	1	3	0
G. Johnson	1b	3	0	1	13	0	0
C. Williams	c	4	0	0	2	0	0
J. Hill	ss	4	0	0	2	4	1
Totals		38	4	8	30	14	1

Habana	Pos	AB	R	H	O	A	E
L. Bustamante	ss	4	0	1	3	8	1
B.P. Carrillo	3b	5	1	2	2	8	0
J. Violá	cf	5	0	0	1	0	0
E. Prats	1b	5	1	2	20	0	2
A. Arcano	lf	4	0	0	0	0	0
G. Sánchez	c	4	0	0	3	0	0
R. Govantes	2b	3	0	0	0	6	1
P. Olave	p	4	0	1	0	0	0
M. Prats	rf	4	1	1	1	0	0
Totals		38	3	7	30	22	4

Cuban X-Giants	001	000	010	2 : 4 (10 innings)
Habana	001	000	001	1 : 3

Earned runs: Cuban X-Giants (2), Habana (2)
Three-base hits: C. Winston
Two-base hits: H. Buckner
Sacrifice hits: E. Bowman
Stolen Bases: L. Bustamante, B.P. Carrillo, M. Prats, C. Winston (2), J.P. Hill, B. Petway
Double-plays: B.P. Carrillo and E. Prats; L. Bustamante, R. Govantes and E. Prats
Bases on balls: H. Buckner 2 (L. Bustamantes, R. Govantes), P. Olave 1 (J. Johnson)
Strikeouts: H. Buckner 2 (L. Bustamante, M. Prats), P. Olave 2 (H. Moore, W. Gatewood)
Hit by pitcher: P. Olave 1 (W. Gatewood)
Winning pitcher: W. Gatewood
Losing pitcher: P. Olave
Time: 1 hour 40 minutes
Umpires: Bobadilla (home) and Antonio Maria García (bases)
Scorers: Ramon Mendoza and Francisco Rodríguez

GAME FIVE: THURSDAY, NOVEMBER 13, 1906, AT ALMENDARES PARK

Cuban X-Giants	Pos	AB	R	H	O	A	E
C. Winston	lf	3	0	1	2	0	1
J.P. Hill	cf	3	0	0	3	0	0
H. Buckner	p	4	0	0	1	6	2
H. Moore	3b	4	0	0	0	2	0
W. Gatewood	rf	4	0	0	0	0	0
E. Bowman	2b	4	0	1	2	0	1

Almendares	Pos	AB	R	H	O	A	E
A. Marsans	lf	3	1	1	0	0	0
J. Muñoz	p	3	0	0	0	4	0
E. Palomino	rf	3	0	0	5	0	1
J. Castillo	1b	4	0	1	9	0	0
G. Gomzalez	c	4	1	0	2	0	0
H. Hidalgo	cf	3	0	0	4	0	0

Cuban X-Giants	Pos	AB	R	H	O	A	E
G. Johnson	1b	3	0	1	10	0	1
J. Hill	ss	3	0	0	3	3	0
B. Petway	c	4	0	1	3	2	0
Totals		32	0	4	24	13	5

Almendares	Pos	AB	R	H	O	A	E
R. Valdés	2b	4	1	1	2	2	0
R. Almeida	3b	3	2	2	0	0	2
A. Cabrera	ss	4	1	2	0	0	0
Totals		31	6	7	27	8	3

Cuban X-Giants	000	000	000 : 0
Almendares	003	102	00x : 6

Earned runs: Cuban X-Giants (0), Almendares (1)
Two-base hits: B. Petway
Sacrifice hits: J.P. Hill, H. Hidalgo, J. Muñoz
Stolen bases: R. Almeida (2), G. Johnson
Bases on balls: J. Muñoz 2 (G. Johnson, J. Hill), H. Buckner 3 (A. Marsans, E. Palomino, R. Almeida)
Strikeouts: J. Muñoz 2 (C. Winston, E. Bowman), H. Buckner 3 (G. González, H. Hidalgo, J. Castillo)
Hit by pitcher: J. Muñoz 1 (C. Winston)
Winning pitcher: J. Muñoz
Losing pitcher: H. Buckner
Time: 1 hour 50 minutes
Umpires: Bobadilla (home) and Antonio Maria García (bases)
Scorers: Ramon Mendoza and Francisco Rodríguez

GAME SIX: SUNDAY, NOVEMBER 16, 1906, AT ALMENDARES PARK

Habana	Pos	AB	R	H	O	A	E
L. Bustamante	ss	4	0	0	3	3	0
B.P. Carrillo	3b	4	0	1	2	0	0
J. Violá	cf	3	1	1	3	0	0
E. Prats	1b	3	2	1	9	0	0
V. González	2b	2	1	1	1	0	0
A. Arcano	lf	4	0	1	3	0	0
G. Sánchez	c	4	0	0	2	4	0
L. González	p	1	0	0	0	2	1
P. Olave	p	3	0	0	0	2	0
M. Prats	rf	3	0	0	1	0	0
Totals		30	4	5	24	11	1

Cuban X-Giants	Pos	AB	R	H	O	A	E
C. Winston	lf	4	0	2	4	0	0
J.P. Hill	cf	4	1	2	0	0	0
H. Buckner	rf	3	1	0	0	0	0
H. Moore	3b	3	1	1	3	4	1
W. Gatewood	2b	4	0	1	0	1	0
E. Bowman	p	4	1	2	0	2	0
G. Johnson	1b	2	2	2	9	0	0
C. Williams	c	2	1	1	7	1	0
J. Hill	ss	3	0	1	4	2	0
Totals		29	7	12	27	10	1

Habana	010	300	000 : 4
Cuban X-Giants	211	002	01x : 7

Earned runs: Cuban X-Giants (4), Habana (0)
Three-base hits: J. Johnson
Two-base hits: A. Arcano, J.P. Hill
Sacrifice hits: E. Prats, G. Johnson (2), J. Hill
Stolen base: H. Moore, G. Johnson, L. Bustamante, P. Olave
Double-plays: G. Sánchez, E. Prats and L. González
Bases on balls: E. Bowman 5 (L. Bustamante, J. Violá, E. Prats, V. González 2); L. González 4
  (J.P. Hill, H. Buckner, H. Moore, C. Williams); P. Olave 1 (C. Winston)
Strikeouts: E. Bowman 4 (L. Bustamante, B.P. Carrillo, J. Violá, G. Sánchez); L. González 1
  (H. Buckner), P. Olave 0
Hit by pitcher: E. Bowman 1 (M. Prats) and P. Olave 1 (C. Williams)
Passed balls: C. Williams (2)
Hits: L. González 6 in 3.2 innings
Winning pitcher: E. Bowman
Losing pitcher: L. González
Time: 1 hour, 55 minutes
Umpires: Marrero (home) and Antonio Maria García) bases)
Scorers: Ramon Mendoza and Francisco Rodríguez

GAME SEVEN: MONDAY, NOVEMBER 17, 1906, AT ALMENDARES PARK

Almendares	Pos	AB	R	H	O	A	E
A. Marsans	lf	5	2	1	3	0	0
R. Almeida	3b	4	1	3	0	5	0
E. Palomino	rf	5	0	1	0	0	0
J. Castillo	1b	4	0	0	15	0	1
G. González	c	5	0	0	5	0	0
H. Hidalgo	cf	4	1	2	2	0	0
R. Valdés	2b	4	0	1	1	1	2
A. Cabrera	ss	4	1	1	1	8	0
R. Figarola	p	4	1	1	0	2	0
Totals		39	6	10	27	16	3

Cuban X-Giants	Pos	AB	R	H	O	A	E
C. Winston	lf	2	0	0	4	0	0
J. Hill	ss	2	0	0	5	3	2
H. Buckner	rf	4	0	1	0	0	0
H. Moore	3b	4	0	0	2	1	2
W. Gatewood	p	4	0	0	1	5	1
E. Bowman	2b	4	0	1	0	3	2
G. Johnson	1b	3	0	0	9	1	1
C. Wiliiams	c	2	0	0	4	0	0
B. Petway	cf	3	0	0	2	0	1
Totals		28	0	2	27	13	9

Almendares	001	010	130 : 6
Cuban X-Giants	000	000	000 : 0

Earned runs: Almendares (3), Cuban X-Giants (0)
Two-base hits: R. Figarola
Sacrifice hits: J. Hill (2), R. Almeida
Stolen bases: E. Palomino, J. Castillo
Double-plays: R. Figarola and R. Almeida
Bases on balls: W. Gatewood 1 (H. Hidalgo), R. Figarola 3 (C. Winston 2, C. Williams)
Strikeouts: W. Gatewood 3 (H. Hidalgo, R. Figarola 2); R. Figarola 4 (J. Hill, H. Moore 2, G. Johnson)
Hit Batsmen: W. Gatewood 1 (J. Castillo)
Passed balls: C. Williams 1, G. González 1
Winning pitcher: R. Figarola
Losing pitcher: W. Gatewood
Time: 2 hours
Umpires: Bobadilla (home) and Antonio Maria García (bases)
Scorers: Francisco Rodríguez and Ramon Mendoza

GAME EIGHT: SUNDAY, NOVEMBER 22, 1906, AT ALMENDARES PARK

Cuban X-Giants	Pos	AB	R	H	O	A	E
C. Winston	lf	3	0	1	2	0	1
J. Hill	ss	4	0	0	1	3	0
H. Buckner	rf	3	1	0	0	0	0
H. Moore	3b	3	0	1	1	2	2
W. Gatewood	2b	3	0	0	0	3	0
E. Bowman	p	4	1	1	0	7	0
G. Johnson	c	4	0	1	10	0	0
C. Williams	1b	3	0	0	12	2	1
B. Petway	cf	4	0	0	1	1	1
Totals		31	2	4	27	18	5

Habana	Pos	AB	R	H	O	A	E
L. Bustamante	ss	3	0	0	6	3	0
B.P. Carrillo	3b	4	1	0	2	1	1
J. Violá	cf	3	0	1	3	0	0
E. Prats	1b	3	0	0	4	0	1
R. Govantes	rf	3	0	1	1	0	0
V. González	2b	2	0	2	4	2	1
A. Arcano	lf	4	0	1	3	0	0
G. Sánchez	c	4	0	0	4	1	0
L. González	p	3	0	1	0	2	1
Totals		29	1	5	27	9	4

Cuban X-Giants	010	001	000 : 2
Habana	001	000	000 : 1

Earned runs: Cuban X-Giants (1), Habana (0)
Three-base hits: G. Johnson
Sacrifice hits: C. Winston and L. Bustamante
Stolen bases: H. Buckner
Bases on balls: E. Bowman 5 (J. Violá, E. Prats, R. Govantes, V. González 2); L.González 4
   (H. Buckner, H. Moore, W. Gatewood, C. Williams)
Strikeouts: E. Bowman 6 (L. Bustamante, B. Carrillo, J. Violá, R. Govantes, A. Arcano, L. González);
   L. González 4 (J. Hill, H. Buckner, H. Moore, W. Gatewood)
Wild pitches: E. Bowman 1
Winning pitcher: E. Bowman

Losing pitcher: L. González
Time: 1 hour 40 minutes
Umpires: Marrero (home) and Antonio Maria García (bases)
Scorers: R.Rodríguez and Ramon Mendoza

GAME NINE: SUNDAY, NOVEMBER 29, 1906, AT ALMENDARES PARK

Cuban X-Giants	Pos	AB	R	H	O	A	E
C. Winston	lf	4	1	1	2	0	1
J.P. Hill	cf	5	0	2	1	0	0
L. Bustamante	ss	5	0	0	2	4	1
R. García	c	5	0	2	5	1	0
H. Buckner	p	4	0	1	3	2	1
H. Moore	3b	3	0	1	1	5	0
W. Gatewood	rf,1b	5	1	2	5	0	0
E. Bowman	2b	2	1	1	1	8	1
G. Johnson	1b	3	0	0	10	0	1
B. Petway	rf	2	0	2	0	0	0
Totals		38	3	12	30	20	5

Almendares	Pos	AB	R	H	O	A	E
R. Valdés	ss	4	1	1	4	3	1
A. Marsans	lf	5	1	0	2	1	0
R. Almeida	3b	4	2	1	2	2	0
E. Palomino	rf	5	0	1	2	0	0
G. González	c	4	0	0	8	4	0
H. Hidalgo	cf	4	0	1	2	1	0
A. Cabañas	2b	4	0	1	3	2	1
J. Muñoz	p	4	0	0	0	3	0
A. Cabrera	1b	4	0	2	10	0	0
Totals		38	4	7	33	16	2

Cuban X-Giants	100	001	001	0 : 3
Almendares	300	000	000	1 : 4

One out when winning run
Earned runs: Cuban X-Giants (1), Almendares (0)
Three-base hits: J.P. Hill
Two-base hits: W. Gatewood
Sacrifice hits: C. Winston, E. Bowman, R. Almeida
Stolen bases: R. Valdés, R. Almeida
Double-plays: E. Bowman, L. Bustamante and G. Johnson
Bases on balls: H. Buckner 1 (R. Valdés), J. Muñoz 7 (C. Winston, J.P. Hill, H. Buckner, H. Moore 2, E. Bowman 2)
Strikeouts: H. Buckner 2 (G. González, A. Cabrera, J. Muñoz 5 (J.P. Hill, L. Bustamante 2, W. Gatewood, G. Johnson)
Wild pitches: J. Muñoz 1
Winning pitcher: J. Muñoz
Losing pitcher: H. Buckner
Time: 2 hours 20 minutes
Umpires: Bobadilla (home) and Antonio Maria García (bases)
Scorers: Francisco Rodríguez and Ramon Mendoza

GAME TEN: MONDAY, NOVEMBER 30, 1906, AT ALMENDARES PARK

Almendares	Pos	AB	R	H	O	A	E
R. Valdés	2b	4	0	0	3	2	2
A. Marsans	1b	4	0	1	12	0	1
R. Almeida	3b	4	0	0	1	3	0
E. Palomino	rf	4	0	0	0	0	0
G. González	c	4	0	0	3	0	1
H. Hidalgo	cf	1	1	0	3	0	1
A. Cabañas	2b	2	0	0	1	0	0
A. Cabrera	1b	3	0	0	0	3	0
A. D'Meza	p	3	0	0	0	4	1
J. Muñoz	p	0	0	0	0	0	0
Totals		29	1	1	24	12	6

Cuban X-Giants	Pos	AB	R	H	O	A	E
C. Winston	lf	5	2	3	2	0	1
J.P. Hill	cf	5	2	3	0	0	0
H. Buckner	rf	3	1	0	1	0	0
H. Moore	3b	4	1	0	1	2	1
R. García	c	4	1	2	6	1	0
W. Gatewood	p	4	1	1	1	3	0
E. Bowman	2b	4	0	0	3	4	0
L. Bustamante	ss	4	0	0	1	5	1
G. Johnson	1b	3	2	1	12	1	1
Totals		36	10	10	27	16	4

Almendares	010	000	000 : 1
Cuban X-Giants	000	005	32x : 10

Earned runs: Cuban X-Giants (2), Almendares (0)
Sacrifice hits: H. Buckner, A. Cabañas
Stolen bases: R. Almeida, H. Hidalgo, A. Cabrera, C. Winston 2. J.P. Hill 2, H. Buckner, G. Johnson
Double-plays: H. Moore and W. Gatewood
Bases on balls: W. Gatewood 2 (H. Hidalgo 2); A. D'Meza 0, J. Muñoz 1 (G. Johnson)
Strikeouts: W. Gatewood 6 (A. Marsans, R. Alemida, G. González 2, A. Cabrera, A. D'Meza)
Passed balls: R. García 1
Hits: A. D'Meza 10 in 7.2 innings
Winning pitcher: W. Gatewood
Losing pitcher: A. D'Meza
Time: 1 hour 45 minutes
Umpires: Bobadilla (home) and Antonio Maria García (bases)
Scorers: Francisco Rodríguez and Ramon Mendoza

Final Statistics

CUBAN X-GIANTS

Individual Pitching

Pitcher	G	GS	GC	W	L	Pct	IP	R	H	W	K	ERA
Emmett Bowman	3	3	3	2	1	.667	27.0	12	18	15	13	ND
Harry Buckner	4	4	4	2	2	.500	37.0	14	25	7	14	ND
William Gatewood	4	4	4	2	2	.500	34.2	19	27	9	16	ND
Totals	11	11	11	6	5	.545	98.2	45	70	31	43	ND

Individual Batting

Player	Pos	G	AB	R	H	2B	3B	HR	SH	SB	Pct
Emmett Bowman	2b,p	11	40	5	10	0	0	0	2	0	.250
Harry Buckner	cf,p	11	44	6	9	1	0	0	1	5	.205
William Gatewood	rf,p	11	44	5	7	1	1	0	1	1	.159
John A. Hill	ss	9	30	1	3	0	0	0	5	0	.100
J.Preston Hill	cf	9	37	9	13	1	1	0	1	5	.351
George Johnson	1b	11	36	7	12	0	3	0	3	3	.333
Harry Moore	3b	11	42	6	9	0	0	0	0	3	.214
Bruce Petway	c	7	22	3	5	1	0	0	1	2	.227
Clarence Williams	c	7	17	3	2	0	0	0	1	0	.118
Clarence Winston	lf	11	40	9	13	0	1	0	2	6	.325
Luis Bustamante	ss	2	9	0	0	0	0	0	0	0	.000
Regino García	c	2	9	1	4	0	0	0	0	0	.400
Totals		11	370	55	90	4	6	0	17	25	.243

Individual Fielding

Player	Pos	G	O	A	E	Pct
Emmett Bowman	2b,p	11	12	38	6	.893
Harry Buckner	cf,p	11	10	17	4	.871
William Gatewood	rf,p	11	11	21	2	.941
John A. Hill	ss	9	23	21	6	.870
J.Preston Hill	cf	9	20	1	2	.905
George Johnson	1b	11	109	4	6	.950
Harry Moore	3b	11	17	32	12	.797
Bruce Petway	c	7	22	5	3	.900
Clarence Williams	c	7	35	9	1	.971
Clarence Winston	lf	11	26	1	6	.818
Luis Bustamante	ss	2	3	9	2	.857
Regino García	c	2	11	2	0	1.000
Totals		11	299	160	49	.905

ALMENDARES

Individual Pitching

Pitchers	G	C	W	L	Pct	IP	R	H	W	SO	ERT
A. D'Meza	2	0	0	2	.000	11.2	8	16	3	2	...
J. Muñoz	4	2	2	0	1.000	25.1	6	19	11	5	...
E. Palomino	1	1	1	0	1.000	9.0	4	9	3	4	...
R. Figarola	1	1	1	0	1.000	9.0	0	2	3	4	...
Totals	8	4	4	2	.667	555.0	18	46	20	15	...

Individual Batting

Almendares	Pos	G	AB	R	H	2b	3b	HR	SH	SB	Pct
A. Marsans	lf(),1b(1)	6	26	5	4	0	0	0	0	0	.154
A. Cabañas	2b(4)	4	13	2	1	0	0	0	2	1	.077
E. Palomino	rf(4),lf(1),p(p)	6	25	1	5	1	0	0	0	2	.200
J. Castillo	1b(4)	4	16	2	4	0	0	0	0	1	.250
G. Gonalez	c(6)	6	23	2	2	0	0	0	1	1	.087
H. Hidalgo	cf(6)	6	20	5	6	0	0	0	2	5	.300
R. Valdés	2b(),b(1),ss(2)	6	24	3	4	0	0	0	0	1	.167
A. Cabrera	1b(2),ss(4)	6	22	2	7	0	0	0	0	2	.318
R. Almeida	3b(4),rf(1)	5	18	5	7	0	0	0	2	4	.389
J. Muñoz	p(4)	4	9	0	0	0	0	0	2	0	.000
A. D'Meza	p(2)	2	4	0	0	0	0	0	0	0	.000
R. Figarola	p(1)	1	4	1	1	1	0	0	0	0	.250
Totals		6	203	28	41	2	0	0	9	17	.202

Individual Fielding

Almendares	Pos	G	O	A	E	Pct
A. Marsans	lf(),1b(1)	6	22	2	2	.923
A. Cabañas	2b(4)	4	6	2	1	.889
E. Palomino	rf(4),lf(1),p(p)	6	8	3	1	.917
J. Castillo	1b(4)	4	42	0	2	.955
G. Gonalez	c(6)	6	32	7	1	.975
H. Hidalgo	cf(6)	6	18	3	1	.955
R. Valdés	2b(),b(1),ss(2)	6	12	9	5	.808
A. Cabrera	1b(2),ss(4)	6	14	21	1	.972
R. Almeida	3b(4),rf(1)	5	5	10	2	.882
J. Muñoz	p(4)	4	0	8	0	1.000
A. D'Meza	p(2)	2	0	4	3	.571
R. Figarola	p(1)	1	0	2	0	1.000
Totals		6	135	73	19	.878

HABANA

Individual Pitching

Pitcher	G	CG	W	L	Pct	IP	R	H	W	K
L.González	4	2	1	3	.250	22.2	17	25	13	10
P.Olave	3	1	0	1	.000	21.1	13	21	5	5
Totals	7	3	1	4	.200	44.0	30	46	18	15

Individiual Batting

Habana	Pos	Pos	AB	R	H	2b	3b	HR	SH	SB	Pct
L. Bustamante	ss(5)	5	19	2	3	0	0	0	1	2	.158
B.P. Carrillo	3b(5)	5	20	2	4	0	0	0	1	1	.200
J. Violá	cf()	5	19	3	3	0	0	0	0	1	.158

Habana	Pos	Pos	AB	R	H	2b	3b	HR	SH	SB	Pct
E. Prats	1b(5)	5	19	4	5	0	0	0	1	1	.263
G. Sánchez	c(5)	5	19	2	1	0	0	0	0	0	.053
V. González	2b(4)	4	8	2	3	0	0	0	0	0	.375
A. Arcano	lf(50	5	20	0	4	1	0	0	0	1	.200
P. Olave	p(3)	3	9	1	2	0	0	0	0	1	.222
L. González	p(4)	4	9	0	2	0	0	0	0	0	.222
M. Prats	rf(4)	4	12	1	1	0	0	0	1	1	.833
R. Govantes	2b(2),rf(1)	3	8	0	2	0	1	0	0	0	.250
Totals		6	161	17	29	1	1	0	4	7	.180

Individual Fielding

Habana	Pos	G	O	A	E	Pct
L. Bustamante	ss(5)	5	16	21	4	.902
B.P. Carrillo	3b(5)	5	6	14	3	.870
J. Violá	cf()	5	10	0	1	.909
E. Prats	1b(5)	5	55	0	5	.917
G. Sánchez	c(5)	5	19	6	1	.962
V. González	2b(4)	4	8	6	1	.933
A. Arcano	lf(50)	5	9	0	0	1.000
P. Olave	p(3)	3	0	8	0	1.000
L. González	p(4)	4	0	7	2	.778
M. Prats	rf(4)	4	8	0	2	.800
R. Govantes	2b(2),rf(1)	3	1	7	1	.889
Totals		6	132	69	20	.910

♦ 6 ♦

1907
Philadelphia Giants

The U.S. champion Philadelphia Giants had been assembled by player-manager Sol White, the man who later wrote the first history of black baseball. White was absent from Cuba, however; and while the Giants' lineup was formidable, it included a number of players not on their regular season roster. And after November 20, the names changed once again, as four players (Bill Gatewood, Nate Harris, Andrew Payne, and Bobby Winston) replaced departing stars Grant "Home Run" Johnson, Pete Hill, Dan McClellan, and Bill Holland. Both versions of the club lost more games than they won, with the ad hoc Giants going 5–7 with their first lineup and 4–6 with the substitute players onboard.

First Round

Roster

Player	Position	Regular Season Club, 1907
Emmett Bowman	3b	Philadelphia Giants
John Davis	p	Chicago Leland Giants
Charles B. Earle	cf	Independent
Pete Hill	lf	CHI Leland Giants and Philadelphia Giants
William Holland	p,rf	Brooklyn Royal Giants
Grant Johnson	ss	Brooklyn Royal Giants
John Henry Lloyd	ss	Philadelphia Giants
Daniel McClellan	p	Philadelphia Giants
Bruce Petway	rf,1b	Philadelphia Giants
Felix Wallace	1b,2b	Famous Cuban Giants
Clarence Williams	c,1b	Philadelphia Giants

Emmett "Scotty" Bowman played with the Philadelphia Giants in 1905. This was his second trip to Cuba.

John Davis began with the Leland Giants in 1905. He also played with the Cuban Giants before joining the Philadelphia Giants.

C.B. Earle played with the Wilmington Giants, Cuban Giants and Philadelphia Giants before his trip to Cuba.

Pete Hill started with the Philadelphia Giants in 1903.

William "Billy" Holland began with the Page Fence Giants in 1896. He played for the Chicago Unions and Brooklyn Royal Giants.

Grant "Home Run" Johnson earned the nickname "Home Run" by his powerful righthanded swing in the dead-ball era. He began a career in 1895 that took him to the best of the early twentieth century clubs. He played with the Page Fence Giants of Adrian, Michigan, the Columbia Giants and the Brooklyn Royal Giants before joining the Cuban X Giants.

Pop Lloyd began his career in 1905 as a twenty-year-old professional ball player, a catcher for the Macon Acmes, Georgia. He also played with the Cuban X Giants and Philadelphia Giants. The 1907 trip was his first to Cuba.

Dan McClellan started with the Cuban X Giants.

Bruce Petway, began with the Leland Giants in 1906. This was his second trip to Cuba. Felix Wallace was on his first trip to Cuba.

Clarence Williams started with the Cuban Giants in 1886. He played with the New York Gorhams, Cuban X Giants and Philadelphia Giants.

Games Played

Date	Winning Club		Losing Club		Winning Pitcher	Losing Pitcher
Oct 10	Almendares	6	PHI Giants	0	J. Muñoz 1–0	W. Holland 0–1
Oct 13	PHI Giants	9	Habana	4	J. Davis 1–0	L. González 0–1
Oct 14	Almendares	2	PHI Giants	1	C. Royer 1–0	W. Holland 0–2
Oct 17	PHI Giants	5	Habana	1	D. McClellan 1–0	I. Pérez 0–1
Oct 20	Almendares	1	PHI Giants	0	A. Ortega 1–0	J. Davis 1–1
Oct 21	Habana	3	PHI Giants	1	L. González 1–1	W. Holland 0–3
Oct 24	PHI Giants	3	Almendares	1	J. Davis 2–1	J. Muñoz 1–1
Oct 27	Habana	7	PHI Giants	5	I. Pérez 1–1	W. Holland 0–4
Oct 28	Almendares	4	PHI Giants	4	–Tied-A. Ortega-J. Davis	
Oct 31	PHI Giants	12	Habana	1	W. Holland 1–4	L. González 1–2
Nov 3	Almendares	5	PHI Giants	4	C. Royer 2–0	J. Davis 2–2
Nov 4	Habana	5	PHI Giants	1	L. González 2–2	D. McClellan 1–1
Nov 8	PHI Giants	8	Almendares	2	J. Davis 3–2	A. Ortega 1–1
(13)						

Club Standings

Pos	Club	G	W	L	T	Pct
1.	Almendares	7	4	2	1	.667
2.	Habana	6	3	3	0	.500
3.	Philadelphia Giants	13	5	7	1	.417
	Totals	26	12	12	2	.500

The Games

GAME ONE: THURSDAY, OCTOBER 10, 1907, AT ALMENDARES PARK

Almendares	Pos	AB	R	H	O	A	E
R. Valdés	lf	4	1	1	2	0	0
J. Muñoz	p	3	1	0	2	1	0
G. González	c	4	1	1	5	0	0
J. Castillo	1b	4	0	2	15	1	0
R. Almeida	3b	4	1	0	2	7	1
A. Cabañas	2b	4	1	1	0	5	0
H. Hidalgo	cf	3	0	0	0	0	0
A. Cabrera	ss	4	1	1	1	0	0
A. Marsans	cf	4	0	2	0	0	0
Totals		34	6	8	27	4	1

PHI Giants	Pos	AB	R	H	O	A	E
C.B. Earle	cf	3	0	1	0	0	0
J.P. Hill	lf	3	0	0	3	0	1
D. McClellan	rf	4	0	0	0	0	0
J.H. Lloyd	2b	4	0	0	1	3	0
E. Bowman	3b	4	0	0	3	3	1
F. Wallace	ss	3	0	0	1	2	0
B. Petway	1b	3	0	0	6	1	0
W. Holland	p	3	0	1	0	5	0
C. Williams	c	3	0	2	3	0	1
Totals		30	0	4	27	0	3

Almendares	000	002	004 : 6
Philadelphia Giants	000	000	000 : 0

Earned runs: Almendares (4), PHI Giants (0)
Two-base hits: A. Cabrera
Sacrifice hits: J.P. Hill
Stolen bases: G. González (2) and J. Castillo
Bases on balls: W. Holland 1, J. Muñoz 1
Strikeouts: W. Holland 1, J. Muñoz 4
Dead balls: W. Holland 2 (H. Hidalgo and R. Valdés)
Winning pitcher: J. Muñoz
Losing pitcher: W. Holland
Time: 1 hour 45 minutes
Umpires: Antonio Maria García (home) and Eustaquio Gutiérrez (bases)
Scorer: Francisco Rodríguez

On Tuesday, October 11, *El Diario de la Marina* published an account of Monday's first game on page 5 of the afternoon edition. The reporter, identified only as "Mendoza," makes no mention of Monday's second game, which the hometown Habana club lost. The article is reproduced below, translated by Peter Bjarkman.

The Thrashed Masters
Before a large crowd at the Carlos III ballpark yesterday afternoon, this year's new series of contests was inaugurated between visiting North American ball clubs and two teams of stars from local championship nines.

The local outfit known as the "Blues" first opened fire against the American Negro League champions, the Philadelphia Giants, and the fire of our own "Boys" was so deadly that none of the Philadelphians remained standing. That is to say, none of the opposition reached home plate, because all were cut down on the base paths, such was the skill and the attack of our own blue birds.

This is not at all to say that the visiting champions were of low quality, nothing like that, but instead they were an exceptionally strong team that played well in the field. But the visitors lacked an offensive attack; at least that was our impression of this opening match.

The very strength of the Philadelphia club was precisely why the match with the local professional "Blues" team was so vitally important, especially for the American "imports" (who play with Cuban teams during the winter). But these imports never could break through and were shut out for nine innings.

Among the "imports" that we are already most familiar with was Pete Hill, who in last year's Cuban championship season played with Club Fe; "Rascun" (Dan McClellan) who was with Team Habana; and the great "Pinta-Copa" (Bruce Petway), the well-known and talented ballplayer who is heftier than our own "Tinti" (Molina).

The Americans, as we have said, are excellent in the field, particularly in their play at third base [a reference to Emmett Bowman], but they are all not very dexterous at the plate.

As for the teams waiting on deck, all—definitely all—are probably superior, to the degree that yesterday we would have liked to see big leaguers from Chicago or Detroit play against us, because those guys would likely have discovered just how tough the local Cuban players actually are.

On the mound for the Blues was the likeable José Muñoz, who proved to be the talented moundsman that he always seems to be, in other words, an absolutely great hurler, especially in championship games.

Almeida, Cabrera and Castillo were the heroes of the afternoon, and their professional play brought great cheers from the crowd.

GAME TWO: SUNDAY, OCTOBER 13, 1907, AT ALMENDARES PARK

PHI Giants	Pos	AB	R	H	O	A	E	Habana	Pos	AB	R	H	O	A	E
C.B. Earle	cf	4	1	1	0	0	0	C. Morán	3b	4	1	2	1	1	2
J.P. Hill	lf	4	2	2	1	0	1	S. Valdés	2b	3	0	0	3	3	0
D. McClellan	rf	4	1	2	0	0	1	R. García	c	2	1	0	3	1	1
J.H. Lloyd	2b	4	2	1	3	2	0	L. González	p	3	0	1	0	1	0
E. Bowman	3b	5	1	1	0	3	2	L. Padrón	p,lf	5	0	0	2	3	0
F. Wallace	ss	5	1	2	5	1	1	V. González	cf	4	0	1	1	0	0
B. Petway	c,1b	5	0	1	8	2	1	M. Prats	rf	4	0	2	0	0	0

PHI Giants	Pos	AB	R	H	O	A	E
C. Williams	1b,c	2	1	0	10	0	0
J. Davis	p	3	0	0	0	3	1
Totals		36	9	10	27	11	7

Habana	Pos	AB	R	H	O	A	E
L. Bustamante	ss	3	0	0	1	5	1
F. Morán	lf,1b	4	1	0	7	0	1
A. Molina	c	3	1	0	0	0	1
Totals		35	4	6	27	14	6

Philadelphia Giants	004	310	010 : 9
Habana	200	000	002 : 4

Earned runs: Philadelphia Giants (9), Habana (0)
Two-base hits: J.H. Lloyd
Sacrifice hits: J. Davis and S. Valdés
Stolen bases: J.P. Hill (2), D. McClellan and L. Padrón
Double-plays: J.H. Lloyd, B. Petway and F. Wallace; S. Valdés, L. Bustamante and F. Morán
Bases on balls: L. Padrón 3, L. González 1, J. Davis 3
Strikeouts: L. Padrón 3, L. González 2, J. Davis 7
Dead balls: L. Padrón 1 (C.Williams) and L.González 1 (C.Williams)
Wild pitches: J. Davis
Winning pitcher: J.Davis
Losing pitcher: Luis Padrón
Passed balls: B.Petway
Time: 1 hour 50 minutes
Umpires: Antonio Maria García (home) and Eustaquio Gutiérrez (bases)
Scorer: Francisco Rodríguez

As it had for Game One, the local newpaper *Diario de la Marina* published an account for the series' second game.

October 14, 1907
Diario de la Marina
Afternoon Edition
Page 5

Baseball
And What About the Reds?
The masters (translator's note: meaning the American pros) did to the Reds yesterday what the Blues did to them last Thursday.
The Americans, except in the first inning, in which they substituted for both the first and third basemen, played well and showed more batting skills than they had in their first outing.
In the field they made splendid plays, especially Wallace who plays third base and who robbed Miguel Prats of a base hit, a play that earned an ovation from the large crowd attending the match.
The pitcher named Davis was very effective and completely dominated the Reds batters, especially with his fast ball which showed top speed.
He alone struck out the opposing side, putting away the majority of the Reds batters with ease.
The Reds played very carelessly and without any signs of cohesion.
Luis Padrón was blasted, to the degree that if he had not been taken from the mound the slugging would never have stopped.
He was replaced by his namesake Luis González, who was able to shut down Philadelphia for a while.
[Translation by Peter Bjarkman]

GAME THREE: MONDAY, OCTOBER 14, 1907, AT ALMENDARES PARK

PHI Giants	Pos	AB	R	H	O	A	E
C.B. Earle	cf	4	0	0	1	0	0
J.P. Hill	lf	3	0	0	3	0	1
D. McClellan	rf	3	0	0	1	0	0
J.H. Lloyd	2b	3	1	1	4	2	0

Almendares	Pos	AB	R	H	O	A	E
R. Valdés	lf	4	1	2	2	0	0
A. Cabañas	2b	3	0	1	2	2	0
E. Palomino	rf	4	0	0	0	0	0
J. Castillo	1b	3	1	2	10	1	0

PHI Giants	Pos	AB	R	H	O	A	E
G. Johnson	ss	3	0	0	1	1	0
E. Bowman	1b	3	0	1	8	2	0
F. Wallace	3b	3	0	1	2	2	0
W. Holland	p	3	0	0	0	3	0
B. Petway	c	2	0	1	4	0	0
C. Williams	c	0	0	0	0	0	0
Totals		27	1	4	24	10	1

Almendares	Pos	AB	R	H	O	A	E
G. González	c	4	0	1	5	2	0
R. Almeida	3b	3	0	0	1	3	0
H.Hidalgo	cf	2	0	2	1	0	0
A. Cabrera	ss	3	0	0	3	3	0
C. Royer	p	3	0	0	0	2	0
Totals		29	2	8	24	13	0

Philadelphia Giants	000	010	00 : 1 (eight innings)
Almendares	000	100	00 : 2

Earned runs: Philadelphia Giants (1), Almendares (1)
Sacrifice hits: A. Cabañas and H. Hidalgo
Stolen bases: F. Wallace and J. Castillo
Double-plays: J. Castillo, A. Cabañas and A. Cabrera
Bases on balls: C. Royer 2, W. Holland 1
Strikeouts: C. Royer 5, W. Holland 3
Dead balls: W. Holland 1 (R. Almeida)
Winning pitcher: C. Royer
Losing pitcher: W. Holland.
Passed balls: B. Petway
Time: 1 hour 50 minutes
Umpires: Antonio Maria García (home) and Eustaquio Gutiérrez (bases)
Scorer: Francisco Rodríguez

A third game report, and the final one known to have been published, appeared on Friday, October, 15.

October 15, 1907
Diario de la Marina
Afternoon Edition

Baseball
A Professional Game
Before a huge crowd yesterday afternoon transpired the second meeting between the baseball nines the Blues, comprised of Cuban players, and the Philadelphia Black Giants. The teams played in so professional a manner that the first-mentioned Blues gained the victory with only two runs to a single tally made by their opponents.

The game was of superior quality as both clubs played to full potential and defended their respective fields palm to palm (translator's note: that is, with equal skill).

The pitchers for both teams were most effective, especially Carlos Royer, the great "Baby," who reminded us of his best previous outings, performing a superior work on the mound.

All the players performed well, but of all the great individual plays performed, those of the fifth inning especially stood out, as explained here:

Rogelio Valdés made a spectacular base hit; Cabañas, the irreplaceable second baseman, made an out by flying to left field; Palomino hit a sharp grounder which the second baseman grabbed and then threw him out at first. Castillo, who would not be satisfied with a single hit, swung mightily at a pitch from the American hurler, and lashed the ball over third base; as a result Rogelio Valdés raced home to score the second and final run for the Blues.

The inning ended when Muñoz, who ran for Castillo, was forced out at second, after the American third sacker grabbed a hard bouncer hit by Strike González and tossed over to second for the force.

Philadelphia's only run was made in this same inning on consecutive base hits by Lloyd, Wallace and Bowman.

[Translation by Peter Bjarkman]

GAME FOUR: SUNDAY, OCTOBER 17, 1907, AT ALMENDARES PARK

Habana	Pos	AB	R	H	O	A	E
L. Bustamante	ss	4	0	2	1	1	0

PHI Giants	Pos	AB	R	H	O	A	E
C.B. Earle	cf	3	1	1	2	0	0

Habana	Pos	AB	R	H	O	A	E
S. Valdés	2b	4	1	1	2	3	2
L. Padrón	lf	2	0	0	3	1	0
V. González	cf	4	0	1	3	0	1
F. Morán	1b	3	0	0	8	0	0
C. Morán	3b	4	0	0	1	2	0
A. Molina	c	3	0	0	3	0	0
M. Prats	rf	4	0	0	2	0	1
J. Pérez	p	3	0	1	1	0	0
Totals		31	1	5	24	10	4

PHI Giants	Pos	AB	R	H	O	A	E
J.P. Hill	lf	3	1	2	5	0	0
D. McClellan	p	2	1	1	0	2	0
J.H. Lloyd	2b	4	1	2	4	4	0
G. Johnson	ss	4	1	2	4	4	2
E. Bowman	1b	4	0	1	11	1	0
F. Wallace	3b	4	0	1	0	4	0
B. Petway	rf	4	0	0	0	0	0
C. Williams	c	2	0	0	1	0	0
Totals		30	5	9	27	15	2

Habana 100 000 000 : 1
Philadelphia Giants 203 000 000 : 5

Earned runs: Philadelphia Giants (1), Habana (0)
Home runs: G. Johnson
Two-Base hits: G. Johnson
Sacrifice hits: D. McClellan
Stolen bases: J.P. Hill and D. McClellan
Double-plays: J.H. Lloyd, G. Johnson and E. Bowman (2)
Bases on balls: J. Pérez 4, D. McClellan 3
Strikeouts: J. Pérez 1, D. McClellan 1
Wild pitches: J. Pérez 1, D. McClellan 1
Winning pitcher: D. McClellan
Losing pitcher: J. Pérez
Time: 1 hour 50 minutes
Umpires: Antonio Maria García (home), Eustaquio Gutiérrez (bases)
Scorer: Francisco Rodríguez

GAME FIVE: SUNDAY, OCTOBER 30, 1907, AT ALMENDARES PARK

Almendares	Pos	AB	R	H	O	A	E
R. Valdés	lf	4	1	1	2	0	0
A. Cabañas	2b	4	0	2	1	5	0
G. González	c	4	0	0	2	1	0
J. Castillo	1b	2	0	0	14	0	0
R. Almeida	3b	4	0	1	1	1	0
A. Marsans	lf	1	0	0	2	0	0
E. Palomino	rf	2	0	0	0	0	0
H. Hidalgo	cf	3	0	1	3	0	0
A. Cabrera	ss	2	0	0	2	4	0
A. Ortega	p	3	0	0	0	5	1
Totals		29	1	5	27	16	1

PHI Giants	Pos	AB	R	H	O	A	E
J.P. Hill	lf	4	0	0	3	0	0
D. McClellan	rf	4	0	0	0	0	0
G. Johnson	ss	3	0	1	2	6	2
J.H. Lloyd	2b	4	0	0	2	2	0
C.B. Earle	cf	3	0	2	2	1	0
E. Bowman	1b	3	0	0	12	1	0
F. Wallace	3b	3	0	1	0	1	1
C. Williams	c	3	0	0	5	0	1
J. Davis	p	2	0	0	1	4	0
Totals		29	0	4	27	15	2

Almendares 001 000 000 : 1
Philadelphia Giants 000 000 000 : 0

Two-base hits: H. Hidalgo
Sacrifice hits: J. Castillo and A. Cabrera
Doubles-plays: J.H. Lloyd, G. Johnson and E. Bowman
Bases on balls: A. Ortega 1, J. Davis 3
Strikeouts: A. Ortega 1, J. Davis 3
Wild pitches: J. Davis
Dead balls: A. Ortega 1 (J. Davis)
Winning pitcher: A. Ortega
Losing pitcher: J. Davis
Time: 1 hour 45 minutes
Umpires: Antonio Maria García (home) and Eustaquio Gutiérrez (bases)
Scorer: Francisco Rodríguez

The run in the third inning was produced by a single of Simon Valdés to the third base, and after arrived to third base by error of Felix Wallace, later he scored subsequently for a wild pitches of Davis. Everything these registered after two outs.

GAME SIX: MONDAY, OCTOBER 1, 1907, AT ALMENDARES PARK

PHI Giants	Pos	AB	R	H	O	A	E
J.P. Hill	lf	4	0	1	2	0	1
D. McClellan	rf	2	0	0	0	0	0
G. Johnson	ss	3	0	0	0	1	2
J.H. Lloyd	2b	4	0	1	2	2	1
C.B. Earle	cf	3	0	0	1	0	0
E. Bowman	c	4	0	0	9	1	0
F. Wallace	3b	3	0	0	2	0	0
B. Petway	1b	3	1	1	7	1	0
W. Holand	p	3	0	0	1	6	0
Totals		29	1	3	24	11	4

Habana	Pos	AB	R	H	O	A	E
L. Bustamante	ss	4	0	1	4	1	2
F. Morán	1b	4	0	1	10	0	0
C. Morán	3b	4	1	1	2	3	0
R. García	c	3	1	0	3	1	1
L. Padrón	lf	3	1	0	5	0	0
V. González	cf	3	0	1	1	0	0
S. Valdés	2b	3	0	1	2	4	0
M. Prats	rf	3	0	0	0	0	0
L. González	p	3	0	0	0	3	0
Totals		30	3	5	27	12	3

Philadelphia Giants	000	000	010 : 1
Habana	000	030	00x : 3

Two-base hits: B. Petway and V. González
Sacrifice hits: D. McClellan and C. Morán
Stolen bases: C.B. Earle, F. Morán (2), R. García (2), V. González and S. Valdés
Bases on balls: L. González 2, W. Holland 6
Strikeouts: L. González 1, W. Holland 7
Dead balls: W. Holland 2 (R. García and V. González)
Winning pitcher: L. González
Losing pitcher: W. Holland
Passed balls: E. Bowman
Time: 1 hour 45 minutes
Umpires: Antonio Maria García (home) and Eustaquio Gutiérrez (bases)
Scorer: Francisco Rodríguez

GAME SEVEN: THURSDAY, OCTOBER 24, 1907, AT ALMENDARES PARK

PHI Giants	Pos	AB	R	H	O	A	E
G. Johnson	ss	4	0	2	2	9	2
J.P. Hill	lf	3	1	0	2	0	0
D. McClellan	rf	4	1	1	1	0	0
J.H. Lloyd	2b	4	1	0	5	2	1
C.B. Earle	cf	4	0	0	2	0	2
E. Bowman	1b	4	0	0	13	1	0
F. Wallace	3b	4	0	0	2	2	0
C. Williams	c	3	0	0	0	3	0
J. Davis	p	3	0	0	0	0	0
Totals		33	3	3	27	17	5

Almendares	Pos	AB	R	H	O	A	E
R. Valdés	lf	3	0	0	1	0	0
J. Muñoz	p	4	1	0	0	4	0
G. González	c	3	0	1	3	0	0
A. Marsans	1b	4	0	1	15	0	0
E. Palomino	rf	4	0	0	1	0	0
R. Almeida	3b	3	0	0	3	3	3
H. Hidalgo	cf	3	0	0	1	0	0
A. Cabrera	ss	3	0	0	1	6	1
A. Cabañas	2b	3	0	0	2	5	1
Totals		30	1	2	27	16	5

Philadelphia Giants	300	000	000 : 3
Almendares	000	100	000 : 1

Stolen bases: J.P. Hill, D. McClellan, J. Muñoz, G. González and A. Cabañas
Double-plays: J.H. Lloyd and E. Bowman; J.H. Lloyd, G. Johnson and E. Bowman
Bases on balls: J. Muñoz 1, J. Davis 1
Strikeouts: J. Muñoz 1, J. Davis 0
Winning pitcher: J. Davis
Losing pitcher: J. Muñoz
Dead balls: J. Davis (S. Valdés)

Time: 1 hour 40 minutes
Umpires: Antonio Maria García (home) and Eustaquio Gutiérrez (bases)
Scorer: Francisco Rodríguez

GAME EIGHT: SUNDAY, OCTOBER 7, 1907, AT ALMENDARES

Habana	Pos	AB	R	H	O	A	E
L. Bustamante	ss	5	0	1	4	3	0
F. Morán	1b	4	0	0	10	0	0
C. Morán	3b	2	3	2	2	1	0
R. García	c	3	1	1	3	1	1
L. Padrón	lf	5	1	1	5	0	0
V. González	cf	5	0	2	1	0	1
S. Valdés	2b	4	1	1	2	0	0
M. Prats	rf	4	1	1	0	0	0
I. Pérez	p	4	0	0	0	2	1
Totals		36	7	9	27	7	3

PHI Giants	Pos	AB	R	H	O	A	E
G. Johnson	ss	4	0	2	1	2	2
J.P. Hill	lf	5	0	2	2	0	2
D. McClellan	rf	5	0	0	0	0	0
J.H. Lloyd	2b	5	1	2	3	1	0
C.B. Earle	cf	3	2	1	1	0	0
E. Bowman	1b	3	0	1	8	0	0
F. Wallace	3b	3	1	0	4	4	0
W. Holland	p	4	0	0	1	3	0
C. Williams	c	4	1	1	7	2	0
Totals		36	5	9	27	12	4

Habana	000	301	111 : 7
Philadelphia Giants	010	000	220 : 5

Sacrifice hits: E. Bowman, R. García (2) and S. Valdés
Stolen bases: G. Johnson, C.B. Earle and M. Prats
Double-plays: R. García and S. Valdés
Bases on balls: I. Pérez 3, W. Holland 4
Strikeouts: I. Pérez 3, W. Holland 7
Winning pitcher: I. Pérez
Losing pitcher: W. Holland
Time: 2 hours 10 minutes
Umpires: Antonio Maria García (home) and Eustaquio Gutiérrez (bases)
Scorer: Francisco Rodríguez

GAME NINE: MONDAY, OCTOBER 28, 1907, AT ALMENDARES PARK

Almendares	Pos	AB	R	H	O	A	E
R. Valdés	lf	2	2	2	0	0	0
A. Cabañas	c	4	1	2	6	1	0
E. Palomino	rf	3	0	1	2	0	0
G. González	2b	4	0	1	3	1	0
J. Castillo	1b	4	0	0	12	1	1
A. Marsans	3b	3	1	0	1	2	1
H. Hidalgo	cf	3	0	2	4	1	0
A. Cabrera	ss	3	0	0	2	4	3
A. Ortega	p	1	0	0	0	2	0
C. Royer	p	2	0	0	0	4	2
Totals		29	4	8	27	16	7

PHI Giants	Pos	AB	R	H	O	A	E
G. Johnson	ss	4	2	1	1	5	0
J.P. Hill	lf	3	2	1	1	0	0
J.H. Lloyd	2b	5	0	2	5	0	0
D. McClellan	rf	3	0	1	2	0	0
C.B. Earle	cf	4	0	1	4	0	0
E. Bowman	1b	4	0	0	9	0	0
F. Wallace	3b	3	0	1	1	2	0
B. Petway	c	4	0	1	3	5	0
J. Davis	p	4	0	0	1	1	0
Totals		34	4	8	27	13	0

Almendares	000	011	002 : 4
Philadelphia Giants	200	000	200 : 4

Earned runs: Almendares (3), Philadelphia Giants (1)
Three-base hits: J.P. Hill
Two-base hits: S. Valdés
Sacrifice hits: D. McClellan
Stolen bases: S. Valdés, G. González and C.B. Earle
Double-plays: G. González, A. Ortega and J. Castillo
Bases on balls: J. Davis 4, A. Ortega 2, C. Royer 3
Strikeouts: J. Davis 2, A. Ortega 0, C. Royer 1

Dead balls: C. Royer 1 (C.B. Earle)
Passed balls: A. Cabañas (3)
Time: 2 hours
Umpires: Antonio Maria García (home) and Eustaquio Gutiérrez (bases)
Scorer: Francisco Rodríguez

GAME TEN: THURSDAY, OCTOBER 31, 1907, AT ALMENDARES PARK

Habana	Pos	AB	R	H	O	A	E
L. Bustamante	ss	4	1	1	3	4	0
F. Morán	2b	3	0	0	0	4	0
R. García	c	2	1	0	5	3	1
L. Padrón	3b,p	3	0	2	2	0	1
V. González	lf,3b	4	0	0	3	2	2
L. González	p,cf	4	0	0	2	0	0
A. Molina	1b	3	0	0	7	0	0
M. Martinez	cf,lf	4	0	0	2	0	0
M. Prats	rf	4	0	0	0	0	0
Totals		30	2	6	24	13	4

PHI Giants	Pos	AB	R	H	O	A	E
G. Johnson	ss	4	1	1	3	6	1
J.P. Hill	lf	4	2	2	2	0	0
D. McClellan	p	4	2	2	0	2	0
J.H. Lloyd	2b	5	2	3	4	5	0
C.B. Earle	cf	5	2	4	2	0	0
E. Bowman	1b	5	1	0	12	0	0
F. Wallace	3b	5	3	2	0	3	0
B. Petway	c	4	0	0	4	0	1
W. Holland	rf	4	0	3	0	0	0
Totals		40	12	17	27	16	2

Habana	100	000	010 : 1
Philadelphia Giants	521	013	00x : 12

Earned runs: Philadelphia Giants (5), Habana (0)
Two-base hits: L. Padrón, D. McClellan and C.B. Earle
Sacrifice hits: F. Morán
Stolen bases: L. Bustamante, R. García (2), J.H. Lloyd, G. Johnson
Bases on balls: D. McClellan 4, L. González 1, L. Padrón 3
Strikeouts: D. McClellan 3, L. González 0, L. Padrón 1
Dead balls: D. McClellan 1 (R. García) and L. Padrón 1 (B. Petway)
Wild pitches: L. Padrón
Winning pitcher: D. McClellan
Losing pitcher: L. González
Time: 1 hour 40 minutes
Umpires: Antonio Maria García (home) and Eustaquio Gutiérrez (bases)
Scorer: Francisco Rodríguez

GAME ELEVEN: SUNDAY, NOVEMBER 3, 1907, AT ALMENDARES PARK

PHI Giants	Pos	AB	R	H	O	A	E
G. Johnson	ss	4	0	1	3	4	1
D. McClellan	cf	4	1	1	1	0	0
J.H. Lloyd	2b	3	1	1	3	1	1
C.B. Earle	cf	3	0	0	1	1	0
E. Bowman	1b	4	2	2	12	0	1
F. Wallace	3b	4	0	0	1	6	2
W. Holland	lf	4	0	2	1	0	1
C. Williams	c	4	0	1	2	1	0
J. Davis	p	4	0	0	0	1	0
Totals		34	4	8	24	14	6

Almendares	Pos	AB	R	H	O	A	E
R. Valdés	lf	3	1	0	3	1	0
R. Almeida	3b	4	0	1	2	3	1
E. Palomino	rf	4	1	2	1	0	0
J. Castillo	1b	4	0	1	14	0	0
G. González	c	4	0	0	4	0	0
A. Cabañas	2b	4	1	1	0	2	1
H. Hidalgo	cf	4	0	1	2	0	1
A. Cabrera	ss	3	1	2	1	5	0
C. Royer	p	4	1	2	0	4	0
Totals		34	5	10	27	15	3

Philadelphia Giants	010	030	000 : 4
Almendares	100	100	12x : 5

Earned runs: Philadelphia Giants (2) and Almendares (1)
Two-base hits: J.H. Lloyd, W.Bowman (2) and W. Holland
Sacrifice hits: A. Cabrera
Stolen bases: G. Johnson and C.B. Earle

Double-plays: S.Valdés and J. Castillo
Bases on balls: C.Royer 3, J. Davis 1
Strikeouts: C. Royer 1, J. Davis 0
Dead balls: C. Royer 1 (J.H. Lloyd)
Wild pitches: J. Davis 1
Winning pitcher: C. Royer
Losing pitcher: J. Davis
Time: 2 hours 10 minutes
Umpires: Antonio Maria García (home) and Eustaquio Gutiérrez (bases)
Scorer: Francisco Rodríguez

GAME TWELVE: TUESDAY, NOVEMBER 4, AT ALMENDARES PARK

PHI Giants	Pos	AB	R	H	O	A	E		Habana	Pos	AB	R	H	O	A	E
G. Johnson	ss	3	1	1	2	4	1		L. Bustamante	ss	4	2	2	6	4	0
D. McClellan	p	3	0	0	0	4	1		F. Morán	1b	4	1	2	8	0	0
J.H. Lloyd	2b	3	0	1	1	1	1		R. García	c	3	0	1	0	3	0
C.B. Earle	cf	3	0	0	3	0	0		L. Padrón	3b	4	0	0	2	3	0
E. Bowman	1b	4	0	1	9	0	0		V. González	cf	4	2	3	3	0	0
F. Wallace	3b	4	0	1	2	1	0		S. Valdés	2b	3	0	1	4	1	1
W. Holland	lf	3	0	1	3	0	1		M. Martinez	cf	4	0	1	2	0	0
B. Petway	rf	3	0	1	1	0	0		M. Prats	rf	4	0	1	2	0	0
C. Williams	c	3	0	0	5	0	0		L. González	p	4	0	0	0	0	1
Totals		29	1	6	24	10	4		Totals		34	5	11	27	11	2

Philadelphia Giants	100	000	000 : 1
Habana	101	100	11x : 5

Earned runs: Habana (2), Philadelphia Giants (0)
Three-base hits: L. Bustamantw
Two-base hits: M. Martinez
Sacrifice hits: D. McClellan, R. García and S. Valdés
Stolen bases: G. Johnson and J.H. Lloyd
Double-plays: S. Valdés, L. Bustamante and R. García
Bases on balls: L. González 5, D. McClellan 0
Strikeouts: L. González 3, D. McClellan 4
Winning pitcher: L. González
Losing pitcher: D. McClellan
Pased balls: C. Williams
Time: 1 hour 35 minutes
Umpires: Antonio Maria García (home) and Eustaquio Gutiérrez (bases)
Scorer: Francisco Rodríguez

GAME THIRTEEN: THURSDAY, NOVEMBER 4, AT ALMENDARES PARK

Almendares	Pos	AB	R	H	O	A	E		PHI Giants	Pos	AB	R	H	O	A	E
R. Valdés	lf	2	0	0	0	0	0		G. Johnson	ss	2	2	0	2	2	2
G. González	2b	2	0	0	2	3	1		C.B. Earle	cf	4	1	1	3	0	0
R. Almeida	3b	4	1	3	0	1	1		J.H. Lloyd	2b	4	1	1	3	4	0
E. Palomino	rf	4	0	0	0	0	0		E. Bowman	1b	5	0	1	10	2	0
A. Cabañas	c	4	0	1	8	1	1		F. Wallace	3b	3	1	1	1	3	0
H. Hidalgo	cf	4	0	2	3	0	0		W. Holland	lf	4	1	2	2	0	0
A. Marsans	2b	1	0	1	0	0	0		B. Petway	rf	4	1	1	2	0	0
C. Royer	1b	2	0	0	8	0	2		C. Williams	c	3	1	1	4	0	0
J. Muñoz	1b,lf	4	0	1	2	0	0		J. Davis	p	4	0	0	0	3	0
A. Ortega	p	4	1	0	0	2	1		Totals		33	8	8	27	14	2
Totals		34	2	9	24	9	7									

Almendares	110	000	000 : 2	
Philadelphia Giants	010	200	41x : 8	

Earned runs: Almendares (2), Philadelphia Giants (0)
Three-base hits: R. Almeida
Sacrifice hits: E. Bowman
Stolen bases: R. Almeida 2 and C. Williams
Double-plays: J.H. Lloyd, G. Johnson and E. Bowman; J.H. Lloyd, F. Wallace and E. Bowman
Bases on balls: J. Davis 2, A. Ortega 5
Strikeouts: J. Davis 4, A. Ortega 4
Wild pitches: A. Ortega
Winning pitcher: J. Davis
Losing pitcher: A. Ortega
Time: 2 hours.
Umpires: Antonio Maria García (home) and Eustaquio Gutiérrez (bases)
Scorer: Francisco Rodríguez

Final Statistics

PHILADELPHIA GIANTS
Individual Pitching

Pitcher	G	GS	GC	W	L	Pct	IP	R	H	W	K	HP	WP
William Holland	4	4	4	0	4	.000	34.0	18	30	12	18	5	0
John Davis	6	6	6	2	3	.400	53.0	17	40	14	18	2	1
Daniel McClellan	3	3	3	2	1	.333	26.0	8	22	7	8	1	1
Totals	13	13	13	4	8	.333	113.0	43	92	33	44	8	2

Individual Batting

Player	Pos	G	AB	R	H	2B	3B	HR	SH	SB	Pct
Charles B. Earle	cf	13	46	7	12	1	0	0	0	4	.261
J. Preston Hill	lf	10	38	8	10	1	0	0	1	4	.263
Daniel McClellan	rf,p	12	42	6	7	1	0	0	4	4	.167
Grant Johnson	ss	11	38	5	11	1	0	1	0	4	.289
John Henry Lloyd	ss,2b	13	52	10	15	2	0	0	0	2	.288
Emmett Bowman	2b,1b	13	52	4	8	2	0	0	2	1	.154
Felix Wallace	3b	13	47	6	10	0	0	0	0	1	.213
Bruce Petway	1b,rf,c	9	32	2	6	1	0	0	0	0	.187
William Holland	p,rf	8	28	1	9	1	0	0	0	0	.321
Clarence Williams	c,1b	10	27	3	5	0	0	0	0	1	.185
John Davis	p	6	20	0	0	0	0	0	1	0	.000
Totals		13	422	52	93	10	0	1	8	21	.220

Individual Fielding

Player	Pos	G	O	A	E	Pct
Charles B. Earle	cf	13	22	2	2	.923
J.Preston Hill	lf	10	21	0	5	.808
Daniel McClellan	rf,p	12	5	8	2	.867
Grant Johnson	ss	11	18	44	15	.805
John Henry Lloyd	ss,2b	13	42	29	4	.948
Emmett Bowman	2b,1b	13	116	14	4	.973
Felix Wallace	3b	13	21	32	4	.930
Bruce Petway	1b,rf,c	9	45	10	3	.948
William Holland	p,rf	8	12	14	1	.963
Clarence Williams	c,1b	10	37	6	4	.915

Player	Pos	G	O	A	E	Pct
John Davis	p	6	2	12	1	.933
Totals		13	341	171	45	.919

ALMENDARES

Individual Pitching

Pitcher	G	CG	W	L	Pct	IP	R	H	W	K	ERA
J. Muñoz	2	2	1	1	.500	18.0	3	7	2	5	1.50
C. Royer	3	2	2	0	1.000	20.0	5	13	8	7	2.25
A. Ortega	3	2	1	1	.500	23.0	12	19	8	5	4.70
Totals	8	6	4	2	.667	61.0	20	39	18	17	2.95

Individual Batting

Almendares	Pos	G	AB	R	H	2B	3B	HR	SH	SB	Pct
R. Valdés	lf(7)	7	22	6	6	1	0	0	0	1	.272
J. Muñoz	p(2),1b-lf(1)	3	11	2	1	0	0	0	0	1	.091
G. González	c(7)	7	25	1	4	0	0	0	0	4	.160
J. Castillo	1b(5)	5	17	1	5	0	0	0	1	2	.294
R. Almeida	3b(6)	6	22	2	5	0	1	0	0	2	.227
A. Cabañas	2b(5),c(2)	7	26	4	8	0	0	0	1	1	.308
A. Cabrera	ss(6)	6	18	2	3	1	0	0	2	0	.167
A. Marsans	lf(2),1b(1),2b(1),3b(1)	5	13	1	4	0	0	0	0	0	.308
E. Palomino	rf(6)	6	21	1	3	0	0	0	0	0	.143
H. Hidalgo	cf(7)	7	22	0	8	1	0	0	1	0	.373
C. Royer	p(3),1b(1)	4	11	1	2	0	0	0	0	0	.191
A. Ortega	p(3)	3	8	1	0	0	0	0	0	0	.000
Totals		7	219	21	50	3	1	0	5	11	.228

Individual Fielding

Almendares	Pos	G	O	A	E	Pct
R. Valdés	lf(7)	7	10	1	0	1.000
J. Muñoz	p(2),1b-lf(1)	3	4	5	0	1.000
G. González	c(7)	7	24	7	1	.969
J. Castillo	1b(5)	5	65	3	1	.986
R. Almeida	3b(6)	6	7	11	5	.783
A. Cabañas	2b(5),c(2)	7	19	21	3	.930
A. Cabrera	Ss(6)	6	10	22	4	.889
A. Marsans	lf(2),1b(1),2b(1),3b(1)	5	18	2	1	.952
E. Palomino	rf(6)	6	4	0	0	1.000
H. Hidalgo	cf(7)	7	16	1	1	.944
C. Royer	p(3),1b(1)	4	8	10	4	.818
A. Ortega	p(3)	3	0	9	2	.818
Totals		2	183	89	24	.919

HABANA

Individual Pitching

Pitcher	G	CG	W	L	Pct	IP	R	H	W	K	ERA
I. Pérez	2	2	1	1	.500	18.0	10	18	7	4	5.00
L. Padrón	2	0	0	1	.000	9.0	11	13	6	1	11.00
L. González	4	2	2	1	.667	26.0	12	23	8	7	4.15
Totals	8	4	3	3	.500	53.0	33	54	21	12	5.68

Individual Batting

Habana	Pos	POS	AB	R	H	2B	3B	HR	SH	SB	Pct
L. Bustamante	ss(6)	6	24	3	7	0	1	0	0	1	.292
F. Morán	1b(5),2b(1),lf(1)	6	22	2	3	0	0	0	1	2	.136
C. Morán	3b(4)	4	14	5	5	0	0	0	1	0	.357
R. García	c(5)	5	13	4	2	0	0	0	3	4	.154
L. Padrón	lf(4),p(2),3b(2)	6	22	2	3	0	0	0	0	1	.136
V. González	cf(5),lf-3b(1)	6	24	2	8	1	0	0	0	1	.333
S. Valdés	2b(5)	5	17	2	4	0	0	0	3	1	.235
M. Prats	rf(6)	6	23	1	4	0	0	0	0	1	.174
I. Pérez	p(2)	2	7	0	1	0	0	0	0	0	.143
M. Martinez	cf(2),lf(1)	2	8	0	1	1	0	0	0	0	.125
L. González	p(4),cf(1)	4	14	0	1	0	0	0	0	0	.071
A. Molina	c(2),1b(1)	3	9	1	0	0	0	0	0	0	.000
Totals		6	196	22	42	2	1	0	8	11	.214

Individual Fielding

Habana	Pos	G	O	A	E	Pct
L. Bustamante	ss(6)	6	15	19	3	.919
F. Morán	1b(5),2b(1),lf(1)	6	33	4	1	.974
C. Morán	3b(4)	4	6	7	2	.867
R. García	c(5)	5	14	9	4	.852
L. Padrón	lf(4),p(2),3b(2)	6	19	4	1	.958
V. González	cf(5),lf-3b(1)	6	12	2	4	.800
S. Valdés	2b(5)	5	13	11	3	.889
M. Prats	rf(6)	6	4	0	1	.800
I. Pérez	p(2)	2	1	2	0	1.000
M. Martinez	cf(2),lf(1)	2	4	0	0	1.000
L. González	p(4),cf(1)	4	2	4	1	.857
A. Molina	c(2),1b(1)	3	10	0	1	.909
Totals		1	156	67	22	.910

Second Round

On November 20, Clarence Winston, Andrew H. Payne, William Gatewood and Nathan "Nate" Harris arrived in Havana as reinforcements for the Giants, substituting for departing players Grant Johnson, J. Preston Hill, Daniel McClellan and William Holland, who returned to the United States. The new team played a series of matches in Matanzas City.

Roster

John Davis	p,rf,1b	Chicago Leland Giants
Charles B. Earle	p,2b,rf	Independent
William Gatewood	p,lf,1b	Chicago Leland Giants
Emmett Bowman	3b	Philadelphia Giants
Nathan Harris	2b	Chicago Leland Giants
John Henry Lloyd	ss	Philadelphia Giants
Andrew H. Payne	cf	Chicago Leland Giants
Bruce Petway	rf,1b	Philadelphia Giants
Felix Wallace	1b,2b	Famous Cuban Giants' 906
Clarence Williams	c,1b	Philadelphia Giants
Clarence Winston	lf	Chicago Leland Giants
Luis González	rf	Cuban Stars

William "Bill," Gatewood began with the Cuban X Giants in 1905. He played with Philadelphia Giants in 1907.

Nathan "Nate" Harris started with the Philadelphia Giants in 1906.

Andrew H. "Jap" Payne began with the Philadelphia Giants in 1902.
Clarence "Bobby" Winston started with the Philadelphia Giants in 1906.

Games Played (Second trip)

Date	Winning Club		Losing Club		Winning Pitcher	Losing Pitcher
Dec 5	PHI Giants	6	Almendares	2	J. Davis 1–0	A. Ortega 0–1
Dec 8	Almendares	3	PHI Giants	2	C. Royer 1–0	J. Davis 1–1
Dec 9	Habana	8	PHI Giants	7	A. D'Meza 1–0	W. Gatewood 0–1
Dec 12	PHI Giants	3	Almendares	1	J. Davis 2–1	J. Muñoz 0–1
Dec 15	Habana	3	PHI Giants	2	L. González 1–0	W. Gatewood 0–2
Dec 16	Almendares	2	PHI Giants	0	A. Ortega 1–0	J. Davis 2–2
Dec 19	Habana	9	PHI Giants	8	L. González 2–0	W. Gatewood 0–3
Dec 22	PHI Giants	5	Almendares	1	J. Davis 3–2	E. Palomino 0–1
Dec 23	PHI Giants	8	Habana	2	C.B. Earle 1–0	A. D'Meza 1–1
Dec 29	PHI Giants	3	Habana	2	J. Davis 4–2	A. D'Meza 1–2
(10)						

Dec 30 no information available

Club Standings

Pos	Clubs	G	W	L	Pct
1-2.	Almendares	5	3	2	.600
1-2.	Habana	5	3	2	.600
3.	Philadelphia Giants	10	4	6	.400
	Totals	20	10	10	.500

These totals do not include the final game, on which no information was available.

GAME ONE: THURSDAY, DECEMBER 5, 1907, AT ALMENDARES PARK

Almendares	Pos	AB	R	H	O	A	E
E. Santa Cruz	cf	3	0	1	0	0	0
J. Muñoz	lf	3	0	0	1	0	0
A. Marsans	rf	4	0	0	1	0	0
G. González	c	4	0	1	2	2	1
H. Hidalgo	3b	4	0	0	3	3	1
A. Cabañas	2B	4	0	0	1	1	1
A. Ortega	p	3	1	1	0	3	0
A. Cabrera	ss	3	1	0	4	1	0
E. Prats	1b	2	0	1	12	1	0
Totals		30	2	4	24	11	3

PHI Giants	Pos	AB	R	H	O	A	E
C. Winston	lf	4	1	1	0	0	0
C.B. Earle	2b	3	2	2	3	4	0
J.H. Lloyd	ss	4	1	1	3	4	1
E. Bowman	3b	4	1	1	1	2	1
A. Payne	cf	4	0	1	4	0	0
B. Petway	rf	4	0	1	0	0	0
C. Williams	c	3	0	1	4	2	1
W. Gatewood	1b	3	0	0	12	0	1
J. Davis	p	3	1	1	0	0	0
Totals		32	6	9	27	12	4

Almendares	001	010	000 : 2
Philadelphia Giants	000	210	03x : 6

Earned runs: Philadelphia Giants (2), Almendares (0)
Two-base hits: A. Ortega and J. Davis
Sacrifice hits: J. Muñoz and E. Prats
Stolen bases: A. Cabrera
Bases on balls: J. Davis 1, A. Ortega 0
Strikeouts: J. Davis 4, A. Ortega 1
Dead balls: A.Ortega 1 (C.B. Eale)
Wild pitches: A. Ortega 1
Winning pitcher: J. Davis
Losing pitcher: A. Ortega
Time: 1 hour 40 minutes
Umpires: Eustaquio Gutiérrez (home) and Antonio Maria García (base)
Scorer: Francisco Rodríguez

GAME TWO: SUNDAY, DECEMBER 8, 1907, AT ALMENDARES PARK

PHI Giants	Pos	AB	R	H	O	A	E
C. Winston	lf	4	1	0	0	0	0
C.B. Earle	2b	3	0	1	3	2	2
J.H. Lloyd	ss	4	1	2	2	4	0
E. Bowman	3b	4	0	1	0	4	2
A. Payne	cf	4	0	0	2	0	0
B. Petway	c	3	0	0	0	2	0
C. Williams	1b	3	0	3	11	0	1
W. Gatewood	rf	3	0	0	0	0	0
J. Davis	p	3	0	0	0	2	0
Totals		31	2	7	24	14	5

Almendares	Pos	AB	R	H	O	A	E
A. Cabrera	ss	3	0	0	2	3	0
J. Muñoz	lf	4	1	0	2	0	0
E. Palomino	rf	3	0	0	1	0	0
G. González	c	4	1	2	4	1	1
H. Hidalgo	3b	3	1	0	0	2	0
A. Cabañas	2b	2	0	0	6	2	1
A. Marsans	cf	3	0	0	3	0	0
E. Prats	1b	4	0	2	9	3	1
C. Royer	p	2	0	0	0	3	1
Totals		28	3	4	27	14	4

Philadelphia Giants	100	001	000 : 2
Almendares	100	000	02x : 3

Three-base hits: J.H. Lloyd.
Sacrifice hits: C.B. Earle, H. Hidalgo, A. Marsans and C. Royer
Stolen bases: C. Williams and A. Marsans
Double-plays: G. González, A. Cabañas and E. Prats; A. Cabrera, A. Cabañas and E. Prats; C. Williams, B. Petway and J. Davis
Bases on balls: J. Davis 4, C. Royer 0
Strikeouts: J. Davis 3, C. Royer 2
Winning pitcher: C. Royer
Losing pitcher: J. Davis
Passed balls: G. González 1
Time: 1 hour 50 minutes
Umpires: Eustaquio Gutiérrez (home) and Antonio Maria García (bases)
Scorer: Francisco Rodríguez

GAME THREE: MONDAY, DECEMBER 9, 1907, AT ALMENDARES PARK

Habana	Pos	AB	R	H	O	A	E
L. Bustamante	ss	4	2	0	2	0	0
C. Morán	rf	4	0	2	3	0	0
R. García	c	3	1	0	4	3	0
J. Castillo	1b	4	0	1	9	2	1
L. Padrón	3b	4	1	1	2	2	0
F. Morán	lf	3	1	1	0	1	1
S. Valdés	2b	2	0	0	4	3	2
M. Martinez	cf	1	2	0	2	0	0
A. D'Meza	p	3	1	1	1	0	0
Totals		28	8	6	27	13	6

PHI Giants	Pos	AB	R	H	O	A	E
C. Winston	lf	4	2	2	0	0	0
J.H. Lloyd	ss	5	1	2	4	7	1
E. Bowman	3b	5	1	2	3	4	1
A. Payne	2b	5	0	0	4	3	0
B. Petway	cf	5	1	1	2	1	0
C. Williams	c	3	0	1	1	0	0
W. Gatewood	p	2	0	0	0	2	0
J. Davis	rf,1b	3	1	1	4	0	0
F. Wallace	1b	2	0	1	9	1	2
L. González	rf	2	1	0	0	0	0
Totals		7	7	10	27	18	4

Habana	000	050	201 : 8
Philadelphia Giants	100	100	401 : 7

Earned runs: Philadelphia Giants (2), Habana (2)
Two-base hits: J.H. Lloyd and J. Davis
Sacrifice hits: J. Davis, R. García, S. Valdés, M. Martinez and A. D'Meza
Stolen bases: C. Winston 2, E. Bowman, C. Williams, L. González, R. García, F. Morán 2 and A. D'Meza
Double-plays: E. Bowman (sin asistencia); L. Padrón, L. Bustamante and J. Castillo; J. Castillo (sin asistencia)
Bases on balls: A. D'Meza 1, W. Gatewood 9
Strikeouts: A. D'Meza 1, W. Gatewood 1
Dead balls: A. D'Meza 2 (C. Winston and W. Gatewood)

Wild pitches: W. Gatewood 1
Winning pitcher: A. D'Meza
Losing pitcher: W. Gatewood
Time: 2 hours 10 minutes
Umpires: Antonio Maria García (home) and Eustaquio Gutiérrez (bases)
Scorer: Francisco Rodríguez

GAME FOUR: THURSDAY, DECEMBER 1, 1907, AT ALMENDARES PARK

Almendares	Pos	AB	R	H	O	A	E
A. Cabrera	ss	4	0	1	2	4	1
R. Valdés	cf	4	0	1	1	0	0
E. Palomino	rf	3	1	2	0	0	0
G. González	c	4	0	0	3	1	0
H. Hidalgo	3b	4	0	1	1	2	0
A. Cabañas	2b	3	0	0	3	2	1
A. Marsans	lf	4	0	1	1	0	0
E. Prats	1b	3	0	0	11	0	1
J. Muñoz	p	3	0	0	2	1	1
Totals		32	1	6	24	10	4

PHI Giants	Pos	AB	R	H	O	A	E
C. Winston	lf	4	1	1	1	0	1
C.B. Earle	cf	4	1	2	1	0	0
J.H. Lloyd	ss	4	0	0	6	3	1
E. Bowman	3b	4	1	0	1	3	0
A. Payne	2b	3	0	1	3	1	0
B. Petway	c	3	0	0	5	3	0
C. Williams	1b	3	0	1	7	0	1
W. Gatewood	rf	2	0	0	3	0	0
J. Davis	p	3	0	1	0	1	0
Totals		30	3	6	27	11	2

Almendares	000	001	000 : 1
Philadelphia Giants	300	000	000 : 3

Earned runs: Philadelphia Giants (1), Almendares (0)
Three-base hits: A. Cabrera
Two-base hits: A. Payne
Sacrifice hits: E. Prats
Stolen bases: R. Vadles, H. Hidalgo, C. Winston and E. Bowman
Double-plays: A. Cabañas, A. Cabrera and E. Prats (2)
Bases on balls: J. Davis 2, J. Muñoz 1
Strikeouts: J. Davis 3, J. Muñoz 3
Winning pitcher: J. Davis
Losing pitcher: J. Muñoz
Time: 1 hour 45 minutes
Umpires: Eustaquio Gutiérrez (home) and Antonio Maria García (bases)
Scorer: Francisco Rodríguez

GAME FIVE: SUNDAY, DECEMBER 15, 1907, AT ALMENDARES PARK

PHI Giants	Pos	AB	R	H	O	A	E
C. Winston	lf	2	1	0	0	0	0
C.B. Earle	cf	2	0	1	2	0	0
J.H. Lloyd	ss	3	1	1	0	4	1
E. Bowman	3b	4	0	1	1	4	1
A. Payne	2b	4	0	0	0	2	1
B. Petway	c	4	0	1	5	0	0
C. Williams	1b	4	0	0	17	0	0
W. Gatewood	p	4	0	0	0	6	0
J. Davis	rf	3	0	1	0	0	1
Totals		30	2	5	25	16	4

Habana	Pos	AB	R	H	O	A	E
L. Bustamante	ss	4	1	1	1	3	1
C. Morán	rf	3	1	1	1	0	0
R. García	c	3	0	0	3	1	0
J. Castillo	1b	4	0	1	10	1	0
L. Padrón	3b	4	0	1	1	3	0
V. González	2b	3	0	0	7	5	1
M. Prats	cf	3	1	1	0	0	0
L. González	p	3	0	2	0	2	0
M. Martinez	lf	4	0	1	4	0	0
Totals		31	3	7	27	15	2

Philadelphia Giants	100	001	000 : 2
Habana	100	001	001 : 3

Earned runs: Philadelphia Giants (1), Habana (0)
Sacrifice hits: C.B. Earle, R. García, E. Prats, V. González
Stolen bases: C. Winston, C.B. Earle

Double-plays: L. Bustamante, V. González and J. Castillo
Bases on balls: W. Gatewood 3, L. González 4
Strikeouts: W. Gatewood 4, L. González 0
Passed balls: R. García 1
Winning pitcher: L. González
Losing pitcher: W. Gatewood
Time: 1 hour 50 minutes
Umpires: Eustaquio Gutiérrez (home) and Antonio Maria García (bases)
Scorer: Francisco Rodríguez
The winning run was scored with one out.

GAME SIX: MONDAY, DECEMBER 16, 1907, AT ALMENDARES PARK

Almendares	Pos	AB	R	H	O	A	E
A. Marsans	2b	5	1	2	0	4	1
J. Muñoz	lf	4	0	0	1	0	0
E. Palomino	rf	5	1	2	1	0	0
G. González	c	5	0	1	5	1	0
R. Valdés	cf	4	0	0	0	0	0
A. Cabrera	ss	4	0	1	3	5	0
E. Prats	1b	2	0	1	14	1	0
A. Ortega	p	2	0	1	1	5	1
S. Valdés	3b	3	0	0	2	1	0
Totals		34	2	8	27	17	2

PHI Giants	Pos	AB	R	H	O	A	E
C. Winston	lf	4	0	2	2	0	0
C.B. Earle	cf	3	0	0	0	0	0
J.H. Lloyd	ss	4	0	1	4	3	0
E. Bowman	3b	3	0	0	3	1	1
A. Payne	2b	4	0	0	3	3	0
B. Petway	c,rf	2	0	0	1	0	0
C. Williams	1b,c	2	0	0	7	1	1
W. Gatewood	rf,1b	3	0	0	7	0	2
J. Davis	p	3	0	0	0	2	0
Totals		30	0	3	27	10	4

Almendares	100	010	000 : 2
Philadelphia Giants	000	000	000 : 0

Earned runs: Almendares (1), Philadelphia Giants (0)
Sacrifice hits: J. Muñoz and E. Prats
Stolen bases: E. Palomino (2), G. González
Double-plays: G. González, A. Ortega and E. Prats
Bases on balls: A. Ortega 2, J. Davis 3
Strikeouts: A. Ortega 4, J. Davis 3
Dead balls: A. Ortega 1 (J. Davis), J. Davis 1 (A. Ortega)
Winning pitcher: A. Ortega
Losing pitcher: J. Davis
Time: 1 hour 50 minutes
Umpires: Eustaquio Gutiérrez (home) and Antonio Maria García (bases)
Scorer: Francisco Rodríguez

GAME SEVEN: THURSDAY, DECEMBER 19, 1907, AT ALMENDARES PARK

Habana	Pos	AB	R	H	O	A	E
L. Bustamante	ss	5	1	1	2	3	2
C. Morán	1b,cf	3	2	1	0	0	1
R. García	c	4	1	0	6	1	0
L. Padrón	3b	4	2	1	1	3	0
V. González	cf,1b	5	1	1	12	1	0
S. Valdés	2b	5	1	1	2	3	0
M. Martinez	lf	4	1	2	0	0	0
J.M. Magrinat	rf	4	0	3	4	0	0
A. D'Meza	p	3	0	0	0	2	1
L. González	p	1	0	0	0	1	0
Totals		34	8	10	27	14	4

PHI Giants	Pos	AB	R	H	O	A	E
C. Winston	lf	5	2	2	4	1	0
C.B. Earle	cf	4	1	0	2	0	1
J.H. Lloyd	ss	5	1	3	4	5	2
E. Bowman	3b	5	2	2	4	6	0
A. Payne	2b	2	0	0	5	1	0
B. Petway	c	4	0	1	2	1	1
C. Williams	1b	1	1	1	2	1	1
W. Gatewood	p	4	0	0	0	0	0
J. Davis	rf	4	1	1	0	0	0
Totals		38	9	10	27	14	4

Habana	200	300	013 : 9
Philadelphia Giants	201	012	002 : 8

Earned runs: Habana (3), Philadelphia Giants (3)
Three-base hits: J. Davis
Two-base hits: J.M. Magrinat
Sacrifice hits: R. García and A. Payne
Stolen bases: L. Bustamante (2), F. Morán (2), R. García, L. Padrón (2), V. González, C. Winston,
    C. Williams and J. Davis
Double-plays: A. Payne, E. Bowman and C. Williams; S. Valdés, L. Padrón and V. González; S. Valdés,
    L. Bustamante and V. González; L. Padrón and V. González
Bases on balls: W. Gatewood 3, A. D'Meza 2, L. González 2
Strikeouts: W. Gatewood 2, A. D'Meza 1, L. González 3
Dead balls: W. Gatewood 1 (L. Padrón), A. D'Meza 1 (C. Williams), L. González 1 (A. Payne)
Passed balls: B. Petway
Winning pitcher: L. González
Losing pitcher: W. Gatewood
Time: 2 hours 18 minutes
Umpires: Antonio Maria García (home) and Eustaquio Gutiérrez (bases)
Scorer: Francisco Rodríguez

GAME EIGHT: SUNDAY, DECEMBER 22, 1907, AT ALMENDARES PARK

Almendares	Pos	AB	R	H	O	A	E
E. Santa Cruz	cf	3	0	0	0	0	0
J. Muñoz	lf	3	0	0	2	0	0
E. Palomino	p	4	1	2	0	4	0
G. González	c	3	0	0	3	0	0
M. Prats	rf	3	0	0	0	1	0
A. Cabrera	ss	2	0	0	3	3	2
E. Prats	1b	3	0	0	13	0	0
A. Ortega	2b	3	0	0	1	5	2
E. Valdés	3b	2	0	1	2	2	1
Totals		26	1	3	24	15	5

PHI Giants	Pos	AB	R	H	O	A	E
C. Winston	lf	5	1	2	2	0	0
C.B. Earle	cf	3	0	1	0	0	0
J.H. Lloyd	ss	4	1	0	5	4	1
E. Bowman	3b	4	0	2	0	2	0
A. Payne	2b	3	1	2	2	0	0
B. Petway	1b	4	1	1	15	1	0
F. Wallace	3b	3	1	0	2	8	0
C. Williams	c	3	0	0	0	0	0
J. Davis	p	4	0	0	1	3	0
Totals		33	5	8	27	18	1

Almendares	000	000	100 : 1
Philadelphia Giants	110	000	12x : 5

Three-base hits: A. Payne
Sacrifice hits: J. Muñoz, M. Prats, C.B. Earle and F. Wallace
Stolen bases: R. Valdés, C. Winston and F. Wallace
Double-plays: F. Wallace and B. Petway
Bases on balls: J. Davis 4, E. Palomino 1
Strikeouts: J. Davis 0, E. Palomino 3
Dead balls: E. Palomino 2 (C.B. Earle and C. Winston)
Winning pitcher: J. Davis
Losing pitcher: E. Palomino
Time: 1 hour 50 minutes
Umpires: Eustaquio Gutiérrez (home) and Antonio Maria García (bases)
Scorer: Francisco Rodríguez

GAME NINE: MONDAY, DECEMBER 23, 1907, AT ALMENDARES PARK

Habana	Pos	AB	R	H	O	A	E
L. Bustamante	ss	1	0	0	0	0	1
E. Ramos	ss	2	0	0	0	1	0
S. Valdés	2b	2	1	1	1	0	0
R. García	c	1	0	0	2	1	0
J. Castillo	1b	0	1	0	6	0	0
L. Padrón	3b	2	0	0	0	0	2
V. González	cf	2	0	0	1	0	0

PHI Giants	Pos	AB	R	H	O	A	E
C. Winston	lf	1	2	0	0	0	0
C.B. Earle	p	3	2	2	1	2	0
J.H. Lloyd	ss	3	1	1	2	3	1
E. Bowman	3b	3	1	0	0	0	0
A. Payne	cf	3	1	1	0	0	0
B. Petway	1b	2	0	0	8	0	0
F. Wallace	2b	2	1	1	2	2	2

Habana	Pos	AB	R	H	O	A	E
J.M. Magrinat	rf	2	0	0	2	0	0
M. Martinez	lf	2	0	0	0	0	0
A. D'Meza	p	2	0	0	1	0	0
Totals		16	2	1	13	2	3

PHI Giants	Pos	AB	R	H	O	A	E
C. Williams	c	2	0	0	2	2	0
J. Davis	rf	1	0	0	0	0	0
Totals		20	8	5	15	9	3

Habana	010	10	: 2
Philadelphia Giants	521	00	: 8

Game called at end of fifth inning on account of rain, with one out.

Earned runs: Philadelphia Giants (3), Habana (0)
Two-base hits: A. Payne
Sacrifice hits: R. García
Stolen bases: J. Castillo 2, C. Winston, C.B. Earle 2, E. Bowman, A. Payne, B. Petway
Bases on balls: C.B. Earle 2, A. D'Meza 4
Strikeouts: C.B. Earle 1, A. D'Meza 2
Winning pitcher: C.B. Earle
Losing pitcher: A. D'Meza
Time: 1 hour 50 minutes
Umpires: Antonio Maria García (home) and Eustaquio Gutiérrez (bases
Scorer: Francisco Rodríguez

GAME TEN: SUNDAY, DECEMBER 29, 1897, AT ALMENDARES PARK

Habana	Pos	AB	R	H	O	A	E
J.P. Hill	lf,3b	4	1	1	1	2	1
S. Valdés	2b	2	0	0	2	0	0
R. García	c	4	1	2	3	1	0
J. Castillo	1b	4	0	1	8	0	1
L. Padrón	ss	4	0	0	7	4	1
V. González	3b	1	0	0	0	0	0
A. Arcano	lf	3	0	0	1	1	0
J.M. Magrinat	rf	4	0	2	0	0	0
M. Martinez	cf	2	0	0	1	0	0
A. D'Meza	p	3	0	0	1	2	0
Totals		31	2	6	24	16	3

PHI Giants	Pos	AB	R	H	O	A	E
C. Winston	lf	4	1	1	2	0	0
C.B. Earle	rf	4	2	3	0	0	0
J.H. Lloyd	2b	4	0	0	6	7	0
E. Bowman	3b	4	0	1	0	2	1
A. Payne	cf	2	0	0	0	2	0
B. Petway	1b	3	0	1	15	0	2
F. Wallace	ss	3	0	0	3	8	0
C. Williams	c	2	0	1	1	2	0
J. Davis	p	3	0	0	0	4	0
Totals		30	3	7	27	23	3

Habana	100	001	000	: 2
Philadelphia Giants	001	000	02x	: 3

Earned runs: Philadelphia Giants (1), Habana (1)
Home-runs: C.B. Earle
Sacrifice hits: S. Valdés
Stolen bases: R. García, C.B. Earle and E. Bowman
Double-plays: L. Padrón, S. Valdés and J. Castillo; J.P. Hill and J. Castillo;
J.H. Lloyd, F. Wallace and B. Petway
Bases on balls: J. Davis 1, A. D'Meza 1
Strikeouts: J. Davis 1, A. D'Meza 2
Winning pitcher: J. Davis
Losing pitcher: A. D'Meza
Time: 1 hour 30 minutes
Umpires: Eustaquio Gutiérrez (home) and Antonio Maria García (bases)
Scorer: Francisco Rodríguez

GAME ELEVEN: MONDAY, DECEMBER 30, AT ALMENDARES PARK

No information appeared in the newspapers

Final Statistics

PHILADELPHIA GIANTS

Individual Pitching

Pitcher	G	GS	GC	W	L	Pct	IP	R	H	BB	SO	HP	WP
John Davis	6	6	6	4	2	.667	53.0	11	31	15	14	0	0
Charles B. Earle	1	1	1	1	0	1.000	8.0	2	1	2	1	0	0
William Gatewood	3	3	3	0	3	.000	26.1	20	23	15	7	1	1
Totals	10	10	10	5	5	.500	87.1	33	55	32	22	1	1

Individual Batting

Players	Pos	G	AB	R	H	2B	3B	HR	SH	SB	Pct
Emmett Bowman	3b	10	40	6	10	0	0	0	0	4	.250
John Davis	p,rf,1b	10	30	3	5	2	1	0	1	1	.167
Charl B. Earle	2b,p,rf	9	29	8	12	0	0	1	3	4	.414
Nathan Harris	(Did not play)										
William Gatewood	p,lf,1b	7	21	0	0	0	0	0	0	0	.000
Luis González	rf	1	2	1	0	0	0	0	0	1	.000
John Henry Lloyd	ss	10	40	7	11	2	0	0	0	0	.275
Andrew H. Payne	cf	10	34	2	5	2	1	0	1	1	.147
Bruce Petway	rf,1b	10	36	2	6	0	0	0	0	1	.167
Felix Wallace	1b,2b	3	7	2	2	0	0	0	1	0	.286
Clarence Williams	c,1b	10	26	1	8	0	0	0	0	3	.307
Clarence Winston	lf	10	37	12	11	0	0	0	0	6	.297
Totals		10	302	44	70	6	2	1	6	20	.232

Individual Fielding

Players	Pos	G	O	A	E	Pct
Emmett Bowman	3b	10	13	28	6	.872
John Davis	p,rf,1b	10	5	8	1	.929
Charl B. Earle	2b,p,rf	9	12	8	3	.870
Nathan Harris	(Did not Play)					
William Gatewood	p,lf,1b	7	22	8	3	.909
Luis González	rf	1	3	0	0	1.000
John Henry Lloyd	ss	10	30	37	8	.893
Andrew H. Payne	cf	10	23	10	1	.971
Bruce Petway	rf,1b	10	44	8	1	.981
Felix Wallace	1b,2b	3	13	11	4	.857
Clarence Williams	c,1b	10	55	5	6	.909
Clarence Winston	lf	10	9	1	1	.909
Totals		10	229	124	34	.912

ALMENDARES

Individual Pitching

Pitcher	G	CG	W	L	Pct	IP	R	H	W	K	ERA
A. Ortega	2	2	1	1	.500	17.0	6	12	2	5	3.18
C. Royer	1	1	1	0	1.000	9.0	2	7	0	2	2.00
J. Muñoz	1	1	0	1	.000	9.0	3	6	1	3	3.00
E. Palomino	1	1	0	1	.000	8.0	5	8	1	3	5.63
Totals	5	5	2	3	.400	43.0	16	33	4	13	3.35

Individual Batting

Almendares	Pos	G	AB	R	H	2B	3B	HR	SH	SB	Pct
E. Santa Cruz	cf(2)	2	6	0	1	0	0	0	0	0	.167
J. Muñoz	lf(5),p(1)	5	17	1	0	0	0	0	3	0	.000
A. Marsans	of(3),2b(1)	4	16	1	3	0	0	0	1	1	.188
G. González	c(2)	5	20	1	4	0	0	0	0	1	.200
H. Hidalgo	3b(3)	3	11	1	1	0	0	0	1	1	.091
A. Cabañas	2b(3)	3	9	0	0	0	0	0	0	0	.000
A. Ortega	p(2),2b(1)	3	8	1	2	1	0	0	0	0	.250
E. Valdés	3b(2)	2	5	0	1	0	0	0	0	0	.200
R. Valdés	cf(2)	2	8	0	1	0	0	0	0	2	.125
M. Prats	rf(1)	1	3	0	0	0	0	0	0	0	.000
A. Cabrera	ss(5)	5	16	1	2	0	1	0	1	1	.125
E. Prats	1b(5)	5	14	0	4	0	0	0	4	0	.286
E. Palomino	rf(3),p(1)	4	15	3	6	0	0	0	0	2	.400
C. Royer	p(1)	1	2	0	0	0	0	0	1	0	.000
Totals		5	150	9	25	1	1	0	11	8	.167

Individual Fielding

Almendares	Pos	G	O	A	E	Pct
E. Santa Cruz	cf(2)	2	0	0	0	.000
J. Muñoz	lf(5),p(1)	5	8	1	1	.900
A. Marsans	of(3),2b(1)	4	5	4	1	.900
G. González	c(2)	5	17	5	2	.917
H. Hidalgo	3b(3)	3	4	7	0	1.000
A. Cabañas	2b(3)	3	10	5	3	.833
A. Ortega	p(2),2b(1)	3	2	13	3	.833
E. Valdés	3b(2)	2	4	3	0	1.000
R. Valdés	cf(2)	2	1	0	0	1.000
M. Prats	rf(1)	1	0	1	0	1.000
A. Cabrera	ss(5)	5	14	16	3	.909
E. Prats	1b(5)	5	59	5	2	.970
E. Palomino	rf(3),p(1)	4	2	4	0	1.000
C. Royer	p(1)	1	0	3	1	.750
Totals		5	126	67	18	.914

HABANA

Individual Pitching

Pitcher	G	CG	W	L	Pct	IP	R	H	W	K	ERA
A. D'Meza	4	3	1	2	.333	27.1	24	30	8	6	7.90
L. González	2	1	2	0	1.000	12.0	4	7	6	3	3.00
Totals	6	4	3	2	.600	39.1	28	37	14	9	6.41

Individual Batting

Habana	Pos	G	AB	R	H	2B	3B	HR	SH	SB	Pct
L. Bustamante	ss(4)	4	14	4	2	0	0	0	0	2	.143
C. Morán	rf(2),1b-cf(1)	3	10	3	4	0	0	0	0	0	.400
R. García	c(5)	5	15	3	2	0	0	0	4	3	.133
J. Castillo	1b(4)	4	12	1	3	0	0	0	0	2	.250
L. Padrón	3b(4),ss(1)	5	18	3	3	0	0	0	0	2	.167
V. González	cf(2),1b(1),2b(1),3b(1)	4	11	1	1	0	0	0	1	1	.091
F. Morán	lf(1)	1	3	1	1	0	0	0	0	4	.333
S. Valdés	2b(4)	4	11	2	2	0	0	0	2	0	.191
M. Martinez	lf(3),cf(2)	5	13	3	3	0	0	0	1	0	.231

Habana	Pos	G	AB	R	H	2B	3B	HR	SH	SB	Pct
A. D'Meza	p(4)	4	11	1	1	0	0	0	1	1	.091
L. González	p(2)	2	4	0	2	0	0	0	0	1	.500
J.M. Magrinat	rf(3)	3	10	0	5	1	0	0	0	0	.500
E. Ramos	ss(1)	1	2	0	0	0	0	0	0	0	.000
J.P. Hill	lf,3b(1)	1	4	1	1	0	0	0	0	0	.250
A. Arcano	lf(1)	1	3	0	0	0	0	0	0	0	.000
Totals		5	134	24	30	1	0	0	9	16	.224

Individual Fielding

Habana	Pos	G	O	A	E	Pct
L. Bustamante	ss(4)	4	5	6	3	.786
C. Morán	rf(2),1b,cf(1)	3	4	0	1	.800
R. García	c(5)	5	18	7	0	1.000
J. Castillo	1b(4)	4	33	3	2	.947
L. Padrón	3b(4),ss(1)	5	11	12	3	.885
V. González	cf(2),1b(1),2b(1),3b(1)	4	20	6	1	.963
F. Morán	lf(1)	1	0	1	1	.500
S. Valdés	2b(4)	4	9	4	2	.867
M. Martinez	lf(3).cf(2)	5	7	0	0	1.000
A. D'Meza	p(4)	4	3	4	1	.875
L. González	p(2)	2	0	3	0	1.000
J.M. Magrinat	rf(3)	3	6	0	0	1.000
E. Ramos	ss(1)	1	0	1	0	1.000
J.P. Hill	lf-3b(1)	1	1	2	1	.750
A. Arcano	lf(1)	1	1	1	0	1.000
Totals		5	120	60	19	.905

◆ 7 ◆

1908
Brooklyn Royal Giants

Roster

Player	Position	Regular Season Club, 1908
Phil Bradley	c,rf	Brooklyn Royal Giants
Harry Buckner	p	Brooklyn Royal Giants
Ashby Dunbar	cf	Brooklyn Royal Giants
Charles B. Earle	p,rf,lf	Brooklyn Royal Giants
Robert Gans	p,rf	Independent
Ricardo Hernandez	2b	Cuban Stars
J. Preston Hill	lf	Chicago Leland Giants
W. Gus James	c,rf	Brooklyn Royal Giants
Grant Johnson	ss	Brooklyn Royal Giants
Samuel Mongin	2b	Brooklyn Royal Giants
William Monroe	3b	Brooklyn Royal Giants
Agustin Parpetti	1b	Cuban Stars

Phil Bradley started with the Brooklyn Royal Giants in 1908.

Harry Buckner began with the Chicago Unions in 1896. He also played with the Columbia Giants, Philadelphia Giants, and Cuban X Giants. He played with the Brooklyn Royal Giants in Cuba.

Ashby Dunbar started with the Brooklyn Royal Giants in 1908.

C.B. Earle began with the Wilmington Giants in 1906 and also played with the Cuban Giants, Philadelphia Giants and Brooklyn Royal Giants.

Robert Edward "Jude" Gans started with the Brooklyn Royal Giants in 1908.

J. Preston "Pete" Hill started with the Philadelphia Giants in 1903.

Grant Johnson earned the nickname "Home Run" with his powerful righthanded swing in the dead-ball era. In 1895 he began a career that took him to early twentieth century's best clubs. He played with the Page Fence Giants of Adrian, Michigan, the Columbia Giants, the Cuban X Giants and the Brooklyn Royal Giants.

W. Gus "Nux" James began with the Brooklyn Royal Giants in 1909.

Sam Mongin started with the Brooklyn Royal Giants in 1909.

William "Bill" Monroe began with the Chicago Unions in 1896. He also played with the Philadelphia Giants and Brooklyn Royal Giants.

Al Robinson started with the Brooklyn Royal Giants in 1909.

Games Played

Date	Winning Club	Losing Club	Winning Pitcher	Losing Pitcher
Oct 10	Almendares 3	Royal Giants 2	J. Mendez 1–0	C.B. Earle 0–1

Date	Winning Club	Losing Club	Winning Pitcher	Losing Pitcher
Oct 11	Habana 6	Royal Giants 4	L. Padrón 1–0	H. Buckner 0–1
Oct 13	Royal Giants 9	Almendares 1	H. Buckner 1–1	A. Ortega 0–1
Oct 15	Habana 3	Royal Giants 2	L. González 1–0	C.B. Earle 0–2
Oct 18	Royal Giants 2	Almendares 0	H. Buckner 2–1	J. Muñoz 0–1
Oct 19	Royal Giants 4	Habana 0	C.B. Earle 1–2	J. Pérez 0–1
Oct 22	Almendares 4	Royal Giants 3	C. Royer 1–0	H. Buckner 2–2
Oct 25	Royal Giants 8	Habana 5	R. Gans 1–0	L. Padrón 1–1
Oct 26	Royal Giants 4	Almendares 2	H. Buckner 3–2	J. Mendez 1–1
Oct 31	Royal Giants 2	Habana 1	R. Gans 2–0	L. Padrón 1–2
Nov 1	Almendares 4	Royal Giants 3	A. Ortega 1–1	H. Buckner 3–3
Nov 2	Habana 6	Royal Giants 0	J. Pérez 1–0	R. Gans 2–1
Nov 7	Royal Giants 4	Almendares 2	C.B. Earle 1–2	J. Muñoz 0–2
Nov 8	Royal Giants 5	Habana 1	H. Buckner 4–3	J. Pérez 1–1
Nov 9	Almendares 2	Royal Giants 0	C. Royer 2–0	R. Gans 2–2
Nov 11	Almendares 8	Royal Giants 3	C. Rodríguez 1–0	C.B. Earle 1–3
(16)				

Club Standings

Pos	Club	G	W	L	Pct
1.	Almendares	9	5	4	.556
2.	Brooklyn Royal Giants	16	8	8	.500
3.	Habana	7	3	4	.429
	Totals	32	16	16	.500

Out of Concours

Date	Winning Club	Losing Club	Winning Pitcher	Losing Pitcher
Nov 20	Royal Giants 9	Cincinnati 1	H. Buckner	J. Dubuc

The Games

GAME ONE: SATURDAY, OCTOBER 10, 1908, AT ALMENDARES PARK

Almendares	Pos	AB	R	H	O	A	E
R. Valdés	lf	4	0	0	0	0	0
A. Marsans	1b	4	0	0	9	0	1
A. Cabañas	2b	4	1	0	2	3	0
G. González	c	2	0	0	12	1	0
J. Violá	rf	4	1	2	1	0	0
H. Hidalgo	cf	3	0	0	1	0	0
J. Muñoz	cf	0	0	0	0	0	1
A. Cabrera	3b	4	1	1	2	0	0
P. Chacon	ss	3	0	1	0	4	0
J. Mendez	p	3	0	0	0	3	0
Totals		31	3	4	27	11	2

Royal Giants	Pos	AB	R	H	O	A	E
W. Monroe	3b	4	0	1	6	2	0
J.P. Hill	lf	2	0	0	2	0	0
G. Johnson	ss	3	0	0	1	5	1
C.B. Earle	p	4	1	1	1	4	1
G. James	c	3	0	0	8	1	0
H. Buckner	c	1	0	0	0	0	0
A. Dunbar	cf	4	1	1	2	0	0
A. Robinson	1b	4	0	0	7	1	0
R. Gans	rf	4	0	0	0	0	1
S. Mongin	2b	3	0	1	0	0	0
Totals		32	2	4	27	13	3

Almendares	100	000	200 : 3	
Brooklyn Royal Giants	000	000	200 : 2	

Earned runs: BRO Royal Giants (1), Almendares (1)
Two-base hits: S. Mongin
Sacrifice hits: A. Cabañas, W. Monroe, J.P. Hill (2), J. Violá (2), A. Cabrera, A. Dunbar
Stolen bases: C.B. Earle and A. Dunbar
Bases on balls: J. Mendez 2, C.B. Earle 2
Strikeouts: J. Mendez 12, C.B. Earle 5

Dead ball: J. Mendez 1 (G. Johnson)
Winning pitcher: J. Mendez
Losing pitcher: C.B. Earle
Umpires: Quesada (home) and Prudencio Benavides (bases)
Scorer: Antonio Conejo

GAME TWO: SUNDAY, OCTOBER 11, 1908, AT ALMENDARES PARK

Habana	Pos	AB	R	H	O	A	E
L. Bustamante	ss	4	3	1	1	2	1
R. Figarola	c	4	0	0	5	2	0
E. Palomino	rf	3	0	0	2	1	0
J. Castillo	1b	4	0	0	8	0	1
L. Padrón	p	4	1	2	2	6	1
R. Hernandez	3b	3	0	2	3	1	2
V. González	cf	3	0	0	2	1	0
E. Pedroso	2b	2	0	0	2	1	1
J.M. Magrinat	lf	4	2	0	2	0	0
Totals		31	6	5	27	13	6

Royal Giants	Pos	AB	R	H	O	A	E
J.P. Hill	lf	3	2	0	1	0	0
C.B. Earle	rf	0	0	0	0	0	0
R. Gans	rf,p	3	0	0	0	1	0
G. Johnson	ss	4	1	1	4	4	0
W. Monroe	3b	2	0	0	3	6	0
A. Dumbar	cf	4	0	1	3	0	0
A. Robinsonz	1b	3	0	1	12	0	0
G. James	c,rf	4	0	0	0	2	0
H. Buckner	p	1	0	0	0	0	0
P. Bradley	rf,c	3	1	0	2	2	0
S. Mongin	2b	4	0	1	2	2	0
Totals		31	4	4	27	17	0

Habana	100	120	200-6
BRO Royal Giants	100	000	030-4

Three-base hits: G. Johnson
Sacrifice hits: R. Hernandez. C.B. Earle
Stolen bases: R. Hernandez, L. Bustamante, L. Padrón, J.M. Magrinat
Double-plays: V. González to R. Figarola; W. Monroe to A. Robinson
Bases on balls: L. Padrón 4, H. Buckner 1, R. Gans 1
Strikeouts: L. Padrón 4, H. Buckner 0, R. Gans 2
In three strikes: H. Buckner 1 (L. Bustamante); R. Gans 1 (L. Bustamante)
Dead balls: H. Buckner 1, L. Padrón 1, R. Gans 1
Wild pitches: H. Buckner 1
Hits: H. Buckner 3 in 4.2
Passed balls: G. James 1
Winning pitcher: L. Padrón
Losing pitcher: H. Buckner
Time: 2 hours
Umpires: Prudencio Benavides (home) and Quesada (bases)
Scorer: Antonio Conejo

GAME THREE: TUESDAY, OCTOBER 13, 1908, AT ALMENDARES PARK

Royal Giants	Pos	AB	R	H	O	A	E
J.P. Hill	lf	4	2	2	6	0	0
W. Monroe	3b	5	1	2	1	5	0
G. Johnson	ss	5	1	1	5	2	0
H. Buckner	p	5	1	1	0	3	0
A. Dunbar	cf	4	2	3	1	0	1
A. Robinson	1b	4	0	1	9	0	0
R. Gans	rf	4	1	1	0	0	0
P. Bradley	c	4	0	1	4	1	0
S. Mongin	2b	5	1	2	1	0	0
Totals		40	9	14	27	11	1

Almendares	Pos	AB	R	H	O	A	E
A. Marsans	lf	5	0	3	3	0	0
A. Cabrera	1b	5	0	0	9	0	0
A. Cabañas	2b	4	1	2	3	3	0
G. González	c	4	0	1	7	1	0
J. Violá	rf,p	4	0	1	1	0	0
H. Hidalgo	cf	2	0	0	2	0	0
R. Almeida	3b	4	0	2	0	0	0
P. Chacon	ss	4	0	0	1	3	1
A. Ortega	p	2	0	0	0	4	2
J. Muñoz	rf	2	0	0	1	0	0
Totals		36	1	9	27	11	3

BRK Royal Giants	100	021	500 : 9
Almendares	000	000	001 : 1

Earned runs: BRK Royal Giants (5), Almendares (0)
Two-base hits: A. Dunbar
Sacrifice hits: A. Robinson, P. Bradley
Stolen bases: P. Chacon, W. Monroe
Double-plays: P. Chacon to A. Cabañas to A. Cabrera
Bases on balls: H. Buckner 4, A. Ortega 1, J.Violá 0
Strikeouts: H. Buckner 2, A. Ortega 4, J. Violá 2
Dead balls: A. Ortega 1, H. Buckner 1
Hits: A. Ortega 13 in 7.1 innings (32 AB)
Winning pitcher: H. Buckner
Losing pitcher: A. Ortega
Time: 2 hours
Umpires: Prudencio Benavides (home) and Quesada (bases)
Scorer: Antonio Conejo

GAME FOUR: THURSDAY, OCTOBER 15, 1908, AT ALMENDARES PARK

Royal Giants	Pos	AB	R	H	O	A	E
J.P. Hill	lf	2	0	0	1	0	0
C.B. Earle	p	3	1	1	0	3	0
G. Johnson	ss	3	0	0	1	4	0
W. Monroe	3b	4	0	1	2	4	0
A. Dunbar	cf	4	0	1	1	0	0
A. Robinson	1b	3	0	0	16	0	0
G. James	rf	4	1	2	1	0	0
P. Bradley	c	3	0	0	3	1	0
S. Mongin	2b	3	0	0	1	3	1
Totals		29	2	5	26	15	1

Habana	Pos	AB	R	H	O	A	E
L. Bustamante	ss	3	0	1	0	4	0
R. Figarola	c	4	0	0	6	2	0
E. Palomino	rf	4	0	1	1	0	0
J. Castillo	1b	4	1	0	14	0	0
L. Padrón	lf	2	1	1	4	0	0
R. Hernandez	3b	4	1	1	2	0	0
V. González	cf	3	0	1	0	0	0
E. Pedroso	2b	2	0	1	0	0	0
L. González	p	3	0	0	0	3	1
Totals		29	3	6	27	11	1

BRK Royal Giants	100	010	000 : 2
Habana	000	000	201 : 3

One out when winning run scored in ninth inning.
Earned runs: Habana (1), BRK Royal Giants (0)
Sacrifice hits: A. Robinson, P. Bradley, L. Padrón, E. Pedroso
Double-plays: R. Figarola to R. Hernandez to J. Castillo; G. Johnson to S. Mongin to A. Robinson.
Bases on balls: C.B. Earle 3, L. González 3
Strikeouts: C.B. Earle 3, L. González 3
Winning pitcher: L. González
Losing pitcher: C.B. Earle
Time: 2 hours
Umpires: Antonio Maria García (home) and Prudencio Benavides (bases)

GAME FIVE: SUNDAY, OCTOBER 18, 1908, AT ALMENDARES PARK

Royal Giants	Pos	AB	R	H	O	A	E
J.P. Hill	lf	4	0	1	5	0	0
C.B. Earle	rf	4	0	0	1	0	0
G. Johnson	ss	4	0	0	3	3	0
W. Monroe	3b	3	0	1	2	4	0
A. Dumbar	cf	2	1	0	4	0	0
P. Bradley	c	3	0	1	3	0	0
H. Buckner	p	4	0	0	0	2	0
A. Robinson	1b	3	1	1	9	0	0
C. Mongin	2b	3	0	1	0	0	0
Totals		30	2	6	27	9	0

Almendares	Pos	AB	R	H	O	A	E
A. Marsans	rf	4	0	0	4	1	0
A. Cabañas	2b	4	0	0	4	1	0
R. Almeida	3b	4	0	1	1	2	1
G. González	c	3	0	0	2	2	0
H. Hidalgo	cf	3	0	0	1	0	0
J. Muñoz	p	3	0	0	1	4	0
P. Chacon	ss	3	0	1	2	4	0
E. Prats	p	3	0	0	10	1	0
R. Valdés	lf	2	0	0	2	0	0
Totals		29	0	2	27	15	1

Brooklyn Royal Giants	000	000	200 : 2
Almendares	000	000	000 : 0

Three-base hits: J.P. Hill
Sacrifice hits: P. Bradley
Stolen bases: R. Valdés
Bases on balls: J. Muñoz 3, H. Buckner 1
Strikeouts: J. Muñoz 2, H. Buckner 2
Winning pitcher: H. Bucker
Losing pitcher: J. Muñoz
Time: 1 hour, 40 minutes
Umpires: Prudencio Benavides (home) and Quesada (bases)
Scorer: Antonio Conejo

GAME SIX: MONDAY, OCTOBER 19, 1908, AT ALMENDARES PARK

Royal Giants	Pos	AB	R	H	O	A	E
J.P. Hill	lf	5	0	2	2	0	0
C.B. Earle	p	4	1	2	0	4	0
G. Johnson	ss	2	1	2	1	4	0
W. Monroe	3b	4	1	2	5	3	1
A. Dunbar	cf	5	0	1	2	0	1
G. James	rf	5	0	0	2	0	0
A. Robinson	1b	4	0	0	10	0	0
P. Bradley	c	3	0	1	4	0	0
S. Mongin	2b	3	1	1	1	0	0
Totals		35	4	11	27	15	2

Habana	Pos	AB	R	H	O	A	E
L. Bustamante	ss	4	0	0	1	2	0
R. Hernandez	3b	3	0	0	3	1	1
E. Palomino	rf	4	0	0	1	0	0
J. Castillo	1b	4	0	1	8	2	0
L. Padrón	lf	4	0	0	2	0	1
V. González	cf	2	0	1	0	0	0
E. Pedroso	2b	2	0	0	3	2	0
R. Figarola	c	2	0	0	7	1	0
J. Pérez	p	3	0	1	1	4	0
Totals		28	0	3	26	12	2

BRK Royal Giants	003	100	000 : 4
Habana	000	000	000 : 0

C.B. Earle out, for batter in the first inning.
Earned-runs: BRK Royal Giants (2), Habana (0)
Sacrifice hits: W. Monroe, S. Mongin
Stolen bases: W. Monroe, A. Dunbar (2), L. Padrón, E. Palomino
Bases on balls: C.B. Earle 4, J. Pérez 3
Strikeouts: C.B. Earle 4, J. Pérez 5
Dead balls: J. Pérez 2
Winning pitcher: C.B. Earle
Losing pitcher: J. Pérez
Time: 2 hours
Umpires: Antonio Maria García (home) and Eustaquio Gutiérrez (bases)
Scorer: Antonio Conejo

GAME SEVEN: THURSDAY, OCTOBER 22, 1908, AT ALMENDARES PARK

Royal Giants	Pos	AB	R	H	O	A	E
J.P. Hill	lf	4	0	1	2	0	1
C.B. Earle	rf	3	1	0	1	0	0
G. Johnson	ss	4	1	1	5	3	0
W. Monroe	3b	4	0	0	1	1	0
A. Dunbar	cf	4	1	1	3	0	0
H. Buckner	p	2	0	1	0	1	0
P. Bradley	c	4	0	0	5	1	0
A. Robinson	1b	4	0	0	6	0	0
S. Mongin	2b	4	0	0	1	1	0
Totals		35	3	4	24	7	1

Almendares	Pos	AB	R	H	O	A	E
A. Marsans	rf	4	0	0	0	0	0
A. Cabañas	2b	4	0	0	3	2	1
R. Almeida	3b	3	0	0	2	1	1
G. González	c	2	2	1	1	2	0
H. Hidalgo	cf	2	0	0	5	0	0
R. Valdés	lf	2	1	2	2	0	0
A. Cabrera	ss	3	1	1	2	5	1
E. Prats	1b	3	0	0	11	0	0
C. Royer	p	3	0	0	1	2	0
Totals		26	4	4	27	12	3

BRK Royal Giants	000	100	002 : 3
Almendares	030	000	10x : 4

Earned runs: Almendares (2), BRK Royal Giants (0)
Home-run: R. Valdés
Sacrifice hits: H. Hidalgo
Bases on balls: C. Royer 1, H. Buckner 2
Strikeouts: C. Royer 1, H. Buckner 3
Dead ball: C. Royer 2
Winning pitcher: C. Royer
Losing pitcher: H. Buckner
Time: 2 hours
Umpires: Prudencio Benavides (home) and Antonio Maria García (bases)
Scorer: Antonio Conejo

GAME EIGHT: SUNDAY, OCTOBER 25, 1908, AT ALMENDARES PARK

Habana	Pos	AB	R	H	O	A	E
L. Bustamante	ss	3	2	1	2	5	1
R. Hernandez	3b	4	1	1	2	1	0
E. Palomino	rf	4	0	2	1	0	0
L. Padrón	lf,p	4	1	0	0	2	1
J. Castillo	1b	4	0	2	7	0	1
V. González	cf	4	0	1	1	1	0
E. Pedroso	2b	4	0	0	2	3	1
R. Figarola	c	4	0	0	8	2	0
J. Pérez	p	1	1	0	1	1	0
J.M. Magrinat	lf	2	0	0	0	0	0
Totals		34	5	7	24	15	4

Royal Giants	Pos	AB	R	H	O	A	E
J.P. Hill	lf	3	1	1	0	0	1
C.B. Earle	p,rf	2	3	2	1	2	0
G. Johnson	ss	4	2	1	5	3	0
W. Monroe	3b	4	1	0	0	1	0
A. Dunbar	cf	4	1	2	2	0	0
G. James	rf	3	0	1	1	0	0
R. Gans	p	1	0	1	0	2	0
P. Bradley	c	4	0	1	7	2	0
A. Robinson	1b	4	0	0	10	0	1
S. Mongin	2b	4	0	0	1	4	0
Totals		33	8	9	27	14	3

Habana	220	010	000 : 5
BRK Royal Giants	100	040	30x : 8

Earned runs: BRK Royal Giants (1), Habana (0)
Three-base hits: A. Dunbar
Two-base hits: J.Castillo (2), C.B. Earle
Stolen bases: L. Bustamante, R. Hernandez, J.P. Hill
Double-plays: V. González to R. Figarola
Bases on balls: C.B. Earle 3, R. Gans 2, J. Pérez 4, L. Padrón 1
Strikeouts: C.B. Earle 2, R. Gans 2, J. Pérez 1, L. Padrón 3
Dead ball: J. Pérez 1 (G. Johnson)
Hits: J. Pérez 5 in 5.0 innings; C.B. Earle 6 in 5.0
Passed balls: P. Bradley 1
Winning pitcher: R. Gans
Losing pitcher: L. Padrón
Time: 2 hours
Umpires: Eustaquio Gutiérrez (home) and Prudencio Benavides (bases)
Scorer: Antonio Conejo

GAME NINE: MONDAY, OCTOBER 26, 1908, AT ALMENDARES PARK

Royal Giants	Pos	AB	R	H	O	A	E
J.P. Hill	lf	2	1	0	4	1	1
C.B. Earle	rf	4	0	0	0	0	0
G. Johnson	ss	4	0	1	0	2	0
W. Monroe	3b	4	0	1	3	5	0
A. Dunbar	cf	4	0	0	1	0	0
P. Bradley	c	4	1	1	5	1	0
H. Buckner	p	2	2	2	1	3	0
A. Robinson	1b	3	0	0	9	0	0

Almendares	Pos	AB	R	H	O	A	E
A. Marsans	3b,1b	4	0	2	8	0	0
A. Cabañas	2b	3	0	0	3	1	1
G. González	c,cf	2	0	0	1	0	0
J. Muñoz	lf	2	0	0	0	0	0
Hidalgo	cf,c	3	1	1	4	1	0
R. Valdés	lf	1	0	0	3	0	0
A. Cabrera	ss	3	0	0	4	2	0
J. Violá	rf	3	0	0	1	1	0

Royal Giants	Pos	AB	R	H	O	A	E
S. Mongin	2b	4	0	1	4	0	0
Totals		31	4	6	27	12	1

Almendares	Pos	AB	R	H	O	A	E
E. Prats	1b	0	0	0	2	1	0
R. Almeida	3b	4	0	1	1	1	0
J. Mendez	p	3	1	1	0	6	0
Totals		28	2	5	24	14	1

BRK Royal Giants	100	000	201 : 4
Almendares	010	010	000 : 2

Two-base hits: H. Buckner, R. Almeida
Sacrifice hits: A. Cabañas, A. Cabrera, R. Valdés, A. Robinson
Stolen bases: S. Mongin
Double-plays: E. Prats to A. Cabrera
Bases on balls: J. Mendez 3, H. Buckner 3
Strikeouts: J. Mendez 5, H. Buckner 3
In three strikes: (S. Mongin)
Dead balls: J. Mendez 2 (to H. Buckner 2)
Passed balls: G. González 1, H. Hidalgo 1
Winning pitcher: H. Buckner
Losing pitcher: J. Mendez
Time: 2 hours
Umpires: Quesada (home) and Antonio Maria García (bases)
Scorer: Antonio Conejo

GAME TEN: SATURDAY, OCTOBER 31, 1908, AT ALMENDARES PARK

Royal Giants	Pos	AB	R	H	O	A	E
J.P. Hill	lf	4	0	0	5	0	0
C.B. Earle	rf	3	0	0	1	0	0
G. Johnson	ss	4	0	2	0	1	1
W. Monroe	3b	4	0	0	1	5	0
A. Dunbar	cf	4	1	1	1	0	0
P. Bradley	c	2	1	1	3	0	1
A. Robinson	1b	3	0	0	13	1	0
S. Mongin	2b	3	0	0	2	5	0
R. Gans	p	3	0	0	1	3	0
Totals		30	2	4	27	15	2

Habana	Pos	AB	R	H	O	A	E
R. Hernandez	3b	4	1	1	4	0	0
R. Figarola	c	3	0	0	5	0	0
E. Palomino	rf	4	0	1	1	0	0
L. Padrón	p	4	0	2	1	10	0
J. Castillo	1b	4	0	0	11	0	0
V. González	cf	4	0	0	1	0	0
E. Pedroso	2b	3	0	0	1	1	1
J.M. Magrinat	rf	3	0	1	2	0	1
L. Bustamante	ss	3	0	0	1	0	3
Totals		32	1	6	27	11	5

BRK Royal Giants	000	100	001 : 2
Habana	000	001	000 : 1

Earned-runs: BRK Royal Giants (1), Habana (0)
Two-base hits: A. Dunbar
Sacrifice hits: J.P. Hill, P. Bradley (2), A. Robinson, R. Figarola
Stolen bases: S. Mongin
Double-plays: R. Hernandez (s.a)
Bases on balls: R. Gans 0, L. Padrón 4
Strikeouts: R. Gans 3, l. Padrón 4
Winning pitcher: R. Gans
Losing pitcher: L. Padrón
Time: 2 hours
Umpires: Eustaquio Gutiérrez (home) and Prudencio Benavides (bases)
Scorer: Antonio Conejo

GAME ELEVEN: SUNDAY, NOVEMBER 1, 1908, AT ALMENDARES PARK

Royal Giants	Pos	AB	R	H	O	A	E
J.P. Hill	lf	3	1	1	3	0	0

Almendares	Pos	AB	R	H	O	A	E
A. Marsans	1b	5	0	0	9	1	0

Royal Giants	Pos	AB	R	H	O	A	E
C.B. Earle	rf-p	4	0	1	0	0	0
G. Johnson	ss	4	0	1	4	1	0
W. Monroe	3b	4	1	1	3	3	0
A. Dunbar	cf	4	0	0	4	0	0
P. Bradley	c	4	0	0	2	1	0
A. Robinson	1b	4	0	1	6	0	1
H. Buckner	p	2	0	0	0	1	0
G. James	rf	2	0	0	0	0	0
S. Mongin	2b	4	1	1	2	1	0
Totals		35	3	6	24	7	1

Almendares	Pos	AB	R	H	O	A	E
R. Valdés	lf	2	2	1	2	0	0
G. González	c	3	0	0	9	1	0
R. Almeida	3b	4	0	1	1	1	0
H. Hidalgo	cf	3	0	1	2	0	0
P. Chacon	ss	3	1	0	0	0	2
J. Violá	rf	4	1	1	1	0	0
A. Cabrera	2b	3	0	2	2	1	0
A. Ortega	p	3	0	0	1	4	2
Totals		30	4	6	28	8	4

BRK Royal Giants	010	000	020 : 3		
Almendares	101	002	00x : 4		

Two-base hits: A. Robinson
Sacrifice hits: A. Cabrera
Stolen bases: R. Valdés 2, R. Almeida, G. Johnson, A. Cabrera, W. Monroe, S. Mongin
Bases on balls: A. Ortega 7, H. Buckner 4, C.B. Earle 0
Strikeouts: A. Ortega 7, H. Buckner 0, C.B. Earle 1
Wild pitches: H. Buckner 1
Passed balls: P. Bradley 1
Winning pitcher: A. Ortega
Losing pitcher: H. Buckner
Time: 2 hours
Umpires: Simmmons (home), Quesada and Antonio Maria García (bases)
Scorer: Antonio Conejo

GAME TWELVE: MONDAY, NOVEMBER 2, 1908, AT ALMENDARES PARK

Royal Giants	Pos	AB	R	H	O	A	E
J.P. Hill	lf	3	0	0	3	1	0
C.B. Earle	rf,p	4	0	0	0	0	0
G. Johnson	ss	4	0	0	0	3	2
W. Monroe	3b	4	0	0	1	5	0
A. Dunbar	cf	3	0	0	0	0	0
P. Bradley	c	3	0	0	3	1	0
A. Robinson	1b	3	0	0	13	0	0
S. Mongin	2b	2	0	2	4	1	0
R. Gans	p	2	0	0	0	3	1
G. James	rf	1	0	0	0	0	0
Totals		29	0	3	24	14	3

Habana	Pos	AB	R	H	O	A	E
R. Hernandez	ss	4	1	1	1	1	0
R. Figarola	c	5	1	2	4	1	0
E. Palomino	rf	3	2	1	3	0	0
L. Padrón	3b	3	1	2	3	0	0
J. Castillo	1b	3	1	1	14	0	0
V. González	cf	4	0	1	0	0	0
E. Pedroso	2b	4	0	1	2	8	0
J. Pérez	p	3	0	0	0	3	0
A. Arcano	lf	4	0	1	2	0	0
Totals		33	6	10	27	16	0

BRK Royal Giants	000	000	000 : 0		
Habana	310	000	20x : 6		

Earned runs: Habana (1), BRK Royal Giants (0)
Two-base hits: A. Arcano
Sacrifice hits: J. Castillo
Stolen bases: R. Hernandez
Bases on balls: J. Pérez 2, R. Gans 3, C.B. Earle 1
Strikeouts: J. Pérez 3, R. Gans 2, C.B. Earle 0
Winning pitcher: J. Pérez
Losing pitcher: R. Gans
Time: 2 hours
Umpires: Eustaquio Gutiérrez (home) and Prudencio Benavides (bases)
Scorer: Antonio Conejo

GAME THIRTEEN: SATURDAY, NOVEMBER 7, 1908, AT ALMENDARES PARK

Royal Giants	Pos	AB	R	H	O	A	E
J.P. Hill	lf	4	1	2	1	0	0
C.B. Earle	p	3	0	0	0	1	0
G. Johnson	ss	5	1	3	8	3	0
W. Monroe	3b	4	0	2	1	0	1
A. Dunbar	cf	4	0	0	3	0	0
P. Bradley	c	4	0	0	0	0	1
A. Robinson	1b	4	0	0	9	0	1
G. James	rf	4	0	0	1	0	0
S. Mongin	2b	4	2	1	4	2	1
Totals		36	4	7	27	10	3

Almendares	Pos	AB	R	H	O	A	E
A. Marsans	1b	4	0	1	9	1	1
R. Valdés	lf	2	1	0	0	0	0
G. González	c	3	0	0	0	1	0
A. Cabañas	2b	4	1	1	3	4	0
H. Hidalgo	cf	3	0	1	3	0	0
J. Violá	rf	3	0	0	2	0	0
A. Cabrera	ss	4	0	2	0	2	1
J. Muñoz	p	3	0	0	0	2	0
J. Mendez	3b	4	0	0	1	3	0
Totals		30	2	5	27	13	2

BRK Royal Giants	003	000	100 : 4
Almendares	000	000	110 : 2

Three-base hits: A. Cabrera
Sacrifice hits: C.B. Earle, J. Muñoz
Stolen bases: R. Valdés
Bases on balls: C.B. Earle 4, J. Muñoz 2
Strikeouts: C.B. Earle 2, J. Muñoz 5
Dead ball: C.B. Earle 1 (R. Valdés)
Winning pitcher: C.B. Earle
Losing pitcher: J. Muñoz
Time: 2 hours
Umpires: Antonio Maria García (home) and Prudencio Benavides (bases)
Scorer: Antonio Conejo

GAME FOURTEEN: SATURDAY, NOVEMBER 8, 1908, AT ALMENDARES PARK

Royal Giants	Pos	AB	R	H	O	A	E
J.P. Hill	lf	4	1	1	3	0	0
R. Gans	rf	1	0	0	0	0	0
C.B. Earle	rf,lf	5	0	1	2	0	0
G. Johnson	ss	4	1	0	4	4	1
W. Monroe	3b	4	2	2	0	1	0
A. Dunbar	cf	4	1	3	3	0	0
P. Bradley	c	4	0	0	5	1	0
H. Buckner	p	3	0	0	0	2	0
A. Robinson	1b	4	0	1	9	0	0
S. Mongin	2b	3	0	0	1	3	0
Totals		36	5	8	27	11	1

Habana	Pos	AB	R	H	O	A	E
L. Bustamante	ss	4	0	0	2	3	0
R. Hernandez	3b	4	0	0	2	1	2
E. Palomino	rf	3	0	2	0	0	0
L. Padrón	cf	4	0	0	2	0	0
J. Castillo	1b	4	0	1	11	0	1
V. González	2b	3	0	0	3	1	0
R. Figarola	c	4	1	2	4	1	0
J.M. Magrinat	lf	4	0	0	3	0	0
J. Pérez	p	3	0	1	1	3	0
Totals		34	1	6	27	14	3

BRK Royal Giants	021	020	000 : 5
Habana	000	001	000 : 1

Earned runs: BRK Royal Giants (2), Habana (0)
Two-base hits: A. Dunbar, E. Palomino
Stolen bases: R. Figarola, E. Palomino, W. Monroe, R. Gans
Double-plays: L. Bustamante to V. González to J. Castillo
Bases on balls: J. Pérez 1, H. Buckner 1
Strikeouts: J. Pérez 4, H. Buckner 6
Dead ball: J. Pérez 1 (S. Mongin)
Winning pitcher: H. Buckner
Losing pitcher: J. Pérez
Time: 2 hours
Umpires: Eustaquio Gutiérrez (home) and Quesada (bases)
Scorer: Antonio Conejo

GAME FIFTEEN: MONDAY, NOVEMBER 9, 1908, AT ALMENDARES PARK

Royal Giants	Pos	AB	R	H	O	A	E
J.P. Hill	lf	4	0	2	1	0	0
C.B. Earle	rf	4	0	0	1	0	0
G. Johnson	ss	3	0	0	3	2	0
W. Monroe	3b	2	0	0	2	0	0
A. Dunbar	cf	2	0	0	2	0	0
P. Bradley	c	2	0	0	3	3	0
A. Robinson	1b	3	0	0	8	0	0
S. Mongin	2b	3	0	0	3	1	0
R. Gans	p	3	0	0	1	2	0
P. Chacon	ss	0	0	0	3	0	0
C. Royer	p	3	1	0	0	3	0
Totals		27	2	7	27	9	1

Almendares	Pos	AB	R	H	O	A	E
A. Marsans	rf,2b	4	0	2	2	0	0
R. Valdés	lf	4	0	2	2	0	0
G. González	c	4	0	0	5	1	0
A. Cabañas	2b	3	0	2	5	3	1
J. Muñoz	rf	1	0	0	0	0	0
H. Hidalgo	cf	3	0	0	1	0	0
A. Cabrera	ss	1	0	0	3	0	0
E. Prats	1b	2	1	0	6	0	0
J. Mendez	3b	2	0	1	0	2	0
Totals		26	0	2	27	9	1

Brooklyn Royal Giants	000	000	000 : 6
Almendares	000	020	00x : 2

Earned runs: Almendares (1), Brooklyn Royal Giants (0)
Three-base hits: J.P. Hill
Sacrifice hits: H. Hidalgo
Double-plays: C. Royer to A. Cabañas to E. Prats; G. Johnson to S. Mongin to A. Robinson
Bases on balls: R. Gans 5, C. Royer 3
Strikeouts: R. Gans 2, C. Royer 4
Dead ball: C. Royer 1
Winning pitcher: C. Royer
Losing Pitcher: R. Gans
Time: 2 hours
Umpires: Antonio Maria García (home) and Prudencio Benavides (bases)
Scorer: Antonio Conejo

GAME SIXTEEN: FRIDAY, NOVEMBER 11, 1908, AT ALMENDARES PARK

Royal Giants	Pos	AB	R	H	O	A	E
P.J. Hill	lf	5	0	1	3	0	0
C.B. Earle	p	4	1	1	1	3	0
G. Johnson	ss	3	0	1	0	3	2
A. Dunbar	cf	4	0	0	1	0	0
P. Bradley	c	4	1	1	2	0	0
H. Buckner	rf	2	1	0	0	0	0
R. Hernandez	2b	3	0	0	3	2	0
A. Parpetti	1b	3	0	0	11	0	1
S. Mongin	2b	4	0	2	3	3	0
Totals		32	3	6	24	11	3

Almendares	Pos	AB	R	H	O	A	E
A. Marsans	lf	5	2	1	1	0	0
H. Hidalgo	cf	4	0	0	1	1	0
G. González	c	3	2	1	16	0	0
R. García	1b	4	1	2	6	0	0
R. Almeida	3b	4	2	3	1	0	0
J. Violá	rf	4	1	0	0	1	0
A. Cabrera	ss	4	0	1	1	1	1
A. Cabañas	2b	3	0	1	1	2	1
C. Rodríguez	p	4	0	1	0	2	0
Totals		35	8	10	27	7	2

BRK Royal Giants	001	000	020 : 3
Almendares	114	002	00x : 8

Three-base hits: A. Cabañas
Sacrifice hits: H. Hidalgo
Stolen bases: R. Almeida, A. Cabrera, A. Marsans, G. González, C.B. Earle
Left on bases: BRK Royal Giants (10), Almendares (6)
Bases on balls: C. Rodríguez 6, C.B. Earle 2
Strikeouts: C. Rodríguez 11, C.B. Earle 1
Dead balls: C. Rodríguez 2 (C.B. Earle, A. Dunbar)
Wild pitches: C. Rodríguez 2
Passed balls: P. Bradley 2
Winning pitcher: C. Rodríguez
Losing pitcher: C.B. Earle

Time: 2 hours
Umpire: Settley
Scorer: Antonio Conejo

Out of Concours

FRIDAY, NOVEMBER 20, 1908, AT ALMENDARES PARK

Royal Giants	Pos	AB	R	H	O	A	E
J.P. Hill	lf	2	4	2	0	0	0
C.B. Earle	rf	4	1	2	0	0	0
G. Johnson	ss	4	2	0	1	6	0
W. Monroe	3b	4	2	1	2	3	0
A. Dunbar	cf	5	0	1	0	0	0
P. Bradley	c	5	0	0	5	0	0
H. Buckner	p	5	0	3	1	2	0
A. Robinson	1b	5	0	0	13	0	0
S. Mongin	2b	5	0	0	5	0	0
Totals		39	9	9	27	11	0

Cincinnati	Pos	AB	R	H	O	A	E
J. Kane	cf	4	1	1	0	0	0
M. Huggins	2b	2	0	0	1	3	0
H. Lobert	3b	4	0	1	1	1	1
M. Mitchell	rf	4	0	1	1	0	0
R. Hoblitzel	1b	2	0	1	9	0	0
J. McLean	rf	4	0	1	5	0	0
R. Hulswitt	ss	4	0	1	4	1	2
W. Pearce	c	3	0	0	6	2	1
C. Dubut	p	3	0	0	0	4	1
Totals		30	1	6	27	11	5

BRO Royal Giants	100	034	100 : 9
Cincinnati	001	000	000 : 1

Home-run: J.P. Hill
Three-base hits: H. Buckner, A. Dunbar
Two-base hits: H. Buckner
Stolen bases: C.B. Earle, M. Huggins, R. Hoblitzel, J. Kane
Bases on balls: H. Buckner 2, C.Dubuc 6
Strikeouts: H. Buckner 2, C. Dubuc 4
Dead ball: H. Buckner 1 (R. Hoblitzel)
Wild pitches: C. Dubuc 1
Winning pitcher: H. Buckner
Losing pitcher: C. Dubuc
Time: 2 hours
Umpires: Settley (home)
Scorer: Antonio Conejo

Final Statistics

BROOKLYN ROYAL GIANTS

Individual Pitching

Pitcher	G	GS	GC	W	L	Pct	IP	R	H	W	K	HP	WP	ERA
Charles B. Earle	7	6	5	2	3	.400	50.2	21	35	18	18	1	0	3.73
Harry Buckner	7	7	5	4	3	.571	56.2	16	33	16	16	0	1	2.54
Robert Gans	5	4	2	2	2	.500	30.1	11	25	11	11	1	0	3.26
Totals	19	17	12	8	8	.500	136.2	48	93	45	45	2	1	3.16

Individual Batting

Player	Pos	G	AB	R	H	2B	3B	HR	SH	SB	Pct
William Monroe	3b	15	56	6	13	0	0	0	2	4	.232
J. Preston Hill	lf	16	56	9	15	1	1	0	3	2	.269
Grant Johnson	ss	16	60	8	14	0	1	0	0	1	.233
C.B. Earle	p,rf,lf	15	51	8	9	2	0	0	2	1	.176

Player	Pos	G	AB	R	H	2B	3B	HR	SH	SB	Pct
Asby Dunbar	cf	16	60	8	14	3	1	0	0	3	.233
Gus James	c,rf	8	26	1	3	0	0	0	0	0	.115
Harry Buckner	p	9	22	4	4	1	0	0	0	0	.182
Phil Bradley	c,rf	15	51	2	8	0	0	0	5	0	.157
Robert Gans	p,rf	8	21	1	2	0	0	0	0	1	.095
Samuel Mongin	2b	16	56	3	13	1	0	0	1	3	.232
Ricardo Hernandez	2b	1	3	0	0	0	0	0	0	0	.000
Agustin Parpetti	1b	1	3	0	0	0	0	0	0	0	.000
Totals		16	465	50	95	8	3	0	13	15	.204

Individual Fielding

Player	Pos	G	O	A	E	Pct
William Monroe	3b	15	31	45	3	.974
J. Preston Hill	lf	16	42	2	3	.936
Grant Johnson	ss	16	44	47	8	.919
C.B. Earle	p,rf,lf	15	9	17	1	.963
Asby Dunbar	cf	16	33	0	3	.917
Gus James	c,rf	8	13	3	2	.889
Harry Buckner	p	9	1	12	0	1.000
Phil Bradley	c,rf	15	52	16	1	.986
Robert Gans	p,rf	8	2	11	2	.867
Samuel Mongin	2b	16	31	26	2	.966
Ricardo Hernandez	2b	1	3	2	0	1.000
Agustin Parpetti	1b	1	11	0	1	.917
Totals		16	272	181	26	.946

ALMENDARES

Individual Pitching

Pitcher	G	CG	W	L	Pct	IP	R	H	W	SO	ERA
J. Mendez	2	2	1	1	.500	18.0	4	8	5	18	2.00
A. Ortega	2	1	1	1	.500	15.1	11	19	9	11	6.46
J. Violá	1	0	0	0	.000	2.2	1	1	0	2	3.37
J. Muñoz	2	2	0	2	.000	18.0	6	12	5	7	3.00
C. Royer	2	2	2	0	1.000	18.0	3	6	4	5	1.50
C. Rodríguez	1	1	1	0	1.000	9.0	3	6	6	11	6.00
Totals	10	8	5	4	.556	81.0	28	52	29	54	2.56

Individual Batting

Almendares	Pos	G	AB	R	H	2B	3B	HR	SH	SB	Pct
R. Valdés	lf	7	17	4	5	0	0	1	1	4	.294
A. Marsans	lf,1b,rf,2b,3b	9	39	2	9	0	0	0	0	1	.231
A. Cabañas	2b	8	29	3	6	0	1	0	2	0	.207
G. González	c-rf	9	26	4	3	0	0	0	0	1	.115
J. Violá	p-rf	6	22	3	4	0	0	0	2	0	.182
M. Hidalgo	cf-c	9	26	1	3	0	0	0	3	0	.182
J. Muñoz	p,lf,cf,rf	6	11	0	0	0	0	0	1	0	.000
A. Cabrera	3b,2b,1b,ss	8	27	2	7	0	1	0	3	2	.259
P. Chacon	ss	5	13	1	2	0	0	0	0	1	.154
J. Mendez	p,3b	4	12	1	2	0	0	0	0	0	.167
R. García	1b	1	4	1	2	0	0	0	0	0	.500
R. Almeida	3b	6	23	2	8	1	0	0	0	2	.348

Almendares	Pos	G	AB	R	H	2B	3B	HR	SH	SB	Pct
C. Rodríguez	p	1	4	0	1	0	0	0	0	0	.250
A. Ortega	p(2)	2	5	0	0	0	0	0	0	0	.000
E. Prats	1b(4)	4	8	1	0	0	0	0	0	0	.000
C. Royer	p(2)	2	6	1	0	0	0	0	0	0	.000
Totals		9	272	26	52	1	2	1	12	11	.191

Individual Pitching

Almendares	Pos	G	O	A	E	Pct
R. Valdés	lf(7)	7	11	0	0	1.000
A. Marsans	lf(3),1b(4),rf(2),2b(1),3b(1)	9	45	3	2	.960
A. Cabañas	2b(8)	8	24	19	4	.915
G. González	c(9),rf(1)	9	53	9	0	1.000
J. Violá	p(1),rf(6)	6	6	2	0	1.000
M. Hidalgo	cf(9),c(1)	9	20	2	0	1.000
J. Muñoz	p(2),lf(1),cf(1),rf(2)	6	2	6	1	.889
A. Cabrera	3b(1),2b(1),1b(1),ss(5)	8	23	11	3	.919
P. Chacon	ss(5)	5	6	11	3	.850
J. Mendez	p(2),3b(2)	4	1	14	0	1.000
R. García	1b(1)	1	6	0	0	1.000
R. Almeida	3b(6)	6	6	5	2	.846
C. Rodríguez	p(1)	1	0	2	0	1.000
A. Ortega	p(2)	2	1	8	4	.692
E. Prats	1b(4)	4	29	2	0	1.000
C. Royer	p(2)	2	1	5	0	1.000
Totals		9	248	100	19	.948

HABANA

Individual Pitching

Pitcher	G	CG	W	L	Pct	IP	R	H	W	SO	ERA
L. González	1	1	1	0	1.000	9.0	2	5	3	3	2.00
J. Pérez	4	3	1	2	.333	32.0	14	27	10	13	3.94
L. Padrón	3	2	1	2	.333	32.0	9	8	10	11	2.25
Totals	8	6	3	4	.429	73.0	25	40	23	27	3.08

Individual Batting

Habana	Pos	G	AB	R	H	2B	3B	HR	SH	SB	Pct
L. Bustamante	ss	6	21	5	3	0	0	0	0	1	.143
R. Figarola	c	7	26	2	4	0	0	0	1	1	.154
E. Palomino	rf	7	25	2	7	1	0	0	0	2	.280
J. Castillo	1b	7	27	2	5	2	0	0	1	0	.185
L. Padrón	p,lf,cf,2b	7	25	4	8	0	0	0	1	1	.320
R. Hernandez	3b,ss	7	26	4	6	0	0	0	0	2	.231
V. González	cf,2b	7	23	0	4	0	0	0	0	0	.174
E. Pedroso	2b	6	17	0	2	0	0	0	1	0	.118
L. González	p	1	3	0	0	0	0	0	0	0	.000
J. Pérez	p	4	10	1	2	0	0	0	0	0	.200
J.M. Magrinat	lf,rf	4	13	2	1	0	0	0	0	0	.077
A. Arcano	lf	1	4	0	1	1	0	0	0	0	.250
Totals		7	221	22	43	4	0	0	4	7	.195

Individual Fielding

Habana	Pos	G	O	A	E	Pct
L. Bustamante	ss(6)	6	7	16	5	.821

Habana	Pos	G	O	A	E	Pct
R. Figarola	c(7)	7	39	9	0	1.000
E. Palomino	rf(7)	7	9	1	0	1.000
J. Castillo	1b(7)	7	73	2	3	.962
L. Padrón	p(3),lf(3),cf(1),2b(1)	7	14	18	3	.914
R. Hernandez	3b(6),ss(1)	7	17	5	5	.815
V. González	cf(6),2b(1)	7	7	3	0	1.000
E. Pedroso	2b(6)	6	10	15	3	.893
L. González	p(1)	1	0	3	1	.917
J. Pérez	p(4)	4	3	11	0	1.000
J.M. Magrinat	lf(3),rf(1)	4	7	0	1	.875
A. Arcano	lf(1)	1	2	0	0	1.000
Totals		7	185	92	21	.930

♦ 8 ♦

1910
Chicago Leland Giants

A year before Rube Foster would rename the team the American Giants, splitting from owner Frank Leland, the Chicago Leland Giants again dominated black baseball in the west. And according to the October 8, 1910, issue of the *Chicago Defender*, which announced the club's intentions to sail for Cuba, the East Coast teams fared no better against the star-studded Giants:

Leland Giants to Play Baseball in Cuba

New York, Oct. 3 — After defeating the Ridgewoods, champions of New York City 21 to 7 here, the Leland Giants departed for Jacksonville, Fla., where they play October1 and 5, after which they will sail for a series of games in Havana, Cuba, starting October 9. The Chicago colored clubclosed its Eastern invasion with a clean record having won eighteen straight games.

Stateside, the Lelands would finish with a record of 123 wins against only 6 losses. The team, which manager Foster called "the greatest team ever assembled, black or white," had little trouble with the Philadelphia Giants, Brooklyn Royal Giants, or the Cuban Stars.

In the 14-game American Series, Habana and Almendares would provide much stiffer competition.

Roster

Player	Position	Regular Season Club, 1910
James Booker	1b,lf	Chicago Leland Giants
Phil Bradley	c,1b	Brooklyn Royal Giants
Charles Dougherty	p	Chicago Leland Giants
Frank Duncan	lf,1b	Chicago Leland Giants
Andrew Foster	p	Chicago Leland Giants
J. Preston Hill	cf	Chicago Leland Giants
Grant Johnson	ss,2b	Chicago Leland Giants
Bill Lindsay	p,rf	Chicago Leland Giants
John Henry Lloyd	ss	Chicago Leland Giants
Andrew H. Payne	lf	Chicago Leland Giants
Bruce Petway	c,rf	Chicago Leland Giants
Wes Pryor	3b	Chicago Leland Giants
Frank Wickware	p	Chicago Leland Giants

James "Pete" Booker started with the Philadelphia Giants in 1905. He played with the Leland Giants for this to trip to Cuba.

Phil Bradley started with the Brooklyn Royal Giants in 1908. He played with the Leland Giants for this to trip to Cuba.

Charles "Pat" Dougherty a lefthanded pitcher, earned soubriquet "the Black Marquard" when pitching in Chicago area teams. He played with the Leland Giants in 1909.

Frank Duncan began with the Philadelphia Giants in 1909, and played with the Leland Giants in 1910.

Andrew "Rube" Foster started with the Chicago Union Giants in 1901. Rube is credit with 51 victories in 1902. He also played with the Cuban X Giants, Philadelphia Giants and Leland Giants.

J. Preston "Pete" Hill an extremely consistent left-handed line-drive hitter, was the first great outfielder in black baseball history. He played with the Philadelphia Giants from 1903 to 1908. He also played with the Leland Giants in 1909.

Grant Johnson earned the nickname "Home Run" with his powerful righthanded swing in the dead-ball era. He began a career in 1895 that took him to the early twentieth century's best clubs. He played with the Page Fence Giants of Adrian, Michigan, the Columbia Giants, the Cuban X Giants and the Brooklyn Royal Giants. He played with the Leland Giants for to trip to Cuba.

Bill Lindsay began with the Kansas City Giants in 1910 and also played with the Leland Giants the same year.

John Henry Lloyd began his career in 1905 as a twenty-year-old professional ball player, the catcher for the Macon Acmes, Georgia. He also played with the Cuban X Giants and Philadelphia Giants. The 1910 series was his third trip to Cuba.

Bruce Petway began with the Leland Giants in 1906. He also played with the Brooklyn Royal Giants and Philadelphia Giants.

Andrew H. "Jap" Payne started with the Philadelphia Giants in 1902. He played with the Cuban X Giants and Leland Giants.

Wes Pryor began with the Leland Giants in 1910.

Frank Wickware a righthanded pitcher with great speed, started with the Leland Giants in 1910.

Games Played

Date	Winning Club		Losing Club		Winning Pitcher	Losing Pitcher
Oct 9	Leland Giants	5	Habana	4	W. Lindsay 1-0	P. Pareda 0-1
Oct 10	Almendares	5	Leland Giants	2	E. Pedroso 1-0	F. Wickware 0-1
Oct 16	Leland Giants	7	Almendares	0	A. Foster 1-0	J. Muñoz 0-1
Oct 20	Almendares	1	Leland Giants	0	J. Mendez 1-0	P. Dougherty 0-1
Oct 22	Almendares	3	Leland Giants	1	E. Pedroso 2-0	W. Lindsay 1-1
Oct 23	Leland Giants	3	Habana	1	F. Wickware 1-1	L. Mederos 0-1
Oct 24	Almendares	5	Leland Giants	2	J. Mendez 2-0	A. Foster 1-1
Oct 27	Leland Giants	3	Habana	2	P. Dougherty 1-1	L. González 0-1
Oct 30	Leland Giants	7	Almendares	6	A. Foster 2-1	J. Mendez 2-1
Nov 3	Almendares	1	Leland Giants	1	(Tie) P. Dougherty-E. Pedroso	
Nov 5	Leland Giants	11	Habana	7	F. Wickware 2-1	L. Mederos 0-2
Nov 6	Almendares	1	Leland Giants	0	J. Muñoz 1-1	W. Lindsay 1-2
Nov 6	Leland Giants	6	Habana	1	A. Foster 3-1	L. González 0-2
Nov 7 (14)	Almendares	5	Leland Giants	4	J. Mendez 3-1	P. Dougherty 1-2

Club Standings

Pos	Clubs	G	W	L	T	Pct
1.	Almendares	9	6	2	1	.750
2.	Leland Giants	13	7	5	1	.583
3.	Habana	5	0	5	0	.000
	Totals	26	12	12	2	.500

The Games

GAME ONE: SUNDAY, OCTOBER 9, 1910, AT ALMENDARES PARK LELAND

Giants	Pos	AB	R	H	O	A	E
F. Duncan	1b	4	0	0	8	0	0
J.P. Hill	cf	4	0	2	0	0	0
G. Johnson	ss	2	1	0	5	1	1
J. Booker	lf	4	0	0	2	0	0
A. Payne	rf	4	1	3	1	0	0
P. Bradley	2b	3	1	1	1	1	0
W. Pryor	3b	4	0	0	2	3	0
B. Petway	c	2	0	0	9	3	0
B. Lindsay	p	4	0	1	0	0	0
Totals		30	5	7	27	8	1

Habana	Pos	AB	R	H	O	A	E
R. Hernandez	2b	3	1	1	2	3	0
C. Morán	3b	2	1	0	3	3	0
L. Bustamante	ss	4	1	1	1	1	0
R. García	c	4	1	1	6	1	0
A. Parpetti	1b	3	0	1	12	0	1
L. Padrón	rf	3	0	0	0	0	1
V. González	cf	3	0	0	3	0	0
J.M. Magrinat	lf	3	0	1	0	0	0
P. Pareda	p	3	0	0	0	7	1
Totals		28	4	5	27	15	4

Leland Giants	000	112	100 : 5
Habana	003	010	000 : 4

Two-base hits: L. Bustamante, A. Payne (2), J.M. Magrinat
Sacrifice hits: C. Morán, B. Petway, G. Johnson
Sacrifice fly: J.P. Hill
Stolen bases: P. Bradley
Double-plays: R. García and A. Parpetti; C. Morán and R. Hernandez
Left on bases: Leland Giants (6), Habana (4)
Bases on balls: B. Lindsay 3, P. Pareda 2
Strikeout: B. Lindsay 7, P. Pareda 4
Wild pitches: P. Pareda 1, B. Lindsay 2
Hit by pitcher: P. Pareda 2 (F. Duncan and B. Lindsay); B. Lindsay 2 (V. González, A. Parpetti)
Passed balls: R. García 1, B. Petway 1
Winning pitcher: B. Lindsay
Losing pitcher: P. Pareda
Time: 1 hour 35 minutes
Umpires: Prudencio Benavides (home) and Eustaquio Gutiérrez (bases)
Scorer: Antonio Conejo

GAME TWO: MONDAY, OCTOBER 10, 1910, AT ALMENDARES PARK

Leland Giants	Pos	AB	R	H	O	A	E
F. Duncan	lf	3	0	1	1	1	0
J.P. Hill	cf	4	1	1	5	0	0
G. Johnson	ss	4	0	0	3	1	0
J. Booker	1b	3	1	1	11	1	0
A. Payne	rf	4	0	4	0	0	0
P. Bradley	2b	4	0	1	0	4	0
W. Pryor	3b	4	0	1	0	4	0
B. Petway	c	4	0	0	4	2	0
F. Wickware	p	2	0	0	0	2	0
P. Dougherty	(x)	1	0	0	0	0	0
Totals		33	2	9	24	13	0

(x)—Out for F. Wickware in ninth.

Almendares	Pos	AB	R	H	O	A	E
A. Marsans	2b	3	1	1	2	2	0
A. Cabrera	ss	4	1	1	2	8	1
R. Almeida	3b	4	1	3	2	1	0
E. Palomino	rf	4	2	3	1	0	0
J. Castillo	1b	4	0	2	11	0	0
G. González	c	2	0	1	4	1	0
H. Hidalgo	cf	4	0	2	0	0	0
R. Valdés	lf	3	0	0	5	1	0
E. Pedroso	p	3	0	0	0	1	0
Totals		31	5	12	27	14	3

Leland Giants	000	200	000 : 2
Almendares	012	001	10x : 5

Two-Base hits: R. Almeida
Sacrifice hits: G. González
Sacrifice fly: G. González
Stolen bases: J. Castillo, A. Marsans, G. González, E. Palomino, F. Duncan, A. Cabrera
Double-plays: A. Cabrera, A. Marsans and J. Castillo; G. Johnsob and J. Booker

Left on bases: Leland Giants (6), Almendares (5)
Bases on balls: F. Wickware 2, E. Pedroso 3
Strikeouts: F. Wickware 3, E. Pedroso 3
Hit by pitcher: Wickware 1 (A. Marsans), E. Pedroso 2 (J. Booker, F. Wickware)
Passed balls: B. Petway 1
Winning pitcher: E. Pedroso
Losing pitcher: F. Wickware
Time: 1 hour 4 minutes
Umpires: Prudencio Benavides (home) and Eustaquio Gutiérrez (bases)
Scorer: Antonio Conejo

GAME THREE: SUNDAY, OCTOBER 16, 1910, AT ALMENDARES PARK

Almendares	Pos	AB	R	H	O	A	E
A. Marsans	2b	2	0	0	3	8	1
A. Cabrera	ss	3	0	0	0	4	1
R. Almeida	3b	3	0	0	1	0	0
E. Palomino	rf	3	0	1	1	1	0
J. Castillo	1b	3	0	0	15	0	1
G. González	c	3	0	2	3	0	0
H. Hidalgo	cf	3	0	0	0	0	2
R. Valdés	lf	3	0	2	1	0	0
J. Muñoz	p	3	0	0	0	4	0
Totals		26	0	5	24	17	5

Leland Giants	Pos	AB	R	H	O	A	E
F. Duncan	lf	2	1	0	1	0	0
J.P. Hill	cf	3	0	0	0	0	0
G. Johnson	ss	3	1	0	4	4	2
J. Booker	1b	4	0	2	10	0	0
A. Payne	rf	4	0	1	0	0	0
P. Bradley	2b	4	0	0	1	1	1
W. Pryor	3b	4	3	3	1	3	0
B. Petway	c	4	1	1	7	4	0
A. Foster	p	3	1	2	0	2	1
Totals		34	7	9	24	14	4

```
Almendares     000  000  00 : 0 (eight innings)
Leland Giants  000  010  51 : 7
```

Two-base hits: A. Foster, B. Petway
Sacrifice hits: A. Foster
Stolen bases: G. González, F. Duncan
Left on bases: Almendares (3); Leland Giants (5)
Double-plays: G. Johnson, P. Bradley and J. Booker; J. Muñoz, A. Marsans and J. Castillo; B. Petway and J. Booker
Bases on balls: A. Foster 2, J. Muñoz 2
Strikeouts: A. Foster 4, J. Muñoz 3
Hit by pitcher: J. Muñoz 2 (F. Duncan and J.P. Hill)
Winning pitcher: A. Foster
Losing pitcher: J. Muñoz
Time: 2 hours
Umpires: Prudencio Benavides (home) and Eustaquio Gutiérrez (bases)
Scorer: Antonio Conejo

GAME FOUR: THURSDAY, OCTOBER 0, 1910, AT ALMENDARES PARK

Leland Giants	Pos	AB	R	H	O	A	E
F. Duncan	lf	4	0	0	2	0	0
J.P. Hill	cf	4	0	0	0	0	0
G. Johnson	2b	4	0	0	3	6	1
J.H. Lloyd	ss	2	0	0	0	3	0
J. Booker	1b	4	0	0	11	0	1
A. Payne	rf	3	0	0	0	1	0
W. Pryor	3b	3	0	0	2	2	0
B. Petway	c	3	0	0	6	0	1
C. Dougherty	p	3	0	0	0	1	0
Totals		30	0	3	24	13	3

Almendares	Pos	AB	R	H	O	A	E
R. Valdés	lf	4	0	0	3	0	0
A. Marsans	2b	4	0	0	1	4	0
R. Almeida	3b	2	1	0	1	1	2
E. Palomino	rf	3	0	1	2	0	0
J. Castillo	1b	3	0	1	10	0	0
G. González	c	2	0	1	8	1	0
A. Cabañas	rf	3	0	1	1	0	0
A. Cabrera	ss	3	0	0	0	2	0
J. Mendez	p	3	0	0	0	2	0
Totals		28	1	4	27	11	2

```
Leland Giants  000  000  000 : 0
Almendares     000  100  00x : 1
```

Stolen bases: R. Valdés
Double-plays: W. Pryos (without assistance); A. Cabrera, A. Marsans and J. Castillo
Left on bases: Leland Giants (5), Almendares (5)
Bases on balls: C. Dougherty 2, J. Mendez 2
Strikeouts: C. Dougherty 6, J. Mendez 6
Winning pitcher: J. Mendez
Losing pitcher: C. Dougherty
Time: 1 hour 50 minutes
Umpires: Eustaquio Gutiérrez (home) and Prudencio Benavides (bases)
Scorer: A. Conejo

GAME FIVE: SATURDAY, OCTOBER 22, 1910, AT ALMENDDARES

Almendares	Pos	AB	R	H	O	A	E
E. Palomino	rf	4	0	0	0	0	0
A. Marsans	2b	3	1	0	1	3	0
R. Almeida	3b	3	1	3	2	1	0
J. Castillo	1b	3	0	0	14	1	2
G. González	c	2	1	0	3	2	0
A. Cabañas	cf	2	0	0	1	0	0
A. Cabrera	ss	4	0	1	3	8	0
E. Pedroso	p	4	0	1	0	4	0
R. Valdés	lf	4	0	0	3	0	0
Totals		29	3	5	27	19	2

Leland Giants	Pos	AB	R	H	O	A	E
F. Duncan	lf	4	0	1	1	1	1
J.P. Hill	cf	4	0	0	1	0	0
G. Johnson	2b	4	0	0	1	3	0
J.H. Lloyd	ss	4	1	3	3	3	0
J. Booker	c	4	0	1	16	0	0
A. Payne	rf	3	0	0	0	0	2
W. Pryor	3b	2	0	0	2	5	0
B. Petway	c	3	0	0	0	2	0
B. Lindsay	p	3	0	0	1	4	0
Totals		31	1	7	27	8	3

Almendares	001	000	110 : 3
Leland Giants	010	000	000 : 1

Sacrifice hits: A. Payne
Stolen bases: B. Petway. W. Pryor, R. Almeida (2)
Double-plays: A. Marsans, A. Cabrera to J. Castillo (2); F. Duncan to J.H. Lloyd
Left on bases: Almendares (6); Leland Giants (3)
Bases on balls: J. Lindsay 5, E. Pedroso 1
Strikeouts: J. Lindsay 2, E. Pedroso 2
Balk: E. Pedroso Passed balls: B. Petway
Winning pitcher: E. Pedroso
Losing pitcher: B. Lindsay
Time: 1 hour 50 minutes
Umpires: Prudencio Benavides (home) and Eustaquio Pedroso (bases)
Scorer: Antonio Conejo

GAME SIX: SUNDAY, OCTOBER 23, 1910, AT ALMENDARES PARK

Habana	Pos	AB	R	H	O	A	E
R. Hernandez	2b	3	0	0	1	1	0
C. Morán	3b	2	0	1	1	2	0
L. Bustamante	ss	3	0	1	2	1	1
R. García	c	4	0	0	4	3	2
A. Parpetti	1b	4	0	0	8	0	0
L. Padrón	rf	3	0	0	2	0	0
V. González	cf	3	1	0	3	0	0
J.M. Magrinat	lf	3	0	0	2	0	0
L. Mederos	p	3	0	1	1	2	0
Totals		28	1	3	24	9	3

Leland Giants	Pos	AB	R	H	O	A	E
F. Duncan	lf	4	1	1	2	0	1
J.P. Hill	cf	4	1	1	0	0	0
G. Johnson	2b	3	0	0	0	2	1
J.H. Lloyd	ss	3	1	2	3	6	0
J. Booker	1b	4	0	1	14	0	0
A. Payne	rf	3	0	0	2	0	0
W. Pryor	3b	3	0	0	0	1	0
B. Petway	c	2	1	1	4	2	0
F. Wickware	p	3	0	1	0	2	0
Totals		29	4	7	27	13	2

Habana	000	000	010 : 1
Leland Giants	000	100	02x : 3

Sacrifice hits: A. Payne and L. Bustamante
Stolen bases: J.H. Lloyd, B. Petway, J.P. Hill, F. Duncan, V. González and J. Booker
Double-plays: B. Petway and J.H. Lloyd
Left on bases: Habana (3), Leland Giants (5)
Bases on balls: F. Wickware 3, L. Mederos 2 Strikeouts: F. Wickware 4, L. Mederos 3
Winning pitcher: F. Wickware
Losing pitcher: L. Mederos
Time: 1 hour 40 minutes
Umpires: Eustaquio Gutiérrez (home) and Prudencio Benavides (bases)
Scorer: Antonio Conejo

GAME SEVEN: MONDAY, OCTOBER 8, 1910, AT ALMENDARES PARK

Leland Giants	Pos	AB	R	H	O	A	E
F. Duncan	lf	4	0	0	3	0	0
J.P. Hill	cf	3	0	1	1	1	0
G. Johnson	2b	3	1	0	1	0	0
J.H. Lloyd	ss	4	1	2	4	2	0
J. Booker	1b	4	0	1	8	0	0
A. Payne	rf	3	0	1	0	0	0
W. Pryor	3b	3	0	1	0	0	0
B. Lindsay	(x)	1	0	0	0	0	0
B. Petway	c	3	0	0	6	0	0
A. Foster	p	3	0	0	0	4	2
Totals		31	2	5	24	10	2

(x)—Out for W. Pryor in ninth.

Almendares	Pos	AB	R	H	O	A	E
R. Valdés	lf	4	0	0	1	0	0
A. Marsans	2b	4	0	0	3	3	1
R. Almeida	3b	4	1	1	1	0	1
E. Palomino	rf	4	2	2	1	0	0
J. Castillo	1b	3	1	1	10	2	0
G. González	c	3	1	2	3	0	0
A. Cabañas	cf	3	0	1	5	0	0
A. Cabrera	ss	3	0	0	1	4	0
J. Mendez	p	3	0	1	2	3	0
Totals		31	5	8	27	12	2

Leland Giants	200		000		000 : 2	
Almendares	010		301		00x : 5	

Two-base hits: J. Booker and J. Mendez
Double-plays: J. Mendez, A. Marsans and J. Castillo
Left on bases: Leland Giants (4), Almendares (2)
Bases on balls: A. Foster 0, J. Mendez 1
Strikeouts: A. Foster 6, J. Mendez 2
Hit by pitcher: J. Mendez 1 (G. Johnson)
Balk: A. Foster 1
Winning pitcher: J. Mendez
Losing pitcher: A. Foster
Time: 1 hour 50 minutes
Umpires: Eustaquio Gutiérrez (home) and Prudencio Benavides (bases)
Scorer: Antonio Conejo

GAME EIGHT: THURSDAY, OCTOBER 27, 1910, AT ALMENDARES PARK

Leland Giants	Pos	AB	R	H	O	A	E
F. Duncan	lf	4	3	1	3	0	1
J.P. Hill	cf	2	0	0	4	1	0
G. Johnson	2b	4	0	1	2	1	1
J.H. Lloyd	ss	2	0	0	3	2	0
J. Booker	1b	4	0	1	11	0	0
A. Payne	rf	4	0	1	3	1	0
W. Pryor	3b	3	0	1	1	3	1
P. Bradley	c	2	0	0	1	1	0
B. Petway	c	1	0	0	1	1	1
C. Dougherty	p	4	0	0	0	3	1
Totals		30	3	5	27	13	5

(x)—Hit for G. Sánchez in ninth.

Habana	Pos	AB	R	H	O	A	E
R. Hernandez	2b	3	0	1	4	2	0
L. Bustamante	ss	4	0	1	4	3	1
R. García	rf	4	0	0	1	0	0
A. Parpetti	1b	4	0	0	7	1	1
L. Padrón	3b	3	2	1	2	4	1
V. González	cf	4	0	0	1	0	0
J.M. Magrinat	lf	4	0	1	3	1	0
G. Sánchez	c	3	0	0	5	1	2
L. Mederos	(x)	1	0	1	0	0	0
L. González	p	2	0	0	0	0	0
Totals		32	2	5	27	18	5

Leland Giants	101	010	000 : 3
Habana	010	100	000 : 2

Two-base hits: W. Pryor
Sacrifice hits: J.P. Hill
Sacrifice fly: J.P. Hill
Stolen bases: L. Bustamante, L. Padrón, J.H. Lloyd, J. Booker
Left on bases: Leland Giants (7), Habana (4)
Double-plays: A. Payne and P. Bradley
Bases on balls: C. Dougherty 5, L. González 3
Strikeouts: C. Dougherty 1, L. González 3
Hit by pitcher: L. González 1 (J.H. Lloyd)
Winning pitcher: C. Dougherty
Losing pitcher: L. González
Time: 2 hours 10 minutes
Umpires: Eustaquio Gutiérrez (home) and Prudencio Benavides (bases)
Scorer: Antonio Conejo

GAME NINE: WEDNESDAY, OCTOBER 30, 1910, AT ALMENDARES PARK

Almendares	Pos	AB	R	H	O	A	E
A. Cabrera	ss	3	1	1	4	4	1
A. Marsans	2b	4	1	2	4	0	0
R. Almeida	3b	5	2	2	2	0	0
E. Palomino	rf	3	0	2	2	0	0
J. Castillo	1b	4	0	2	6	0	5
G. González	c	4	0	2	1	2	0
A. Cabañas	lf	4	0	0	2	0	0
H. Hidalgo	cf	3	2	2	2	0	1
J. Muñoz	p	1	0	0	0	2	0
J. Mendez	p	2	0	0	1	3	1
Totals		33	6	13	24	11	9

Leland Giants	Pos	AB	R	H	O	A	E
F. Duncan	lf	3	1	2	3	0	0
B. Lindsay	rf	1	0	0	0	0	0
J.P. Hill	cf	5	0	2	0	1	1
G. Johnson	2b	5	1	1	5	4	0
J.H. Lloyd	ss	3	0	1	6	2	0
J. Booker	1b	3	0	0	8	1	0
A. Payne	rf,lf	3	2	2	2	0	0
W. Pryor	3b	3	2	1	0	1	0
B. Petway	c	3	1	1	3	1	0
F. Wickware	p	2	0	2	0	2	0
A. Foster	p	2	0	0	0	0	0
Totals		33	7	12	27	13	1

Almendares	201	011	010 : 6
Leland Giants	120	012	01x : 7

Home run: R. Almeida
Two-base hits: J.P. Hill, H. Hidalgo, J. Castillo, A. Marsans
Sacrifice hits: E. Palomino, A. Payne, W. Pryor, B. Petway, J. Mendez
Sacrifice fly: J.H. Lloyd
Stolen bases: G. González, G. Johnson, H. Hidalgo
Double-plays: J.H. Lloyd to J. Booker (2); G. Johnson to J. Booker; J. Mendez to A. Cabrera;
　　J. Mendez, A. Cabrera to J. Castillo
Left on bases: Almendares (9), Leland Giants (7)
Bases on balls: F. Wickware 4, A. Foster 1, J. Muñoz 0, J. Mendez 1
Strikeouts: F. Wickware 0, A. Foster 1, J. Muñoz 0, J. Mendez 1
Hit by pitcher: F. Wickware 2 (A. Marsans and G. González) and J. Mendez 1 (J. Booker)
Hits: J. Muñoz 6 in 2.0 innings, J. Mendez 6 in 6.0, F. Wickware 7 in 5.0, A. Foster 6 in 4.0
Winning pitcher: A. Foster
Losing pitcher: J. Mendez
Time: 2 hours
Umpires: Eustaquio Gutiérrez (home) and Prudencio Benavides (bases)

GAME TEN: THURSDAY, NOVEMBER 3, 1910, AT ALMENDARES PARK

Leland Giants	Pos	AB	R	H	O	A	E
A. Payne	lf	4	1	0	1	0	0
J.P. Hill	cf	4	0	2	1	0	0

Almendares	Pos	AB	R	H	O	A	E
A. Cabrera	ss	5	0	0	1	5	0
A. Marsans	2b	4	0	0	2	1	0

Leland Giants	Pos	AB	R	H	O	A	E
G. Johnson	2b	4	0	0	2	3	1
J.H. Lloyd	ss	5	0	0	2	2	0
J. Booker	1b	5	0	1	11	1	0
F. Duncan	rf	4	0	0	1	0	0
W. Pryor	3b	3	0	1	1	2	0
B. Petway	c	3	0	1	11	2	0
C. Dougherty	p	2	0	1	0	3	0
Totals		34	1	6	30	13	1

Almendares	Pos	AB	R	H	O	A	E
R. Almeida	c	4	0	1	3	3	1
E. Palomino	rf	4	0	0	0	0	0
J. Castillo	1b	2	0	0	15	0	1
R. Valdés	lf	3	1	1	6	0	0
H. Hidalgo	cf	3	0	1	2	0	0
J. Mendez	3b	4	0	0	1	5	0
E. Pedroso	p	3	0	0	0	4	0
Totals		32	1	3	30	18	2

Leland Giants	100	000	000	0 : 1 (10 innings)
Almendares	000	000	001	0 : 1

Sacrifice hits: G. Johnson, C. Dougherty, B. Petway
Stolen bases: J. Booker (2), A. Payne, J.P. Hill, J.H. Lloyd and R. Valdés
Left on bases: Leland Giants (11), Almendares (6)
Bases on balls: E. Pedroso 4, C. Dougherty 5
Strikeouts: E. Pedroso 1, C. Dougherty 9
Hit by pitcher: E. Pedroso 1 (W. Pryor)
Time: 2 hours 15 minutes
Umpires: Eustaquio Gutiérrez (home) and Prudencio Benavides (bases)
Scorer: Antonio Conejo
Game called at end of tenth inning on account of darkness

GAME ELEVEN: SATURDAY, NOVEMBER 5, 1910, AT ALMENDARES PARK

Leland Giants	Pos	AB	R	H	O	A	E
A. Payne	lf	5	2	1	4	0	0
J.P. Hill	cf	6	3	2	1	0	0
G. Johnson	2b	4	2	2	4	3	0
J.H. Lloyd	ss	6	3	3	4	1	1
J. Booker	1b	6	0	2	7	1	0
W. Pryor	3b	4	0	1	1	1	0
B. Petway	c	5	0	0	6	5	2
P. Bradley	rf	4	0	0	0	0	0
F. Wickware	p	5	1	1	0	5	0
Totals		45	11	12	27	13	4

Habana	Pos	AB	R	H	O	A	E
C. Morán	3b	5	1	2	1	0	1
R. Hernandez	2b	5	1	1	1	1	1
L. Bustamante	ss	4	1	0	3	5	5
A. Parpetti	1b	4	2	1	9	2	3
L. Padrón	p,lf	4	2	2	2	1	1
R. García	rf	3	0	1	1	0	0
V. González	cf	3	0	1	1	0	1
G. Sánchez	c	4	0	0	1	2	1
J.M. Magrinat	lf	1	0	0	1	0	0
L. Mederos	p	3	0	1	1	5	0
Totals		36	7	9	27	16	13

Leland Giants	303	201	200 : 11
Habana	502	000	000 : 7

Two-base hits: J.H. Lloyd
Sacrifice hits: G. Johnson
Stolen bases: J.P. Hill, J. Booker, R. García
Left on bases: Leland Giants (11), Habana (4)
Bases on balls: F. Wickware 4, L. Padrón 4, L. Mederos 2
Strikeouts: F. Wickares 4, L. Padrón 1, L. Mederos 4
Passed balls: B. Petway 1 Hits: L. Pedron 3 in 3.0 innings
Winning pitcher: F. Wickware
Losing pitcher: L. Mederos
Time: 2 hours 30 minutes
Umpires: Prudencio Benavides (home) and Eustaquio Gutiérrez (bases)
Scorer: Antonio Conejo

GAME TWELVE: SUNDAY, NOVEMBER 6, 1910,
AT ALMENDARES PARK (FIRST GAME)

Almendares	Pos	AB	R	H	O	A	E
A. Cabrera	ss	4	0	0	1	7	0

Leland Giants	Pos	AB	R	H	O	A	E
A. Payne	lf	2	0	0	4	0	1

Almendares	Pos	AB	R	H	O	A	E
A. Cabañas	2b	4	0	1	1	4	0
R. Almeida	c	3	0	1	4	2	0
E. Palomino	rf	4	0	2	2	0	1
J. Castillo	1b	4	0	0	14	0	0
R. Valdés	lf	3	1	2	2	0	0
H. Hidalgo	cf	3	0	0	1	0	0
J. Mendez	3b	4	0	0	1	2	0
J. Muñoz	p	3	0	0	1	0	0
Totals		32	1	6	27	21	1

Leland Giants	Pos	AB	R	H	O	A	E
J.P. Hill	cf	4	0	0	1	0	0
G. Johnson	2b	3	0	0	2	4	0
J.H. Lloyd	ss	4	0	1	3	3	0
J. Booker	1b	4	0	0	12	0	0
W. Pryor	3b	3	0	0	0	2	0
P. Bradley	rf	3	0	1	1	0	0
C. Dougherty	(x)	1	0	1	0	0	0
B. Petway	c	3	0	0	4	2	0
A. Foster	(xx)	1	0	0	0	0	0
B. Lindsay	p	2	0	1	0	4	0
Totals		30	0	4	27	15	1

(x)— Hit for P. Bradley in Ninth
(xx)— Out for B. Petway in Ninth

Almendares	000	010	000 : 1
Leland Giants	000	000	000 : 0

Sacrifice hits: A. Payne (2)
Stolen bases: W. Pryor, G. Johnson, R. Valdés
Left on bases: Almendares (7), Leland Giants (6)
Bases on balls: Off J. Muñoz 2, B. Lindsay 3
Strikeouts: J. Muñoz 4, B. Lindsay 2
Hit by pitcher: J. Munnz 1 (G. Johnson)
Winning pitcher: J. Muñoz
Losing pitcher: B. Lindsay
Time: 1 hour 50 minutes
Umpires: Eustaquio Gutiérrez (home) and Prudencio Benavides (bases)
Scorer: Antonio Conejo

GAME THIRTEEN: SUNDAY, NOVEMBER , 1910, AT ALMENDARES PARK (SECOND GAME)

Habana	Pos	AB	R	H	O	A	E
R. Hernandez	ss	4	0	1	2	5	1
C. Morán	3b	4	0	0	1	2	0
R. García	rf	4	0	1	1	0	1
L. Padrón	3b	3	1	1	3	3	1
A. Parpetti	1b	4	0	1	10	0	0
J.M. Magrinat	lf	3	0	0	4	0	0
V. González	cf	3	0	0	3	0	1
G. Sánchez	c	2	0	0	0	0	0
L. González	p	2	0	0	0	5	0
Totals		29	1	4	24	15	4

Leland Giants	Pos	AB	R	H	O	A	E
A. Payne	lf	5	0	0	2	0	0
J.P. Hill	cf	5	2	1	0	0	0
G. Johnson	2b	4	3	4	2	3	0
J.H. Lloyd	ss	3	1	2	2	6	0
J. Booker	1b	2	0	1	18	0	0
W. Pryor	3b	4	0	2	0	5	0
P. Bradley	c	3	0	1	2	1	0
B. Petway	rf	3	0	0	1	0	0
A. Foster	p	4	0	0	0	5	1
Totals		33	6	4	27	20	1

Habana	000	000	100 : 1
Leland Giants	002	030	10x : 6

Sacrifice hits: J. Booker, J.H. Lloyd and P. Bradley
Stolen bases: J.M. Magrinat, A. Payne, J.H. Lloyd, C. Morán, L. Padrón
Double-plays: R. Hernandez, L. Padrón and A. Parpetti
Left on bases: Habana (3), Leland Giants (5)
Bases on balls: A. Foster 2, L. González 4
Strikeouts: A. Foster 1, L. González 1
Hit by pitcher: A. Foster 1 (L. Padrón)
Winning pitcher: A. Foster
Losing pitcher: L. González
Time: 1 hour 40 minutes
Umpires: Prudencio Benavides (home) and Eustaquio Gutiérrez (bases)
Scorer: Antonio Conejo

GAME FOURTEEN: SUNDAY, NOVEMBER 7, 1910, AT ALMENDARES PARK

Leland Giants	Pos	AB	R	H	O	A	E
A. Payne	lf	5	1	2	1	0	0
J.P. Hill	cf	5	1	1	3	0	0
G. Johnson	2b	4	1	0	0	4	1
J.H. Lloyd	ss	5	1	2	2	0	1
J. Booker	1b	5	0	2	12	0	0
W. Pryor	3b	4	0	1	1	5	1
B. Petway	rf	3	0	0	4	1	0
P. Bradley	c	1	0	0	1	1	0
C. Dougherty	p	4	0	3	0	1	1
Totals		40	4	11	24	12	4

Almendares	Pos	AB	R	H	O	A	E
A. Cabrera	ss	3	1	0	2	6	0
A. Marsans	2b	5	2	1	3	2	0
R. Almeida	c	4	1	2	8	0	0
E. Palomino	rf	3	1	0	1	0	0
J. Castillo	1b	4	0	0	8	0	1
R. Valdés	3b	3	0	0	0	5	0
A. Cabañas	lf	3	0	0	3	0	0
H. Hidalgo	cf	3	0	0	1	0	1
C. Royer	p	1	0	0	0	0	1
J. Mendez	p	0	0	0	1	1	0
Totals		29	5	3	27	14	3

Leland Giants	300	100	000 : 4
Almendares	410	000	00x : 5

Two-base hits: R. Almeida, J.H. Lloyd
Sacrifice hits: A. Cabañas, A. Cabrera
Stolen bases: J.P. Hill, W. Pryor (2), J. Booker, A. Payne, H. Hidalgo, J. Mendez
Double-plays: J. Mendez, A. Cabrera and J. Castillo
Left on bases: Leland Giants (10), Almendares (9)
Bases on balls: C. Dougherty 5, C. Royer 1, J. Mendez 0
Strikeouts: C. Dougherty 6, C. Royer 1, J. Mendez 4
Hits: C. Royer 2 in 1.0 innings, J. Mendez 9 in 8.0
Winning pitcher: J. Mendez
Losing pitcher: C. Dougherty
Time: 2 hours
Umpires: Eustaquio Gutiérrez (home) and Prudencio Benavides (bases)
Scorer: Antonio Conejo

Final Statistics

CHICAGO LELAND GIANTS

Individual Pitching

Pitcher	G	GS	GC	W	L	Pct	IP	R	H	W	K	ERA
Charles Dougherty	4	4	4	1	2	.333	35.0	9	15	17	22	ND
Andrew Foster	4	3	3	3	1	.750	29.0	9	23	5	12	ND
Bill Lindsay	3	3	3	1	2	.333	27.0	8	16	11	11	ND
Frank Wickware	4	4	3	2	1	.667	31.0	15	31	13	11	ND
Totals	15	14	13	7	6	.538	122.0	41	85	46	56	ND

Individual Batting

Player	Pos	G	VB	R	H	2B	3B	HR	SH	SB	Pct	O	A	E	Pct
James Booker	1b,lf	14	56	1	13	1	0	0	1	6	.232	151	4	3	.956
Phil Bradley	c,rf	8	25	1	4	0	0	0	2	0	.160	7	9	1	.941
Charles Dougherty	p	6	15	0	5	0	0	0	1	0	.333	0	8	2	.800
Frank Duncan	lf,1b	10	36	6	6	0	0	0	0	3	.167	25	2	3	.900
Andrew Foster	p	5	13	1	2	1	0	0	1	0	.154	0	11	4	.733
John Preston Hill	cf	14	58	8	13	1	0	0	2	4	.224	17	3	1	.952
Grant Johnson	ss,2b	14	51	10	8	0	0	0	3	1	.157	38	37	6	.926
Bill Lindsay	p,rf	5	11	0	2	0	0	0	0	0	.182	1	8	0	1.000
John Henry Lloyd	ss	11	41	8	16	2	0	0	2	4	.390	31	30	3	.953
Andrew H. Payne	lf	14	52	7	15	2	0	0	5	3	.288	20	2	3	.880

Player	Pos	G	VB	R	H	2B	3B	HR	SH	SB	Pct	O	A	E	Pct
Bruce Petway	c,rf	14	41	3	4	1	0	0	3	2	.098	69	22	4	.958
Wes Pryor	3b	14	47	5	11	1	0	0	1	4	.234	11	40	2	.962
Frank Wickware	p	4	12	1	4	0	0	0	0	0	.333	0	11	0	1.000
Totals		14	458	51	103	10	0	0	21	27	.225	370	187	32	.946

Individual Fielding

Players	Pos	G	O	A	E	Pct
James Booker	1b,lf	14	151	4	3	.956
Phil Bradley	c,rf	8	7	9	1	.941
Charles Dougherty	p	6	0	8	2	.800
Frank Duncan	lf,1b	10	25	2	3	.900
Andrew Foster	p	5	0	11	4	.733
John Preston Hill	cf	14	17	3	1	.952
Grant Johnson	ss,2b	14	38	37	6	.926
Bill Lindsay	p,rf	5	1	8	0	1.000
John Henry Lloyd	ss	11	31	30	3	.953
Andrew H. Payne	lf	14	20	2	3	.880
Bruce Petway	c,rf	14	69	22	4	.958
Wes Pryor	3b	14	11	40	2	.962
Frank Wickware	p	4	0	11	0	1.000
Totals		14	370	187	32	.946

ALMENDARES

Individual Pitching

Pitcher	G	CG	W	L	Pct	IP	R	H	W	SO	ERA
E. Pedroso	3	3	2	0	1.000	28.0	4	22	8	5	1.29
J. Mendez	4	2	3	1	.750	32.0	7	22	4	13	1.97
J. Muñoz	3	2	1	1	.500	19.0	10	19	4	7	4.74
C. Royer	1	0	0	0	.000	1.0	3	2	1	1	27.00
Totals	10	7	6	2	.750	80.0	24	65	17	26	2.70

Individual Batting

Player	Pos	G	AB	R	H	2B	3B	HR	SH	SB	Pct
A. Marsans	2b	8	29	5	4	1	0	0	0	1	.138
A. Cabañas	ss,of,2b	6	20	1	4	0	0	0	1	0	.200
R. Almeida	3b,c	9	32	7	13	2	0	1	0	2	.406
E. Palomino	rf	9	32	5	11	0	0	0	1	1	.344
J. Castillo	1b	9	30	1	6	1	0	0	0	1	.200
A. Cabrera	ss	8	27	2	2	0	0	0	1	0	.074
G. González	c	6	16	2	8	0	0	0	2	3	.500
M. Hidalgo	cf	6	19	2	6	1	0	0	0	2	.316
R. Valdés	lf,2b	9	30	2	5	0	0	0	0	3	.167
E. Pedroso	p	3	10	0	1	0	0	0	0	0	.100
J. Mendez	p,3B	6	16	0	1	1	0	0	1	1	.063
C. Royer	P	1	1	0	0	0	0	0	0	0	.000
J. Muñoz	p	3	7	0	0	0	0	0	0	0	.000
Totals		9	271	27	59	6	0	1	6	14	.218

Individual Fielding

Player	Pos	G	O	A	E	Pct
A. Marsans	2b(8)	8	19	15	2	.944
A. Cabañas	ss(1),rf(1),cf(2),lf(1),2b(1)	6	12	4	1	.941
R. Almeida	3b(6),c(3)	9	24	8	5	.865

Player	Pos	G	O	A	E	Pct
E. Palomino	rf(9)	9	10	1	1	.917
J. Castillo	1b(9)	9	103	3	10	.914
A. Cabrera	ss(8)	8	12	40	2	.963
G. González	c(6)	6	22	8	0	1.000
M. Hidalgo	cf(6)	6	6	0	4	.600
R. Valdés	lf(8),2b(1)	9	24	6	0	1.000
E. Pedroso	p(3)	3	0	9	0	1.000
J. Mendez	p(4),3b(2)	6	6	16	1	.957
C. Royer	P(1)	1	0	0	1	.000
J. Muñoz	p(3)	3	1	6	0	1.000
Totals		9	240	137	29	.929

HABANA

Individual Pitching

Pitcher	G	CG	W	L	Pct	IP	R	H	W	SO	ERT
L. Padrón	1	0	0	0	.000	3.0	6	3	4	1	18.00
P. Pareda	1	1	0	1	.000	9.0	5	7	2	4	5.00
L. Mederos	2	1	0	2	.000	16.0	8	16	4	7	4.50
L. González	2	2	0	2	.000	17.0	9	9	7	4	4.76
Totals	6	4	0	5	.000	45.0	28	35	17	16	5.50

Individual Batting

Habana	Pos	G	AB	R	H	2B	3B	HR	SH	SB	Pct
R. Hernandez	2b,ss	5	18	2	4	0	0	0	0	0	.222
C. Morán	3b	4	13	2	3	0	0	0	1	1	.231
L. Bustamante	ss	4	15	2	3	1	0	0	1	1	.200
R. García	rf,c	5	19	1	3	0	0	0	0	1	.158
A. Parpetti	1b	5	19	2	3	0	0	0	0	0	.158
L. Padrón	p,cf,3b,lf	5	16	5	4	0	0	0	0	2	.250
V. González	cf	5	16	1	1	0	0	0	0	1	.063
J.M. Magrinat	lf	5	14	0	2	1	0	0	0	1	.143
P. Pareda	p	1	3	0	0	0	0	0	0	0	.000
L. Mederos	p,ph	3	7	0	3	0	0	0	0	0	.429
G. Sánchez	c	3	9	0	0	0	0	0	0	0	.000
L. González	p	2	4	0	0	0	0	0	0	0	.000
Totals		5	153	15	26	2	0	0	2	7	.170

Individual Fielding

Habana	Pos	G	O	A	E	Pct
R. Hernandez	2b(4),ss(1)	5	10	12	2	.917
C. Morán	3b(4)	4	6	7	1	.929
L. Bustamante	ss(4)	4	10	10	7	.741
R. García	rf(3),c(2)	5	13	4	3	.850
A. Parpetti	1b(5)	5	46	3	5	.907
L. Padrón	p(1),cf(2),3b(2),lf(1)	5	9	8	4	.810
V. González	cf(5)	5	11	0	2	.846
J.M. Magrinat	lf(5)	5	10	1	0	1.000
P. Pareda	p(1)	1	0	7	1	.938
L. Mederos	p(2),ph(1)	3	2	7	0	1.000
G. Sánchez	c(3)	3	12	3	3	.833
L. González	p(2)	2	0	5	0	1.000
Totals		5	129	73	29	.874

◆ 9 ◆

1912
Lincoln Giants of New York

Roster

Player	Position	Regular Season Club, 1912
James Booker	c,1b	Lincoln Giants
William Francis	3b	Lincoln Giants
Robert Gans	lf	Lincoln Giants
LeRoy Grant	1b	Lincoln Giants
John Henry Lloyd	ss	Lincoln Giants
Harry Moore	cf	Lincoln Giants
Spottswood Poles	rf	Lincoln Giants
Richard Redding	p	Lincoln Giants
Louis Santop	c	Lincoln Giants
Frank Wickware	p	Brooklyn Royal Giants
Joseph Williams	p	Lincoln Giants
George C. Wright	2b	Lincoln Giants
Rafael Figarola	c	Cuban Stars

James "Pete" Booker started with the Philadelphia Giants in 1905. He played with the Leland Giants and Lincoln Giants. The 1912 series was his second trip to Cuba.

William "Billy" Francis began with the Wilmington Giants in 1906. He played with the Cuban Giants, Philadelphia Giants and Lincoln Giants.

Robert Edward "Jude" Gans started with the Brooklyn Royal Giants in 1908. He played with the Cuban Giants, Smart Set and Lincoln Giants.

Leroy Grant began with the Lincoln Giants in 1911. He played with the Chicago American Giants.

John Henry Lloyd began his career in 1905 as a twenty-year-old professional ball player, a catcher for the Macon Acmes, Georgia. He also played with the Cuban X Giants, Philadelphia Giants, Leland Giants and Lincoln Giants. The 1912 series was his third trip to Cuba.

Harry "Mike" Moore began with the Chicago Unions in 1896. He played with the Algona Brownies, Cuban X-Giants, Philadelphia Giants, Leland Giants, Chicago Giants and Lincoln Giants. He played in Cuba four times.

Spottswood Poles started with the Philadelphia Giants in 1909 and played with them two seasons before joining the new Lincoln Giants in 1911. Labeled "the Black Ty Cobb," he starred as the centerfielder of the great Lincoln Giants in 1912.

Richard "Cannonball Dick" Redding as his nickname suggests, was a pitcher noted for overpowering speed. A right-hander, he started with the Lincoln Giants in 1911. In 1912, he won an astounding 43 games, losing 12. According to historian Kabert Peterson, Redding's wins that season included a perfect game against the Eastern League's Jersey City Skeeters and a 3-hit, 24-strikeout game against a picked nine of minor leaguers (Only the Ball Was White, 213-214).

Louis "Top" Santop was a lefthanded power hitter and skilled catcher. After beginning with the Fort Worth Wonders in 1909, he played with the Oklahoma Monarchs, Philadelphia Giants and Lincoln Giants.

Frank Wickware, a righthanded pitcher with great speed, started with the Leland Giants in 1910. He also played with the Saint Louis Giants, Mohawk Giants and Lincoln Giants.

Joe "Cyclone" or "Smokey" Williams is regarded by many as the greatest black pitcher. There are those who say that his fastball at its best compared only with that of Walter Johnson. This right-hander began with the San Antonio Bronchos in 1897. He also played with the Leland Giants, Chicago Giants and Lincoln Giants.

George Wright started with the Quaker Giants in 1906. He played with the Brooklyn Royal Giants, Leland Giants, Chicago Giants and Lincoln Giants.

Also playing with the Lincoln Giants in Cuba was Rafael Figarola (catcher).

Also playing with the Lincoln Giants in Cuba was Rafael Figarola (catcher).

Games Played

Date	Winning Club		Losing Club		Winning Pitcher	Losing Pitcher
Dec 1	Almendares	10	Lincoln Giants	1	E. Pedroso 1–0	J. Williams 0–1
Dec 3	Lincoln Gs	3	Habana	0	F. Wickware 1–0	F. Muñoz 0–1
Dec 5	Lincoln Gs	8	Almendares	2	F. Wickware 2–0	J. Mendez 0–1
Dec 8	Habana	14	Lincoln Giants	0	P. Pareda 1–0	F. Wickware 2–1
Dec 9	Almendares	1	Lincoln Giants	0	E. Pedroso 2–0	J. Williams 0–2
Dec 12	Habana	3	Lincoln Giants	2	F. Muñoz 1–1	F. Wickware 2–2
Dec 15	Almendares	6	Lincoln Giants	2	J. Muñoz 1–0	J. Williams 0–3
Dec 17	Lincoln Gs	10	Habana	7	R. Redding 1–0	A. Villazon 0–1
Dec 19	Almendares	6	Lincoln Giants	0	J. Mendez 1–1	F. Wickware 2–3
Dec 22	Lincoln Gs	7	Habana	6	F. Wickware 3–3	F. Muñoz 1–2
Dec 23	Lincoln Gs	7	Almendares	4	R. Redding 2–0	E. Pedroso 2–1
Dec 26	Habana	6	Lincoln Giants	5	F. Muñoz 2–2	J. Williams 0–4
Dec 29	Habana	4	Lincoln Giants	3	A. Villazon 1–1	R. Redding 2–1
(13)						

Club Standings

Pos	Clubs	G	W	L	Pct
1.	Almendares	6	4	2	.667
2.	Habana	7	4	3	.571
3.	Lincoln Giants	13	5	8	.385
	Totals	26	13	13	.500

The Games

GAME ONE: MONDAY, DECEMBER 2, 1912, AT ALMENDARES PARK

Lincoln Giants	Pos	AB	R	H	O	A	E		Almendares	Pos	AB	R	H	O	A	E
S. Poles	rf	2	1	1	1	0	0		A. Marsans	lf	4	1	3	2	0	0
L. Grant	1b	4	0	0	13	0	0		M. Cueto	3b	3	1	1	0	0	0
R. Gans	lf	4	0	2	2	0	0		E. Palomino	rf	3	1	1	1	0	0
J.H. Lloyd	ss	2	0	1	1	4	0		J. Castillo	1b	3	0	0	12	0	0
G. Wright	2b	4	0	0	1	4	0		G. González	c	3	1	0	6	1	0
H. Moore	cf	4	0	0	1	0	1		H. Hidalgo	cf	3	1	0	1	1	1
W. Francis	3b	4	0	1	3	2	0		J. Mendez	2b	3	2	1	3	2	0

Lincoln Giants	Pos	AB	R	H	O	A	E
J. Booker	c	3	0	0	1	3	1
J. Williams	p	3	0	0	1	5	0
Totals		30	1	5	24	18	2

Almendares	Pos	AB	R	H	O	A	E
T. Romanach	ss	4	1	1	1	3	1
E. Pedroso	p	3	2	1	0	5	0
T. Calvo	lf	1	0	0	0	0	0
Totals		30	10	8	27	12	2

Lincoln Giants	001	000	000 :1
Almendares	000	001	09x : 10

Home-run: J. Mendez
Sacrifice hits: M. Cueto
Sacrifice fly: J. Castillo
Stolen bases: J.H. Lloyd, H. Moore, M. Cueto, E. Palomino
Double-plays: G. González and J. Castillo
Bases on balls: E. Pedroso 3, J. Williams 3
Strikeouts: E. Pedroso 1, J. Williams 4
Hit by pitcher: E. Pedroso 1, J. Williams 1
Winning pitcher: E. Pedroso
Losing pitcher: J. Williams
Time: 1 hour 50 minutes
Umpires: Eustaquio Gutiérrez (home) and Alfredo Arcano (bases)
Scorer: Antonio Conejo

GAME TWO: TUESDAY, DECEMBER 3, 1912, AT ALMENDARES PARK

Lincoln Giants	Pos	AB	R	H	O	A	E
S. Poles	rf	4	0	0	2	0	0
L. Grant	1b	3	0	2	7	0	0
R. Gans	lf	4	0	1	3	0	0
J.H. Lloyd	ss	3	1	1	1	2	0
G. Wright	2b	4	1	2	1	3	0
H. Moore	cf	3	1	1	3	1	0
W. Francis	3b	4	0	1	0	0	0
J. Booker	c	2	0	1	7	0	0
F. Wickware	p	2	0	0	0	2	0
Totals		29	3	9	24	8	0

Habana	Pos	AB	R	H	O	A	E
C. Morán	3b	3	0	0	0	2	0
M. Villa	2b	3	0	0	1	7	0
R. García	lf,rf	2	0	2	2	0	0
J. Violá	lf	1	0	0	0	0	0
R. Almeida	1b	2	0	0	13	0	1
R. Hernandez	cf	3	0	0	1	1	0
L. Padrón	2b,lf	3	0	0	0	1	0
P. Chacon	ss	3	0	0	2	2	0
M.A. González	c	2	0	0	5	1	0
F. Muñoz	p	2	0	0	0	4	0
A. Cabañas	(a)	1	0	1	0	0	0
Totals		25	0	3	24	18	1

Lincoln Giants	021	001	00 : 3 (Eight innings)
Habana	000	000	00 : 0

Two-base hits: L. Grant, H. Moore
Sacrifice hits: H. Moore
Stolen bases: R. García, R. Hernandez, L. Grant
Double-plays: H. Moore and L. Grant; R. Hernandez and M.A. González
Bases on balls: F. Wickware 4, F. Muñoz 2
Strikeouts: F. Wickware 4, f.Muñoz 2
Wild pitches: J. Muñoz 1
Winning pitcher: F. Wickware
Losing pitcher: F. Muñoz
Time: 1 hour 35 minutes
Umpires: Valentin González (home) and Alfredo Arcano (bases)
Scorer: Antonio Conejo

GAME THREE: THURSDAY, DECEMBER 5, 1912, AT ALMENDARES PARK

Lincoln Giants	Pos	AB	R	H	O	A	E
S. Poles	rf	5	0	1	1	0	0

Almendares	Pos	AB	R	H	O	A	E
A. Marsans	lf	5	2	3	3	0	0

Lincoln Giants	Pos	AB	R	H	O	A	E
L. Grant	1b	4	1	1	11	0	1
R. Gans	lf	5	1	2	5	0	0
J.H. Lloyd	ss	4	2	1	1	4	0
G. Wright	2b	4	1	0	2	4	2
H. Moore	cf	4	1	1	0	0	0
W. Francis	3b	4	1	2	0	4	0
J. Booker	c	4	0	1	7	2	0
J. Williams	p	4	1	1	0	1	1
Totals		38	8	10	27	15	4

Almendares	Pos	AB	R	H	O	A	E
M. Cueto	3b	4	0	0	0	2	1
E. Palomino	rf	3	0	0	3	0	1
J. Castillo	1b	4	0	0	4	2	1
G. González	c	3	0	1	3	0	1
H. Hidalgo	cf	2	0	0	1	0	0
T. Calvo	ss	4	0	0	0	5	2
T. Romanach	2b	2	0	0	3	6	0
J. Mendez	p	4	0	0	3	3	1
Totals		31	2	6	27	18	7

Lincoln Giants	000	200	024 : 8
Almendares	001	000	010 : 2

Three-base hits: R. Gans, J.H. Lloyd
Two-base hits: A. Marsans, J. Booker, W. Francis
Sacrifice hits: H. Hidalgo
Stolen bases: J.H. Lloyd, H. Hidalgo, A. Marsans (2), S. Poles, E. Palomino, T. Calvo, J. Mendez
Double-plays: J.H. Lloyd, G. Wright and L. Grant
Bases on balls: J. Mendez 4, J. Williams 4
Strikeouts: J. Mendez 1, J. Williams 6
Winning pitcher: J. Williams
Losing Pitcher: J. Mendez
Time: 2 hours
Umpires: Eustaquio Gutiérrez (home) and Alfredo Arcano (bases)
Scorer: Antonio Conejo

GAME FOUR: SUNDAY, DECEMBER 8, 1912, AT ALMENDARES PARK

Lincoln Giants	Pos	AB	R	H	O	A	E
S. Poles	cf	3	0	1	2	0	0
L. Grant	1b	2	0	0	3	0	0
J. Booker	1b	2	0	1	7	0	1
R. Gans	lf	4	0	0	1	0	0
J.H. Lloyd	ss	4	0	2	4	7	1
G. Wright	2b	3	0	0	1	2	0
H. Moore	rf	4	0	2	1	0	0
W. Francis	3b	2	0	0	2	2	0
R. Figarola	c	3	0	0	3	0	0
F. Wickware	p	3	0	0	0	1	1
Totals		30	0	6	24	12	3

Habana	Pos	AB	R	H	O	A	E
C. Morán	3b	4	1	1	1	2	0
A. Cabañas	rf	1	0	1	1	0	0
B. Acosta	lf	2	1	1	1	0	0
M. Villa	2b	5	1	1	0	4	0
J. Violá	lf,rf	4	2	2	2	0	0
A. Parpetti	1b	5	2	2	11	1	0
R. Hernandez	cf	5	2	2	3	0	0
P. Chacon	ss	3	2	1	2	2	0
M.A. González	c	4	2	2	5	3	0
P. Pareda	p	3	1	1	1	0	0
Totals		36	14	14	27	12	0

Lincoln Giants	000	000	000 : 0
Habana	024	000	08x : 14

Three-base hits: A. Parpetti
Two-base hits: P. Chacon
Sacrifice hits: P. Pareda, P. Chacon
Stolen bases: M.A. González
Double-plays: J.H. Lloyd and J. Booker; A. Parpetti and P. Pareda
Bases on balls: F. Wickware 4, P. Pareda 2
Strikeouts: F. Wickware 2, P. Pareda 2
Hit by pitcher: P. Pareda 1, F. Wickware 1
Winning pitcher: P. Pareda
Losing pitcher: F. Wickware
Time: 2 hours
Umpires: Eustaquio Gutiérrez (home) and Alfredo Arcano (bases)
Scorer: Antonio Conejo

GAME FIVE: MONDAY, DECEMBER 9, 1912, AT ALMENDARES PARK

Lincoln Giants	Pos	AB	R	H	O	A	E
S. Poles	cf	3	0	1	1	1	0
H. Moore	rf	4	0	0	1	0	0
R. Gans	lf	3	0	1	3	0	0
J.H. Lloyd	ss	4	0	0	1	5	0
G. Wright	2b	4	0	0	0	1	0
L. Grant	1b	4	0	0	12	1	0
W. Francis	3b	3	0	2	1	3	0
J. Booker	c	2	0	0	5	1	0
J. Williams	p	3	0	0	0	2	0
Totals		30	0	4	24	14	0

Almendares	Pos	AB	R	H	O	A	E
A. Marsans	lf	2	1	0	2	0	0
M. Cueto	3b	2	0	0	0	4	0
E. Palomino	rf	3	0	1	1	0	0
J. Castillo	1b	3	0	1	9	0	0
G. González	c	3	0	0	8	2	0
H. Hidalgo	cf	3	0	1	2	0	0
T. Calvo	ss	3	0	0	3	1	0
T. Romanach	2b	3	0	0	2	2	0
E. Pedroso	p	3	0	0	0	2	0
Totals		28	1	5	27	11	0

Lincoln Giants	000	000	000 : 0
Almendares	100	000	00x : 1

Sacrifice hits: M. Cueto
Bases on balls: J. Williams 1, E. Pedroso 2
Strikeouts: J. Williams 4, E. Pedroso 7
Hit by pitcher: E. Pedroso 1
Winning pitcher : E. Pedroso
Losing pitcher: J. Williams
Time: 1 hour 40 minutes
Umpires Eustaquio Gutiérrez (home) and Alfredo Arcano (bases)
Scorer: Antonio Conejo

GAME SIX: THURSDAY, DECEMBER 1, 1912, AT ALMENDARES PARK

Lincoln Giants	Pos	AB	R	H	O	A	E
S. Poles	cf	3	0	1	3	0	0
G. Wright	2b	4	1	2	1	0	1
R. Gans	lf	4	1	1	0	0	0
J.H. Lloyd	ss	4	0	2	4	4	0
H. Moore	rf	4	0	0	0	0	0
L. Grant	1b	4	0	1	10	3	0
W. Francis	3b	4	0	0	1	3	1
L. Santop	c	4	0	1	5	0	0
W. Wickware	p	1	0	0	0	0	0
J. Williams	(a)	1	0	1	0	0	0
R. Redding	(b)	1	0	0	0	0	0
Totals		34	2	8	24	10	2

Habana	Pos	AB	R	H	O	A	E
C. Morán	3b	2	2	0	1	1	1
A. Cabañas	rf	0	1	0	2	0	0
M. Villa	2b	3	0	2	2	2	1
J. Violá	lf	4	0	0	2	0	0
A. Parpetti	1b	3	0	2	11	1	0
R. Hernandez	cf	2	0	0	1	0	0
P. Chacon	ss	3	0	0	5	7	0
M.A. González	c	2	0	0	3	2	0
F. Muñoz	p	3	0	0	0	2	1
Totals		24	3	4	27	15	3

Lincoln Giants	100	000	010 : 2
Habana	101	010	00x : 2

Two-base hits: A. Parpetti, M. Villa
Sacrifice hits: A. Cabañas, R. Hernandez, P. Chacon, F. Muñoz
Stolen bases: C. Morán, A. Cabañas, A. Parpetti
Bases on balls: F. Wickware 4, F. Muñoz 2
Strikeouts: F. Wickware 4, F. Muñoz 3
Hit by pitcher: F. Wickware 1
Wild pitches: F. Muñoz 1
Passed balls: L. Santop 1
Winning pitcher: F. Muñoz
Losing pitcher: F. Wickware
Time: 2 hours
Umpires: Eustaquio Gutiérrez (home) and Alfredo Arcano (bases)
Scorer: Antonio Conejo

GAME SEVEN: SUNDAY, DECEMBER 15, 1912, AT ALMENDARES PARK

Lincoln Giants	Pos	AB	R	H	O	A	E
S. Poles	cf,lf	3	0	0	1	0	0
G. Wright	2b	4	0	0	3	2	2
R. Gans	lf	1	0	0	0	0	0
R. Redding	(x)	1	0	0	0	0	0
J.H. Lloyd	ss	3	1	1	3	3	0
H. Moore	rf,cf	4	0	1	1	0	0
L. Grant	1b	3	0	1	9	1	3
W. Francis	3b	2	0	0	2	2	0
J. Booker	c	2	0	1	5	2	0
J. Williams	p	1	0	0	0	4	0
F. Wickware	p	3	0	0	0	4	0
Totals		27	1	4	24	18	5

Almendares	Pos	AB	R	H	O	A	E
E. Palomino	rf	3	2	1	4	0	0
M. Cueto	lf	1	0	0	5	0	0
G. González	c	3	0	1	4	1	1
J. Castillo	1b	4	1	0	7	0	0
H. Hidalgo	cf	1	0	1	1	0	0
J. Mendez	cf	3	1	0	3	0	0
A. Cabrera	ss	2	0	2	1	2	0
T. Romanach	2b	3	0	0	2	4	0
E. González	3b	3	1	0	0	1	0
J. Muñoz	p	4	0	2	0	1	1
Totals		27	5	7	27	9	2

(x)-Out for R. Gans in Fifth.

Lincoln Giants	000	000	100 : 1
Almendares	101	002	10x : 5

Three-base hits: A. Cabrera
Sacrifice hits: M. Cueto, A. Cabrera, J. Booker, T. Romanach
Stolen bases: G. González. J.H. Lloyd, S. Poles
Double-plays: J. Williams, J.H. Lloyd and L. Grant; A. Cabrera, T. Romanach and J. Castillo
Bases on balls: F. Muñoz 2, J. Williams 2, F. Wickware 3
Strikeouts: F. Muñoz 2, J. Williams 5, F. Wickare 0
Winning pitcher: F. Muñoz
Losing pitcher: J. Williams
Time: 1 hour 50 minutes
Umpires: Eustaquio Gutiérrez (home) and Alfredo Arcano (bases)
Scorer: Antonio Conejo

GAME EIGHT: TUESDAY, DECEMBER 17, 1912, AT ALMENDARES PARK

Lincoln Giants	Pos	AB	R	H	O	A	E
S. Poles	cf	4	1	2	2	0	0
G. Wright	2b	4	0	1	2	4	0
J. Booker	rf	5	2	1	0	0	0
J.H. Lloyd	ss	4	2	2	2	4	1
H. Moore	lf	3	0	1	3	0	0
L. Grant	1b	3	2	0	14	1	0
W. Francis	3b	5	1	2	2	2	0
L. Santop	c	3	1	1	1	2	0
R. Redding	p	3	1	1	1	4	0
F. Wickware	p	1	0	1	0	1	0
Totals		35	10	12	27	18	1

Habana	Pos	AB	R	H	O	A	E
C. Morán	3b	4	0	0	3	3	0
A. Cabañas	rf	4	0	1	2	0	1
M. Villa	2b	3	1	1	0	1	0
R. Almeida	ss	4	2	2	5	2	1
J. Violá	lf	0	0	0	1	0	0
B. Acosta	lf	1	0	0	0	0	0
A. Parpetti	1b	4	0	1	7	0	2
R. Hernandez	cf	4	0	1	2	1	0
M.A. González	c	4	2	2	7	3	0
A. Villazon	p	0	0	0	0	1	0
P. Pareda	p	3	0	1	0	0	0
R. García	(x)	1	0	0	0	0	0
J. Junco	p	0	0	0	0	1	0
Totals		32	7	11	27	12	4

(x)-Out for P. Pareda.

Lincoln Giants	130	033	000 : 10
Habana	004	120	000 : 7

Two-base hits: J.H. Lloyd, A. Cabañas, R. Almeida (2), M.A. González, P. Pareda
Sacrifice hits: G. Wright
Sacrifice fly: H. Moore
Stolen bases: J.H. Lloyd, H. Moore, J. Violá, S. Poles
Bases on balls: A. Villazon 3, P. Pareda 2, J. Junco 1, F. Wickware 2, R. Redding 1

Strikeouts: A. Villazon 1, P. Pareda 4, J. Junco 1, F. Wickware 1, R. Redding 1
Hit by pitcher: P. Pareda 1, F. Wickware 1
Winning pitcher: R. Redding
Losing pitcher: P. Pareda
Time: 2 hours 30 minutes
Umpires: Eustaquio Gutiérrez (home) and Alfredo Arcano (bases)
Scorer: Antonio Conejo

GAME NINE: THURSDAY DECEMBER 19, 1912, AT ALMENDARES PARK

Lincoln Giants	Pos	AB	R	H	O	A	E
S. Poles	cf,lf	4	0	2	1	0	0
G. Wright	2b	4	0	0	1	3	1
R. Gans	lf	2	0	1	0	0	0
L. Santop	rf	2	0	0	0	0	0
J.H. Lloyd	ss	4	0	0	1	2	0
H. Moore	lf,cf	3	0	1	2	0	0
L. Grant	1b	2	0	0	9	0	1
W. Francis	3b	3	0	1	1	3	0
J. Booker	c	3	0	1	6	0	0
J. Williams	p	2	0	0	0	5	0
Totals		29	0	6	21	13	2

Almendares	Pos	AB	R	H	O	A	E
E. Palomino	rf	4	0	1	1	2	0
M. Cueto	3b	3	1	1	1	1	0
G. González	c	4	0	2	5	0	0
J. Castillo	1b	4	0	1	9	1	0
J. Calvo	lf	4	0	0	1	0	0
A. Cabrera	ss	3	1	1	1	5	0
H. Hidalgo	cf	4	1	1	3	0	0
T. Calvo	2b	3	1	0	1	2	1
J. Mendez	p	1	1	1	1	1	0
J. Muñoz	p	1	0	0	0	0	0
E. Pedroso	p	1	1	1	0	0	0
Totals		31	6	9	24	14	1

Lincoln Giants	000	000	000 : 0
Almendares	001	113	00x : 6

Two-base hits: H. Moore
Stolen bases: S. Poles, J. Mendez, A. Cabrera, E. Pedroso, M. Cueto
Bases on balls: J. Williams 2, J. Mendez 0, J. Muñoz 1, E. Pedroso 1
Strikeouts: J. Williams 6, J. Mendez 0, J. Muñoz 2, E. Pedroso 3
Hit by pitcher: J. Muñoz 1
Passed balls: J. Booker
Hits: J. Mendez 3 in 3.0 innings; J. Muñoz 3 in 3.0; E. Pedroso in 2.0
Winning pitcher: J. Mendez
Losing pitcher: J. Williams
Time: 2 hours
Umpires: Eustaquio Gutiérrez (home) and Alfredo Arcano (bases)
Scorer: Antonio Conejo

GAME TEN: SUNDAY, DECEMBER 22, 1912, AT ALMENDARES PARK

Lincoln Giants	Pos	AB	R	H	O	A	E
S. Poles	cf	4	1	0	1	0	0
G. Wright	2b	4	2	2	0	3	0
R. Gans	lf	3	1	0	1	0	0
J.H. Lloyd	ss	4	2	3	3	4	1
H. Moore	rf	2	1	1	1	0	0
L. Grant	1b	2	0	0	11	2	0
W. Francis	3b	2	0	0	2	1	0
J. Booker	c	4	0	1	7	0	0
L. Santop	c	0	0	0	1	1	1
F. Wickware	p	3	0	0	0	2	0
J. Williams	p	0	0	0	0	0	0
R. Redding	p	0	0	0	0	0	0
Totals		28	7	7	27	13	2

Habana	Pos	AB	R	H	O	A	E
C. Morán	3b	2	1	0	0	3	1
A. Cabañas	2b	2	1	1	1	3	0
M. Villa	ss	4	0	0	4	3	0
R. Almeida	c	5	2	4	1	3	0
J. Violá	rf	3	0	2	2	0	0
A. Parpetti	1b	2	1	0	13	1	2
R. Hernandez	cf	5	1	1	2	0	1
B. Acosta	lf	4	0	2	2	1	0
F. Muñoz	p	2	0	0	1	3	0
A. Villazon	(x)	1	0	0	0	0	0
P. Pareda	p	1	0	0	1	2	0
M.A. González	(xx)	1	0	0	0	0	0
Totals		32	6	10	27	19	4

(x)—Out for F. Muñoz.
(xx)—Out for P. Pareda in Ninth.

Lincoln Giants	200	002	030 : 7
Habana	011	000	112 : 6

Two-base hits: R. Almeida
Sacrifice hits: J. Violá, R. Gans
Sacrifice fly: L. Grant, M. Villa, W. Francis
Stolen bases: R. Almeida, A. Parpetti (2), B. Acosta (2), R. Gans, J.H. Lloyd (3), H. Moore (2), C. Morán
Double-plays: M. Villa (without assistance)
Bases on balls: F. Muñoz 3, P. Pareda 3, F. Wickware 5, J. Williams 3, R. Redding 0
Strikeouts: F. Muñoz 3, P. Pareda 3, F. Wickware 4, J. Williams 2, R. Redding 0
Hit by pitcher: F. Muñoz 1, F. Wickware 1
Passed balls: J. Booker
Winning pitcher: F. Wickware
Losing pitcher: F. Muñoz
Time: 1 hour 55 minutes
Umpires: Eustaquio Gutiérrez (home) and Alfredo Arcano (bases)
Scorer: Antonio Conejo

GAME ELEVEN: MONDAY, DECEMBER 23, 1912, AT ESTADIUM COLUMBIA

Lincoln Giants	Pos	AB	R	H	O	A	E
S. Poles	cf	4	0	2	5	0	0
G. Wright	2b	5	0	0	3	6	0
R. Gans	lf	2	0	1	2	0	0
J.H. Lloyd	ss	3	3	1	0	3	0
H. Moore	rf	2	2	1	1	0	0
L. Grant	1b	2	1	1	10	1	0
J. Booker	c	1	0	0	3	0	1
W. Francis	3b	3	0	0	1	5	0
L. Santop	c	4	0	1	2	0	0
R. Redding	p	4	1	2	0	1	0
Totals		30	7	9	27	16	1

Almendares	Pos	AB	R	H	O	A	E
E. Palomino	rf	4	0	0	1	0	0
M. Cueto	3b	0	0	0	0	0	0
T. Calvo	3b	0	0	0	0	0	0
E. González	3b	2	0	0	1	0	0
G. González	c	4	0	1	4	1	0
J. Castillo	1b	4	1	0	12	0	0
J. Calvo	lf	3	1	1	1	0	1
A. Cabrera	ss	2	0	1	2	7	0
H. Hidalgo	cf	4	1	2	2	0	0
T. Romanach	2b	2	0	0	3	3	0
A. Marsans	(x)	1	0	0	0	0	0
E. Pedroso	p	2	1	1	1	2	2
J. Muñoz	p	2	0	2	0	1	0
J. Mendez	(xx)	1	0	0	0	0	0
Totals		31	4	8	27	17	3

(x)—Out for T. Romanach in Ninth.
(xx)—Out for J. Muñoz in Ninth.

Lincoln Giants	000	312	100 : 7
Almendares	000	001	120 : 4

Sacrifice hits: T. Calvo, S. Poles, H. Moore
Stolen bases: R. Gans, H. Hidalgo
Double-plays: J.H. Lloyd, G. Wright to L. Grant; W. Francis, G. Wright to L. Grant; T. Romanach, A. Cabrera to J. Castillo; W. Francis, G. Wright to J. Booker
Bases on balls: E. Pedroso 1, J. Muñoz 2, R. Redding 6
Strikeouts: E. Pedroso 1, J. Muñoz 2, R. Redding 2
Hit by pitcher: E. Pedroso 1, J. Muñoz 1
Passed balls: L. Santop
Winning pitcher: R. Redding
Losing pitcher: E. Pedroso
Time: 2 hours
Umpires: Eustaquio Gutiérrez (home) and Alfredo Arcano (bases)
Scorer: Antonio Conejo

GAME 12: THURSDAY, DECEMBER 26, 1912, AT ALMENDARES PARK

Lincoln Giants	Pos	AB	R	H	O	A	E
S. Poles	cf	4	1	0	1	0	0

Habana	Pos	AB	R	H	O	A	E
C. Morán	3b	4	1	2	1	0	0

Lincoln Giants	Pos	AB	R	H	O	A	E
G. Wright	2b	4	0	1	2	5	2
R. Gans	lf	4	0	0	1	1	0
J.H. Lloyd	ss	3	1	1	2	3	2
H. Moore	rf	2	1	1	0	0	0
L. Grant	1b	4	1	1	11	0	2
W. Francis	3b	3	1	0	1	1	0
L. Santop	c	3	0	1	5	2	1
J. Williams	p	3	0	0	1	4	1
Totals		30	5	5	24	16	8

Habana	Pos	AB	R	H	O	A	E
A. Cabañas	2b	2	1	1	7	6	2
M. Villa	ss	3	1	1	1	3	0
R. Almeida	c	4	0	1	2	1	1
J. Violá	rf	3	0	0	0	0	0
A. Parpetti	1b	4	0	1	13	1	0
R. Hernandez	cf	4	1	2	2	0	0
B. Acosta	lf	3	1	1	1	1	0
P. Pareda	p	2	1	0	0	3	0
F. Muñoz	p	0	0	0	0	0	0
Totals		29	6	9	27	15	3

Lincoln Giants	000	000	500 : 5
Habana	000	140	01x : 6

Three-base hits: C. Morán, R. Gans
Sacrifice hits: P. Pareda, A. Cabañas, M. Villa
Stolen bases: R. Gans, J.H. Lloyd, H. Moore, R. Almeida, J. Violá
Double-plays: J.H. Lloyd, G. Wright and L. Grant; M. Villa, A. Cabañas and A. Parpetti (2)
Bases on balls: J. Williams 1, P. Pareda 4, F. Muñoz 1
Strikeouts: J. Williams 4, P. Pareda 2, F. Muñoz 0
Hit by pitcher: J. Williams 1
Winning pitcher: F. Muñoz
Losing pitcher: J. Williams
Time: 2 hours 30 minutes
Umpires: Eustaquio Gutiérrez (home) and Alfredo Arcano (bases)
Scorer: Antonio Conejo

GAME THIRTEEN: SUNDAY, DECEMBER 29, 1912

Lincoln Giants	Pos	AB	R	H	O	A	E
S. Poles	cf	5	0	3	5	0	0
G. Wright	2b	4	0	0	2	1	0
R. Gans	lf	3	0	0	0	0	0
J.H. Lloyd	ss	4	1	2	5	3	0
H. Moore	rf	3	1	1	3	0	0
L. Grant	1b	2	0	1	4	1	1
W. Francis	3b	4	0	1	0	3	0
L. Santop	c	4	0	0	6	1	0
R. Redding	p	4	1	1	0	1	0
Totals		33	3	9	25	10	1

Habana	Pos	AB	R	H	O	A	E
C. Morán	3b	3	0	1	3	1	0
A. Cabañas	2b	4	0	1	2	4	0
M. Villa	ss	4	0	1	3	2	0
R. Almeida	c	3	2	2	2	3	1
J. Violá	rf	3	1	1	0	0	0
A. Parpetti	1b	2	0	1	13	0	0
R. Hernandez	cf	4	1	1	1	0	0
B. Acosta	lf	3	0	1	3	0	0
A. Villazon	p	3	0	0	0	4	1
M.A. González	(x)	1	0	1	0	0	0
Totals		30	4	10	27	14	2

(x) — Hit for A. Villazon in ninth.

Lincoln Giants	000	100	110 : 3
Habana	010	000	003 : 4

One out when winning run scored in ninth inning
Sacrifice hits: L. Grant (2), J. Violá and A. Parpetti
Sacrifice fly: A. Parpetti
Stolen bases: M. Villa (2), R. Almeida and S. Poles
Bases on balls: A. Villazon 3, R. Redding 2
Strikeouts: A. Villazon 2, R. Redding 6
Passed balls: L. Santop 1
Winning Pitcher: A. Villazon
Losing pitcher: R. Redding
Time: 2 hours
Umpires: Eustaquio Gutiérrez (home) and Alfredo Arcano (bases)
Anotador: Antonio Conejo

Final Statistics

LINCOLN GIANTS—1912

Individual Pitching

Pitchers	G	GS	GC	W	L	Pct	IP	R	H	W	K	ERA
Joseph Williams	7	5	4	1	4	.200	44.1	27	40	16	31	ND
Frank Wickware	6	5	3	2	3	.400	38.1	26	36	21	15	ND
Richard Redding	4	3	2	2	1	.667	23.2	15	28	9	9	ND
Totals	17	13	9	5	8	.385	106.1	68	104	46	55	ND

Individual Batting

Players	Pos	G	AB	R	H	2B	3B	HR	SH	SB	Pct
Spottswood Poles	rf	13	48	4	14	0	0	0	1	6	.292
LeRoy Grant	1b	13	39	5	8	1	0	0	4	1	.205
Robert Gans	lf	12	39	3	9	0	2	0	1	2	.231
John Henry Lloyd	ss	13	46	13	17	1	1	0	0	8	.370
George C. Wright	2b	13	52	5	8	0	0	0	1	0	.154
Harry Moore	cf	13	42	7	11	2	0	0	3	5	.262
William Francis	3b	15	43	3	10	1	0	0	1	0	.233
James Booker	c,1b	10	28	2	7	1	0	0	1	0	.250
Joseph Williams	p	8	17	1	1	0	0	0	0	0	.059
Frank Wickware	p	6	13	0	1	0	0	0	0	0	.077
Louis Santop	c	7	20	1	4	0	0	0	0	0	.200
Richard Redding	p	6	13	3	4	0	0	0	0	0	.308
Rafael Figarola	c	1	3	0	0	0	0	0	0	0	.000
Totals		13	403	47	94	6	3	0	12	22	.244

Individual Fielding

Players	Pos	G	O	A	E	Pct
Spottswood Poles	rf	13	26	1	0	1.000
LeRoy Grant	1b	13	124	10	8	.942
Robert Gans	lf	12	18	1	0	1.000
John Henry Lloyd	ss	13	28	48	6	.938
George C. Wright	2b	13	19	38	6	.905
Harry Moore	cf	13	17	1	1	1.000
William Francis	3b	15	16	31	2	.979
James Booker	c,1b	10	48	8	3	.949
Joseph Williams	p	8	2	21	2	.920
Frank Wickware	p	6	0	10	1	.909
Louis Santop	c	7	20	6	2	.933
Richard Redding	p	6	1	6	0	1.000
Rafael Figarola	c	1	3	0	0	1.000
Totals		13	322	181	31	.948

ALMENDARES

Individual Pitching

Pitchers	G	CG	W	L	Pct	IP	R	H	W	SO
J. Mendez	2	1	1	1	.500	12.0	8	13	4	1
E. Pedroso	4	2	2	1	.667	27.0	7	16	7	12
J. Muñoz	3	1	1	1	.500	15.0	2	9	5	6
Totals	9	4	4	3	.571	54.0	17	38	16	19

Individual Batting

Almendares	Pos	G	AB	R	H	2B	3B	HR	SH	SB	Pct
A. Marsans	lf(3),ph(1)	4	12	4	6	1	0	0	0	2	.500
M. Cueto	3b(6)	6	13	2	2	0	0	0	3	2	.154
E. Palomino	rf(6)	6	20	3	4	0	0	0	0	2	.200
J. Castillo	1b(6)	6	22	2	2	0	0	0	1	0	.091
G. González	c(6)	6	20	1	5	0	0	0	0	1	.250
H. Hidalgo	cf(6)	6	17	3	5	0	0	0	1	2	.294
J. Mendez	p(2),2b(1),cf(1),ph(1)	5	12	4	2	0	0	1	0	2	.167
T. Romanach	2b(4),ss(1)	5	14	1	1	0	0	0	1	0	.071
E. Pedroso	p(4)	4	9	4	4	0	0	0	0	1	.444
T. Calvo	ss(2),2b(1),3b(1)	4	10	1	0	0	0	0	1	0	.000
J. Calvo	lf(3)	3	8	1	1	0	0	0	0	1	.125
A. Cabrera	ss(3)	3	7	1	4	0	1	0	1	1	.571
E. González	3b(2)	2	5	1	0	0	0	0	0	0	.000
J. Muñoz	p(3)	3	7	0	4	0	0	0	0	0	.571
Totals		6	178	28	40	1	1	1	8	14	.225

Individual Fielding

Almendares	Pos	G	O	A	E	Pct
A. Marsans	lf(3),ph(1)	4	7	0	0	1.000
M. Cueto	3b(6)	6	6	7	1	.929
E. Palomino	rf(6)	6	11	2	1	.929
J. Castillo	1b(6)	6	53	3	1	.982
G. González	c(6)	6	30	5	2	.946
H. Hidalgo	cf(6)	6	10	1	1	.917
J. Mendez	p(2),2b(1),cf(1),ph(1)	5	10	6	1	.941
T. Romanach	2b(4),ss(1)	5	11	18	1	.967
E. Pedroso	p(4)	4	1	9	2	.833
T. Calvo	ss(2),2b(1),3b(1)	4	4	8	3	.800
J. Calvo	lf(3)	3	2	0	1	.667
A. Cabrera	ss(3)	3	4	14	0	1.000
E. González	3b(2)	2	1	1	0	1.000
J. Muñoz	p(3)	3	0	2	1	.667
Totals		6	150	76	15	.934

HABANA

Individual Pitching

Players	Pos	G	CG	W	L	Pct	IP	R	H	W	SO
P. Pareda	p(4)	4	1	2	1	.667	22.0	11	19	11	11
F. Muñoz	p(4)	4	2	1	2	.333	26.0	9	21	8	8
A. Villazon	p(2)	2	1	1	0	.000	11.0	7	13	6	3
J. Junco	p(1)	1	0	0	0	.000	4.0	3	3	1	1
Totals		11	4	4	3	.571	63.0	30	48	26	23

Individual Batting

Players	Pos	G	VB	R	H	2B	3B	HR	SH	SB	Pct
C. Morán	3b(7)	7	22	5	4	0	1	0	0	2	.182
A. Cabañas	2b(3),rf(3),ph(1)	7	14	3	6	1	0	0	2	1	.429
B. Acosta	lf(5)	5	13	2	5	0	0	0	0	2	.385
M. Villa	2b(4e),ss(3)	7	25	3	6	1	0	0	1–1	2	.240
J. Violá	lf(4),rf(4)	7	18	3	5	0	0	0	0	2	.278
A. Parpetti	1b(6)	6	20	3	7	1	1	0	1–1	3	.350
R. Hernandez	cf(7)	7	27	5	7	0	0	0	1	1	.259

Players	Pos	G	VB	R	H	2B	3B	HR	SH	SB	Pct
M.A. González	c(4),ph(2)	6	14	4	5	1	0	0	0	1	.357
P. Pareda	p(4)	4	9	2	2	1	0	0	2	0	.222
R. Almeida	c(3(,1b(1),ss(1)	5	18	6	9	3	0	0	0	3	.500
L. Padrón	3b)1),lf(1)	1	3	0	0	0	0	0	0	0	.000
F. Muñoz	p(4)	4	7	0	0	0	0	0	0	0	.000
R. García	lf(1),rf(1),ph(1)	2	3	0	2	0	0	0	0	1	.667
P. Chacon	ss(3)	3	9	2	1	1	0	0	2	0	.111
A. Villazon	p(2),ph(1)	3	4	0	0	0	0	0	0	0	.000
J. Junco	p(1)	1	0	0	0	0	0	0	0	0	.000
Totals		6	208	40	61	9	2	0	9–2	18	.293

Individual Fielding

Players	Pos	G	O	A	E	Pct
C. Morán	3b(7)	7	9	12	2	.913
A. Cabañas	2b(3),rf(3),ph(1)	7	15	13	3	.903
B. Acosta	lf(5)	5	7	2	0	1.000
M. Villa	2b(4e),ss(3)	7	11	22	1	.971
J. Violá	lf(4),rf(4)	7	7	0	0	1.000
A. Parpetti	1b(6)	6	68	3	4	.947
R. Hernandez	cf(7)	7	12	2	1	.933
M.A. González	c(4),ph(2)	6	20	9	0	1.000
P. Pareda	p(4)	4	2	5	0	1.000
R. Almeida	c(3),1b(1),ss(1)	5	23	9	4	.889
L. Padrón	3b)1),lf(1)	1	0	1	0	1.000
F. Muñoz	p(4)	4	1	9	0	1.000
R. García	lf(1),rf(1),ph(1)	2	2	0	0	1.000
P. Chacon	ss(3)	3	9	11	0	1.000
A. Villazon	p(2),ph(1)	3	0	5	1	.833
J. Junco	p(1)	1	0	1	0	1.000
Totals		6	186	105	14	.950

◆ 10 ◆

1914
Lincoln Stars of New York

Roster

Player	Position	Regular Season Club, 1914
Dell Clark	2b,ss	Lincoln Giants/Brooklyn Royal Giants
William Dismukes	p	Lincoln Giants/Brooklyn Royal Giants
Joe Forbes	3b	Lincoln Stars
Peter "Ed" Green	p,rf	Independent
William Handy	ss,2b	Brooklyn Royal Giants
Frank Harvey	p,rf	Lincoln Giants
William Parks	1b,3b,rf	Lincoln Stars
Spottswood Poles	cf	Lincoln Giants
Dick Redding	p,rf	Lincoln Giants
Louis Santop	c,1b	Lincoln Giants/Brooklyn Royal Giants
Jules Thomas	lf	Brooklyn Royal Giants
Pearl Webster	1b,c	Brooklyn Royal Giants

Dell Clark began with the Brooklyn Royal Giants in 1914. He played with the Lincoln Stars for this trip to Cuba.

William "Dizzy" Dismukes started with the Philadelphia Giants in 1913. This right-handed pitcher played with the Lincoln Stars for the 1914 trip to Cuba.

Joe Forbes started with the Lincoln Stars in 1914.

Peter "Ed" Green started with the Lincoln Stars in 1914.

William "Bill" Handy started with the New York Black Sox in 1910. He played with the Brooklyn Royal Giants, Saint Louis Giants and Lincoln Giants.

Frank Harvey began with the Saint Louis Giants in 1912 and also played with the Brooklyn Royal Giants and the Lincoln Giants.

William Parks started his career in 1911 with the Chicago Giants. He also played with the Lincoln Giants.

Spottswood Poles started with the Philadelphia Giants in 1909 and played with them two seasons before joining the new Lincoln Giants in 1911. Labeled "the Black Ty Cobb," he starred as the centerfielder of the great Lincoln Giants in 1912.

Richard "Cannonball Dick" Redding as his nickname suggests, was a pitcher noted for overpowering speed. A right-hander, he started with the Lincoln Giants in 1911. In 191 winning 43 games and losing 12.

Louis "Top" Santop was a lefthanded power hitter and skilled catcher. He began with the Fort Worth Wonders in 1909 and later played with the Oklahoma Monarchs, Philadelphia Giants and Lincoln Giants.

Jules Thomas started with the Brooklyn Royal Giants in 1914. He played with the Lincoln Stars for this trip to Cuba.

Pearl Webster began with the Brooklyn Royal Giants in 1912. He also played with Hilldale.

Games Played

Date	Winning Club		Losing Club		Winning Pitcher	Losing Pitcher
Oct 9	Almendares	5	Lincoln Stars	1	E. Pedroso 1-0	R. Redding 0-1
Oct 10	Lincoln Stars	6	Habana	4	W. Dismukes 1-0	P. Pareda 0-1
Oct 11	Almendares	10	Lincoln Stars	4	A. Luque 1-0	F. Harvey 0-1
Oct 12	Habana	4	Lincoln Stars	3	J. Acosta 1-0	R. Redding 0-2
Oct 13	Lincoln Stars	3	Almendares	1	W. Dismukes 2-0	J. Mendez 0-1
Oct 15	Lincoln Stars	1	Habana	0	R. Redding 1-2	G. Ballesteros 0-1
Oct 18	Almendares	3	Lincoln Stars	2	E. Pedroso 2-0	W. Dismukes 2-1
Oct 19	Lincoln Stars	3	Habana	0	R. Redding 2-2	P. Pareda 0-2
Oct 22	Almendares	3	Lincoln Stars	1	J. Mendez 1-1	W. Dismukes 2-2
Oct 25	Lincoln Stars	1	Habana	1	(Tie) Redding-Acosta	
Oct 26	Almendares	10	Lincoln Stars	5	A. Luque 2-0	W. Dismukes 2-3
Oct 29	Habana	2	Lincoln Stars	1	G. Ballesteros 1-0	R. Reding 2-3
Nov 2	Almendares	4	Lincoln Stars	2	F. López 1-0	R. Redding 2-4
Nov 2	Habana	2	Lincoln Stars	1	E. Palmero 1-0	W. Dismukes 2-4
(14)						

Club Standings

Clubs	G	W	L	T	Pct
Almendares	7	6	1	0	.857
Habana	7	3	3	1	.500
Lincoln Stars	14	4	9	1	.308
Totals	28	13	13	2	.500

The Games

GAME ONE: FRIDAY, OCTOBER 9, 1914, AT ALMENDARES PARK

Lincoln Stars	Pos	AB	R	H	O	A	E
S. Poles	cf	3	1	3	1	0	0
P. Webster	1b	2	0	0	13	0	1
W. Parks	rf	3	0	0	1	0	0
L. Santop	c	4	0	0	5	1	1
J. Thomas	lf	4	0	1	0	0	0
D. Clark	ss	3	0	0	2	2	1
W. Handy	2b	2	0	0	2	0	1
J. Forbes	3b	3	0	0	0	2	0
R. Redding	p	3	0	0	0	4	0
F. Harvey	(x)	1	0	0	0	0	0
Totals		28	1	5	24	9	4

(x)—Out for W. Handy in ninth.

Almendares	Pos	AB	R	H	O	A	E
M. Cueto	c	3	0	0	11	0	0
R. Almeida	3b	2	2	2	0	1	0
R. García	rf	2	1	1	1	0	0
J. Castillo	1b	1	0	0	6	0	0
E. Pedroso	p	3	0	0	1	4	1
A. Cabrera	ss	3	2	0	1	3	1
A. Luque	cf	3	0	0	3	0	0
J. Violá	lf	4	0	2	4	0	0
F. Hungo	2b	4	0	1	0	0	0
H. Hidalgo	lf	1	0	0	0	0	0
Totals		27	5	6	27	8	2

Lincoln Stars	100	000	000 : 1
Almendares	002	110	01x : 5

Sacrifice hits: W. Webster, W. Parks, E. Pedroso, A. Luque, R. García
Stolen bases: A. Cabrera (2), J. Thomas (2)
Double-plays: S. Poles and L. Santop; W. Webster, D. Clark and W. Handy
Bases on balls: E. Pedroso 2, R. Redding 5
Strikeouts: E. Pedroso 10, R. Redding 5
Hit by pitcher: R. Redding 1

Passed balls: L. Santop 1
Winning pitcher: E. Pedroso
Losing pitcher: R. Redding
Time: 1 hour 55 minutes
Umpires: Alfredo Arcano (home) and Valentin González (bases)
Scorer: Julio E. López

GAME TWO: SATURDAY, OCTOBER 10, 1914, AT ALMENDARES PARK

Lincoln Stars	Pos	AB	R	H	O	A	E		Habana	Pos	AB	R	H	O	A	E
S. Poles	cf	3	1	2	0	0	0		A. Marsans	1b	4	1	2	16	1	0
P. Webster	c	5	2	1	9	2	2		J. Calvo	cf	4	0	1	0	0	0
W. Parks	rf,1b	5	1	1	6	1	3		T. Calvo	lf	5	0	0	1	0	0
L. Santop	1b,rf	5	1	2	7	1	0		L. Padrón	rf	3	0	1	0	0	0
J. Thomas	lf	5	1	2	1	0	0		E. González	3b	4	1	0	2	2	1
W. Handy	2b	5	0	0	2	2	1		M.A. González	c	5	0	1	9	1	0
D. Clark	ss	5	0	2	4	3	0		R. Seiglie	2b	2	1	0	0	3	1
J. Forbes	3b	2	0	0	1	1	0		T. Romanach	ss	4	1	0	1	6	1
W. Dismukes	p	3	0	0	0	3	0		P. Pareda	p	3	0	0	0	2	0
Totals		38	6	10	30	13	6		Totals		34	4	5	30	15	3

Lincoln Stars	202	000	000	2 : 6 (10 innings)		
Habana	000	000	400	0 : 4		

Two-base hits: J. Thomas, S. Poles
Sacrifice hits: E. González, W. Dismukes
Stolen bases: W. Webster (2), J. Calvo, S. Poles (2), T. Romanach, A. Marsans (2)
Double-plays: W. Parks and D. Clark; R. Seiglie, A. Marsans and E. González
Bases on balls: P. Pareda 4, W. Dismukes 5
Strikeouts: P. Pareda 7, W. Dismukes 6
Hit by pitcher: W. Dismukes 1
Winning pitcher: W. Dismukes
Losing pitcher: P. Pareda
Time: 2 hours 30 minutes
Umpires: Alfredo Arcano (home) and Valentin González (bases)
Scorer: Julio E. López

GAME THREE: SUNDAY, OCTOBER 11, 1914, AT ALMENDARES PARK

Lincoln Stars	Pos	AB	R	H	O	A	E		Almendares	Pos	AB	R	H	O	A	E
S. Poles	2b,cf	4	1	2	0	1	0		M. Cueto	lf	3	2	1	1	0	0
F. Webster	1b,c	3	2	2	9	1	1		R. Almeida	3b	4	0	1	0	1	0
W. Parks	rf	4	0	0	0	0	0		H. Hidalgo	cf	4	1	2	2	0	0
L. Santop	c,1b	2	0	0	4	0	1		C. Torriente	rf	3	1	0	1	0	0
J. Thomas	lf	4	0	0	0	0	0		A. Cabrera	ss	3	2	2	0	6	0
W. Handy	2b,ss	3	0	0	1	5	0		G. González	c	2	1	0	8	0	0
D. Clark	ss	1	0	0	1	0	2		J. Violá	1b	4	0	1	10	1	1
J. Forbes	3b	4	0	1	2	1	0		F. Hungo	2b	3	2	2	4	3	0
F. Harvey	p	2	0	0	1	2	0		A. Luque	p	5	1	1	0	1	0
R. Redding	rf	2	0	0	0	0	0		Azcarraga	rf	0	0	0	1	0	0
P. Green	p	1	1	1	0	2	0		Totals		31	10	10	27	12	1
Totals		30	4	6	24	11	6									

Lincoln Stars	000	102	010 : 4		
Almendares	300	222	01x : 10		

Three-base hits: P. Webster, S. Poles
Two-base hits: H. Hidalgo, P. Webster, and F. Hungo

Sacrifice hits: A. Cabrera
Sacrifice fly: L. Santop
Stolen bases: M. Cueto, C. Torriente, W. Handy, J. Thomas
Double-plays: W. Handy and L. Santop
Bases on balls: F. Harvey 8, P. Green 0, A. Luque 3
Strikeouts: F. Harvey 8, P. Green 0, A. Luque 7
Hit by pitcher: F. Harvey 1, Green 1, A. Luque 1
Passed balls: P. Webster 1
Winning pitcher: A. Luque
Losing pitcher: F. Harvey
Time: 2 hours 20 minutes
Umpires: Alfredo Arcano (home) and Valentin González (bases)
Scorer: Julio E. López

GAME FOUR: MONDAY, OCTOBER 12, 1914, AT ALMENDARES PARK

Lincoln Stars	Pos	AB	R	H	O	A	E
S. Poles	cf	4	1	2	2	0	1
P. Webster	1b	3	0	1	8	0	1
W. Parks	rf	4	0	1	2	0	0
L. Santop	c	2	0	2	6	0	1
J. Thomas	lf	3	0	0	1	0	0
W. Handy	ss	4	0	1	3	0	0
D. Clark	2b	4	0	0	0	1	0
J. Forbes	3b	3	0	0	1	0	0
R. Redding	p	2	2	1	1	6	0
F. Harvey	(a)	0	0	0	0	0	0
P. Green	(b)	1	0	0	0	0	0
Totals		30	3	8	24	7	3

Habana	Pos	AB	R	H	O	A	E
A. Marsans	1b	4	1	2	13	0	1
J. Calvo	cf	3	0	2	2	0	0
T. Calvo	lf	4	0	1	2	0	0
L. Padrón	rf	3	1	0	4	0	0
E. González	3b	4	0	1	3	1	0
M.A. González	c	4	0	0	1	3	0
R. Seiglie	2b	1	1	0	0	2	0
T. Romanach	ss	2	1	0	1	5	2
J. Acosta	p	2	0	0	1	0	0
Totals		27	4	6	27	11	3

Lincoln Stars	000	002	100 : 3
Habana	001	200	01x : 4

Two-base hits: W. Handy, L. Santop
Sacrifice hits: J. Calvo, J. Acosta, P. Webster
Stolen bases: J. Calvo, R. Seiglie, A. Marsans (2), T. Calvo, E. González, L. Padrón
Double-plays: W. Handy and P. Webster; J. Acosta and A. Marsans
Bases on balls: R. Redding 5, J. Acosta 3
Strikeouts: R. Redding 5, J. Acosta 0
Passed balls: L. Santop 1
Winning pitcher: J. Acosta
Losing pitcher: R. Redding
Umpires: Valentin González (home) and Cubillas (bases)
Scorer: Julio E. López

GAME FIVE: TUESDAY, OCTOBER 13, 1914, AT ALMENDARES PARK

Lincoln Stars	Pos	AB	R	H	O	A	E
S. Poles	cf	4	1	1	4	0	0
P. Webster	1b	4	0	1	10	0	0
W. Parks	rf,3b	4	0	1	2	2	0
L. Santop	c	4	1	0	3	0	0
J. Thomas	lf	4	1	2	4	0	0
W. Handy	ss	3	0	1	0	3	1
D. Clark	2b	4	0	1	3	2	0
J. Forbes	3b	1	0	0	1	0	1
W. Dismukes	p	3	0	0	0	4	0

Almendares	Pos	AB	R	H	O	A	E
M. Cueto	lf	3	0	2	2	0	0
R. Almeida	3b	4	0	0	1	0	0
H. Hidalgo	cf	4	0	0	3	0	0
C. Torriente	rf	4	0	0	2	0	1
A. Cabrera	ss	4	0	1	0	3	0
G. González	c	4	1	1	7	0	0
J. Violá	1b	4	0	1	7	0	1
F. Hungo	2b	4	0	0	2	3	0
J. Mendez	p	3	0	1	1	2	0

Lincoln Stars	Pos	AB	R	H	O	A	E
F. Harvey	rf	2	0	0	0	0	0
Totals		33	3	6	27	11	2

Almendares	Pos	AB	R	H	O	A	E
Azcarraga	cf	2	0	0	2	0	0
Totals		34	1	6	27	6	2

Lincoln Stars	012	000	000 : 3
Almendares	000	100	000 : 1

Three-base hits: J. Thomas
Two-base hits: G. González and J. Thomas
Sacrifice hits: F. Harvey
Stolen bases: W. Webster, J. Mendez
Double-plays: W. Handy, D. Clark and P. Webster
Bases on balls: W. Dismukes 1, J. Mendez 1
Strikeouts: W. Dismukes 2, J. Mendez 5
Winning pitcher: W. Dismukes
Losing pitcher: J. Mendez
Time: 1 hour 53 minutes
Umpires: Valentin González (home) and Cubillas (bases)
Scorer: Julio E. López

GAME SIX: THURSDAY, OCTOBER 15, 1914, AT ALMENDARES PARK

Lincoln Stars	Pos	AB	R	H	O	A	E
S. Poles	cf	3	1	0	2	1	0
P. Webster	1b	3	0	1	10	0	2
W. Parks	rf	4	0	0	2	1	0
L. Santop	c	4	0	0	4	1	0
J. Thomas	lf	3	0	1	3	0	0
W. Handy	ss	1	0	0	2	1	0
D. Clark	2b	3	0	0	2	4	0
J. Forbes	3b	4	0	1	2	2	0
R. Redding	p	3	0	1	0	2	0
Totals		28	1	4	27	12	3

Habana	Pos	AB	R	H	O	A	E
A. Marsans	1b	4	0	0	11	0	1
J. Calvo	cf	4	0	0	1	0	0
R. Torres	rf	3	0	0	1	0	0
L. Padrón	lf	4	0	1	1	0	0
E. González	2b	3	0	1	2	0	0
M.A. González	c	3	0	1	8	1	0
R. Seiglie	2b	1	0	0	2	1	0
T. Romanach	ss	2	0	0	1	3	0
G. Ballesteros	p	2	0	0	0	2	0
J. Acosta	(x)	1	0	1	0	0	0
Totals		27	0	4	27	7	1

(x)— Hit for R.Torres in Ninth.

Lincoln Stars	000	000	010 : 1
Habana	000	000	000 : 0

Two-base hits: R. Redding, P. Webster
Sacrifice hits: P. Webster, W. Handy, E. González, G. Ballesteros
Stolen bases: L. Padrón, R. Seiglie, P. Webster
Double-plays: R. Redding, L. Santop to W. Webster; E. González to A. Marsans; D. Clark to W. Handy
Bases on balls: R. Redding 2, G. Ballesteros 5
Strikeouts: R. Redding 2, G. Ballesteros 3
Winning pitcher: R. Redding
Losing pitcher: G. Ballesteros
Time: 1 hour 40 minutes
Umpires: Valentin González (home) and Alfredo Arcano (bases)
Scorer: Julio E. López

GAME SEVEN: SUNDAY, OCTOBER 18, 1914, AT ALMENDARES PARK

Lincoln Stars	Pos	AB	R	H	O	A	E
S.Poles	cf	5	0	0	1	1	0
P. Webster	c	5	0	0	8	2	0
W. Parks	rf	5	1	1	1	0	0
L. Santop	1b	4	1	1	10	0	0

Almendares	Pos	AB	R	H	O	A	E
M.Cueto	lf	5	0	0	3	0	0
R. Almeida	3b	5	1	1	1	1	0
H. Hidalgo	cf	4	0	0	1	0	0
C. Torriente	rf	4	1	1	1	0	0

Lincoln Stars	Pos	AB	R	H	O	A	E
J. Thomas	lf	4	0	1	3	0	1
W. Handy	ss	3	0	1	3	5	1
D. Clark	2b	2	0	0	3	2	0
J. Forbes	3b	4	0	0	2	0	1
W. Dismukes	p	3	0	0	1	2	1
Totals		35	2	4	31	13	4

Almendares	Pos	AB	R	H	O	A	E
A. Cabrera	ss	4	0	0	1	4	0
G. González	c	4	0	0	15	0	0
J. Violá	1b	4	0	0	9	0	0
F. Hungo	2b	3	1	2	1	2	0
A. Luque	p	2	0	0	1	2	0
E. Pedroso	p	1	0	1	0	1	0
Totals		36	3	5	33	10	0

Lincoln Stars	000	002	000	00 : 2 (11 innings)		
Almendares	110	000	000	01 : 3		

One out when winning run scored.
Sacrifice hits: A. Luque
Stolen bases: L. Santop, F. Hungo, H. Hidalgo, C. Torriente
Double-plays: J. Thomas and P. Webster; A. Luque, R. Almeida and J. Violá
Bases on balls: W. Dismukes 3, A. Luque 4, E. Pedroso 0
Strikeouts: W. Dismukes 5, A. Luque 9, E. Pedroso 1
Hit by pitcher: W. Dismukes 1, A. Luque 1
Passed balls: G. González 1
Winning pitcher: E. Pedroso
Losing pitcher: W. Dismukes
Time: 2 hours 15 minutes
Umpires: Valentin González (home) and Alfredo Arcano (bases)
Scorer: Julio E. López

GAME EIGHT: MONDAY, OCTOBER 19, 1914, AT ALMENDARES PARK

Lincoln Stars	Pos	AB	R	H	O	A	E
S. Poles	cf	4	1	2	1	0	1
P. Webster	1b	3	1	1	9	0	0
W. Parks	3b	3	0	0	0	2	0
L. Santop	c	4	0	1	6	2	0
J. Thomas	lf	4	0	1	2	0	0
W. Handy	ss	3	1	2	3	2	1
D. Clark	2b	1	0	0	3	2	0
F. Harvey	rf	4	0	1	2	0	0
R. Redding	p	3	0	0	1	3	0
Totals		29	3	8	27	11	2

Habana	Pos	AB	R	H	O	A	E
B. Acosta	lf	4	0	1	2	0	0
J. Calvo	cf	3	0	1	2	0	0
A. Marsans	1b	4	0	0	10	2	0
L. Padrón	rf	3	0	0	3	0	0
E. González	2b	3	0	0	2	1	0
M.A. González	c	3	0	1	5	1	0
R. Seiglie	2b	3	0	0	1	1	1
T. Romanach	ss	3	0	0	1	4	0
P. Pareda	p	2	0	0	1	0	0
T. Calvo	(x)	1	0	0	0	0	0
Totals		29	0	3	27	12	1

(x)—Out for P. Pareda in Ninth.

Lincoln Stars	200	000	100 : 3			
Habana	000	000	000 : 0			

Two-base hits: S. Poles
Sacrifice hits: W. Park, D. Clark (2), W. Handy
Double-plays: R. Seiglie, E. González and A. Marsans
Bases on balls: R. Redding 1, P. Pareda 2
Strikeouts: R. Redding 6, P. Pareda 4
Winning pitcher: R. Redding
Losing pitcher: P. Pareda
Time: 1 hour 40 minutes
Umpires: Valentin González (home) and Cubillas (bases)
Scorer: Julio E. López

GAME NINE: THURSDAY, OCTOBER 22, 1914, AT ALMENDARES PARK

Lincoln Stars	Pos	AB	R	H	O	A	E
S. Poles	cf	4	0	2	3	0	0

Almendares	Pos	AB	R	H	O	A	E
M. Cueto	lf	4	1	1	1	0	0

Lincoln Stars	Pos	AB	R	H	O	A	E
P. Webster	c	3	0	0	5	0	0
W. Parks	3b	3	0	0	2	1	0
L. Santop	1b	2	0	1	7	1	0
J. Thomas	lf	4	0	0	3	0	0
W. Handy	ss	3	0	0	1	1	1
D. Clark	2b	3	0	0	1	2	1
F. Harvey	rf	3	0	0	2	0	0
W. Dismukes	p	2	1	0	0	3	0
R. Redding	(x)	1	0	0	0	0	0
Totals		28	1	3	24	8	2

(x)— Out for W. Dismukes in Ninth.

Almendares	Pos	AB	R	H	O	A	E
R. Almeida	3b	4	0	1	2	2	0
H. Hidalgo	cf	4	0	1	2	0	0
C. Torriente	rf	3	1	1	0	0	0
A. Cabrera	ss	4	0	2	3	5	0
G. González	c	4	1	1	9	1	0
J. Violá	1b	4	0	1	6	0	1
F. Hungo	2b	3	0	1	4	1	0
J. Mendez	p	2	0	0	0	2	0
Totals		32	3	9	27	11	1

Lincoln Stars	000	001	000 : 1
Almendares	011	000	10x : 3

Two-base hits: C. Torriente, A. Cabrera
Sacrifice hits: J. Mendez
Stolen bases: W. Webster
Double-plays: J. Mendez, A. Cabrera and J. Violá; R. Almeida, F. Hungo and J. Violá; W. Parks, L. Santop and W. Webster
Bases on balls: W. Dismukes 1, J. Mendez 6
Strikeouts: W. Dismukes 2, J. Mendez 8
Winning pitcher: J. Mendez
Losing pitcher: W. Dismukes
Time: 1 hour 50 minutes
Umpires: Valentin González (home) and Alfredo Arcano (bases)
Scorer: Julio E. López

GAME TEN: SUNDAY, OCTOBER 25, 1914, AT ALMENDARES PARK

Lincoln Stars	Pos	AB	R	H	O	A	E
S. Poles	cf	3	1	0	3	0	0
P. Webster	1b	3	0	1	3	0	0
W. Parks	3b	2	0	1	1	0	0
L. Santop	c	2	0	0	3	0	0
J. Thomas	lf	2	0	0	0	0	0
W. Handy	ss	2	0	1	0	0	0
D. Clark	2b	2	0	1	2	0	1
F. Harvey	rf	2	0	0	3	0	0
R. Redding	p	2	0	1	0	2	0
Totals		20	1	5	15	2	1

Habana	Pos	AB	R	H	O	A	E
B. Acosta	lf	3	0	1	1	0	0
J. Calvo	cf	3	0	0	1	0	0
A. Marsans	1b	2	0	1	3	0	1
L. Padrón	3b	2	0	1	1	1	0
T. Calvo	rf	2	0	1	0	0	0
M.A. González	c	2	0	0	3	1	0
E. González	2b	2	0	0	0	3	0
T. Romanach	ss	1	1	1	3	0	0
J. Acosta	p	1	0	0	0	2	0
Totals		18	1	5	15	7	1

Lincoln Stars	001	00 : 1
Habana	000	01 : 1

Game called at end of fifth inning on account of rain.
Two-base hits: A. Marsans
Stolen bases: D. Clark, L. Padrón (2)
Bases on balls: R. Redding 0, J. Acosta 0
Strikeouts: R. Redding 3, J. Acosta 1
Hit by pitcher: R. Redding 1 (T. Romanach)
Umpires: Valentin González (home) and Alfredo Arcano (bases)
Scorer: Antonio Conejo

GAME ELEVEN: MONDAY, OCTOBER 26, 1914, AT ALMENDARES PARK

Lincoln Stars	Pos	AB	R	H	O	A	E
S. Poles	cf	4	0	1	1	0	0

Almendares	Pos	AB	R	H	O	A	E
M. Cueto	lf	3	2	0	1	0	0

Lincoln Stars	Pos	AB	R	H	O	A	E
P. Webster	c	4	0	0	2	1	1
W. Parks	3b	4	0	1	1	7	3
L. Santop	1b	4	1	2	12	1	1
J. Thomas	lf	3	1	0	1	1	0
W. Handy	ss	1	0	0	0	3	2
D. Clark	2b	2	1	0	5	3	0
F. Harvey	rf,p	4	1	0	0	0	0
W. Dismukes	p	1	0	0	0	1	0
P. Green	p,rf	3	0	1	2	1	0
J. Forbes	(x)	1	1	1	0	0	0
R. Redding	p	1	0	0	0	0	0
Totals		32	5	6	24	18	7

Almendares	Pos	AB	R	H	O	A	E
R. Almeida	3b	4	0	1	1	3	1
H. Hidalgo	cf	0	1	0	0	0	0
C. Torriente	rf	3	3	3	1	0	0
A. Cabrera	ss	4	0	0	3	1	0
G. González	c	3	1	1	6	1	0
J. Violá	1b	3	1	0	10	0	1
F. Hungo	2b	4	0	2	3	2	1
A. Luque	p	4	0	1	0	3	0
Azcarraga	cf	2	2	1	2	0	1
Totals		30	10	9	27	10	5

Lincoln Stars	000	400	001 : 5
Almendares	303	112	00x : 10

Sacrifice hits: R. Almeida (2), W. Handy, A. Cabrera and J. Violá
Stolen bases: M. Cueto, G. González, C. Torriente
Double-plays: D. Clark and L. Santop (2); F. Hungo and J. Violá
Bases on balls: F. Harvey 3, P. Green 1, W. Dismukes 2, A. Luque 3
Strikeouts: F. Harvey 1, P. Green 0, W. Dismukes 0, A. Luque 5
Hit by pitcher: F. Harvey 1, W. Dismukes 1, A. Luque 1
Winning pitcher: A. Luque
Losing pitcher: F. Harvey
Time: 2 hours
Umpires: Valetin González (home) and Cubillas (bases)
Scorer: Antonio Conejo

GAME TWELVE: THURSDAY, OCTOBER 29, 1914, AT ALMENDARES PARK

Lincoln Stars	Pos	AB	R	H	O	A	E
S. Poles	cf	4	0	1	0	0	0
P. Webster	1b	4	0	2	9	0	0
W. Parks	rf	4	1	1	4	0	0
L. Santop	c	4	0	1	5	3	1
J. Thomas	lf	3	0	0	2	0	0
W. Handy	ss	3	0	0	2	2	0
D. Clark	2b	3	0	0	1	1	0
J. Forbes	3b	3	0	0	1	2	0
F. Harvey	p	2	0	0	0	1	0
R. Redding	p	1	0	0	0	1	0
Totals		31	1	5	24	10	1

Habana	Pos	AB	R	H	O	A	E
B. Acosta	lf	2	0	1	4	0	0
J. Calvo	cf	4	0	0	4	0	1
A. Marsans	1b	3	1	1	11	0	0
A. Aragon	3b	3	0	0	2	2	0
L. Padrón	rf	4	0	1	3	0	0
M.A. González	c	4	0	0	6	1	0
E. González	2b	4	0	0	0	2	0
T. Romanach	ss	1	1	0	1	1	0
J. Acosta	p	1	0	1	0	1	1
R. Seiglie	(x)	0	0	0	0	0	0
G. Ballesteros	p	1	0	1	0	0	0
Totals		27	2	5	27	7	2

(x)— Run for J. Acosta in Fifth.

Lincoln Stars	100	000	000 : 1
Habana	000	001	10x : 2

Sacrifice hits: A. Aragon
Stolen bases: R. Seiglie
Bases on balls: F. Harvey 5, R. Redding 0, J. Acosta 0, G. Ballesteros 0
Strikeouts: F. Harvey 3, R. Redding 2, J. Acosta 4, G. Ballesteros 2
Hit by pitcher: F. Harvey 1
Winning pitcher: G. Ballesteros
Losing pitcher: R. Redding
Time: 1 hour 40 minutes
Umpires: Valentin González (home) and Alfredo Arcano (bases)
Scorer: Antonio Conejo

GAME THIRTEEN: SUNDAY, NOVEMBER 1, 1914, AT ALMENDARES PARK (FIRST GAME)

Lincoln Stars	Pos	AB	R	H	O	A	E
P. Webster	1b	4	1	1	13	0	0
W. Parks	rf	3	0	0	0	0	1
S. Poles	cf	3	0	2	1	0	0
L. Santop	c	3	0	2	5	1	0
J. Thomas	lf	4	0	0	2	1	0
W. Handy	ss	3	1	0	0	2	0
D. Clark	2b	3	0	1	2	4	1
J. Forbes	3b	4	0	0	1	3	0
R. Redding	p	3	0	1	0	5	0
P. Green	(x)	1	0	0	0	0	0
F. Harvey	(xx)	1	0	1	0	0	0
Totals		31	2	8	24	16	2

Almendares	Pos	AB	R	H	O	A	E
M. Cueto	lf	2	1	1	0	0	0
A. Luque	p	1	0	0	0	0	0
R. Almeida	3b	3	0	0	0	2	1
H. Hidalgo	cf	3	1	0	1	0	0
C. Torriente	rf	3	2	2	0	1	0
F. Hungo	2b	3	0	0	4	4	0
G. González	c	4	0	2	6	3	0
J. Mendez	ss	3	0	1	1	2	0
J. Violá	1b	3	0	1	9	1	2
F. López	p	2	0	0	0	3	0
Azcarraga	lf	0	0	0	0	0	0
Totals		27	4	7	27	16	3

Lincoln Stars	000	110	000 : 2
Almendares	010	003	00x : 4

Home runs: C. Torriente
Sacrifice hits: F. Hungo, R. Almeida, M. Cueto, D. Clark
Stolen bases: P. Webster (2)
Double-plays: J. Forbes, D. Clark and P. Webster; G. González and F. Hungo
Bases on balls: R. Redding 3, A. Luque 1, F. López 1
Strikeouts: R. Redding 4, A. Luque 3, F. López 0
Passed balls: L. Santop 2
Winning pitcher: A. Luque
Losing pitcher: R. Redding
Time: 2 hours
Umpires: Valentin González (home) and Cubillas (bases)
Scorer: Antonio Conejo

GAME FOURTEEN: SUNDAY, NOVEMBER 1, 1914, AT ALMENDARES PARK (SECOND GAME)

Lincoln Stars	Pos	AB	R	H	O	A	E
P. Webster	c	4	0	0	2	2	0
W. Parks	rf	4	0	1	1	0	0
S. Poles	cf	4	0	0	3	3	0
L. Santop	c	4	1	1	9	1	0
J. Thomas	lf	3	0	0	1	0	0
W. Handy	ss	3	0	2	2	1	0
D. Clark	2b	2	0	0	3	2	0
J. Forbes	3b	2	0	0	3	1	0
W. Dismukes	p	2	0	0	0	3	0
Totals		28	1	4	24	12	0

Habana	Pos	AB	R	H	O	A	E
B. Acosta	lf	4	0	1	2	0	0
J. Calvo	cf	2	1	2	2	0	0
A. Marsans	1b	4	0	1	9	2	0
A. Aragon	3b	4	0	1	2	1	1
L. Padrón	rf	2	0	0	1	0	0
M.A. González	c	3	1	1	8	1	0
E. González	2b	3	0	0	0	1	0
T. Romanach	ss	3	0	0	1	5	0
E. Palmero	p	2	0	1	1	2	0
Totals		27	2	7	27	11	1

Lincoln Stars	000	000	100 : 1
Habana	011	000	000 : 2

Three-base hits: W. Handy
Sacrifice hits: J. Forbes
Stolen bases: J. Calvo (2), M.A. González (2), T. Romanach, A. Marsans
Double-plays: S. Poles to L. Santop; M.A. González, A. Marsans to M.A. González; S. Poles to D. Clark
Bases on balls: W. Dismukes 4, E. Palmero 2
Strikeouts: W. Dismukes 1, E. Palmero 7
Hit by pitcher: W. Dismukes 1

Winning pitcher: E. Palmero
Losing pitcher: W. Dismukes
Time: 1 hour 35 minutes
Umpires: Valentin González (home) and Alfredo Arcano (bases)
Scorer: Antonio Conejo

Final Statistics

Club Batting

Club	G	AB	R	H	SH	SB	Pct
Almendares	7	221	36	52	11	11	.235
Lincoln Stars	14	425	34	79	11	9	.208
Habana	7	190	13	35	20	6	.180

Individual Batting (All Clubs)

Player	Club	G	AB	R	H	Pct
Emilio Palmero	Hab	1	2	0	1	.500
José Acosta	Hab	4	5	0	2	.400
Gerardo Ballesteros	Hab	2	3	0	1	.333
Fidelio Hungo	Alm	7	25	3	8	.320
Spottswood Poles	Lin	15	52	8	16	.308
Baldomero Acosta	Hab	4	13	0	4	.308
Cristobal Torriente	Alm	6	20	8	6	.300
Armando Marsans	Hab	7	26	3	7	.269
Louis Santop	Lin	14	49	5	13	.265
Jacinto Calvo	Hab	7	23	7	6	.261
José Mendez	Alm	3	8	0	2	.250
Azcarraga	Alm	3	4	1	1	.250
Peter "Ed" Green	Lin	3	4	0	1	.250
Alfredo Cabrera	Alm	7	21	4	5	.238
Gervasio González	Alm	6	21	3	5	.238
Juan Violá	Alm	7	27	0	6	.222
Manuel Cueto	Alm	7	23	6	5	.217
Rafael Almeida	Alm	7	28	3	6	.216
Pearl Webster	Lin	14	51	6	11	.215
Miguel Angel González	Hab	7	24	1	5	.208
Luis Padrón	Hab	7	20	1	4	.200
Tomas Calvo	Hab	3	10	0	2	.200
Eustaquio Pedroso	Alm	2	5	0	1	.200
Richard Redding	Lin	10	23	2	4	.173
William Handy	Lin	14	41	2	7	.171
Heliodoro Hidalgo	Alm	7	18	2	3	.167
William Parks	Lin	14	52	3	8	.154
Jules Thomas	Lin	14	52	3	8	.154
Angel Aragon	Hab	2	7	0	1	.143
Adolfo Luque	Alm	5	15	1	2	.133
Dell Clark	Lin	14	38	2	5	.132
Frank Harvey	Lin	10	18	0	2	.111
Joseph Forbes	Lin	11	32	1	3	.096
Eusebio González	Hab	7	23	1	2	.090
Tomas Romanach	Hab	7	16	4	1	.063
William Dismukes	Lin	5	14	1	0	.000
Ramiro Seiglie	Hab	5	7	2	0	.000
Pastor Pareda	Hab	2	5	0	0	.000
Ricardo Torres	Hab	1	3	0	0	.000
T. López	Alm	1	2	0	0	.000

(40)

Lincoln Stars
Individual Pitching

Pitcher	G	GS	GC	W	L	Pct	IP	R	H	W	K	ERT
William Dismukes	6	6	6	2	4	.333	48.1	19	37	16	16	3.54
Peter "Ed" Green	2	0	0	0	0	.000	5.0	5	5	1	0	9.00
Frank Harvey	3	2	0	0	2	.000	14.0	11	14	16	12	7.07
Richard Redding	8	6	6	2	3	.400	49.0	14	31	16	27	2.57
Totals	19	14	12	4	9	.308	116.1	49	87	39	55	2.65

Individual Batting

Players	Pos	G	AB	R	H	2B	3B	HR	SH	SB	Pct
Dell Clark	2b,ss	14	38	2	5	0	0	0	3	1	.132
William Dismukes	p	6	14	1	0	0	0	0	1	0	.000
Joe Forbes	3b	11	32	1	3	0	0	0	1	0	.094
Peter "Ed" Green	p,rf	4	4	0	1	0	0	0	0	0	.250
William Handy	ss,2b	14	41	2	7	1	1	0	4	1	.171
Frank Harvey	p,rf	10	18	0	2	0	0	0	0	0	.111
William Parks	1b,3b,rf	14	52	3	8	0	0	0	2	0	.154
Spottswood Poles	cf	14	52	8	16	1	2	0	0	2	.308
Richard Redding	p,rf	10	23	2	4	1	0	0	0	0	.173
Louis Santop	c,1b	14	44	5	13	1	0	0	1	1	.265
Jules Thomas	lf	14	52	3	8	2	1	0	0	3	.154
William Webster	1b,c	14	51	6	11	3	0	0	3	7	.215
Totals		14	425	34	79	9	4	0	15	15	.208

Individual Fielding

Players	Pos	G	O	A	E	Pct
Dell Clark	2b,ss	14	32	28	6	.909
William Dismukes	p	6	1	16	1	.944
Joe Forbes	3b	11	14	12	2	.929
Peter "Ed" Green	p,rf	4	2	3	0	1.000
William Handy	ss,2b	14	20	27	9	.839
Frank Harvey	p,rf	10	7	2	2	.818
William Parks	1b,3b,rf	14	24	14	4	.905
Spottswood Poles	cf	14	22	6	2	.933
Richard Redding	p,rf	10	8	23	0	1.000
Louis Santop	c,1b	14	93	12	5	.955
Jules Thomas	lf	14	23	2	1	.962
William Webster	1b,c	14	110	8	8	.937
Totals		14	356	153	50	.911

Almendares
Individual Pitching

Player	G	CG	W	L	Pct	IP	R	H	W	SO	ERT
José Mendez	2	2	1	1	.500	18.	4	9	7	13	2.00
Eustaquio Pedroso	2	1	2	0	1.000	12.	1	5	2	11	0.75
Adolfo Luque	3	2	2	0	1.000	26.	11	16	10	21	3.81
Totals	7	5	5	1	.833	56.	16	30	19	44	2.57

Individual Batting

Player	Club	G	AB	R	H	2B	3B	HR	SH	SB	Pct
Regino García	Alm	1	2	1	1	0	0	0	0	0	.500
Fidelio Hungo	Alm	7	25	3	8	1	0	0	1	1	.320

Player	Club	G	AB	R	H	2B	3B	HR	SH	SB	Pct
Cristobal Torriente	Alm	6	20	8	6	0	0	1	0	3	.300
José Mendez	Alm	3	8	0	2	0	0	0	0	1	.250
Azcarraga	Alm	3	4	1	1	0	0	0	0	0	.250
Alfredo Cabrera	Alm	7	21	4	5	0	0	0	2	2	.238
Gervasio González	Alm	6	21	3	5	1	0	0	0	1	.238
Juan Violá	Alm	7	27	0	6	0	0	0	1	0	.222
Manuel Cueto	Alm	7	23	6	5	0	0	0	1	2	.217
Rafael Almeida	Alm	7	28	3	6	0	0	0	3	0	.216
Eustaquio Pedroso	Alm	2	5	0	1	0	0	0	1	0	.200
Heliodoro Hidalgo	Alm	7	18	2	3	1	0	0	0	1	.167
Adolfo Luque	Alm	5	15	1	2	0	0	0	2	0	.133
T. López	Alm	1	2	0	0	0	0	0	0	0	.000
Julian Castillo	Alm	1	0	0	0	0	0	0	0	0	.000
Totals		7	221	36	52	3	0	1	11	11	.235

Individual Fielding

Player	Pos	Club	G	O	A	E	Pct
Regino García	rf(1)	Alm	1	1	0	0	1.000
Fidelio Hungo	2b(7)	Alm	7	18	15	1	.971
Cristobal Torriente	rf(6)	Alm	6	5	1	1	.857
José Mendez	p(2),ss(1)	Alm	3	2	6	0	1.000
Azcarraga	of(4)	Alm	4	5	0	1	.843
Alfredo Cabrera	ss(7)	Alm	7	8	26	1	.971
Gervasio González	c(6)	Alm	6	51	5	0	1.000
Juan Violá	1b(6),lf(1)	Alm	7	55	2	6	.906
Manuel Cueto	lf(6),c(1)	Alm	7	19	0	0	1.000
Rafael Almeida	3b(7)	Alm	7	5	10	2	.882
Eustaquio Pedroso	p(2)	Alm	2	1	5	1	.857
Heliodoro Hidalgo	cf(6),lf(1)	Alm	7	9	0	0	1.000
Adolfo Luque	p(4),cf(1)	Alm	5	4	6	0	1.000
T. López	p(1)	Alm	1	0	3	0	1.000
Julian Castillo	1b(1)	Alm	1	6	0	0	1.000
Totals			7	189	79	13	.954

HABANA

Individual Pitching

Player	G	CG	W	L	Pct	IP	R	H	W	SO	ERT
Emilio Palmero	1	1	1	0	1.000	9.0	1	4	2	7	1.00
José Acosta	3	2	1	0	1.000	19.0	5	16	3	13	2.37
Gerardo Ballesteros	2	1	1	1	.600	13.0	1	6	5	5	0.69
Pastor Pareda	2	2	0	2	.000	20.0	9	18	6	11	4.05
Totals	8	6	3	3	.500	61.0	16	44	16	36	2.36

Individual Batting

Players	Club	G	AB	R	H	2B	3B	HR	SH	SB	Pct
Emilio Palmero	Hab	1	2	0	1	0	0	0	0	0	.500
José Acosta	Hab	4	5	0	2	0	0	0	1	0	.400
Gerardo Ballesteros	Hab	2	3	0	1	0	0	0	1	0	.333
Baldomero Acosta	Hab	4	13	0	4	0	0	0	0	0	.308
Armando Marsans	Hab	7	26	3	7	0	0	0	0	5	.269
Jacinto Calvo	Hab	7	23	7	6	0	0	0	1	4	.261
Miguel Angel González	Hab	7	24	1	5	0	0	0	0	2	.208
Luis Padrón	Hab	7	20	1	4	0	0	0	0	4	.200
Tomas Calvo	Hab	3	10	0	2	0	0	0	0	1	.200

Players	Club	G	AB	R	H	2B	3B	HR	SH	SB	Pct
Angel Aragon	Hab	2	7	0	1	0	0	0	1	0	.143
Eusebio González	Hab	7	23	1	2	0	0	0	2	1	.090
Tomas Romanach	Hab	7	16	4	1	0	0	0	0	2	.063
Ramiro Seiglie	Hab	5	7	2	0	0	0	0	0	3	.000
Pastor Pareda	Hab	2	5	0	0	0	0	0	0	0	.000
Ricardo Torres	Hab	1	3	0	0	0	0	0	0	0	.000
Totals		7	190	13	35	0	0	0	6	22	.180

Individual Fielding

Player	Pos	Club	G	O	A	E	Pct
Emilio Palmero	p(1)	Hab	1	1	2	0	1.000
José Acosta	p(3),ph(1)	Hab	4	1	3	1	.800
Gerardo Ballesteros	p(2)	Hab	2	0	2	0	1.000
Baldomero Acosta	lf(4)	Hab	4	9	0	0	1.000
Armando Marsans	1b(7)	Hab	7	73	5	3	.963
Jacinto Calvo	cf(7)	Hab	7	12	0	1	.923
Miguel Angel González	c(7)	Hab	7	40	9	0	1.000
Luis Padrón	rf(4)	Hab	7	8	0	0	1.000
Tomas Calvo	lf(2),ph(1)	Hab	3	3	0	0	1.000
Angel Aragon	3b(2)	Hab	2	4	3	1	.875
Eusebio González	2b(5),3b(2)	Hab	7	10	9	1	.950
Tomas Romanach	ss(7)	Hab	7	9	24	3	.917
Ramiro Seiglie	2b(4),pr(1)	Hab	5	3	9	2	.857
Pastor Pareda	p(2)	Hab	2	1	2	0	1.000
Ricardo Torres	rf(1)	Hab	1	1	0	0	1.000
Totals			7	175	66	12	.952

♦ 11 ♦

1915
Indianapolis ABCs

Roster

Player	Position	Regular Season Club, 1915
Todd Allen	3b,1b	Indianapolis ABCs
Oscar Charleston	cf,p	Indianapolis ABCs
Morten Clark	ss	Indianapolis ABCs
Elwood DeMoss	2b	Indianapolis ABCs
James C. Jeffries	p,rf	Indianapolis ABCs
Louis Johnson	p	Indianapolis ABCs
Dan Kennard	c	Indianapolis ABCs
James Lyons	rf,cf,1b,lf	Indianapolis ABCs
Russell Powell	c,3b,1b	Indianapolis ABCs
Richard Redding	p	Indianapolis ABCs
George Shively	lf,rf	Indianapolis ABCs
Benjamin Taylor	1b,p	Indianapolis ABCs
Charles I. Taylor	rf	Indianapolis ABCs

Todd Allen started with the Indianapolis ABCs in 1915.

Oscar Charleston, a superstar blend of power and speed, started with the Indianapolis ABCs in 1915.

Morten Clark started with the Indianapolis ABCs in 1915.

Elwood "Bingo" DeMoss began a playing career in 1905 with the Topeka Giants, then went on to the Giants of Kansas City, Kansas, the Oklahoma Giants and the Indianapolis ABCs.

James C. Jeffries started with the Indianapolis ABCs in 1915.

Louis "Dicta" Johnson began with the Twin City Gophers in 1911. He played with the American Giants and the Indianapolis ABCs.

Dan Kennard started with the Indianapolis ABCs in 1915.

James "Jimmie" Lyons, a fleet baserunner and fielder, started in 1911 with the Lincoln Giants. He played with the Saint Louis Giants, Chicago Giants, Brooklyn Royal Giants and Indianapolis ABCs.

Russell Powell started with the Indianapolis ABCs in 1915.

Richard "Cannonball Dick" Redding, as his nickname implies, was a pitcher noted for overpowering speed. This right-hander started with the Lincoln Giants in 1911. In 1912 he won 43 games and lost 12. Later he played with the Lincoln Stars and Indianapolis ABCs.

George Shively began with the Indianapolis ABCs in 1915.

Benjamin H. "Ben" Taylor started with the West Baden, Indiana, Sprudels in 1910. He played with the Chicago American Giants and Indianapolis ABCs.

Charles I. "C.I" Taylor a player-manager for the ABC's, began with the Birmingham

Giants in 1904. He played with the West Baden, Indiana, Sprudels as well as the Indianapolis ABCs.

Games Played

Date	Winning Club		Losing Club		Winning Pitcher	Losing Pitcher
Oct 30	Indianapolis	5	Almendares	4	R. Redding 1–0	A. Luque 0–1
Oct 31	Indianapolis	5	Habana	4	R. Redding 2–0	J. Acosta 0–1
Nov 1	Almendares	8	Indianapolis	1	A. Luque 1–1	L. Johnson 0–1
Nov 4	Indianapolis	7	Habana	3	R. Redding 3–0	E. Palmero 0–1
Nov 6	Habana	6	Indianapolis	4	P. Pareda 1–0	R. Redding 3–1
Nov 7	Almendares	6	Indianapolis	2	A. Luque 2–1	R. Redding 3–2
Nov 8	Indianapolis	8	Habana	3	L. Johnson 1–1	J. Acosta 0–2
Nov 11	Almendares	6	Indianapolis	3	E. Pedroso 1–0	L. Johnson 1–2
Nov 13	Almendares		Indianapolis		Suspendido	
Nov 14	Habana	10	Indianapolis	4	E. Palmero 1–1	L. Johnson 1–3
Nov 15	Indianapolis	8	Almendares	1	R. Redding 4–2	A. Luque 2–2
Nov 18	Habana	6	Indianapolis	1	P. Pareda 2–0	R. Redding 4–3
Nov 20	Habana	14	Indianapolis	6	J. Acosta 1–2	J. Jeffries 0–1
Nov 21	Almendares	5	Indianapolis	3	A. Luque 3–2	R. Redding 4–4
Nov 22	Habana	4	Indianapolis	2	Ballesteros 1–0	B. Taylor 0–1
Nov 25	Indianapolis	5	Almendares	4	R. Redding 5–4	J. Mendez 0–1
Nov 27	Indianapolis	12	Almendares	9	R. Redding 6–4	E. Pedroso 1–1
Nov 28	Almendares	7	Indianapolis	4	A. Luque 4–2	R. Redding 6–5
Nov 28	Habana	10	Indianapolis	4	J. Acosta 2–2	O. Charleston 0–1
Nov 29	Indianapolis	9	San Francisco	5	J. Jeffries 1–1	J. Junco 0–1
Dec 2	San Francisco	5	Indianapolis	4	E. Pedroso 2–1	J. Jeffries 1–2
(20)						

Club Standings

Clubs	G	W	L	Pct
Habana	9	6	3	.667
Almendares	9	5	4	.556
San Francisco	2	1	1	.500
Indianapolis ABCs	20	8	12	.400
Totals	40	20	20	.500

The Games

GAME ONE: SATURDAY, OCTOBER 30, 1915, AT ALMENDARES PARK

Ind ABCs	Pos	AB	R	H	O	A	E
G. Shively	lf	4	1	1	0	0	0
E. DeMoss	2b	3	1	2	1	3	0
J. Lyons	rf	4	0	2	0	0	0
B. Taylor	1b	4	0	2	13	1	1
O. Charleston	cf	4	1	0	3	0	1
M. Clark	ss	4	0	0	1	3	0
R. Powell	c	4	0	1	5	7	1
T. Allen	3b	4	1	1	4	3	0
L. Johnson	p	3	1	1	0	0	1
R. Redding	p	0	0	0	0	0	0
Totals		34	5	10	27	17	4

Almendares	Pos	AB	R	H	O	A	E
P. Chacon	ss	4	1	1	2	1	1
G. González	rf	3	0	0	2	0	0
M. Villa	2b	4	1	1	1	2	0
C. Torriente	cf	4	2	2	4	1	0
B. Baro	lf	4	0	2	1	0	0
A. Cabrera	1b	4	0	0	7	0	1
M. Cueto	3b	4	0	2	3	2	1
V. Rodríguez	c	4	0	1	7	3	0
E. Pedroso	p	0	0	0	0	0	0
A. Luque	p	1	0	0	0	0	0
Totals		32	4	9	27	12	3

Indianapolis ABCs	103	000	001 : 5
Almendares	000	002	110 : 4

Three-base hits: E. DeMoss, C. Torriente
Two-base hits: B. Taylor, V. Rodríguez
Stolen bases: T. Allen, P. Chacon, B. Baro
Double-plays: C. Torriente and V. Rodríguez
Bases on balls: L. Johnson 3, R. Redding 1, E. Pedroso 0, A. Luque 1
Strikeouts: L. Johnson 4, R. Redding 1, E. Pedroso 2, A. Luque 4
Hits: L. Johnson 8 in 7.0 innings; E. Pedroso 7 in 3.0 innings
Passed balls: V. Rodríguez 1
Winning pitcher: R. Redding
Losing pitcher: A. Luque
Time: 2 hours 13 minutes
Umpires: Eustaquio Gutiérrez (home) and José M. Magrinat (bases)
Scorer: Hilario Franquiz

GAME TWO: SUNDAY, OCTOBER 31, 1915, AT ALMENDARES PARK

Ind ABCs	Pos	AB	R	H	O	A	E
G. Shively	lf	5	1	2	0	0	0
E. DeMoss	2b	5	1	2	4	2	0
J. Lyons	rf	5	0	0	1	1	0
B. Taylor	1b	5	1	2	11	3	0
O. Charleston	cf	5	1	1	1	0	1
M. Clark	ss	4	1	1	0	2	1
R. Powell	c	4	0	1	8	1	0
T. Allen	3b	3	0	2	1	3	0
R. Redding	p	2	0	0	1	1	0
Totals		38	5	11	27	13	2

Habana	Pos	AB	R	H	O	A	E
B. Acosta	lf	3	0	1	0	1	0
A. Marsans	1b	3	1	1	7	1	0
J. Calvo	cf	4	0	0	0	0	0
M.A. González	c	3	0	0	12	2	0
E. González	2b	4	0	3	3	1	0
A. Aragon	3b	3	1	0	2	1	0
T. Calvo	rf	3	2	1	1	0	0
T. Romanach	ss	2	0	0	1	1	0
J. Acosta	p	2	0	1	1	1	0
R. Herrera	(x)	1	0	1	0	0	0
R. Torres	(xx)	1	0	0	0	0	0
Totals		29	4	8	27	8	0

(x)—Hit for T. Romanach in Ninth.
(xx)—Out for J. Acosta in Ninth.

Indianapolis ABCs	101	000	030 : 5
Habana	120	000	100 : 4

Three-base hits: E. González
Two-base hits: B. Taylor, T. Allen, M. Clark
Sacrifice hits: T. Romanach, B. Acosta, R. Redding
Stolen bases: A. Marsans (2), M.A. González, G. Shively, T. Calvo, E. González
Double-plays: E. DeMoss (no assist); B. Taylor and E. DeMoss
Bases on balls: R. Redding 6, J. Acosta 1
Strikeouts: R. Redding 3, J. Acosta 10
Hit by pitcher: J. Acosta 1
Winning pitcher: R. Redding
Losing pitcher: J. Acosta
Time: 2 hours 12 minutes
Umpires: Eustaquio Gutiérrez (home) and José M. Magrinat (bases)
Scorer: Julio Franquiz

GAME THREE: MONDAY, NOVEMBER 1, 1915, AT ALMENDARES PARK

Ind ABCs	Pos	AB	R	H	O	A	E
G. Shively	lf	4	1	2	2	1	0
E. DeMoss	2b	2	0	0	1	2	1
J. Lyons	rf	4	0	0	0	0	0
B. Taylor	1b	4	0	2	12	1	0
O. Charleston	cf	4	0	0	2	1	1
M. Clark	ss	3	0	1	0	6	1

Almendares	Pos	AB	R	H	O	A	E
B. Baro	lf	4	1	1	0	0	0
M. Villa	rf	2	2	1	0	1	0
G. González	c	4	0	1	7	0	0
C. Torriente	cf	3	2	1	1	0	0
E. Pedroso	1b	4	0	2	10	2	0
R. Herrera	2b	4	1	0	3	0	1

Ind ABCs	Pos	AB	R	H	O	A	E
R. Powell	c	3	0	0	5	1	1
T. Allen	3b	3	0	0	2	3	1
L. Johnson	p	3	0	0	0	2	0
Totals		30	1	5	24	17	5

Almendares	Pos	AB	R	H	O	A	E
P. Chacon	ss	4	0	1	2	2	0
M. Cueto	3b	4	1	2	2	3	0
A. Luque	p	4	1	1	0	3	0
Totals		33	8	10	27	12	1

Indianapolis ABCs	100	000	000 : 1
Almendares	021	020	21x : 8

Three-base hits: A. Luque
Two-base hits: E. Pedroso
Sacrifice hits: E. DeMoss (2), M. Villa
Stolen bases: C. Torriente, M. Cueto (3), M. Villa
Double-plays: R. Powell and T. Allen; C. Torriente and R. Herrera
Bases on balls: A. Luque 0, L. Johnson 2
Strikeouts: A. Luque 4, L. Johnson 4
Balk: L. Johnson 1
Winning pitcher: A. Luque
Losing pitcher: L. Johnson
Time: 1 hour 46 minutes
Umpires: Eustaquio Gutiérrez (home) and José M. Magrinat (bases)
Scorer: Hilario Franquiz

GAME FOUR: THURSDAY, NOVEMBER 4, 1915, AT ALMENDARES PARK

Ind ABCs	Pos	AB	R	H	O	A	E
G. Shively	lf	4	0	1	5	0	0
E. DeMoss	2b	5	1	2	1	2	1
J. Lyons	rf	4	2	2	1	0	0
B. Taylor	1b,p	4	2	3	9	0	0
O. Charleston	cf	4	0	1	1	0	0
M. Clark	ss	2	1	1	0	4	1
R. Powell	3b	3	0	1	2	1	0
D. Kennard	c	4	0	2	5	1	0
R. Redding	p,1b	1	0	0	0	0	0
L. Johnson	p	0	1	0	0	0	0
Totals		39	7	13	24	9	2

Habana	Pos	AB	R	H	O	A	E
A. Marsans	lf	3	1	0	0	0	0
J. Calvo	cf	3	0	0	1	0	0
E. González	2b	2	1	1	1	2	2
M.A. González	c	4	0	0	7	3	0
A. Aragon	3b	2	0	0	2	2	0
T. Calvo	rf	3	0	0	1	0	0
R. Torres	1b	4	0	0	8	1	0
T. Romanach	ss	2	0	0	3	0	0
E. Palmero	p	3	0	0	0	5	1
R. González	3b	1	0	0	1	1	1
Totals		27	3	1	24	14	4

Indianapolis ABCs	210	020	11 : 7 (Eight innings)
Habana	200	001	00 : 3

Sacrifice hits: R. Powell, J. Lyons, R. Redding
Stolen bases: J. Lyons (2), B. Taylor (3), A. Marsans
Double-plays: R. Powell and B. Taylor
Bases on balls: R. Redding 5, L. Johnson 2, B. Taylor 0, E. Palmero 5
Strikeouts: R. Redding 3, L. Johnson 7, B. Taylor 0, E. Palmero 5
Hit by pitcher: L. Johnson 1
Wild pitches: E. Palmero 2
Hits: R. Redding 1 in 5.2 innings
Winning pitcher: R. Redding
Losing pitcher: E. Palmero
Time: 2 hours 10 minutes
Umpires: Eustaquio Gutiérrez (home) and José M. Magrinat (bases)
Scorer: Hilario Franquiz

GAME FIVE: SATURDAY, NOVEMBER 6, 1915, AT ALMENDARES PARK

Ind ABCs	Pos	AB	R	H	O	A	E
G. Shively	lf	3	0	0	1	0	0

Habana	Pos	AB	R	H	O	A	E
A. Marsans	1b	5	0	1	14	1	0

Ind ABCs	Pos	AB	R	H	O	A	E
E. DeMoss	2b	2	2	0	5	4	0
J. Lyons	rf	3	1	0	3	1	0
B. Taylor	1b	4	0	3	9	0	1
O. Charleston	cf	4	0	0	2	0	0
M. Clark	ss	4	0	1	1	5	1
R. Powell	3b	4	0	0	1	1	0
D. Kennard	c	3	0	0	3	0	0
J. Jeffries	p	2	1	1	0	0	0
R. Redding	p	0	0	0	1	0	0
Totals		29	4	5	24	10	2

Habana	Pos	AB	R	H	O	A	E
B. Acosta	lf	3	0	0	0	0	0
E. González	2b	3	0	0	1	4	0
M.A. González	c	3	0	0	4	1	0
T. Calvo	rf	4	1	1	3	0	0
J. Calvo	cf	4	1	2	4	0	0
T. Romanach	ss	2	1	1	1	6	0
R. González	3b	2	1	1	0	0	0
G. Ballesteros	p	1	0	0	0	1	0
P. Pareda	p	1	0	0	0	0	0
Totals		30	6	7	27	13	0

Indianapolis ABCs	103	000	000 : 4 (Eight innings)
Habana	020	000	22x : 6

Two-base hits: B. Taylor (2)
Sacrifice hits: G. Shively
Stolen bases: E. DeMoss, M.A. González, J. Calvo
Double-plays: M. Clark, E. DeMoss and B. Taylor; E. DeMoss (unassisted); T. Romanach, A. Marsans and M.A. González; M. Clark and B. Taylor
Bases on balls: J. Jeffries 6, R. Redding 3, G. Ballesteros 3, P. Pareda 0
Strikeouts: J. Jeffries 2, R. Redding 0, G. Ballesteros 1, P. Pareda 1
Wild pitches: R. Redding 1
Hits surrendered: G. Ballesteros 1 in 2.1 innings; J. Jeffries 3 in 6.1 innings
Winning pitcher: P. Pareda
Losing pitcher: R. Redding
Time: 1 hour 57 minutes
Umpires: Eustaquio Gutiérrez (home) and José M. Magrinat (bases)
Scorer: Hilario Franquiz

GAME SIX: SUNDAY, NOVEMBER 7, 1915, AT ALMENDARES PARK

Ind ABCs	Pos	AB	R	H	O	A	E
G. Shively	lf	3	0	0	2	0	2
E. DeMoss	2b	4	1	1	4	3	1
J. Lyons	rf	2	1	1	2	0	0
B. Taylor	1b	4	0	1	10	0	0
O. Charleston	cf	3	0	1	1	0	0
M. Clark	ss	5	0	0	2	2	1
R. Powell	c	4	0	2	3	1	1
T. Allen	3b	1	0	0	4	2	0
R. Redding	p	3	0	0	0	2	0
Totals		29	2	6	24	12	7

Almendares	Pos	AB	R	H	O	A	E
B. Baro	lf	4	2	2	1	0	0
H. Hidalgo	rf	3	0	1	0	0	0
G. González	c	4	0	1	11	1	0
C. Torriente	cf	4	0	1	2	0	1
E. Pedroso	1b	4	0	0	9	0	1
R. Herrera	2b	3	2	1	2	3	0
M. Cueto	3b	4	1	1	1	1	0
P. Chacon	ss	4	1	3	1	3	0
A. Luque	p	4	0	0	0	4	0
Totals		34	6	10	27	12	2

Indianapolis ABCs	000	010	001 : 2
Almendares	000	400	11x : 6

Two-base hits: R. Powell
Sacrifice hits: R. Redding, H. Hidalgo
Sacrifice fly: O. Charleston
Stolen bases: P. Chacon, B. Baro, R. Herrera, E. DeMoss, J. Lyons
Double-plays: J. Lyons and B. Taylor; P. Chacon, R. Herrera and E. Pedroso
Bases on balls: A. Luque 11, R. Redding 1
Strikeouts: A. Luque 9, R. Redding 4
Passed balls: G. González 1
Winning pitcher: A. Luque
Losing pitcher: R. Redding
Time: 2 hours 10 minutes
Umpires: Eustaquio Gutiérrez (home) and José M. Magrinat (bases)
Scorer: Hilario Franquiz

GAME SEVEN: MONDAY, NOVEMBER 8, 1915, AT ALMENDARES PARK

Ind ABCs	Pos	AB	R	H	O	A	E
G. Shively	lf	4	1	2	5	0	0
E. DeMoss	2b	4	1	0	0	2	0
J. Lyons	rf	5	0	1	0	0	0
B. Taylor	1b	5	0	0	8	0	0
O. Charleston	cf	5	0	0	7	0	0
M. Clark	ss	4	2	2	1	3	0
R. Powell	c	4	1	1	4	2	0
T. Allen	3b	3	2	2	2	1	0
L. Johnson	p	2	1	0	0	0	1
Totals		36	8	8	27	8	1

Habana	Pos	AB	R	H	O	A	E
A. Marsans	1b	4	1	1	12	0	1
B. Acosta	lf	5	1	1	2	0	0
J. Calvo	cf	4	0	0	0	0	1
M.A. González	c	2	0	1	5	0	0
E. González	2b	4	0	1	2	5	0
A. Aragon	3b	3	0	1	2	0	0
T. Calvo	rf	3	0	0	2	0	2
T. Romanach	ss	4	0	0	2	9	2
J. Acosta	p	4	1	2	0	1	0
Totals		33	3	7	27	15	6

Indianapolis ABCs	010		250		000 : 8
Habana	100		000		200 : 3

Three-base hits: A. Aragon, G. Shively
Two-base hits: G. Shively
Sacrifice hits: E. DeMoss
Stolen bases: A. Marsans, J. Calvo, M.A. González (2), T. Allen, B. Acosta
Bases on balls: J. Acosta 5, L. Johnson 6
Strikeouts: J. Acosta 5, L. Johnson 4
Winning pitcher: L. Johnson
Losing pitcher: J. Acosta
Time: 2 hours
Umpires: Eustaquio Gutiérrez (home) and José M. Magrinat (bases)
Scorer: Hilario Franquiz

GAME EIGHT: THURSDAY, NOVEMBER 11, 1915, AT ALMENDARES PARK

Ind ABCs	Pos	AB	R	H	O	A	E
G. Shively	lf	3	0	0	0	0	0
E. DeMoss	2b	4	0	1	2	4	3
J. Lyons	rf,cf	5	0	1	1	0	0
B. Taylor	1b	4	0	1	10	1	1
O. Charleston	cf	3	0	0	1	0	0
M. Clark	ss	4	0	0	6	5	1
R. Powell	c	4	1	1	3	2	0
T. Allen	3b	2	2	0	0	2	2
L. Johnson	p	1	0	0	1	3	0
C.I. Taylor	(x)	1	0	0	0	0	0
J. Jeffries	rf	0	0	0	0	0	0
Totals		31	3	4	24	17	7

Almendares	Pos	AB	R	H	O	A	E
B. Baro	lf,p	4	0	2	5	0	0
M. Villa	rf	4	1	0	2	0	0
G. González	1b	3	1	1	9	0	0
C. Torriente	cf	4	1	1	3	0	1
R. Almeida	3b	4	0	0	2	1	0
E. Pedroso	p	4	1	3	0	0	0
R. Herrera	2b	4	1	0	0	3	1
P. Chacon	ss	3	0	1	0	3	0
V. Rodríguez	c	4	1	1	6	1	1
A. Luque	p	0	0	0	0	0	0
Totals		34	6	9	27	8	3

(x)—Out for O. Charleston in seventh.

Indianapolis ABCs	000		010		002 : 3
Almendares	024		000		00x : 6

Two-base hits: C. Torriente, P. Chacon
Sacrifice fly: E. DeMoss
Stolen bases: J. Lyons, T. Allen
Double-plays: P. Chacon, R. Herrera and G. González; E. DeMoss, M. Clark and B. Taylor; T. Allen, E. DeMoss and B. Taylor
Bases on balls: L. Johnson 2, E. Pedroso 7, B. Baro 0, A. Luque 0
Strikeouts: L. Johnson 3, E. Pedroso 6, B. Baro 0, A. Luque 0
Wild pitches: L. Johnson 1
Winning pitcher: E. Pedroso
Losing pitcher: L. Johnson
Time: 2 hours

Umpires: Eustaquio Gutiérrez (home) and José M. Magrinat (bases)
Scorer: Hilario Franquiz

An account of the game was published in the November 27 edition of the *Chicago Defender*:

Johnson Wild; Havana Stars Win

A.B.C.'s Lose to Havana Stars, 10–4, But Get Even Break in Number of Games Played — Equals McGraw's Record.

Havana, Cuba, Nov. 26.— Pitching wretched ball, Johnson let the A.B.C.'s slip back into a tie with the Havana team here Sunday, Nov. 14. The boys from the United States had the lead on the islanders, but today's defeat made a tie. The New York Giants, under the leadership of the famous John McGraw, is the only club that has visited over here and broke even. The A.B.C.'s to date equal the Giants' record. The work of Johnson was fierce, he having no effectiveness whatever, and the thirteen men that compose the A.B.C. were used in efforts to stem the tide, but it was no use. Jefferies worked after Johnson's poor start, but the lead was too great. Palmero held the Hoosiers to eight hits and kept them pretty well apart. Taylor's men made a spurt in the eighth, but it fell away short. Charleston regrets the trouble he had before he left, and says that he will try to be more careful hereafter. The score:

```
A.B.C.'s...............000        001        030 — 4  8  3
Havana Stars.......500        302        00* — 10 10  2
```

Batteries— For Havana Stars: Palmero and González. For A.B.C.'s: Johnson, Jefferies and Kennard.

GAME NINE: SUNDAY, NOVEMBER 14, 1915, AT ALMENDARES PARK

Ind ABCs	Pos	AB	R	H	O	A	E		Habana	Pos	AB	R	H	O	A	E
G. Shively	lf	5	0	0	1	0	1		B. Acosta	lf	4	2	2	2	0	0
E. DeMoss	2b	5	0	1	3	2	0		J. Calvo	cf	3	2	2	1	0	0
T. Allen	3b	0	0	0	0	0	0		A. Marsans	1b,cf	4	2	1	4	0	0
B. Taylor	rf,p	1	0	0	0	4	1		M.A. González	c,1b	5	2	3	9	4	1
J. Lyons	1b	4	1	0	2	0	0		E. González	2b	3	0	1	3	4	0
M. Clark	ss	3	1	1	2	1	1		A. Aragon	3b	4	1	0	1	2	0
R. Powell	c,3b	4	0	2	1	0	0		T. Calvo	rf	3	0	1	2	0	1
O. Charleston	rf	3	0	1	6	0	0		T. Romanach	ss	3	0	1	3	2	2
L. Johnson	p	1	0	0	0	0	1		E. Palmero	p	3	1	1	1	2	0
D. Kennard	c	3	2	2	4	3	1		R. Torres	c	0	0	0	1	0	0
J. Jeffries	p	1	0	0	0	2	0		Totals		32	10	12	27	14	4
C.I. Taylor	rf	2	0	0	1	0	0									
Totals		32	4	7	24	9	4									

```
Indianapolis ABCs        000        001        030 : 4
Habana                   500        302        00x : 10
```

Three-base hits: D. Kennard
Two-base hits: B. Acosta, T. Romanach, R. Powell
Sacrifice hits: R. Torres
Sacrifice fly: A. Marsans, E. González
Stolen bases: A. Marsans, J. Calvo, E. Palmero, B. Acosta, E. DeMoss, R. Powell, O. Charleston
Double-plays: A. Aragon and A. Marsans; D. Kennard and E. DeMoss
Bases on balls: E. Palmero 6, L. Johnson 1, J. Jeffries 2, B. Taylor 1
Strikeouts: E. Palmero 5, L. Johnson 1, J. Jeffries 0, B. Taylor 2
Hit by pitcher: L. Johnson 1
Wild pitches: L. Johnson
Passes balls: R. Torres 1
Winning pitcher: E. Palmero
Losing pitcher: L. Johnson
Hits: Off L. Johnson 9 in 3.1 innings; J. Jeffries 0 in 1.2 innings
Time: 2 hours 5 minutes
Umpires: Eustaquio Gutiérrez (home) and José M. Magrinat (bases)
Scorer: Hilario Franquiz

GAME TEN: MONDAY, NOVEMBER 12, 1915, AT ALMENDARES PARK

Ind ABCs	Pos	AB	R	H	O	A	E
G. Shively	rf	4	1	0	3	1	1
E. DeMoss	2b	4	2	3	3	1	0
T. Allen	3b	5	1	2	3	2	1
B. Taylor	1b	4	0	2	7	0	0
J. Lyons	lf	4	0	1	1	0	0
M. Clark	ss	2	1	0	3	6	1
R. Powell	c	4	0	0	2	2	0
O. Charleston	cf	4	2	3	2	0	0
R. Redding	p	3	1	2	0	0	0
Totals		34	8	13	24	12	3

Almendares	Pos	AB	R	H	O	A	E
B. Baro	rf	2	0	0	1	0	0
M. Villa	lf	4	0	1	0	0	1
G. González	c,1b	4	0	1	5	1	1
E. Pedroso	1b,p	3	0	0	4	0	0
R. Herrera	2b	4	0	1	4	2	0
R. Cueto	cf	3	1	2	2	0	0
A. Cabrera	3b	2	0	0	1	1	0
P. Chacon	ss	3	0	0	3	4	1
A. Luque	p	1	0	0	1	1	0
V. Rodríguez	c	1	0	1	3	3	0
Totals		27	1	6	24	12	0

Indianapolis ABCs	241	000	01 : 8 (Eight innings)
Almendares	000	010	00 : 1

Three-base hits: B. Taylor
Two-base hits: T. Allen (2), G. González
Sacrifice hits: R. Redding
Stolen bases: O. Charleston
Double-plays: P. Chacon, R. Herrera and E. Pedroso; M. Clark and B. Taylor; T. Allen and B. Taylor
Bases on balls: R. Redding 2, A. Luque 2, E. Pedroso 2
Strikeouts: R. Redding 1, A. Luque 0, E. Pedroso 3
Winning pitcher: R. Redding
Losing pitcher: A. Luque
Time: 2 hours 10 minutes
Umpires: Eustaquio Gutiérrez (home) and José M. Magrinat (bases)
Scorer: Hilario Franquiz

GAME ELEVEN: THURSDAY, NOVEMBER 18, 1915, AT ALMENDARES PARK

Ind ABCs	Pos	AB	R	H	O	A	E
G. Shively	rf	3	1	0	1	0	0
E. DeMoss	2b	4	0	1	1	2	1
T. Allen	3b	5	0	3	1	1	0
B. Taylor	1b	3	0	1	8	0	0
J. Lyons	lf	4	0	0	5	1	1
M. Clark	ss	4	0	2	2	4	1
R. Powell	c	3	0	0	3	1	0
O. Charleston	cf	4	0	0	3	1	0
R. Redding	p	3	0	0	0	3	0
C.I. Taylor	(x)	1	0	0	0	0	0
Totals		34	1	7	24	13	3

(x) — Out for R. Redding in Ninth.

Habana	Pos	AB	R	H	O	A	E
B. Acosta	lf	4	0	1	3	0	0
J. Calvo	cf	3	0	1	5	0	1
A. Marsans	1b	3	2	2	9	0	1
M.A. González	c	3	2	1	3	0	0
E. González	2b	3	1	1	3	1	0
A. Aragon	3b	4	1	2	0	3	0
T. Calvo	rf	3	0	1	1	0	0
T. Romanach	ss	4	0	0	2	5	0
P. Pareda	p	3	0	1	1	2	0
Totals		30	6	10	27	11	2

Indianapolis ABCs	100	000	000 : 1
Habana	300	002	01x : 6

Two-base hits: A. Aragon (2), T. Allen
Stolen bases: B. Taylor, T. Allen
Double-plays: T. Romanach, E. González and A. Marsans
Bases on balls: P. Pareda 3, R. Redding 5
Strikeouts: P. Pareda 1, R. Redding 2
Winning pitcher: P. Pareda
Losing pitcher: R. Redding
Time: 1 hour 35 minutes
Umpires: Eustaquio Gutiérrez (home) and José Maria Magrinat (bases)
Scorer: Hilario Franquiz

GAME TWELVE: SATURDAY NOVEMBER 20, 1915, AT ALMENDARES PARK

Ind ABCs	Pos	AB	R	H	O	A	E
G. Shively	rf	4	0	1	1	0	0
E. DeMoss	2b	1	1	0	4	6	1
T. Allen	3b	2	1	0	3	3	0
B. Taylor	1b	3	0	0	10	0	0
J. Lyons	lf	3	1	0	2	1	0
M. Clark	ss	4	1	2	0	3	0
R. Powell	c	3	0	1	3	2	0
O. Charleston	cf	3	1	2	0	1	1
J. Jeffries	p	2	1	0	0	1	0
L. Johnson	p	1	0	0	0	0	0
C.I. Taylor	rf	0	0	0	1	0	0
D. Kennard	(x)	1	0	0	0	0	0
R. Redding	p	0	0	0	0	1	0
Totals		27	6	8	24	18	2

Habana	Pos	AB	R	H	O	A	E
B. Acosta	lf	5	1	2	0	0	0
A. Marsans	1b	4	1	1	11	1	0
E. González	2b	5	2	2	0	2	0
M.A. González	c	4	3	2	5	3	0
A. Aragon	3b	3	1	2	1	1	1
J. Calvo	cf	4	2	4	3	1	0
T. Calvo	rf	3	1	1	1	1	0
T. Romanach	ss	4	1	2	1	6	2
J. Acosta	p	2	1	1	1	2	0
R. González	2b	2	0	1	0	0	0
R. Torres	1b	1	1	0	1	0	0
E. Palmero	p	0	0	0	0	0	0
Totals		37	14	18	24	13	3

(x)—Out for G. Shively in Eighth.

Indianapolis ABCs	002	000	04 : 6
Habana	000	006	14 : 14

Game called on account of darkness.
Two-base hits: E. González, A. Aragon, O. Charleston, B. Acosta
Sacrifice hits: B. Taylor
Sacrifice flies: T. Allen, T. Calvo
Stolen bases: J. Jeffries, E. DeMoss, M.A. González
Double-plays: J. Acosta and A. Marsans; M. Clark, E. DeMoss to B. Taylor
Bases on balls: J. Acosta 8, E. Palmero 0, J. Jeffries 3, R. Redding 2
Strikeouts: J. Acosta 2, E. Palmero 0, J. Jeffries 1, R. Redding 1
Hits: J. Acosta 8 in 7.2 innings; J. Jeffries 11 in 5.1 innings
Winning pitcher: J. Acosta
Losing pitcher: J. Jeffries
Time: 2 hours, 15 minutes
Umpires: Eustaquio Gutiérrez (home) and José Maria Magrinat (bases)
Scorer: Hilario Franquiz

GAME THIRTEEN: SUNDAY, NOVEMBER 21, 1915, AT ALMENDARES PARK

Ind ABCs	Pos	AB	R	H	O	A	E
G. Shively	lf	5	1	0	3	0	0
E. DeMoss	2b	3	1	1	2	1	0
T. Allen	3b	4	0	0	1	5	0
B. Taylor	1b	4	0	1	13	0	1
J. Lyons	rf	4	1	1	0	0	0
M. Clark	ss	4	0	1	1	3	1
R. Powell	c	3	0	0	2	2	0
O. Charleston	cf	4	0	1	2	0	0
R. Redding	p	4	0	2	0	4	0
C.I. Taylor		1	0	0	0	0	0
Totals		36	3	7	24	15	2

Almendares	Pos	AB	R	H	O	A	E
M. Villa	lf	4	1	0	0	0	0
G. González	c	3	0	2	14	0	0
R. Almeida	3b	4	1	1	2	2	0
C. Torriente	cf	3	1	1	2	0	0
E. Pedroso	1b	4	1	1	5	0	0
R. Herrera	2b	4	0	2	2	1	0
M. Cueto	rf	4	0	0	1	0	0
P. Chacon	ss	4	1	2	1	3	1
A. Luque	p	2	0	0	0	0	0
Totals		32	5	10	27	6	1

Indianapolis ABCs	000	000	030 : 3
Almendares	310	100	00x : 5

Two-base hits: P. Chacon, G. González
Sacrifice hits: A. Luque
Stolen bases: E. DeMoss (2), A. Luque, G. Shively, P. Chacon
Bases on balls: A. Luque 2, R. Redding 2

Strikeouts: A. Luque 9, R. Redding 2
Wild pitches: A. Luque
Passed balls: G. González 1, R. Powell 1
Winning pitcher: A. Luque
Losing pitcher: R. Redding
Time: 1 hour 55 minutes
Umpires: Eustaquio Gutiérrez (home) and José Maria Magrinat (bases)
Scorer: Hilario Franquiz

GAME FOURTEEN: MONDAY, NOVEMBER 22, 1915, AT ALMENDARES PARK

Ind ABCs	Pos	AB	R	H	O	A	E
G. Shively	lf	4	0	1	3	1	0
E. DeMoss	2b	2	0	2	4	4	0
T. Allen	1b	3	0	0	9	0	0
B. Taylor	p	4	1	1	1	1	0
J. Lyons	rf	2	1	0	0	0	0
M. Clark	ss	2	0	1	2	2	1
O. Charleston	cf	1	0	0	2	0	0
R. Powell	3b	4	0	0	0	0	0
D. Kennard	c	2	0	0	3	0	0
R. Redding	(x)	1	0	0	0	0	0
Totals		26	2	5	24	8	1

(x)—Out for D. Kennard in Ninth.

Habana	Pos	AB	R	H	O	A	E
B. Acosta	lf	4	1	2	2	0	0
J. Calvo	cf	4	1	1	2	0	0
A. Marsans	1b	4	0	1	9	1	0
M.A. González	c	4	0	2	5	1	0
E. González	2b	2	0	0	2	1	0
A. Aragon	3b	4	0	0	2	3	0
T. Calvo	rf	3	0	0	3	0	0
T. Romanach	ss	2	0	1	2	0	0
G. Ballesteros	p	2	2	0	0	4	0
R. González	2b	2	0	0	0	0	0
Totals		31	4	7	27	10	0

Indianapolis ABCs   010   000   010 : 2
Habana   001   030   00x : 4

Sacrifice hits: T. Allen, O. Charleston
Sacrifice fly: M. Clark
Stolen bases: J. Lyons (2), M. Clark, J. Calvo
Double-plays: A. Aragon and E. González
Bases on balls: G. Ballesteros 8, B. Taylor 2
Strikeouts: G. Ballesteros 5, B. Taylor 2
Winning pitcher: G. Ballesteros
Losing pitcher: B. Taylor
Time: 1 hour 58 minutes
Umpires: Eustaquio Gutiérrez (home) and José Maria Magrinat (bases)
Scorer: Hilario Franquiz

GAME FIFTEEN: THURDAY, NOVEMBER 25, 1915, AT ALMENDARES PARK

Ind ABCs	Pos	AB	R	H	O	A	E
G. Shively	lf	2	2	1	0	0	0
E. DeMoss	2b	2	0	0	5	3	0
T. Allen	3b	1	0	0	3	1	2
B. Taylor	1b	4	1	1	6	2	0
J. Lyons	rf,cf	2	1	1	3	1	0
M. Clark	ss	3	0	0	0	3	0
O. Charleston	cf	1	0	0	0	0	0
R. Powell	c,rf	2	0	1	2	0	0
L. Johnson	p	1	0	0	0	1	0
D. Kennard	c	3	0	2	6	2	1
R. Redding	p	3	1	0	1	2	0
Totals		34	5	6	27	14	3

(x)—Out for A. Cabrera in Ninth.

Almendares	Pos	AB	R	H	O	A	E
P. Chacon	ss	4	1	2	2	4	0
M. Villa	lf	4	1	1	0	0	0
G. González	c	2	1	1	8	5	0
C. Torriente	cf	3	0	1	2	0	1
R. Almeida	rf	1	0	0	1	0	0
R. Herrera	2b	4	0	1	2	3	0
M. Cueto	3b	4	0	0	1	0	0
A. Cabrera	1b	2	1	0	10	2	0
J. Padrón	p	2	0	0	1	1	2
J. Mendez	p	1	0	0	0	5	0
P. Pareda	(x)	1	0	0	0	0	0
Totals		28	4	6	27	20	3

Indianapolis ABCs   001   011   110 : 5
Almendares   310   000   000 : 4

Three-base hits: D. Kennard
Two-base hits: J. Lyons, D. Kennard, G. González
Sacrifice hits: E. DeMoss, J. Lyons. R. Powell
Sacrifice flies: T. Allen (2)
Stolen bases: G. Shively, E. DeMoss, M. Clark, R. Redding, P. Chacon
Double-plays: P. Chacon, R. Herrera and A. Cabrera; D. Kennard and E. DeMoss; E. DeMoss to
   T. Allen and D. Kennard; G. González and R. Herrera
Bases on balls: L. Johnson 4, R. Redding 2, J. Padrón 8, J. Mendez 2
Strikeouts: L. Johnson 2, R. Redding 5, J. Padrón 5, J. Mendez 3
Wild pitches: L. Johnson (2), R. Redding 1
Passed balls: R. Powell
Winning pitcher: R. Redding
Losing pitcher: J. Mendez
Hits: L. Johnson 5 in 2.0 innings; J. Padrón 2 in 5.0 innings
Time: 2 hours 10 minutes
Umoires: Eustaquio Gutiérrez (home) and José Maria Magrinat (bases)
Scorer: Hilario Franquiz

Game Sixteen: Saturday, November 27, 1915, at Almendares Park

Ind ABCs	Pos	AB	R	H	O	A	E
G. Shively	lf	5	2	1	2	0	0
E. DeMoss	2b	5	1	2	6	6	0
J. Lyons	rf	5	1	3	2	0	0
B. Taylor	1b	4	1	2	8	0	0
O. Charleston	cf	4	0	0	1	0	0
M. Clark	ss	3	2	2	0	1	1
R. Powell	c	5	1	0	5	1	0
T. Allen	3b	5	2	4	3	2	0
R. Redding	p	5	2	1	0	1	0
C.I. Taylor	rf	1	0	0	0	0	0
Totals		42	12	15	27	11	1

Almendares	Pos	AB	R	H	O	A	E
B. Baro	lf,p	5	0	2	1	1	2
M. Villa	2b	4	1	1	4	2	0
G. González	1b,lf	4	1	1	4	0	0
C. Torriente	cf	3	2	2	4	0	0
E. Pedroso	p,1b	4	1	0	2	0	0
R. Almeida	3b	5	0	1	3	0	0
R. Herrera	ss	4	1	1	2	1	4
R. Figarola	c	0	0	0	2	2	0
M. Cueto	rf	4	1	2	1	0	0
V. Rodríguez	c	2	2	1	4	1	1
Totals		35	9	11	27	7	7

Indianapolis ABCs   221   051   100 : 12
Almendares   020   020   122 : 9

Three-base hits: J. Lyons. M. Clark, C. Torriente, M. Cueto
Two-base hits: B. Baro, G. González
Sacrifice flies: M. Villa, V. Rodríguez
Stolen bases: G. González, C. Torriente (3), J. Lyons, B. Taylor, R. Redding
Double-plays: R. Herrera, M. Villa and E. Pedroso
Left on bases: Indianapolis ABCs (10), Almendares (6)
Bases on balls: E. Pedroso 3, B. Baro 4, R. Redding 5
Strikeouts: E. Pedroso 3, B. Baro 2, R. Redding 4
Hit by pitcher: B. Baro 1 (O. Charleston)
Passed balls: R. Powell 1
Winning pitcher: R. Redding
Losing pitcher: E. Pedroso
Time: 2 hours 11 minutes
Umpires: Eustaquio Gutiérrez (home) and José Maria Magrinat (bases)
Scorer: Hilario Franquiz

Game Seventeen: Sunday, November 28, 1915,
at Almendares Park (First game)

Ind ABCs	Pos	AB	R	H	O	A	E
G. Shively	lf	5	0	2	1	0	0

Almendares	Pos	AB	R	H	O	A	E
P. Chacon	ss	3	1	0	5	0	1

Ind ABCs	Pos	AB	R	H	O	A	E
E. DeMoss	2b	3	0	0	2	1	0
T. Allen	3b	5	1	2	4	1	0
B. Taylor	1b	4	1	1	6	0	2
J. Lyons	rf	1	0	0	1	0	0
M. Clark	ss	4	1	1	2	2	0
O. Charleston	cf	4	1	0	1	1	0
R. Powell	c	2	0	2	7	1	0
R. Redding	p	4	0	0	0	1	0
Totals		32	4	8	24	7	2

Almendares	Pos	AB	R	H	O	A	E
M. Villa	cf	4	1	1	1	0	0
G. González	c	4	1	2	7	1	0
C. Torriente	cf	2	3	1	1	0	1
R. Almeida	rf	4	1	2	2	0	0
R. Herrera	2b	3	0	0	2	5	1
M. Cueto	3b	4	0	1	4	1	0
D. Hernandez	1b	3	0	1	4	1	0
A. Luque	p	3	0	0	1	3	0
Totals		30	7	9	27	11	3

```
Indianapolis ABCs  200    002    000 : 4
Almendares         501    000    10x : 7
```

Sacrifice hits: R. Herrera
Stolen bases: C. Torriente, R. Almeida, E. DeMoss, M. Cueto
Double-plays: R. Herrera and D. Hernandez; M. Clark and B. Taylor; R. Herrera, D. Hernandez and G. González
Bases on balls: A. Luque 7, R. Redding 2
Strikeouts: A. Luque 5, R. Redding 6
Hit by pitcher: R. Redding (2)
Winning pitcher: A. Luque
Losing pitcher: R. Redding
Time: 2 hours
Umpires: Eustaquio Gutiérrez (home) and José Maria Magrinat (bases)
Scorer: Hilario Franquiz

GAME EIGHTEEN: SUNDAY, NOVEMBER 28, 1915, AT ALMENDARES PARK (SECOND GAME)

Ind ABCs	Pos	AB	R	H	O	A	E
G. Shively	lf	4	0	1	2	0	2
E. DeMoss	2b	4	2	2	0	4	0
T. Allen	3b	4	0	1	1	1	0
B. Taylor	1b	4	0	2	10	2	1
J. Lyons	rf	4	0	2	0	0	0
M. Clark	ss	2	0	0	1	2	0
D. Kennard	c	4	1	2	4	1	0
R. Powell	rf	2	0	0	0	0	0
O. Charleston	p	3	1	1	2	2	0
C.I. Taylor	rf	2	0	0	0	0	0
Totals		33	4	11	20	12	3

Habana	Pos	AB	R	H	O	A	E
B. Acosta	lf	4	2	1	4	0	0
J. Calvo	cf	4	1	2	3	0	0
E. González	2b	4	2	2	1	3	1
M.A. González	c	4	1	1	4	0	0
A. Aragon	3b	3	1	0	1	0	0
T. Calvo	rf	3	2	3	1	1	0
T. Romanach	ss	3	0	0	3	0	0
R. Torres	1b	4	1	3	7	0	0
J. Acosta	p	3	0	0	0	4	0
Totals		32	10	12	28	8	1

```
Indianapolis ABCs    110    000    20 : 4 (Eight innings)
Habana               232    003    0x : 10
```

E. González out; hit by batted ball.
Three-base hits: M.A. González
Two-base hits: B. Taylor, E. González, B. Acosta
Sacrifice fly: T. Romanach
Stolen bases: B. Acosta, J. Calvo, E. González, M.A. González, A. Aragon, T. Calvo (3)
Double-plays: E. DeMoss, B. Taylor and D. Kennard
Bases on balls: O. Charleston 5, J. Acosta 1
Strikeouts: O. Charleston 2, J. Acosta 2
Hit by pitcher: J. Acosta 1
Passed balls: M.A. González 1
Winning pitcher: J. Acosta
Losing pitcher: O. Charleston
Time: 1 hour 40 minutes

Umpires: Eustaquio Gutiérrez (home) and José Maria Magrinat (bases)
Scorer: Hilario Franquiz

GAME NINETEEN: MONDAY, NOVEMBER 19, 1915, AT ALMENDARES PARK

Ind ABCs	Pos	AB	R	H	O	A	E
G. Shively	lf	3	2	0	2	0	0
E. DeMoss	2b	4	3	2	4	3	3
T. Allen	3b	3	0	2	1	3	0
B. Taylor	1b	5	1	1	12	0	0
J. Lyons	cf	5	1	4	1	0	1
M. Clark	ss	3	0	0	2	7	0
D. Kennard	c	4	0	1	4	1	0
R. Powell	rf	4	1	2	0	0	0
L. Johnson	p	1	0	0	0	0	0
J. Jeffries	p	3	1	1	1	2	0
Totals		35	9	13	27	16	3

San Francisco	Pos	AB	R	H	O	A	E
M. Guerra	1b,rf	4	1	1	6	0	0
R. Teran	ss	4	1	0	4	1	0
B. Baro	lf	2	1	0	2	0	0
E. Pedroso	rf,p	4	1	1	7	0	3
H. Hidalgo	cf	5	0	1	4	1	0
V. Rodríguez	c	4	0	1	2	0	0
F. Rivas	2b	4	1	1	0	2	0
S. Cordova	3b	4	0	1	1	2	0
J. Junco	p	1	0	0	1	2	0
F. Campos	p	1	0	0	0	5	0
Totals		35	5	6	27	13	3

Indianapolis ABCs	400	302	000 : 9
San Francisco	202	010	000 : 5

Three-base hits: T. Allen
Two-base hits: B. Taylor, J. Lyons, F. Rivas, E. DeMoss
Sacrifice hits: T. Allen, M. Clark, J. Jeffries
Stolen bases: B. Baro, J. Lyons, E. Pedroso
Double-plays: M. Clark, E. DeMoss and B. Taylor
Bases on balls: J. Junco 2, F. Campos 1, E. Pedroso 0, L. Johnson 4, J. Jeffries 4
Strikeouts: J. Junco 1, F. Campos 1, E. Pedroso 0, L. Johnson 0, J. Jeffries 3
Hits: J. Junco 8 in 3.0 innings; F. Campos 5 in 5.0 innings; L. Johnson 0 in 0.0 inning
Winning pitcher: J. Jeffries
Losing pitcher: J. Junco
Time: 1 hour 47 minutes
Umpires: Eustaquio Gutiérrez (home) and José Maria Magrinat (bases)
Scorer: Hilario Franquiz

GAME TWENTY: THURSDAY, DECEMBER 2, 1915, AT ALMENDARES PARK

Ind ABCs	Pos	AB	R	H	O	A	E
G. Shively	lf	5	2	2	3	0	1
E. DeMoss	2b	2	1	0	3	7	0
D. Kennard	c	3	0	1	1	1	0
B. Taylor	1b	5	0	3	11	0	1
J. Lyons	rf	5	0	2	1	0	0
M. Clark	3b	4	0	1	2	3	0
O. Charleston	cf	4	0	1	3	0	0
R. Powell	ss	3	1	1	0	2	0
J. Jeffries	p	3	0	0	0	0	1
C.I. Taylor		1	0	0	0	0	0
Totals		38	4	11	24	13	3

San Francisco	Pos	AB	R	H	O	A	E
M. Guerra	rf	5	1	2	2	1	0
H. Hidalgo	cf	3	1	1	0	0	1
B. Baro	lf	3	0	1	2	0	1
E. Pedroso	p	2	0	1	1	2	0
A. Parpetti	1b	3	0	0	8	0	0
L. Padrón	3b,cf	4	0	2	1	0	0
V. Rodríguez	c	4	1	1	5	5	0
R. Rivas	2b	4	1	2	2	1	0
R. Teran	ss	2	1	1	5	0	2
F. Campos	3b	1	0	1	0	0	2
Totals		31	5	12	26	9	6

Indianapolis ABCs	100	000	003 : 4
San Francisco	001	000	04x : 5

O. Charleston out for rules infraction.
Two-base hits: L. Padrón
Sacrifice hits: E. DeMoss, B. Baro
Stolen bases: D. Kennard, B. Taylor, H. Hidalgo, F. Rivas, V. Rodríguez
Double-plays: R. Powell, E. DeMoss and B. Taylor; M. Guerra, V. Rodríguez to R. Teran

Bases on balls: E. Pedroso 5, J. Jeffries 4
Strikeouts: E. Pedroso 5, J. Jeffries 1
Passed balls: V. Rodríguez
Winning pitcher: E. Pedroso
Losing pitcher: J. Jeffries
Time: 1 hour 40 minutes
Umpires: Eustaquio Gutiérrez (home) and José Maria Magrinat (bases)
Scorer: Hilario Franquiz

Final Statistics

Club Batting

Clubs	G	AB	R	H	Pct
Habana	9	282	60	82	.290
Almendares	9	288	50	80	.275
Indianapolis ABCs	20	647	97	173	.267
San Francisco	2	65	10	16	.246

Individual Pitching (All Clubs)

Pitcher	Club	G	GC	W	L	Pct	IP	R	H	W	K	PCP
Pastor Pareda	HAB	2	1	2	0	1.000	15.2	1	10	3	2	0.57
Gerardo Ballesteros	HAB	2	1	1	0	1.000	11.1	6	7	9	8	4.77
Eustaquio Pedroso	SFO	2	1	1	0	1.000	10.0	4	11	5	5	3.60
Adolfo Luque	ALM	7	4	4	2	.667	46.0	18	39	23	31	3.52
Richard Redding	IND	12	7	6	5	.545	79.1	49	81	33	33	5.56
José Acosta	HAB	4	3	2	2	.500	34.0	23	38	15	19	6.09
Eustaquio Pedroso	ALM	4	1	1	1	.500	19.0	13	20	11	15	6.16
Emilio Palmero	HAB	3	2	1	1	.500	18.0	11	15	11	10	5.50
James C. Jeffries	IND	5	2	1	2	.333	30.1	18	28	19	7	5.34
Louis Johnson	IND	9	3	1	3	.250	41.1	39	41	23	25	4.29
Benjamin Taylor	IND	3	1	0	1	.000	12.0	7	10	3	4	5.25
Oscar Charleston	IND	1	1	0	1	.000	8.0	10	12	5	2	11.25
Francisco Campos	SFO	1	0	0	0	.000	5.0	2	5	1	1	3.60
José Mendez	ALM	1	0	0	1	.000	4.0	3	3	2	3	6.75
José Junco	SFO	1	0	0	1	.000	3.0	7	8	2	1	21.00
Totals		57	27	20	20	.500						

Individual Batting (All Clubs)

Player	Club	G	AB	R	H	2B	3B	HR	SH	SB	Pct
Ramon Herrera	HAB	1	1	0	1	0	0	0	0	0	1.000
Luis Padrón	SFO	1	4	0	2	0	0	0	0	0	.500
Francisco Campos	SFO	2	2	0	1	0	0	0	0	0	.500
Cristobal Torriente	ALM	8	26	13	11	1	3	0	0	7	.423
Todd Allen	IND	17	57	12	23	4	1	0	1	6	.404
Bernardo Baro	ALM	7	28	2	11	2	0	0	0	2	.393
Manuel Cueto	ALM	8	31	5	12	0	2	0	0	4	.387
Vicente Rodríguez	ALM	5	13	5	5	1	0	0	1	0	.385
Benjamin Taylor	IND	20	79	8	30	6	1	0	1	7	.380
Francisco Rivas	SFO	2	8	1	3	1	0	0	0	1	.375
Eusebio González	HAB	9	30	6	11	2	1	0	0	2	.367
Jacinto Calvo	HAB	8	33	7	12	0	0	0	0	7	.364
José Acosta	HAB	5	11	2	4	0	0	0	0	0	.364
James C. Jeffries	IND	7	11	3	4	0	0	0	0	2	.364
Elwood DeMoss	IND	20	72	19	24	1	1	0	2	10	.333
Miguel Angel González	HAB	9	33	10	11	6	1	0	0	6	.333

Player	Club	G	AB	R	H	2B	3B	HR	SH	SB	Pct
Dan Kennard	IND	8	24	3	8	0	1	0	0	1	.333
Marcelino Guerra	SFO	2	9	2	3	0	0	0	0	0	.333
Heliodoro Hidalgo	ALM	3	3	0	1	0	0	0	1	0	.333
Pelayo Chacon	ALM	7	25	4	8	2	0	0	0	3	.320
Baldomero Acosta	HAB	8	32	7	10	3	0	0	1	3	.313
Gervasio González	ALM	9	33	4	10	2	0	0	0	2	.303
Ricardo Torres	HAB	5	10	2	3	0	0	0	1	0	.300
James Lyons	IND	20	78	11	23	0	1	0	3	8	.295
Richard Redding	IND	13	21	5	6	0	0	0	4	2	.286
Ramon González	HAB	4	7	2	2	0	0	0	0	0	.286
Morten Clark	IND	20	68	11	19	2	2	0	1	3	.279
Tomas Calvo	HAB	9	28	6	8	0	0	0	0	4	.286
Armando Marsans	HAB	8	30	8	8	0	0	0	0	5	.267
Heliodoro Hidalgo	SFO	2	8	1	2	0	0	0	0	1	.250
Vicente Rodríguez	SFO	2	8	1	2	0	0	0	0	1	.250
S. Cordova	SFO	1	4	0	1	0	0	0	0	0	.250
Manuel Villa	ALM	8	30	8	7	0	0	0	2	1	.233
Rafael Almeida	ALM	5	22	3	5	0	0	0	0	2	.227
Eustaquio Pedroso	ALM	8	27	4	6	1	0	0	0	1	.222
Russell Powell	IND	20	72	7	15	2	0	0	1	1	.208
George Shively	IND	20	82	15	17	0	1	0	1	5	.207
Ramon Herrera	ALM	8	30	5	6	0	0	0	1	0	.200
Bernardo Baro	SFO	2	5	1	1	0	0	0	1	1	.200
Pastor Pareda	HAB	2	5	0	1	0	0	0	0	0	.200
Tomas Romanach	HAB	9	26	2	5	1	0	0	2	0	.192
Angel Aragon	HAB	8	26	5	5	3	1	0	0	1	.192
Oscar Charleston	IND	19	69	7	12	1	0	0	1	2	.174
Emilio Palmero	HAB	3	6	1	1	0	0	0	1	0	.167
Julio Teran	SFO	2	6	2	1	0	0	0	0	0	.167
Eustaquio Pedroso	SFO	2	6	1	1	0	0	0	0	1	.167
Louis Johnson	IND	8	11	3	1	0	0	0	0	0	.091
Adolfo Luque	ALM	7	14	1	1	0	1	0	1	1	.071
Charles I. Taylor	IND	9	10	0	0	0	0	0	0	0	.000
Alfredo Cabrera	ALM	2	6	0	0	0	0	0	0	0	.000
Gerardo Ballesteros	HAB	2	3	2	0	0	0	0	0	0	.000
Agustin Parpetti	SFO	1	3	0	0	0	0	0	0	0	.000
Rafael Figarola	ALM	2	0	0	0	0	0	0	0	0	.000
José Junco	SFO	1	0	1	0	0	0	0	0	0	.000

Players Who Played on Two Teams

Bernardo Baro	ALM-SFO	8	28	4	10	.352
Joseito Rodríguez	ALM-SFO	6	19	4	6	.315
Eustaquio Pedroso	ALM-SFO	10	33	5	7	.212

INDIANAPOLIS ABCs

Individual Pitching

Pitcher	G	GS	GC	W	L	Pct	IP	R	H	W	K	ERA
Richard Redding	12	8	7	6	5	.545	79.1	49	81	33	33	5.56
James C. Jeffries	5	4	2	1	2	.333	30.1	18	28	19	7	5.34
Louis Johnson	9	6	3	1	3	.250	41.1	39	41	23	25	4.29
Benjamin Taylor	3	1	1	0	1	.000	12.0	7	10	3	4	5.25
Oscar Charleston	1	1	1	0	1	.000	8.0	10	12	5	2	11.25
Totals	30	20	14	8	12	.400	171.0	123	172	83	71	6.47

Individual Batting

Player	Pos	G	AB	R	H	2B	3B	HR	SH	SB	Pct
George Shively	lf,rf	20	82	15	17	0	1	0	1	5	.207
James Lyons	rf,cf,1b,lf	20	78	11	23	0	1	0	3	8	.295
Elwood DeMoss	2b	20	72	19	24	1	1	0	2	10	.333
Benjamin Taylor	1b,p	20	79	8	30	6	1	0	1	7	.380
Oscar Charleston	cf,p	19	69	7	12	1	0	0	1	2	.174
Morten Clark	ss	20	68	11	19	2	2	0	1	3	.279
Russell Powell	c,3b,1b	20	72	7	15	2	0	0	1	1	.208
Todd Allen	3b,1b	17	57	12	23	4	1	0	1	6	.404
Louis Johnson	p	8	11	3	1	0	0	0	0	0	.091
Richard Redding	p	13	21	5	6	0	0	0	4	2	.286
Dan Kennard	c	8	24	3	8	0	1	0	0	1	.333
James C. Jeffries	p,rf	7	11	3	4	0	0	0	0	2	.364
Charles I. Taylor	rf	9	10	0	0	0	0	0	0	0	.000
Totals		20	634	104	182	16	8	0	15	47	.287

Individual Fielding

Player	Pos	G	O	A	E	Pct
George Shively	lf,rf	20	39	3	7	.857
James Lyons	rf,cf,1b,lf	20	23	3	2	.929
Elwood DeMoss	2b	20	60	66	11	.920
Benjamin Taylor	1b,p	20	182	11	8	.960
Oscar Charleston	cf,p	19	41	6	4	.922
Morten Clark	ss	20	29	65	13	.879
Russell Powell	c,3b,1b	20	59	29	3	.967
Todd Allen	3b,1b	17	38	32	6	.921
Louis Johnson	p	8	1	5	3	.667
Richard Redding	p	13	2	14	1	.941
Dan Kennard	c	8	24	7	1	.969
James C. Jeffries	p,rf	7	1	5	1	.857
Charles I. Taylor	rf	9	4	2	1	.857
Totals			206	470	240	57	.926

ALMENDARES

Individual Pitching

Pitcher	G	CG	W	L	Pct	IP	R	H	W	SO	.PCA
Adolfo Luque	7	4	4	2	.667	46.0	18	39	23	31	3.52
Eustaquio Pedroso	4	1	1	1	.500	19.0	13	20	11	15	6.16
José Mendez	1	4	0	1	.000	4.0	3	3	2	3	6.75
Totals	12	9	5	4	.556	69.0	34	62	36	39	4.34

Individual Batting

Player	Pos	G	AB	R	H	2B	3B	HR	SH	SB	Pct
Pelayo Chacon	ss	7	25	4	8	2	0	0	0	3	.320
Gervasio González	c,1b,of	9	33	4	10	2	0	0	0	2	.303
Manuel Villa	2b,rf,p,lf	8	30	8	7	0	0	0	2	1	.233
Cristobal Torriente	cf	8	26	13	11	1	3	0	0	7	.423
Bernardo Baro	lf,p,rf	7	28	2	11	2	0	0	0	2	.393
Alfredo Cabrera	1b,3b	2	6	0	0	0	0	0	0	0	.000
Manuel Cueto	3b,rf,cf	8	31	5	12	0	2	0	0	4	.387
Vicente Rodríguez	c	5	13	5	5	1	0	0	1	0	.385
Eustaquio Pedroso	p,1b	8	27	4	6	1	0	0	0	1	.222
Adolfo Luque	p	7	14	1	1	0	1	0	1	1	.071

Player	Pos	G	AB	R	H	2B	3B	HR	SH	SB	Pct
Ramon Herrera	2b,ss	8	30	5	6	0	0	0	1	0	.200
Heliodo Hidalgo	rf	3	3	0	1	0	0	0	1	0	.333
Rafael Almeida	3b	5	22	3	5	0	0	0	0	2	.227
Rafael Figarola	c	2	0	0	0	0	0	0	0	0	.000
Totals		9	292	55	85	11	6	0	6	23	.291

Individual Fielding

Player	Pos	G	O	A	E	Pct
Pelayo Chacon	ss	7	15	16	4	.886
Gervasio González	c,1b,of	9	59	3	2	.969
Manuel Villa	2b,rf,p,lf	8	12	7	1	.950
Cristobal Torriente	cf	8	21	2	3	.885
Bernardo Baro	lf,p,rf	7	9	2	3	.786
Alfredo Cabrera	1b,3b	2	8	1	1	.900
Manuel Cueto	3b,rf,cf	8	15	7	1	.957
Vicente Rodríguez	c	5	35	3	2	.950
Eustaquio Pedroso	p,1b	8	22	8	1	.968
Adolfo Luque	p	7	2	12	0	1.000
Ramon Herrera	2b,ss	8	21	16	11	.771
Heliodo Hidalgo	rf	3	0	0	0	.000
Rafael Almeida	3b	5	12	3	0	1.000
Rafael Figarola	c	2	5	4	0	1.000
Totals		9	240	87	29	.919

HABANA

Individual Pitching

Pitchers	G	CG	W	L	Pct	IP	R	H	W	SO	PCA
Pastor Pareda	2	1	2	0	1.000	15.2	1	10	3	2	0.57
Gerardo Ballesteros	2	1	1	0	1.000	11.1	6	7	9	8	4.77
José Acosta	4	3	2	2	.500	34.0	23	38	15	19	6.09
Emilio Palmero	3	2	1	1	.500	18.0	11	15	11	10	5.50
Totals	11	7	6	3	.667	79.	41	60	38	39	4.67

Individual Batting

Player	Pos	G	AB	R	H	2B	3B	HR	SH	SB	Pct
Baldomero Acosta	lf	8	32	7	10	3	0	0	1	3	.313
Armando Marsans	lf,1b,c	8	30	8	8	0	0	0	0	5	.267
Jacinto Calvo	cf	8	33	7	12	0	0	0	0	7	.364
Miguel Angel González	c	9	33	10	11	6	1	0	0	6	.333
Eusebio González	2b	9	30	6	11	2	1	0	0	2	.367
Angel Aragon	3b	8	26	5	5	3	1	0	0	1	.192
Tomas Calvo	rf	9	28	6	8	0	0	0	0	4	.286
Tomas Romanach	ss	9	26	2	5	1	0	0	2	0	.192
José Acosta	p	5	11	2	4	0	0	0	0	0	.364
Ramon Herrera	ph	1	1	0	1	0	0	0	0	0	1.000
Ricardo Torres	1b,c	5	10	2	3	0	0	0	1	0	.300
Emilio Palmero	p	3	6	1	1	0	0	0	1	0	.167
Ramon González	3b,2b	4	7	2	2	0	0	0	0	0	.286
Gerardo Ballesteros	p	2	3	2	0	0	0	0	0	0	.000
Pastor Pareda	p	2	5	0	1	0	0	0	0	0	.200
Totals		9	281	60	81	15	3	0	3	30	.288

Individual Fielding

Player	Pos	G	O	A	E	Pct
Baldomero Acosta	lf	8	13	1	0	1.000
Armando Marsans	lf,1b,c	8	66	4	2	.972
Jacinto Calvo	cf	8	19	1	2	.909
Miguel Angel González	c	9	54	14	1	.986
Eusebio González	2b	9	16	23	3	.929
Angel Aragon	3b	8	11	12	2	.920
Tomas Calvo	rf	9	15	2	3	.850
Tomas Romanach	ss	9	15	32	6	.887
José Acosta	p	5	2	6	0	1.000
Ramon Herrera	ph	1	0	0	0	.000
Ricardo Torres	1b,c	5	17	1	0	1.000
Emilio Palmero	p	3	1	7	1	.889
Ramon González	3b,2b	4	1	1	1	.667
Gerardo Ballesteros	p	2	0	5	0	1.000
Pastor Pareda	p	2	1	2	0	1.000
Totals		92	237	110	22	.940

SAN FRANCISCO

Individual Pitching

Pitchers	G	CG	W	L	Pct	IP	R	H	W	SO	PRA
Eustaquio Pedroso	2	1	1	0	1.000	10.0	4	11	5	5	3.60
Francisco Campos	1	0	0	0	.000	5.0	2	5	1	1	3.60
José Junco	1	0	0	1	.000	3.0	7	8	2	1	21.00
Totals	4	1	1	1	.500	18.0	13	24	8	7	6.50

Individual Batting

Player	Pos	G	AB	R	H	2B	3B	HR	SH	SB	Pct
Marcelino Guerra	1b,rf	2	9	2	3	0	0	0	0	0	.333
Julio Teran	ss	2	6	2	1	0	0	0	0	0	.167
Bernardo Baro	lf	2	5	1	1	0	0	0	1	1	.200
Eustaquio Pedroso	rf,p	2	6	1	1	0	0	0	0	1	.167
Heliodoro Hidalgo	cf	2	8	1	2	0	0	0	0	1	.250
Vicente Rodríguez	c	2	8	1	2	0	0	0	0	1	.250
Francisco Rivas	2b	2	8	1	3	1	0	0	0	1	.375
S. Cordova	3b	1	4	0	1	0	0	0	0	0	.250
José Junco	p	1	0	1	0	0	0	0	0	0	.000
Francisco Campos	p,3b	2	2	0	1	0	0	0	0	0	.500
Agustin Parpetti	1b	1	3	0	0	0	0	0	0	0	.000
Luis Padrón	3b,cf	1	4	0	2	0	0	0	0	0	.500
Totals		2	66	10	18	2	0	0	1	4	.273

Individual Fielding

Player	Pos	G	O	A	E	Pct
Marcelino Guerra	1b,rf	2	8	1	0	1.000
José Teran	ss	2	9	1	2	.833
Bernardo Baro	lf	2	4	0	1	.800
Eustaquio Pedroso	rf,p	2	8	2	3	.769
Heliodoro Hidalgo	cf	2	4	1	1	.833
Vicente Rodríguez	c	2	7	5	0	1.000
Francisco Rivas	2b	2	2	3	0	1.000
S. Cordova	3b	1	1	2	0	1.000
José Junco	p	1	1	2	0	1.000

Player	Pos	G	O	A	E	Pct
Francisco Campos	p,3b	2	0	5	2	.714
Agustin Parpetti	1b	1	8	0	0	1.000
Luis Padrón	3b,cf	1	1	0	0	1.000
Totals		2	53	22	9	.893

◆ 12 ◆

1920
Bacharach Giants

Roster

Player	Position	Regular Season Club, 1920
Toussaint Allen	1b	Hilldale
Charles Blackwell	lf	Hilldale
Oscar Charleston	cf	Indianapolis ABCs
Morten Clark	2b	Indianapolis ABCs
S.R. "Eddie" DeWith	3b	Indianapolis ABCs
Willis "Pud" Flournoy	p	Hilldale
Richard Lundy	ss	Bacharach Giants
Richard Redding	p	Bacharach Giants
Julio Rojo	rf,c	Bacharach Giants
Merven J. Ryan	p	Bacharach Giants
Louis Santop	c,rf	Hilldale

Toussaint "Tom" Allen started with the Havana Red Sox in 1914. He played with Hilldale, but for this trip to Cuba he played with the Bacharach Giants.

Charles Blackwell started with the Saint Louis Giants in 1916 and later played with the Saint Louis Stars, Birmingham Barons and Indianapolis ABCs. For this trip to Cuba he played with the Bacharach Giants.

Oscar Charleston a superstar blend of power and speed, started with the Indianapolis ABCs in 1915.

Morten "Specs" Clark started with the Indianapolis ABCS in 1910. He also played with the Baltimore Black Sox.

S.R. "Eddie" DeWitt started with the Dayton Giants (1910) and played with the Dayton Marcos and Indianapolis ABCs.

Willis "Pud" Flournoy started with Hilldale (1919) and played with the Brooklyn Royal Giants and Bacharach Giants.

Richard Lundy a shortstop with a wide range and a strong arm, began in 1916 with the Bacharach Giants.

Richard "Cannonball Dick" Redding as his nickname suggests, was a pitcher noted for overpowering speed. This right-hander started with the Lincoln Giants in 1911. In 1912 he won 43 games and lost 12. He played with the Lincoln Stars, Indianapolis ABCs, Chicago American Giants, Brooklyn Royal Giants and Bacharach Giants.

Julio Rojo, a Cuban, began in 1916 with the Cuban Stars and later played with the Havana Stars and Bacharach Giants.

Merven J. "Red" Ryan started with the Pittsburgh Stars of Buffalo (1916) and also played with the Brooklyn Royal Giants, Hilldale, Harrisburg Giants and Bacharach Giants.

Louis "Top" Santop was a left-handed power hitter and skilled catcher. Beginning his career with the Fort Worth Wonders in 1909, he went on to play with the Oklahoma Monarchs, Philadelphia Giants, Lincoln Giants, Chicago American Giants, Lincoln Stars and, for this trip to Cuba, with the Bacharach Giants.

Games Played

Date	Winning Club		Losing Club		Winning Pitcher	Losing Pitcher
Nov 22	Habana	4	Bacharach	1	J. Acosta 1-0	F. Flournoy 0-1
Nov 24	Bacharach	2	Habana	2	Tie-R. Redding-O. Tuero	
Nov 25	Almendares	5	Bacharach	4	E. Palmero 1-0	P. Flournoy 0-2
Nov 27	Bacharach	6	Almendares	6	Tie-R. Redding-E. Palmero	
Nov 29	Habana	3	Bacharach	1	W.C. Stewart 1-0	M.J. Ryan 0-1
Dec 1	Almendares	3	Bacharach	0	I. Fabre 1-0	R. Redding 0-1
(6)						

Club Standings

Clubs	G	W	L	T	Pct
Almendares	3	2	0	1	1.000
Habana	3	2	0	1	1.000
Bacharach Giants	6	0	4	2	.000
Totals	12	4	4	4	.500

The Games

GAME ONE: SUNDAY, NOVEMBER 21, 1920, AT ALMENDARES PARK

Bach Giants	Pos	AB	R	H	O	A	E
M. Clark	2b	4	0	2	2	3	1
S.R. Dewitt	3b	4	0	0	0	2	0
O. Charleston	cf	3	0	0	2	0	0
L. Santop	c	4	0	0	7	0	0
C. Blackwell	lf	4	0	0	1	0	0
R. Lundy	ss	4	0	0	3	1	1
J. Rojo	rf	4	0	2	0	0	0
N. Allen	1b	3	0	0	9	0	1
R. Redding	p	3	0	0	0	4	2
Totals		33	0	4	24	10	5

Almendares	Pos	AB	R	H	O	A	E
B. Portuondo	3b	3	1	1	1	3	0
R. González	2b	4	0	0	4	4	0
B. Baro	rf	4	1	0	2	0	0
P. Chacon	ss	4	0	1	0	3	1
C. Torriente	cf	4	1	2	4	0	0
R. Herrera	rf	4	0	1	1	0	0
A. Luque	1b	1	0	0	7	0	1
E. Abreu	c	3	0	0	8	0	0
I. Fabre	p	2	0	0	0	1	0
Totals		29	3	5	27	10	2

Bacharach Giants	000	000	000 : 0
Almendares	102	000	00x : 3

Two-base hits: C. Torriente
Sacrifice hits: I. Fabre
Stolen bases: B. Portuondo, D. Clark, A. Luque
Left on bases: Almendares (8), Bacharach Giants (7)
Bases on balls: R. Redding 5, I. Fabre 1
Strikeouts: R. Redding 6, I. Fabre 6
Passed balls: L. Santop 1
Winning pitcher: I. Fabre
Losing pitcher: R. Redding
Time: 1 hour 45 minutes
Umpires: Valentin González (home) and José M. Magrinat (bases)
Scorer: Julio Franquiz

GAME TWO: MONDAY, NOVEMBER 22, 1920, AT ALMENDARES PARK

Bach Giants	Pos	AB	R	H	O	A	E
M. Clark	2b	3	0	0	2	1	0
S.R. DeWitt	3b	3	0	0	1	1	0
O. Charleston	cf	4	1	2	6	0	0
L. Santop	rf	4	0	1	0	0	0
C. Blackwell	lf	4	0	0	2	0	0
R. Lundy	ss	3	0	0	3	2	2
J. Rojo	c	4	0	0	3	1	0
T. Allen	1b	2	0	1	6	0	0
P. Flournoy	p	0	0	0	0	0	0
M.J. Ryan	p	3	0	1	1	2	0
Totals		30	1	5	24	7	2

Habana	Pos	AB	R	H	O	A	E
M. Cueto	3b	3	1	2	1	4	0
J. Calvo	cf	4	0	1	1	0	1
G. Burns	lf	3	2	1	2	0	0
L. Doyle	2b	2	0	1	1	4	0
R. Almeida	rf	3	0	0	1	0	0
H.H. Ford	ss	2	1	0	4	3	0
J. Rodríguez	1b	3	0	1	13	1	0
R. Torres	c	4	0	0	3	2	0
J. Acosta	p	3	0	0	1	1	0
Totals		27	4	6	27	15	1

Bacharach Giants	000	100	000 : 1		
Habana	200	001	00x : 3		

Three-base hits: O. Charleston
Two-base hits: G. Burns
Sacrifice hits: M. Clark, H.H. Ford
Stolen bases: J. Calvo, J. Rodríguez
Double-plays: O. Charleston and T. Allen; M. Cueyo, L. Doyle and J. Rodríguez
Bases on balls: P. Flournoy 3, M.J. Ryan 3, J. Acosta 2
Strikeouts: P. Flournoy 0, M.J. Ryan 1, J. Acosta 2
Hit by pitcher: J. Acosta 1 (J. Hewitt)
Winning pitcher: J. Acosta
Losing pitcher: P. Flournoy
Time: 1 hour 35 minutes
Umpires: Valentin González (home) and José M. Magrinat (bases)
Scorer: Julio Franquiz

GAME THREE: WEDNESDAY, NOVEMBER 24, 1920, AT ALMENDARES PARK

Bach Giants	Pos	AB	R	H	O	A	E
M. Clark	2b	5	0	1	1	2	1
S.R. Dewitt	3b	5	0	0	1	0	0
O. Charleston	cf	4	1	1	3	0	0
L. Santop	rf	4	0	2	0	0	1
C. Blackwell	lf	4	1	2	1	0	0
R. Lundy	ss	4	0	0	4	4	1
J. Rojo	c	4	0	0	6	1	0
T. Allen	1b	4	0	0	12	0	1
R. Redding	p	4	0	0	0	5	0
M.J. Ryan	p	0	0	0	2	0	0
Totals		38	2	6	30	12	4

Habana	Pos	AB	R	H	O	A	E
M. Cueto	3b	5	1	0	0	3	0
J. Calvo	rf	5	1	3	0	0	0
G. Burns	lf	4	0	0	3	0	0
L. Doyle	2b	3	0	0	1	6	2
R. Almeida	rf	3	0	0	1	0	0
H.H. Ford	ss	4	0	0	0	3	0
J. Rodríguez	1b	3	0	0	19	0	0
R. Torres	c	4	0	0	6	2	0
O. Tuero	p	1	0	0	0	0	0
F. Hungo	(x)	1	0	0	0	0	0
W.C. Stewart	p	1	0	0	0	3	0
J. López	(xx)	1	0	0	0	0	0
Totals		35	2	3	30	17	2

(x)—Out for O. Tuero in Sixth.
(xx)—Out for W.C. Stewart in Tenth.

Bacharach Giants	010	001	000	0 : 2 (Ten innings)
Habana	000	002	000	0 : 2

Three-base hits: C. Blackwell
Two-base hits: O. Charleston
Bases on balls: R. Redding 2, M.J. Ryan 0, O. Tuero 0, W.C. Stewart 0
Strikeouts: R. Redding 5, M.J. Ryan 0, O. Tuero 2, W.C. Stewart 2
Hit by pitcher: R. Redding 1 (J. Rodríguez)

Passed balls: R. Torres 1
Time: 1 hour 50 minutes
Umpires: Valentin González (home) and José M. Magrinat (bases)
Scorer: Julio Franquiz

GAME FOUR: THURSDAY, NOVEMBER 25, 1920, AT ALMENDARES PARK

Bach Giants	Pos	AB	R	H	O	A	E		Almendares	Pos	AB	R	H	O	A	E
S.R. Dewitt	3b	4	1	0	1	1	0		B. Portuondo	3b	3	1	1	1	1	1
M. Clark	2b	3	0	0	3	4	0		B. Baro	rf	3	1	0	1	1	0
O. Charleston	cf	3	0	0	2	0	1		B. Acosta	lf	3	1	0	1	0	0
L. Santop	c	2	2	0	2	3	1		P. Chacon	ss	4	1	1	5	3	1
C. Blackwell	lf	4	0	1	1	0	0		C. Torriente	cf	3	0	0	4	0	0
R. Lundy	ss	4	0	2	3	2	2		E. González	2b	3	0	1	0	5	0
J. Rojo	rf	4	0	1	2	0	0		M. Guerra	1b	3	0	1	10	0	2
T. Allen	1b	2	0	0	9	0	0		E. Abreu	c	2	0	0	5	3	0
P. Flournoy	p	2	1	0	1	1	0		E. Palmero	p	2	0	0	0	4	0
R. Redding	1b	2	0	0	0	0	0		R. Herrera	(x)	0	1	0	0	0	0
M.J. Ryan	p	1	0	0	0	0	0		I. Fabre	p	1	0	0	0	0	0
Totals		31	4	4	24	11	4		Totals		27	5	4	27	17	4

(x)-Base for Palmero in Seventh.

Bacharach Giants	200	001	100 : 4
Almendares	000	110	30x : 5

Two-base hits: P. Chacon, R. Lundy, C. Blackwell
Sacrifice hits: E. González
Stolen bases: B. Baro (2), M. Guerra, P. Chacon, R. Herrera
Bases on balls: E. Palmero 4, I. Fabre 0, P. Flournoy 8, M.J. Ryan 2
Strikeouts: E. Palmero 2, I. Fabre 2, P. Flournoy 2, M.J. Ryan 1
Hit by pitcher: E. Palmero 1 (L. Santop) and P. Flournoy 1 (M. Guerra)
Winning pitcher: E. Palmero
Losing pitcher: P. Flournoy
Time: 2 hours 10 minutes
Umpires: Valentin González (home) and José M. Magrinat (bases)
Scorer: Julio Franquiz

GAME FIVE: SATURDAY, NOVEMBER 27, 1920, AT ALMENDARES PARK

Bach Giants	Pos	AB	R	H	O	A	E		Almendares	Pos	AB	R	H	O	A	E
S.R. Dewitt	3b	2	1	1	0	1	0		B. Portuondo	3b	2	2	2	1	4	0
M. Clark	2b	4	0	0	3	3	1		B. Baro	rf	3	0	2	3	0	0
O. Charleston	cf	4	0	0	3	0	0		B. Acosta	lf	3	0	1	0	0	0
L. Santop	rf	3	1	1	0	0	0		P. Chacon	ss	4	0	1	6	2	2
C. Blackwell	lf	4	2	1	0	0	0		C. Torriente	cf	4	1	1	1	0	0
R. Lundy	ss	4	1	2	2	3	0		E. González	2b	4	0	0	1	4	2
J. Rojo	c	4	0	1	7	1	0		M. Guerra	1b	4	1	1	10	1	0
T. Allen	1b	4	0	0	9	2	0		E. Abreu	c	3	1	1	2	1	0
R. Redding	p	2	0	0	0	2	0		J. Hernandez	p	0	0	0	0	0	0
M.J. Ryan	rf	0	1	0	0	0	0		E. Palmero	p	2	1	0	0	1	0
Totals		28	6	6	24	10	1		Totals		29	6	9	24	13	4

Bacharach Giants	300	001	02 : 6 (Eight innings)
Almendares	120	120	11 : 6

Three-base hits: M. Guerra
Two-base hits: R. Lundy, J. Rojo
Sacrifice hits: J. Hernandez, B. Portuondo, B. Acosta

Stolen bases: C. Blackwell, J. Rojo, B. Acosta
Bases on balls: R. Redding 3, J. Hernandez 1, E. Palmero 1
Strikeouts: R. Redding 6, J. Hernandez 0, E. Palmero 2
Hit by pitcher: J. Hernandez 1 (J. Hewitt)
Time: 1 hour 55 minutes.
Umpires: Valentin González (home) and José M. Magrinat (bases)
Scorer: Julio Franquiz

GAME SIX: MONDAY, NOVEMBER 29, 1920, AT ALMENDARES PARK

Bach Giants	Pos	AB	R	H	O	A	E
S.R. Dewitt	3b	3	0	0	4	4	0
M. Clark	2b	4	0	1	3	0	1
O. Charleston	cf	4	0	1	1	0	1
L. Santop	rf	4	0	0	2	1	0
C. Blackwell	lf	3	0	0	2	0	0
R. Lundy	ss	3	0	1	1	3	2
J. Rojo	c	3	0	0	6	2	0
T. Allen	1b	3	0	0	5	0	0
M.J. Ryan	p	2	1	0	0	0	0
Totals		29	1	3	24	10	4

Habana	Pos	AB	R	H	O	A	E
J. Rodríguez	1b	4	0	0	14	0	0
J. Calvo	cf	4	1	3	1	0	0
M. Cueto	3b	4	0	1	0	2	0
R. Almeida	rf	2	1	1	3	0	0
H.H. Ford	ss	4	0	1	1	3	0
J. López	lf	4	0	0	2	1	0
F. Hungo	2b	3	1	1	2	4	0
R. Torres	c	4	0	2	4	0	0
W.C. Stewart	p	1	0	0	0	5	0
Totals		31	3	9	27	15	0

Bacharach Giants	000	001	000 : 1
Habana	011	100	00x : 3

Two-base hits: J. Calvo, M. Cueto
Sacrifice hits: W.C. Stewart (2)
Double-plays: J. López and F. Hungo
Bases on balls: M.J. Ryan 3, W.C. Stewart 4
Strikeouts: M.J. Ryan 4, W.C. Stewart 1
Time: 1 hour 38 minutes
Winning Pitcher: W.C. Stewart
Lossing Pitcher: M.J. Ryan
Umpires: Valentin González (home) and José M. Magrinat (bases)
Scorer: Julio Franquiz

Final Statistics

Individual Pitching

Pitcher	G	GS	GC	W	L	Pct	IP	R	H	W	K	HP	ERT
Willis Flournoy	2	1	0	0	1	.000	7.2	7	7	11	2	0	8.21
Richard Redding	3	3	3	0	2	.000	25.0	11	17	10	17	1	3.96
Merven J. Ryan	4	2	1	0	1	.000	19.0	4	12	6	5	0	1.89
Totals	9	6	4	0	4	.000	51.2	22	36	27	24	1	3.83

Ties (2), Redding (2) vs, Habana 1, Almendares 1.

Individual Batting

Player	Pos	G	AB	R	H	2B	3B	HR	SH	SB	Pct
Toussaint Allen	1b	6	18	0	1	0	0	0	0	0	.056
Charles Blackwell	lf	6	23	3	4	1	1	0	0	1	.174
Oscar Charleston	cf	6	22	2	4	1	1	0	0	0	.182
Morten Clark	2b	6	23	0	4	0	0	0	1	1	.174
S.R. Dewitt	3b	6	21	2	1	0	0	0	0	0	.048
Willis Pud Flournoy	p	2	2	1	0	0	0	0	0	0	.000
Richard Lundy	ss	6	22	1	5	2	0	0	0	0	.227

Player	Pos	G	AB	R	H	2B	3B	HR	SH	SB	Pct
Richard Redding	p	4	11	0	0	0	0	0	0	0	.000
Julio Rojo	rf,c	6	23	0	4	1	0	0	0	1	.174
Merven J. Ryan	p	5	6	2	1	0	0	0	0	0	.167
Louis Santop	c,rf	6	21	3	4	0	0	0	0	0	.190
Totals		6	189	14	28	5	2	0	1	3	.148

Individual Fielding

Player	Pos	G	O	A	E	Pct
Toussaint Allen	1b	66	50	2	1	.981
Charles Blackwell	lf	64	7	0	0	1.000
Oscar Charleston	cf	62	17	0	2	.895
Morten Clark	2b	64	13	13	4	.867
S.R. Dewitt	3b	68	7	9	0	1.000
Willis Pud Flournoy	p	20	1	1	0	1.000
Richard Lundy	ss	67	16	15	8	.795
Richard Redding	p	40	0	11	2	.846
Julio Rojo	rf,c	64	24	5	0	1.000
Merven J. Ryan	p	57	3	2	0	1.000
Louis Santop	c,rf	60	12	4	2	.889
Totals		68	150	160	20	.913

ALMENDARES

Individual Pitching

Pitcher	G	CG	W	L	Pct	IP	R	H	W	K	ERT
I. Fabre	2	1	1	0	1.000	11.0	0	4	1	6	0.00
E. Palmero	2	0	1	0	1.000	9.0	6	6	5	4	6.00
J. Hernandez	1	0	0	0	.000	6.0	4	4	1	0	6.00
Totals	4	1	2	0	1.000	26.0	10	14	7	10	3.46

Individual Batting

Almendares	Pos	G	AB	R	H	2B	3B	HR	SH	SB	Pct
B. Portuondo	3b(3)	3	8	4	4	0	0	0	1	1	.500
E. González	2b(3)	3	11	0	1	0	0	0	1	0	.091
B. Baro	rf(3)	3	10	2	2	0	0	0	0	2	.200
P. Chacon	ss(3)	3	12	1	3	1	0	0	0	1	.250
C. Torriente	cf(3)	3	12	1	3	1	0	0	0	0	.250
R. Herrera	rf(1),pr(1)	2	4	1	1	0	0	0	0	1	.250
A. Luque	1B(1)	1	1	0	0	0	0	0	0	1	.000
E. Abreu	c(3)	3	8	1	1	0	0	0	0	0	.125
I. Fabre	p(2)	2	3	0	0	0	0	0	1	0	.000
B. Acosta	lf(2)	2	6	1	1	0	0	0	1	1	.167
M. Guerra	1b(2)	2	7	1	2	0	1	0	0	1	.286
J. Hernandez	p(1)	1	0	0	0	0	0	0	1	0	.000
E. Palmero	p(2)	2	4	1	0	0	0	0	0	0	.000
Totals		3	85	14	18	2	1	0	5	8	.212

Individual Fielding

Almendares	Pos	G	O	A	E	Pct
B. Portuondo	3b(3)	3	3	8	1	.917
E. González	2b(3)	3	5	13	0	1.000
B. Baro	rf(3)	3	6	1	0	1.000
P. Chacon	ss(3)	3	11	8	4	.826
C. Torriente	cf(3)	3	9	0	0	1.000

Almendares	Pos	G	O	A	E	Pct
R. Herrera	rf(1),pr(1)	2	1	0	0	1.000
A. Luque	1B(1)	1	7	0	1	.875
E. Abreu	c(3)	3	15	4	0	1.000
I. Fabre	p(2)	2	0	1	0	1.000
B. Acosta	lf(2)	2	1	0	0	1.000
M. Guerra	1b(2)	2	20	1	2	.913
J. Hernandez	p(1)	1	0	0	0	.000
E. Palmero	p(2)	2	0	5	0	.000
Totals		3	78	40	10	.922

HABANA

Individual Pitching

Pitcher	G	CG	W	L	Pct	IP	R	H	W	K	ERT
J. Acosta	1	1	1	0	1.000	9.0	1	5	2	2	1.00
W.C. Stewart	2	1	1	0	1.000	13.0	1	5	1	6	0.69
O. Tuero	1	0	0	0	.000	6.0	2	4	0	2	3.00
Totals	4	2	2	0	1.000	28.0	4	14	3	10	1.29

Tied: O. Tuero–W.C. Stewart (1)

Individual Batting

Habana	Pos	G	AB	R	H	2B	3B	HR	SH	SB	Pct
M. Cueto	3b(3)	3	12	2	3	1	0	0	0	0	.250
J. Calvo	cf(3)	3	13	2	7	1	0	0	0	1	.538
G. Burns	lf(2)	2	7	2	1	1	0	0	0	0	.143
L. Doyle	2b(2)	2	5	0	1	0	0	0	0	0	.200
R. Almeida	rf(3)	3	8	1	1	0	0	0	0	0	.125
H.H. Ford	ss(3)	3	10	1	1	0	0	0	1	0	.100
J. Rodríguez	1b(3)	3	10	0	1	0	0	0	0	1	.100
R. Torres	c(3)	3	12	0	2	0	0	0	0	0	.167
O. Tuero	p(1)	1	1	0	0	0	0	0	0	0	.000
F. Hungo	2b(1),ph(1)	2	4	1	1	0	0	0	0	0	.250
W.C. Stewart	p(2)	2	2	0	0	0	0	0	2	0	.000
J. López	lf(1),ph(1)	2	5	0	0	0	0	0	0	0	.000
Totals		3	93	9	18	3	0	0	3	2	.194

Individual Fielding

Habana	Pos	G	O	A	E	Pct
M. Cueto	3b(3)	3	1	9	0	1.000
J. Calvo	cf(3)	3	2	0	1	.667
G. Burns	lf(2)	2	5	0	0	1.000
L. Doyle	2b(2)	2	2	10	2	.857
R. Almeida	rf(3)	3	5	0	0	1.000
H.H. Ford	ss(3)	3	5	9	0	1.000
J. Rodríguez	1b(3)	3	46	1	0	1.000
R. Torres	c(3)	3	13	4	0	1.000
O. Tuero	p(1)	1	0	0	0	.000
F. Hungo	2b(1),ph(1)	2	2	4	0	1.000
W.C. Stewart	p(2)	2	0	8	0	1.000
J. López	lf(1),ph(1)	2	2	1	0	1.000
Totals		3	84	7	3	.978

1925
All Yankees

With the Almendares club dominating the competition, a halt to further play was called. It was decided that, instead, a series of nine games would be played between two all-star teams, one Cuban and one North American. The series was to be played in honor of major league commissioner Kenesaw Mountain Landis, who was visiting Havana at the time.

The participating teams would be the "All-Cubans," directed by Adolfo Luque and Miguel Angel González, and the "All Yankees," managed by Pop Lloyd.

Roster, All Yankees

Player	Position	U.S. Club
Newt Allen	3b	Kansas City Monarchs
Oscar Charleston	cf	Harrisburg Giants
Andy Cooper	p	Detroit Stars
Leon Daniels	2b	Detroit Stars
Alexander Gaston	c	Bacharch Giants
Art Henderson	p	Brooklyn Royal Giants
William Holland	p	Baltimore Black Sox
Crush Holloway	rf,cf	Bacharach Giants
Pop Lloyd	1b	Bacharach Giants
Richard Lundy	ss	Hilldale Club
Biz Mackey	c,rf	Kansas City Monarchs
Wilbur Rogan	p	Hilldale Club
Merven J. Ryan	p	Hilldale Club
Clinton Thomas	lf,cf	Hilldale Club
Frank Warfield	2b,lf	Hilldale Club

Roster, All-Cubans

Player	Position	U.S. Club
José Rodríguez	1b	—
Pelayo Chacon	ss	Cuban Stars (East)
Valentin Dreke		Cuban Stars (West)
José M. Fernandez	c	Cuban Stars (East)
Martin Dihigo	p	Cuban Stars (East)
Emilio Palmero	p	—
Cristobal Torriente		—
José Ramos	of	—
Ricardo Torres	c	—
Ramon Herrera	2b	—
Rafael Quintana	if	—
José Mendez	p	—
Oscar Levis(Panamanian)	p	Cuban Stars (East)

Player	Position	U.S. Club
Esteban Montalvo	of	Cuban Stars (West)
Juan Mirabal	p	Cuban Stars (East)
Manuel Cueto	3b	—
Baldomero Acosta	of	—

Games Played

Date	Winning Club		Losing Club		Winning Pitcher	Losing Pitcher
Feb 5	Cubans	6	Yankees	5	E. Palmero 1–0	A. Henderson 0–1
Feb 7	Yankees	6	Cubans	0	W. Rogan 1–0	O. Levis 0–1
Feb 8	Yankees	2	Cubans	1	A. Cooper 1–0	J. Mendez 0–1
Feb 12	Yankees	7	Cubans	4	W. Holland 1–0	O. Levis 0–2
Feb 14	Cubans	10	Yankees	3	J. Mendez 1–1	M.J. Ryan 0–1
Feb 15	Yankees	2	Cubans	1	A. Henderson 1–1	E. Palmero 1–1
Feb 16	Yankees	6	Cubans	4	W. Holland 2–0	M. Dihigo 0–1
Feb 16	Cubans	7	Yankees	7	Tied-J. Mirabal/M. Ryan	
(8)						

Club Standings

Pos	Clubs	G	W	T	T	Pct
1.	All Yankees	8	5	2	1	.714
2.	All-Cubans	8	2	5	1	.286
	Totals	16	7	7	2	.500

The Games

GAME ONE: THURDAY, FEBRUARY 5, 1925, AT ALMENDARES PARK

All Yankees	Pos	AB	R	H	O	A	E
F. Warfield	2b	4	1	2	3	3	0
C. Holloway	rf	4	0	0	2	0	2
R. Lundy	ss	4	1	0	3	3	0
O. Charleston	cf	3	1	2	2	0	0
J.H. Lloyd	1b	4	1	2	5	0	0
R. Mackey	c	2	1	2	7	2	0
C. Thomas	lf	3	0	1	0	1	0
N. Allen	3b	4	0	0	1	3	1
A. Henderson	p	3	0	0	1	2	0
W. Rogan	(x)	1	0	0	0	0	0
Totals		31	5	8	24	14	3

All-Cubans	Pos	AB	R	H	O	A	E
J. Ramos	cf	2	2	1	3	0	0
V. Dreke	lf	4	2	2	0	0	0
M. Cueto	3b	3	1	2	0	1	0
E. Montalvo	rf	4	0	0	1	0	0
P. Chacon	2b,ss	4	0	3	1	2	0
J. Rodríguez	1b	3	0	2	10	2	0
J.M. Fernandez	c	4	0	1	9	1	0
R. Quintana	ss	3	0	0	3	3	0
E. Palmero	p	3	1	2	0	1	0
C. Torriente	(xx)	0	0	0	0	0	0
R. Herrera	2b	0	0	0	0	0	0
Totals		30	6	13	27	10	1

(x)—Out for A. Henderson in Ninth.
(xx)—Base for R. Quintana in eighth.

All Yankees	203	000	000-5
All-Cubans	300	030	00x-6

Three-base hits: V. Dreke
Two-Base hits: J.H. Lloyd, C. Thomas, F. Warfield and O. Charleston
Sacrifice hits: C. Holloway, R. Mackey, M. Cueto, J. Rodríguez and J. Ramos
Stolen bases: F. Warfield (2), R. Lundy
Double-plays: R. Quintana, J. Rodríguez and J.M. Fernandez; R. Lundy and J.H. Lloyd; R. Lundy and R. Mackey
Bases on balls: A. Henderson 3, E. Palmero 6
Strikeouts: A. Hederson 3, E. Palmero 8
Winning Pitcher: E. Palmero

Losing Pitcher: A. Henderson
Time: 2 hours 5 minutes
Umpires: Valentin González (home) and José M. Magrinat (bases)
Scorer: Hilario Franquiz

GAME TWO: SATURDAY, FEBRUARY 7, 1925, AT ALMENDARES PARK

All-Cubans	Pos	AB	R	H	O	A	E		All Yankees	Pos	AB	R	H	O	A	E
J. Ramos	cf	4	0	0	0	1	0		F. Warfield	2b	4	1	2	3	5	0
V. Dreke	lf	4	0	2	1	0	0		C. Holloway	rf	4	1	3	0	0	0
M. Cueto	3b	3	0	2	1	1	1		O. Charleston	cf	5	0	1	3	2	0
C. Torriente	rf	3	0	1	1	0	0		R. Mackey	c	4	0	1	3	2	0
R. Herrera	2b	4	0	1	1	9	3		J.H. Lloyd	1b	4	0	0	12	0	0
J. Rodríguez	1b	3	0	1	11	0	0		R. Lundy	ss	3	1	1	4	3	0
J.M. Fernandez	c	4	0	1	5	2	0		C. Thomas	lf	3	0	0	3	1	0
R. Quintana	ss	3	0	0	4	3	0		N. Allen	3b	4	1	1	0	2	0
O. Levis	p	3	0	0	0	2	0		W. Rogan	p	4	2	2	1	0	0
E. Montalvo	(x)	1	0	0	0	0	0		Totals		35	6	11	27	13	0
Totals		32	0	8	24	18	4									

(x)—Out for R. Quintana in Ninth.

All-Cubans	000	000	000-0
All Yankees	100	000	23x-6

Three-base hits: N. Allen
Two-base hits: O. Charleston
Sacrifice hits: C. Holloway
Stolen Bases: V. Dreke, F. Warfield, J.H. Lloyd and R. Lundy
Bases on balls: O. Levis 3, W. Rogan 3
Strikeouts: O. Levis 3, W. Rogan 3
Passed balls: J.M. Fernandez 1
Winning Pitcher: W. Rogan
Losing Pitcher: O. Levis
Time: 2 hours
Umpires: Valentin González (home) and José M. Magrinat (bases)
Scorer: Hilario Franquiz

GAME THREE: FEBRUARY 8, 1925, AT ALMENDARES PARK II

All Yankees	Pos	AB	R	H	O	A	E		All-Cubans	Pos	AB	R	H	O	A	E
F. Warfield	2b	4	0	0	2	1	0		J. Ramos	cf	3	0	1	1	0	1
C. Holloway	rf	4	0	2	2	0	0		V. Dreke	lf	4	0	2	2	1	0
O. Charleston	cf	4	0	0	4	0	0		M. Cueto	3b	4	0	1	1	1	0
R. Mackey	c	3	1	2	7	0	0		C. Torriente	rf	2	0	0	3	0	0
J.H. Lloyd	1b	3	1	1	8	2	1		R. Herrera	2b	3	1	0	3	2	0
R. Lundy	ss	3	0	0	0	3	0		J. Rodríguez	1b,ss	3	0	0	8	1	1
C. Thomas	lf	4	0	0	1	1	0		J.M. Fernandez	c	2	0	1	2	1	0
N. Allen	3b	4	0	1	2	3	0		R. Quintana	ss	2	0	0	4	3	0
A. Cooper	p	3	0	1	1	3	0		J. Mendez	P	2	0	1	0	2	0
Totals		32	2	7	27	13	1		E. Palmero	p	0	0	0	0	3	0
									M. Dihigo	1b	2	0	1	2	0	0
									E. Montalvo	cf	2	0	0	1	0	0
									J. Mirabal	(x)	0	0	0	0	0	0
									O. Levis	(xx)	1	0	0	0	0	0
									Totals		1	1	7	27	14	2

(x)—Ran for J.M. Fernandez in Ninth.
(xx)—Out for E. Palmero in Ninth.

All Yankees	000	002	000 : 2
All-Cubans	010	000	000 : 1

Three-base hits: R. Mackey, J.H. Lloyd
Two-base hits: J. Ramos, V. Dreke
Sacrifice hits: J. Rodríguez, E. Palmero
Stolen bases: R. Mackey
Double-plays: A. Cooper to J.H. Lloyd to N. Allen; J. Mendez to R. Quintana to J. Rodríguez
Left on bases: All Yankees (6), All-Cubans (8)
Bases on balls: A. Cooper 4, J. Mendez 4, E. Palmero 0
Strikeouts: A. Cooper 5, J. Mendez 0, E. Palmero 2
Hits: J. Mendez 6 in 5.0 innings (19 a.b.)
Winning Pitcher: A. Cooper
Losing Pitcher: J. Mendez
Umpires: Valentin González (home) and José M. Magriinat (bases)
Scorer: Hilario Franquiz

GAME FOUR: THURSDAY, FEBRUARY 12, 1925, AT ALMENDARES PARK

All-Cubans	Pos	AB	R	H	O	A	E
J. Ramos	cf	5	1	1	1	0	1
V. Dreke	lf	3	0	0	1	0	0
P. Chacon	3b	3	1	1	1	1	0
C. Torriente	rf	4	1	1	1	0	0
R. Herrera	2b	4	0	1	2	6	0
J. Rodríguez	1b	4	1	3	12	0	0
J.M. Fernandez	c	3	0	1	5	2	2
R. Quintana	ss	3	0	0	1	2	0
O. Levis	p	3	0	1	0	2	0
E. Palmero	p	1	0	0	0	0	0
M. Cueto	(x)	1	0	1	0	0	0
J. Mendez	p	0	0	0	0	0	0
E. Montalvo	(xx)	0	0	0	0	0	0
Totals		33	4	10	24	13	3

All Yankees	Pos	AB	R	H	O	A	E
F. Warfield	2b	5	1	3	3	2	0
C. Holloway	cf	5	0	2	2	0	0
R. Mackey	rf	3	0	1	1	1	0
J.H. Lloyd	1b	4	1	0	6	1	1
R. Lundy	ss	3	1	2	3	4	0
C. Thomas	lf	3	2	3	4	0	0
N. Allen	3b	4	0	0	4	2	0
A. Gaston	c	3	2	1	4	0	0
W. Holland	p	3	0	0	1	0	1
Totals		33	7	12	27	11	2

(x)— Hit for J.M. Fernandez in ninth.
(xx)— Ran for M. Cueto in ninth.

All-Cubans	300	001	000-4
All Yankees	100	002	13x-7

Three-base hits: J. Rodríguez
Two-base hits: C. Torriente, F. Warfield, A. Gaston, R. Herrera, R. Lundy
Sacrifice hits: C. Thomas, R. Lundy, W. Holland
Double-plays: R. Mackey and J.H. Lloyd; R. Lundy, F. Warfield and J.H. Lloyd
Bases on balls: O. Levis 1, E. Palmero 0, W. Holland 2
Strikeouts: O. Levis 6, E. Palmero 0, W. Holland 4
Hit by pitcher; E. Palmero 1 (A. Gaston)
Wild pitch: W. Holland 1
Hits: O. Levis 9 in 7.0 innings (27 a.b)
Passed balls: J.M. Fernandez 1
Winning Pitcher: W. Holland
Losing Pitcher: O. Levis
Time: 2 hours
Umpires: Valentin González (home) and José M. Magrinat (bases)
Scorer: Hilario Franquiz

GAME FIVE: FEBRUARY 14, 1925, AT ALMENDARES PARK II

All Yankees	Pos	AB	R	H	O	A	E
F. Warfield	2b	4	1	2	2	2	0

All-Cubans	Pos	AB	R	H	O	A	E
J. Rodríguez	1b	5	1	2	10	0	0

All Yankees	Pos	AB	R	H	O	A	E
C. Holloway	cf	4	1	1	2	0	0
R. Mackey	rf	4	1	2	3	0	0
J.H. Lloyd	1b	4	0	1	7	0	2
R. Lundy	ss	4	0	0	1	1	0
C. Thomas	lf	4	0	2	2	0	0
N. Allen	3b	4	0	0	1	2	0
N. Gaston	c	4	0	0	5	0	0
M.J. Ryan	p	3	0	0	1	3	1
L. Daniels	(x)	1	0	0	0	0	0
Totals		36	3	10	24	8	3

(x)—Out for M.J. Ryan in ninth.

All-Cubans	Pos	AB	R	H	O	A	E
V. Dreke	lf	5	2	2	4	0	0
E. Montalvo	rf	3	1	2	0	0	0
C. Torriente	cf	4	1	1	1	0	0
P. Chacon	3b	5	1	1	2	4	1
R. Herrera	2b	5	2	2	6	3	1
J.M. Fernandez	c	4	1	2	2	0	0
R. Quintana	ss	4	1	3	2	2	0
J. Mirabal	p	1	0	0	0	1	0
J. Mendez	P	3	0	0	0	1	0
Totals		38	10	15	27	11	2

All Yankees	003	000	000 : 3
All-Cubans	500	021	20x : 10

Home runs: E. Montalvo, R. Quintan, J.M. Fernandez
Three-base hits: R. Mackey, J.H. Lloyd
Two-base hits: C. Thomas, E. Montalvo
Sacrifice hits: C. Torriente
Double-plays: R. Quintana and J. Rodríguez
Left on bases: All-Cubans (8), All Yankees (6)
Bases on balls: M.J. Ryan 2, J. Mirabal 2, J. Mendez 0
Strikeouts: M.J. Ryan 4, J. Mirabal 0, J. Mendez 1
Hits: J. Mirabal 7 in 3.0 innings (14 a.b.)
Winning Pitcher: J. Mendez
Losing Pitcher: M.J. Ryan
Umpires: Valentin González (home) and José M. Magrinat (bases)
Scorer: Julio Franquiz

GAME SIX: FEBRUARY 15, 1925, AT ALMENDARES PARK

All-Cubans	Pos	AB	R	H	O	A	E
J. Rodríguez	1b	4	0	1	11	0	0
V. Dreke	lf	3	0	0	0	0	0
E. Montalvo	rf	3	1	0	1	1	0
C. Torriente	cf	3	0	1	3	0	0
P. Chacon	3b,ss	4	0	0	0	2	0
R. Herrera	2b	4	0	0	0	2	0
J.M. Fernandez	c	3	0	0	4	1	0
R. Quintana	ss	2	0	0	4	4	0
E. Palmero	p	3	0	0	1	5	0
M. Cueto	3b	1	0	0	0	0	0
Totals		30	1	2	24	15	0

All Yankees	Pos	AB	R	H	O	A	E
F. Warfield	lf	4	0	0	2	0	0
C. Holloway	rf	3	0	0	1	0	1
R. Mackey	c	3	0	0	6	0	0
J.H. Lloyd	1b	3	1	1	15	0	0
R. Lundy	ss	3	0	1	1	5	0
C. Thomas	cf	2	1	1	1	0	0
N. Allen	3b	3	0	2	1	1	1
L. Daniels	2b	3	0	2	0	5	0
A. Henderson	p	2	0	0	0	4	0
Totals		26	2	7	27	15	2

All-Cubans	000	100	000-1
All Yankees	010	100	00x-2

Two-base hits: J.H. Lloyd
Sacrifice hits: C. Thomas, A. Henderson
Double-plays: E. Montalvo to J.M. Fernandez; E. Palmero to R. Quintana to J. Rodríguez
Base on balls: E. Palmero 1, A. Henderson 3
Strikeouts: E. Palmero 2, A. Henderson 5
Passed balls: R. Mackey 1
Winning Pitcher: A. Henderson
Losing Pitcher: E. Palmero
Time: 1 hour 43 minutes
Umpires: Valentin González (home) and José M. Magrinat (bases)
Scorer: Hilario Franquiz

GAME SEVEN: FEBRUARY 16, 1925, AT ALMENDARES PARK (FIRST GAME)

All Yankees	Pos	AB	R	H	O	A	E
F. Warfield	lf	4	0	0	5	0	0
C. Holloway	rf	5	1	2	2	0	0
R. Mackey	c	4	1	0	7	0	1
J.H. Lloyd	1b	3	1	2	8	1	0
R. Lundy	ss	4	0	1	3	4	1
C. Thomas	cf	4	1	0	3	0	0
N. Allen	3b	4	1	1	0	0	1
L. Daniels	2b	4	1	2	0	2	0
W. Holland	p	4	0	1	0	2	0
Totals		36	6	9	27	9	3

All-Cubans	Pos	AB	R	H	O	A	E
R. Herrera	2b	4	0	1	2	3	0
V. Dreke	lf	4	0	0	2	0	0
E. Montalvo	rf	4	0	0	1	0	0
C. Torriente	cf	4	1	1	2	0	0
P. Chacon	3b	4	1	2	1	5	0
R. Torres	1b	2	1	0	11	0	0
J.M. Fernandez	c	4	1	2	8	1	0
R. Quintana	ss	2	0	1	1	3	0
M. Dihigo	p	4	0	0	0	2	0
M. Cueto	(x)	1	0	0	0	0	0
J. Mendez	(xx)	0	0	0	0	0	0
J. Ramos	(xxx)	1	0	0	0	0	0
Totals		34	4	7	27	14	1

(x)—Out for R. Torres in ninth.
(xx)—Ran for M. Cueto in ninth.
(xxx)—Out for R. Quintana in ninth.

All Yankees	012	000	012 : 6
All-Cubans	000	021	001 : 4

Two-base hits: J.M. Fernandez
Sacrifice hits: R. Quintana
Stolen bases: C. Torriente
Double-plays: R. Lundy and J.H. Lloyd
Bases on balls: M. Dihigo 2, W. Holland 1
Strikeouts: M. Dihigo 7, W. Holland 5
Winning Pitcher: W. Holland
Losing Pitcher: M. Dihigo
Time: 1 hour 50 minutes
Umpires: Valentin González (home) and José M. Magrinat (bases)
Scorer: Julio Franquiz

GAME EIGHT: FEBRUARY 16, 1925, AT ALMENDARES PARK (SECOND GAME)

All-Cubans	Pos	AB	R	H	O	A	E
R. Herrera	2b	4	1	0	2	3	0
V. Dreke	lf	4	1	2	1	0	0
E. Montalvo	rf	3	0	1	0	1	0
C. Torriente	cf	1	0	0	1	0	0
P. Chacon	3b	4	1	2	2	3	1
R. Torres	1b	3	1	1	6	0	0
J.M. Fernandez	c	3	0	1	4	1	0
R. Quintana	ss	3	0	0	3	3	0
J. Mirabal	p	0	0	0	0	0	0
J. Mendez	p	2	0	0	0	0	0
J. Ramos	cf	3	1	3	1	0	0
M. Dihigo	p	1	1	1	0	0	0
Totals		31	7	10	21	11	1

All Yankees	Pos	AB	R	H	O	A	E
F. Warfield	lf	4	0	0	4	0	0
C. Holloway	rf	4	1	1	2	0	0
R. Mackey	c	4	2	2	1	0	0
J.H. Lloyd	1b	3	2	2	8	0	0
R. Lundy	ss	4	1	4	2	2	1
C. Thomas	cf	4	0	2	2	0	0
N. Allen	3b	3	0	1	2	1	0
L. Daniels	2b	3	0	1	0	1	0
M.J. Ryan	p	3	1	1	0	2	1
Totals		32	7	14	21	6	2

All-Cubans	000	104	2–7
All Yankees	420	010	0–7

Three-base hits: C. Holloway, R. Mackey, C. Thomas, N. Allen
Two-Base hits: R. Mackey, R. Torres
Stolen bases: J. Ramos, R. Lundy
Double-plays: M.J. Ryan, N. Allen and J.H. Lloyd

Bases on balls: J. Mirabal 1, J. Mendez 1, M. Dihigo 0, M.J. Ryan 1
Strikeouts: J. Mirabal 0, J. Mendez 0, M. Dihigo 1, M.J. Ryan 1
Hits: J. Mirabal 3 in 0.1 innings (4 a.b); J. Mendez 10 in 5.2 (24 a.b.)
Time: 1 hour 25 minutes
Umpires: Valentin González (home) and José M. Magrinat (bases)
Scorer: Hilario Franquiz

Final Statistcs

ALL YANKEES—1925

Individual Pitching

Pitcher	G	GC	W	L	T	Pct	IP	VB	R	H	BB	SO	ERT
Andy Cooper	1	1	1	0	0	1.000	9.0	31	1	7	4	3	1.00
Art Henderson	2	2	1	1	0	.500	17.0	60	7	10	6	8	3.71
William Holland	2	2	2	0	0	1.000	18.0	69	8	17	3	9	4.00
Wilbur Rogan	1	1	1	0	0	1.000	9.0	32	0	8	3	3	0.00
Merven J. Ryan	2	2	0	1	1	.500	15.0	64	17	25	3	5	9.87
Totals	8	8	5	2	1	.714	68.0	256	33	67	19	28	4.37

Individual Batting

Players	Pos	G	AB	R	H	TB	2B	3B	HR	SH	SB	Pct
Newton Allen	3b	8	30	2	8	10	0	1	0	0	0	.267
Oscar Charleston	cf	3	11	1	3	5	2	0	0	0	0	.273
Andy Cooper	P	1	3	0	1	1	0	0	0	0	0	.333
Alexander Gaston	c	2	7	0	1	2	1	0	0	0	1	.143
Art Henderson	p	2	5	0	0	0	0	0	0	1	0	.000
William Holland	p	2	7	0	1	1	0	0	0	1	0	.143
Crush Holloway	rf,cf	8	33	4	11	13	0	1	0	2	0	.333
John H. Lloyd	1b	8	28	7	9	15	2	2	0	0	1	.321
Raleigh Mackey	c,rf	8	27	3	9	16	1	3	0	1	2	.333
Leon Daniels	2b	4	11	1	5	5	0	0	0	0	0	.455
Wilbur Rogan	p	5	5	2	2	2	0	0	0	0	0	.400
Merven J. Ryan	p	2	6	1	1	1	0	0	0	0	0	.167
Clinton Thomas	lf,cf	8	27	4	9	13	2	1	0	2	2	.333
Frank Warfield	2b,lf	8	33	4	8	10	2	0	0	0	3	.242
Totals		8	261	38	78	104	10	8	0	7	9	.299

Individual Fielding

Players	Pos	G	O	A	E	Pct
Newton Allen	3b	8	11	14	3	.893
Oscar Charleston	cf	3	7	0	0	1.000
Andy Cooper	p	1	1	2	0	1.000
Alexander Gaston	c	2	9	0	0	1.000
Art Henderson	p	2	1	6	0	1.000
William Holland	p	2	1	2	1	.750
Crush Holloway	rf,cf	8	13	0	3	.813
John H. Lloyd	1b	8	74	6	2	.976
Raleigh Mackey	c,rf	8	33	3	1	.973
Leon Daniels	2b	4	0	8	0	1.000
Wilbur Rogan	p	5	1	0	0	1.000
Merven J. Ryan	p	2	1	5	2	.750
Clinton Thomas	lf,cf	8	15	3	0	1.000
Frank Warfield	2b,lf	8	24	13	0	1.000
Totals		8	204	89	15	.951

ALL-CUBANS

Individual Pitching

Pitcher	G	GC	W	L	Pct	IP	R	H	W	SO	ERT
José Mendez	3	0	1	1	.500	.	.	.	.	.	....
Emilio Palmero	4	2	1	1	.500	.	.	.	.	.	....
Martin Dihigo	2	1	0	1	.000	.	.	.	.	.	....
Oscar Levis	2	1	0	2	.000	.	.	.	.	.	....
Totals	11	4	2	5	.286	.	.	.	.	.	....

Individual Batting

Players	Club	AB	R	H	TB	2B	3B	HR	SH	SB	Pct
Manuel Cueto	AC	13	1	7	7	0	0	0	1	0	.538
José Rodríguez	AC	22	2	9	11	0	1	0	2	0	.409
Pelayo Chacon	AC	24	4	9	9	0	0	0	0	0	.375
Valentin Dreke	AC	31	5	10	13	1	1	0	0	1	.323
José M. Fernandez	AC	28	2	9	13	1	0	1	0	0	.321
Martin Dihigo	AC	7	1	2	2	0	0	0	0	0	.286
Emilio Palmero	AC	7	1	2	2	0	0	0	0	0	.286
Cristobal Torriente	AC	21	3	5	6	1	0	0	1	1	.238
José Ramos	AC	28	4	6	7	1	0	0	1	1	.214
Ricardo Torres	AC	5	1	1	2	1	0	0	0	0	.200
Ramon Herrera	AC	28	4	5	6	1	0	0	0	0	.179
Rafael Quintana	AC	22	1	4	7	0	0	1	1	0	.186
José Mendez	AC	7	0	1	1	0	0	0	0	0	.143
Oscar Levis	AC	7	0	1	1	0	0	0	0	0	.143
Esteban Montalvo	AC	21	3	2	6	1	0	1	0	0	.095
Juan Mirabal	AC	1	0	0	0	0	0	0	0	0	.000

Individual Fielding (Both Clubs)

Pitcher	Club	G	GC	W	L	Pct
William Holland	AY	2	2	2	0	1.000
Wilbur Rogan	AY	1	1	1	0	.000
Andy Cooper	AY	1	1	1	0	1.000
José Mendez	AC	3	0	1	1	.500
Art Henderson	AY	2	2	1	1	.500
Emilio Palmero	AC	4	2	1	1	.500
Martin Dihigo	AC	2	1	0	1	.000
Merven J. Ryan	AY	2	1	0	1	.500
Oscar Levis	AC	2	1	0	2	.000
Totals		19	11	7	7	.500

Individual Batting (Both Clubs)

Players	Club	AB	R	H	TB	2B	3B	HR	SH	SB	Pct
Manuel Cueto	AC	13	1	7	7	0	0	0	1	0	.538
Leon Daniels	AY	11	1	5	5	0	0	0	0	0	.455
José Rodríguez	AC	22	2	9	11	0	1	0	2	0	.409
Wilbur Rogan	AY	5	2	2	2	0	0	0	0	0	.400
Pelayo Chacon	AC	24	4	9	9	0	0	0	0	0	.375
Crush Holloway	AY	33	4	11	13	0	1	0	2	0	.333
Raleigh Mackey	AY	27	3	9	15	1	3	0	1	2	.333
Clinton Thomas	AY	27	4	9	13	2	1	0	2	2	.333
Andy Cooper	AY	3	0	1	1	0	0	0	0	0	.333
Valentin Dreke	AC	31	5	10	13	1	1	0	0	1	.323
José M. Fernandez	AC	28	2	9	13	1	0	1	0	0	.321
John H. Lloyd	AY	28	7	9	15	2	2	0	0	1	.321

Players	Club	AB	R	H	TB	2B	3B	HR	SH	SB	Pct
Martin Dihigo	AC	7	1	2	2	0	0	0	0	0	.286
Emilio Palmero	AC	7	1	2	2	0	0	0	0	0	.286
Oscar Charleston	AY	11	1	3	5	2	0	0	0	0	.273
Newt Allen	AY	30	2	8	10	0	1	0	0	0	.267
Frank Warfield	AY	33	4	8	10	2	0	0	0	3	.242
Cristobal Torriente	AC	21	3	5	6	1	0	0	1	1	.238
José Ramos	AC	28	4	6	7	1	0	0	1	1	.214
Ricardo Torres	AC	5	1	1	2	1	0	0	0	0	.200
Ramon Herrera	AC	28	4	5	6	1	0	0	0	0	.179
Rafael Quintana	AC	22	1	4	7	0	0	1	1	0	.186
Merven J. Ryan	AY	6	1	1	1	0	0	0	0	0	.167
José Mendez	AC	7	0	1	1	0	0	0	0	0	.143
William Holland	AY	7	0	1	1	0	0	0	0	0	.143
Oscar Levis	AC	7	0	1	1	0	0	0	0	0	.143
Alexander Gaston	AY	7	0	1	7	1	0	0	0	1	.143
Esteban Montalvo	AC	21	3	2	6	1	0	1	0	0	.095
Juan Mirabal	AC	1	0	0	0	0	0	0	0	0	.000
Art Henderson	AY	5	0	0	0	0	0	0	1	0	.000

(30)

◆ 14 ◆
1938
Homestead Grays

In the 1938 season Josh Gibson returned to Cuba wearing the uniform of the famous Homestead Grays, which had easily won the 1938 Negro League Championship. Making up the All-Star team that traveled to Cuba to play six games under the Grays' name were members of the Grays, the New York Black Yankees, the Pittsburgh Crawfords, and the Newark Eagles.

Roster

Player	Position	Regular Season Club, 1938
Samuel Bankhead	of	Pittsburgh Crawfords
Barney Brown	p,ph	NY Black Yankees
Raymond Brown	p, ph	Homestead Grays
Matthew Carlisle	2b	Homestead Grays
Thomas Dukes	c	Homestead Grays
Joshua Gibson	c,1b	Homestead Grays
E. Victor Harris	of	Homestead Grays
Norman Jackson	ss,pr	Homestead Grays
Walter Leonard	1b	Homestead Grays
Terris McDuffie	p	NY Black Yankees
Roy Partlow	p,ph	Homestead Grays
Harry Williams	3b	Homestead Grays
James Williams	of	Homestead Grays
Willie Wells	3b,ss	Newark Eagles

Manager: Vic Harris

Samuel "Sam" Bankhead started with the Birmingham Black Barons (1930). He later played with the Nashville Elite Giants, Pittsburgh Crawfords [and] Homestead Grays.

Barney "Brinquitos" Brown.

Raymond "Jabao" or "Red" Brown.

Matthew Carlisle began with the Birmingham Black Barons (1931) and later played with the Montgomery Sox Flock, Memphis Sox Net and the Homestead Grays.

Thomas Dukes.

Joshua Gibson.

Elander Victor "Vic," Harris began with the Cleveland Tate Stars (1923) and later played with the Cleveland Browns, Chicago American Giants and Homestead Grays.

Norman "Jelly" Jackson began with the Cleveland Sox Net (1934) and went on to play with the Homestead Grays.

Walter F. "Buck" Leonard.

Terris McDuffie played with the Birmingham Black Barons (1930), Baltimore Black Sox, New York Black Yankees and Homestead Grays.

Roy Partlow played with the Cincinnati Tigers (1934), Memphis Red Sox and Homestead Grays.

Willie Wells.

Harry Williams.

James Williams began with the Homestead Grays in 1937.

Playing against the Homestead Grays were the traditional Almendares and Habana.

Almendares: José Maria Fernandez and Ramon Couto (c); A. Silveira (1b); José Abreu (2b); Pedro Arango (3b); Antonio "Pollo" Rodríguez (ss); Manuel Cueto, Lazaro Salazar, Rogelio Linares and Antonio (Helio) Mirabal (of) and Rene Monteagudo, Rodolfo Fernandez and Jorge Comellas (p). Manager: Adolfo Luque.

Habana: Salvador Hernandez (c); Gilberto Torres (1b); Fermin Valdés (2b); Clemente (Sungo) Carrera (3b), Joe Olivares (ss); Mario Veitia, Cando López and Antonio Castano (of) and Silvino Ruiz and Tomas De la Cruz (p). Manager: Julio Rojo.

After four matches (two with Habana and two with Almendares), the series concluded with two matches against a team composed of selected players from the Cuban clubs as well as Silvio García (ss) and Rafael "Sungo" Pedroso (c).

Games Played

Date	Winning Club		Losing Club		Winning Pitcher	Losing Pitcher
Oct 8	Habana	6	Homestead Grays	2	S. Ruiz 1–0	T. McDuffie 0–1
Oct 10	Homestead Grays	2	Almendares	1	R. Brown 1–0	R. Monteagudo 0–1
Oct 11	Habana	7	Homestead Grays	2	T. de la Cruz 1–0	R. Partlow 0–1
Oct 12	Homestead Grays	1	Almendares	0	B. Brown 1–0	J. Comellas 0–1
Oct 15	Picked Nine	3	Homestead Grays	2	R. Monteagudo 1–1	R. Partlow 0–2
Oct 17	Picked Nine	5	Homestead Grays	4	S. Ruiz 2–0	B. Brown 1–1
(6)						

Club Standings

Clubs	G	W	L	Pct
Habana	2	2	0	1.000
Picked Nine	2	2	0	1.000
Homestead Grays	6	2	4	.333
Almendares	2	0	2	.000
Totals	12	6	6	.500

The Games

GAME ONE: OCTOBER 8, 1938, AT LA TROPICAL

Homestead Grays	Pos	AB	R	H	O	A	E	Habana	Pos	AB	R	H	O	A	E
V. Harris	lf	3	0	0	2	0	0	F. Valdés	2b	5	1	3	1	3	0
S. Bankhead	cf	4	0	0	1	0	0	J. Olivares	ss	5	1	2	0	3	0
J. Williams	rf	4	0	0	1	0	0	G. Torres	1b	5	0	1	10	3	0
J. Gibson	c	3	2	1	6	1	0	M. Veitia	lf	4	0	0	3	0	0
W. Leonard	1b	4	0	2	9	0	0	C. Carreras	3b	4	0	0	1	2	0
W. Wells	3b	4	0	1	0	2	0	S. Hernandez	c	3	1	1	5	1	0
L. Carlisle	2b	3	0	0	4	4	0	A. Castano	rf	3	1	1	2	0	0
J. Jackson	ss	2	0	0	1	3	0	C. López	cf	3	2	3	2	0	0
T. McDuffie	p	1	0	0	0	0	0	S. Ruiz	p	2	0	0	3	2	0
H. Williams	3b	1	0	0	0	0	1	Totals		34	6	11	27	14	0
B. Brown	(x)	1	0	0	0	0	0								
R. Partlow	p	0	0	0	0	0	0								
Totals		30	2	4	24	11	1								

(x)—Out for T. McDuffie in eight.

Homestead Grays	010	100	000–2
Habana	022	101	00x–6

Runs batted in: L. Carlisle, C. López (2), J. Olivares, G. Torres, W. Leonard, F. Valdés (2)
Two-base hits: C. López (2), J. Olivares and W. Leonard
Sacrifice hits: S. Ruiz and C. López
Stolen bases: F. Valdés
Bases on balls: T. McDuffie 2, R. Partlow 1, S. Ruiz 3
Strikeouts: T. McDuffie 5, R. Partlow 0, S. Ruiz 3
Hits: T. McDuffie 10 in 7.0 innings (30 vb)
Runs: T. McDuffie (6-6), R. Partlow (0-0), S. Ruiz (2-2)
Winning pitcher: S. Ruiz (1-0)
Losing pitcher: T. McDuffie (0-1)
Time: 1 hour 50 minutes
Umpires: Amado Maestri (home) and Bernardino Rodríguez (bases)
Scorer: Julio Franquiz

GAME TWO: OCTOBER 9, 1838, AT STADIUM LA TROPICAL

Homestead Grays	Pos	AB	R	H	O	A	E
V. Harris	lf	4	0	3	0	0	0
S. Bankhead	cf	4	0	1	0	0	0
J. Williams	rf	3	1	0	1	0	0
J. Gibson	c	4	0	2	4	2	0
W. Leonard	1b	4	0	0	17	0	0
W. Wells	ss	3	0	0	4	2	0
H. Williams	3b	4	1	2	0	2	0
L. Carlisle	2b	3	0	0	1	5	0
R. Brown	p	3	0	0	0	5	0
Totals		32	2	8	27	16	0

Almendares	Pos	AB	R	H	O	A	E
J. Abreu	2b	2	0	0	2	4	0
M. Cueto	lf	4	0	0	2	0	0
L. Salazar	cf	3	0	0	3	0	0
R. Linares	rf	2	0	0	1	1	0
A. Silveira	1b	4	0	1	8	1	0
A. Rodríguez	ss	3	0	0	3	4	0
P. Arango	3b	4	1	1	1	1	0
J.M. Fernandez	c	3	0	0	6	1	0
R. Monteagudo	p	3	0	1	1	1	0
Totals		28	1	3	27	13	0

Homestead Grays	100	000	010 :	2
Almendares	000	001	000 :	1

Runs batted in: G. Gibson, M. Cueto, V. Harris
Two-base Hits: J. Gibson
Stolen bases: H. Williams, M. Cueto
Base on balls: R. Monteagudo 2, R. Brown 6
Strikeouts: R. Monteagudo 3, R. Brown 4
Runs: R. Monteagudo (2–2), R. Brown (1–1)
Winning pitcher: R. Brown (1–0)
Losing pitcher: R. Monteagudo (0–1)
Time: 1 hour 40 minutes
Umpires: Amado Maestri (home) and Bernardino Rodríguez (bases)

GAME THREE: OCTOBER 10, 1938, AT STADIUM LA TROPICAL

Homestead Grays	Pos	AB	R	H	O	A	E
V. Harris	lf	2	1	0	1	0	0
S. Bankhead	cf	4	0	1	2	0	0
J. Williams	rf	3	1	0	3	0	0
J. Gibson	c	4	0	2	4	2	0
W. Leonard	1b	4	0	0	8	0	0
W. Wells	ss	4	0	0	4	5	0
H. Williams	3b	4	0	1	1	0	0
L. Carlisle	2b	3	0	1	3	1	0
R. Partlow	p	2	0	0	0	2	0
T. McDuffie	p	1	0	0	0	1	1

Habana	Pos	AB	R	H	O	A	E
F. Valdés	2b	5	0	1	0	6	0
J. Olivares	ss	5	1	2	5	0	1
G. Torres	1b	5	1	2	9	0	0
M. Veitia	lf	3	2	1	4	0	0
C. Carreras	3b	2	1	1	1	3	0
S. Hernandez	c	3	1	1	1	1	0
A. Castano	rf	3	0	2	2	0	0
C. López	cf	4	0	3	5	0	0
T. de la Cruz	p	4	0	0	0	1	0
S. Ruiz	p	0	0	0	0	0	0

Homestead Grays	Pos	AB	R	H	O	A	E
B. Brown	p	1	0	0	0	0	0
R. Brown	(x)	1	0	0	0	0	0
Totals		32	2	5	24	11	1

(x)—Out for L. Carlisle in ninth.

Habana	Pos	AB	R	H	O	A	E
Totals		34	7	13	27	11	1

Homestead Grays	100	000	010 : 2
Habana	400	020	10x : 7

Runs batted in: C. Carreras 2, A. Castano 2, W. Leonard, W. Wells 1, C. López 2
Two-base hits: J. Olivares, C. Carreras
Three-base hits: A. Castano
Base on balls: R. Partlow 4, T. McDuffie 1, B. Brown 0, T.de la Cruz 2, S. Ruiz 1
Strikeouts: R. Partlow 4, T. McDuffie 0, B. Brown 0, T.de la Cruz 1, S. Ruiz 0
Hits: R. Partlow 6 in 4.0 (17vb); T. McDuffie 5 in 2.0 (9vb); B. Brown 2 in 2.0 8vb); T. de la Cruz 5 in 7.1 (27vb); S. Ruiz 0 in 1.2 (5vb)
Runs: R. Partlow (4-4), T. McDuffie (2-1), B. Brown (1-1), T. de la Cruz (2-2), S. Ruiz (0-0)
Winning pitcher: T.de la Cruz (1-0)
Losing pitcher: R. Partlow (0-1)
Time: 2 hours 5 minutes
Umpires: Amado Maestri (home) and Bernardino Rodríguez (bases)

GAME FOUR: OCTOBER 12, 1938, AT STADIUM LA TROPICAL

Homestead Grays	Pos	AB	R	H	O	A	E
V. Harris	lf	4	0	0	2	0	0
S. Bankhead	cf	4	0	0	4	0	0
H. Williams	3b	4	0	0	1	2	0
J. Gibson	c	4	0	0	4	2	0
W. Leonard	1b	2	1	0	14	0	0
W. Wells	ss	3	0	1	1	3	0
J. Williams	rf	3	0	0	0	0	0
L. Carlisle	2b	2	0	0	1	3	0
B. Brown	p	2	0	1	0	4	0
R. Fernandez	(x)	1	0	0	0	0	0
Totals		28	1	2	27	10	0

(x)—Out for R. Linares in Ninth.

Almendares	Pos	AB	R	H	O	A	E
A. Mirabal	rf	4	0	0	2	0	0
J. Abreu	2b	4	0	0	1	3	1
L. Salazar	cf	4	0	2	4	0	0
R. Linares	1b	3	0	0	12	1	0
S. Amaro	lf	2	0	0	4	0	0
P. Arango	3b	3	0	1	0	5	0
A. Rodríguez	ss	3	0	0	3	5	0
R. Couto	c	3	0	0	1	0	0
J. Comellas	p	2	0	0	0	0	0
Totals		29	0	3	27	16	1

Homestead Grays	010	000	000 : 1
Almendares	000	000	000 : 0

Base on balls: J. Comellas 3, R. Brown 2
Strikeouts: J. Comellas 0, B. Brown 3
Runs: J. Comellas (1–0), B. Brown (0–0)
Winning pitcher: B. Brown (1–0)
Losing pitcher: J. Comellas (0–1)
Time: 1 hour 46 minutes
Umpires: Amado Maestri (home) and Bernardino Rodríguez (bases)

GAME FIVE: OCTOBER 15, 1938, AT STADIUM LA TROPICAL

Homestead Grays	Pos	AB	R	H	O	A	E
S. Bankhead	cf	5	0	2	1	0	0
V. Harris	lf	3	0	0	2	0	0
H. Williams	3b	4	1	2	0	1	0
J. Gibson	c	4	1	2	7	0	0
W. Leonard	1b	3	0	1	7	1	0
W. Wells	ss	4	0	2	1	3	0

Seleccion	Pos	AB	R	H	O	A	E
J. Abreu	2b	5	1	2	3	3	1
J. Olivares	ss	3	0	1	3	2	0
L. Salazar	rf	4	0	1	0	0	0
G. Torres	1b	3	1	3	8	1	0
S. Amaro	lf	4	1	1	1	0	0
S. García	3b	4	0	0	0	1	0

Homestead Grays	Pos	AB	R	H	O	A	E
J. Williams	rf	3	0	0	2	0	0
L. Carlisle	2b	4	0	1	4	1	0
R. Brown	p	2	0	0	0	1	0
T. McDuffie	p	0	0	0	0	0	0
R. Partlow	p	1	0	0	0	0	0
B. Brown	(x)	1	0	0	0	0	0
Totals		34	2	10	24	7	0

Seleccion	Pos	AB	R	H	O	A	E
C. López	cf	3	0	2	4	0	0
J.M. Fernandez	c	2	0	0	6	1	0
R. Monteagudo	p	3	0	0	1	1	0
S. Hernandez	c	1	0	0	1	0	0
Totals		32	3	10	27	9	1

(x)— Out for R. Partlow in ninth.

Runs batted in: W. Leonard, J. Gibson. C. López 2, G. Torres
Two-base hits: J. Gibson, S. Amaro
Stolen base: J. Abreu
Base on balls: R. Monteagudo 2, R. Brown 4, T. McDuffie 0, R. Partlow 0
Strikeouts: R. Monteagudo 4, R. Brown 0, T. McDuffie 0, R. Partlow 5
Hits: R. Brown 3 in 4.2 (16vb), T. McDuffie 0 in 0.0 (0vb), R. Partlow 7 in 3.1(16)
Runs: R. Monteagudo (2-1), R. Brown (0-0), T. McDuffie (0-0), R. Partlow (3-3)
Winning pitcher: R. Monteagudo (1-1)
Losing pitcher: R. Partlow (0-1)
Time: Two hours
Umpires: Amado Maestri (home) and Bernardino Rodríguez (bases)

GAME SIX: OCTOBER 17, 1938, AT STADIUM LA TROPICAL

Homestead Grays	Pos	AB	R	H	O	A	E
S. Bankhead	cf,lf	4	0	2	2	0	0
V. Harris	lf,cf	4	1	1	2	1	0
H. Williams	3b	4	1	1	0	3	0
J. Gibson	1b	4	0	1	8	0	1
T. Dukes	c	4	0	1	6	0	0
W. Wells	ss	4	1	2	1	2	0
J. Williams	lf	3	0	1	4	0	0
L. Carlisle	2b	3	0	0	1	3	0
B. Brown	p	0	1	0	0	0	0
R. Brown	p	2	0	0	0	0	0
W. Leonard	(x)	1	0	0	0	0	0
R. Partlow	(xx)	1	0	1	0	0	0
N. Jackson	(xxx)	0	0	0	0	0	0
Totals		34	4	10	24	9	1

Seleccion	Pos	AB	R	H	O	A	E
F. Valdés	2b,3b	4	1	1	2	2	0
J. Olivares	ss	1	0	0	0	1	1
L. Salazar	rf	3	1	2	1	0	0
G. Torres	1b	4	1	2	13	1	0
S. Amaro	lf	3	0	2	4	0	0
S. García	3b,ss	4	0	0	1	3	1
C. López	cf	3	0	1	0	0	0
S. Hernandez	c	3	0	0	3	1	1
S. Ruiz	p	3	1	1	1	2	0
J. Abreu	2b	3	1	1	1	2	0
R. Pedroso	c	0	0	0	0	1	0
A. Castano	lf	0	0	0	0	0	0
Totals		31	5	9	27	13	3

(x)-Out for J. Williams in ninth.
(xx)-Hit for L. Carlisle in ninth.
(xxx)-Ran for L. Carlisle in ninth.

Homestead Grays	101	001	001–4
Seleccion	004	000	01x–5

Runs batted in: Gibson 2, R. Partlow, T. Dukes, G. Torres, L. Salazar (2), F. Valdés, S. García
Two-base hits: J. Gibson (2), W. Wells
Three-base hit: T. Dukes
Base on balls: B. Brown 0, R. Brown 2, S. Ruiz 0
Strikeouts: B. Brown 2, R. Brown 4, S. Ruiz 3
Hits: B. Brown 6 in 2.1 (4–4), R. Brown 3 in 5.2 (1–1), S. Ruiz 10 in 9.0 (4–4)
Winning pitcher: S. Ruiz (2–0)
Losing pitcher: B. Brown (1–1)

Final Statistics

Batting (All Clubs)

Clubs	G	AB	R	H	HR	RBI	Pct
Habana	2	68	13	24	1	12	.353
Selección	2	63	8	19	2	7	.301
Homestead Grays	6	191	13	39	1	12	.204
Almendares	2	57	1	6	1	1	.105

Fielding (All Clubs)

Clubs	G	O	A	E	TC	Pct
Almendares	2	54	29	1	84	.988
Habana	2	54	25	1	80	.987
Homestead Grays	6	150	68	3	221	.986
Selección	2	54	22	4	80	.952

Individual Pitching (All Clubs)

Pitcher	Club	G	GS	W	L	Pct
S. Ruiz	HAB-SEL	3	2	2	0	1.000
R. Brown	HMS	3	1	1	0	1.000
T.de la Cruz	HAB	1	0	1	0	1.000
R. Monteagudo	ALM-SEL	2	2	1	1	.500
B. Brown	HMS	3	1	1	1	.500
J. Comellas	ALM	1	1	0	1	.000
T. McDuffie	HMS	3	0	0	1	.000
R. Partlow	HMS	3	0	0	2	.000

Individual Batting (All Clubs)

Player	Club	G	AB	R	H	2B	3B	HR	RBI	SB	Pct
C. López	HAB-SEL	4	13	2	8	2	0	0	6	1	.615
A. Castano	HAB-SEL	2	6	1	3	0	1	0	2	0	.500
G. Torres	HAB-SEL	4	17	3	8	0	0	0	3	0	.470
F. Valdés	HAB-SEL	3	14	2	5	0	0	0	2	1	.357
J. Olivares	HAB-SEL	3	14	2	5	2	0	0	1	0	.357
L. Salazar	ALM-SEL	4	14	1	5	0	0	0	2	0	.357
J. Gibson	HSG	6	23	3	8	4	0	0	4	0	.347
S. Amaro	ALM-SEL	3	9	1	3	1	0	0	0	0	.333
H. Williams	HSG	6	21	3	6	0	0	0	0	1	.286
P. Arango	ALM	2	7	1	2	0	0	0	0	0	.286
W. Wells	HSG	6	22	1	6	1	0	0	1	0	.272
R. Partlow	HSG	4	4	0	1	0	0	0	1	0	.250
T. Dukes	HSG	1	4	0	1	0	0	0	0	0	.250
A. Silveira	ALM	1	4	0	1	0	0	0	0	0	.250
S. Bankhead	HSG	6	25	0	6	0	0	0	0	0	.240
J. Abreu	ALM-SEL	4	14	2	3	0	0	0	0	1	.214
V. Harris	HSG	6	20	2	4	0	0	0	1	0	.200
S. Hernandez	HAB-SEL	4	10	2	2	0	0	0	0	0	.200
B. Brown	HSG	5	5	1	1	0	0	0	0	0	.200
S. Ruiz	HAB-SEL	3	5	1	1	0	0	0	0	0	.200
W. Leonard	HSG	6	18	1	3	1	0	0	3	0	.167
C. Carreras	HAB	2	6	2	1	1	0	0	2	0	.167
R. Monteagudo	ALM-SEL	2	6	0	1	0	0	0	0	0	.167
M. Veitia	HAB	2	7	2	1	0	0	0	0	0	.143
L. Carlisle	HSG	6	18	0	2	0	0	0	1	0	.111
J. Williams	HSG	6	19	2	1	0	0	0	0	0	.052
R. Fernandez	ALM	1	1	0	0	0	0	0	0	0	.000

Player	Club	G	AB	R	H	2B	3B	HR	RBI	SB	Pct
N. Jackson	HSG	2	2	0	0	0	0	0	0	0	.000
J. Comellas	ALM-SEL	1	2	0	0	0	0	0	0	0	.000
T. McDuffie	HSG	3	2	0	0	0	0	0	0	0	.000
R. Couto	ALM	1	3	0	0	0	0	0	0	0	.000
T. de la Cruz	HSB-SEL	1	4	0	0	0	0	0	0	0	.000
M. Cueto	ALM	1	4	0	0	0	0	0	1	1	.000
A. Mirabal	ALM	1	4	0	0	0	0	0	0	0	.000
J.M. Fernandez	ALM-SEL	2	5	0	0	0	0	0	0	0	.000
R. Linares	ALM	2	5	0	0	0	0	0	0	0	.000
A. Rodríguez	ALM	2	6	0	0	0	0	0	0	0	.000
S. García	SEL	2	8	0	0	0	0	0	1	0	.000
R. Brown	HSG	4	8	0	0	0	0	0	0	0	.000
R. Pedroso	SEL	1	0	0	0	0	0	0	0	0	.000

HOMESTEAD GRAYS

Individual Pitching

Pitchers	G	GS	GC	GR	W	L	Pct	IP	AB	R	ER	H	W	K	ERA
Terris McDuffie	3	1	0	2	0	1	.000	9.0	39	8	7	15	2	6	7.00
Raymond Brown	3	2	1	1	1	0	1.000	19.1	62	2	2	9	10	8	0.93
Barney Brown	3	2	1	1	1	1	.500	13.1	50	5	5	11	2	5	3.38
Roy Partlow	3	1	0	2	0	2	.000	8.1	37	7	7	14	5	5	7.56
Totals	12	6	2	6	2	4	.333	50.0	188	22	21	49	19	24	3.78

Individual Batting

Players	Pos	G	AB	R	H	TB	2B	3B	HR	RB	SB	Pct
Joshua Gibson	c,1b	6	23	3	8	12	4	0	0	4	0	.347
Thomas Dukes	c	1	4	0	1	3	0	1	0	1	0	.250
Walter Leonard	1b	6	18	1	3	4	1	0	0	3	0	.167
Matthew Carlisle	2b	6	18	0	2	2	0	0	0	1	0	.111
Harry Williams	3b	6	21	3	6	6	0	0	0	0	1	.286
Willie Wells	3b,ss	6	22	1	6	7	1	0	0	1	0	.273
Norman Jackson	ss,pr	2	2	0	0	0	0	0	0	0	0	.000
Samuel Bankhead	of	6	25	0	6	6	0	0	0	0	0	.240
E. Victor Harris	of	6	20	2	4	4	0	0	0	1	0	.200
James Williams	of	6	19	2	1	1	0	0	0	0	0	.053
Roy Partlow	p,ph	4	4	0	1	1	0	0	0	1	0	.250
Barney Brown	p,ph	5	5	1	1	1	0	0	0	0	0	.200
Raymond Brown	p,ph	4	8	0	0	0	0	0	0	0	0	.000
Terris McDuffie	p	3	2	0	0	0	0	0	0	0	0	.000
Totals		6	191	13	39	47	6	1	0	12	1	.204

Individual Fielding

Player	Pos	G	O	A	E	Pct
Gibson, Joshua	c,1b	6	33	7	1	.976
Dukes, Thomas	c	1	6	0	0	1.000
Leonard, Walter	1b	6	55	1	0	1.000
Carlisle, Matthew	2b	6	14	17	0	1.000
Williams, Harry	3b	6	2	7	1	.900
Wells, Willie	3b,ss	6	11	15	0	1.000
Jackson, Norman	ss,pr	2	1	3	0	1.000
Bankhead, Samuel	of	6	10	0	0	1.000
Harris, E. Victor	of	6	9	1	0	1.000
Williams, James	of	6	9	1	0	1.000
Partlow, Roy	p,ph	4	0	9	0	1.000

Player	Pos	G	O	A	E	Pct
Barney Brown	p,ph	5	0	4	0	1.000
Raymond Brown	p,ph	4	0	6	0	1.000
Terris McDuffie	p	3	0	1	1	.500
Totals		6	150	82	3	.987

Manager: Victor "Vic" Elander Harris

♦ 15 ♦
1939
Homestead Grays

Roster

Player	Position	Regular Season Club, 1939
Lamb "Bud" Barbee	p	Brooklyn Royal Giants
Haywood "Harry" Cozart	p	Newark Eagles
Raymond "Smokey" Owens	p	Cleveland Bears
Roy Partlow	p	Homestead Grays
Edsall "Big" Walker	p	Homestead Grays
Henry Kimbro	of	Baltimore Elite Giants
Samuel "Sammy" Bankhead	cf	Toledo Crawfords
Clarence "Fats" Jenkins	of	BRK Royal Giants/Toledo Crawfords
Josh Gibson	c	Homestead Grays
Walter "Buck" Leonard	lb	Homestead Grays
Willie Wells	ss	Newark Eagles
Felton Snow	3b,ss	Baltimore Elite Giants
Samuel "Sammy" Hughes	2b	Baltimore Elite Giants
Elander Victor "Vic" Harris	of	Homestead Grays

Games Played

Date	Winning Club		Losing Club		Winning Pitcher	Losing Pitcher
Oct 7	Homestead Grays	7	Habana	4	Smokey Owens	Luis Tiant
Oct 8	Homestead Grays	6	Almendares	4	Roy Partlow	Silvino Ruiz
Oct 10	Homestead Grays	4	Habana	1	Harry Cozart	Tomas de la Cruz
Oct 12	Homestead Grays	5	Almendares	1	Big Walker	Rene Monteagudo
Oct 14	Homestead Grays	2	All-stars	1	Roy Partlow	Rene Monteagudo
Oct 15	Homestead Grays	5	All-stars	0	Bud Barbee	Martin Dihigo
(6)						

Club Standings

Pos	Club	J	G	P	Pct
1.	Homestead Grays	6	6	0	1.000
2-4.	Almendares	2	0	2	.000
2-4.	Habana	2	0	2	.000
2-4.	Picked Nine	2	0	2	.000
	Totals	12	6	6	.500

The Games

GAME ONE: OCTOBER 7, 1939, AT STADIUM LA TROPICAL

Homestead Grays	Pos	AB	R	H	O	A	E
H. Kimbro	cf	5	0	2	2	0	0
S. Bankhead	lf,rf	5	1	1	0	0	0
F. Jenkins	rf,lf	4	1	1	1	0	0
J. Gibson	c	5	1	1	3	1	0
W. Leonard	1b	4	1	2	10	0	0
W. Wells	ss	3	0	1	3	4	0
F. Snow	3b	4	1	1	2	2	0
S. Hughes	2b	4	2	2	4	3	0
S. Owens	p	4	0	0	0	3	0
Totals		38	7	11	27	13	0

Habana	Pos	AB	R	H	O	A	E
A. Alvarez	rf	5	0	1	1	1	0
J. López	cf	5	1	3	5	0	0
G. Torres	1b	5	0	3	6	1	0
S. Hernandez	c	3	0	0	3	0	0
S. Amaro	3b	4	0	1	1	3	1
R. Ortiz	lf	4	0	0	0	0	0
R. Heredia	2b	3	0	2	4	4	0
F. Valdés	ss	4	2	2	3	4	1
L. Tiant	p	1	0	0	1	1	0
A. Aragon	c	2	0	1	3	0	0
P. Pages	(x)	1	1	0	0	0	0
M. Fortes	p	1	0	0	0	0	0
Totals		38	4	12	27	14	2

(x)—Batted for L. Tiant in seventh.

Homestead Grays	210	010	030–7
Habana	000	000	202–4

Runs batted in: H. Kimbro 3, W. Leonard 3, F. Snow, A. Alvarez 2, J. López, G. Torres
Three-base hits: A. Alvarez
Two-base hits: W. Leonard, G. Torres 2, S. Hughes, H. Kimbro, J. López
Stolen bases: S. Hughes
Left on bases: Homestead Grays 6, Habana 9
Base on balls: S. Owens 2, L. Tiant 2, M. Fortes 0
Strikeouts: S. Owens 2, L. Tiant 2, M. Fortes 0
Hits: L. Tiant 6 in 7.0 (28 vb)
Winning pitcher: S. Owens
Losing pitcher: L. Tiant
Time: 2 hours 15 minutes
Umpires: R. Atan (home) and José M. Magrinat (bases)
Scorer: Julio Franquiz

GAME TWO: OCTOBER 8, 1939, AT STADIUM LA TROPICAL

Homestead Grays	Pos	AB	R	H	O	A	E
H. Kimbro	cf	5	3	3	0	0	0
S. Bankhead	lf	4	0	1	2	1	0
F. Jenkins	rf	5	0	2	4	1	0
J. Gibson	c	4	0	2	2	1	0
W. Leonard	1b	4	0	1	11	1	0
W. Wells	ss	3	0	1	1	3	1
F. Snow	3b	4	0	0	0	3	0
S. Hughes	2b	4	2	0	4	2	1
B. Barbee	p	2	1	1	0	0	0
R. Partlow	p	2	0	1	0	1	0
G. Valdivia	(x)	1	0	0	0	0	0
Totals		38	6	12	27	13	1

(x)—Out for A. Mayor in ninth.

Almendares	Pos	AB	R	H	O	A	E
J.J. Vargas	cf	3	0	0	3	0	0
F. Correa	2b	3	0	0	3	3	0
Williams	ss	3	1	0	4	5	0
R. Linares	1b	4	1	2	11	1	0
M. Veitia	rf	4	1	0	1	0	0
A. Rodríguez	3b	3	1	2	0	3	1
A. Mirabal	lf	4	0	1	2	0	1
F. Guerra	c	4	0	1	3	1	0
S. Ruiz	p	2	0	0	0	1	0
A. Mayor	p	0	0	0	0	0	0
Totals		31	4	6	27	14	2

Homestead Grays	102	000	300–6
Almendares	100	201	000–4

Runs batted in: H. Kimbro, F. Jenkins 3, J. Gibson, W. Leonard, R. Linares, A. Mirabal
Two-base hits: R. Linares 2, H. Kimbro

Sacrifice hits: S. Bankhead
Stolen bases: M. Veitia, A. Rodríguez
Double-plays: S. Ruiz, Williams to R. Linares; S. Bankhead to S. Hughes; C. Jenkins to W. Leonard
Left on bases: Homestead Grays 7, Almendares 5
Base on balls: S. Ruiz 0, B. Barbee 0, A. Mayor 1, R. Partlow 0
Strikeouts: S. Ruiz 2, B. Barbee 0, A. Mayor 1, R. Partlow 0
Hits: B. Barbee 4 in 4.0 (15 vb), S. Ruiz 9 in 6.0 (28 vb)
Winning pitcher: R. Partlow
Losing pitcher: S. Ruiz
Time: 2.05
Umpires: Amado Maestri (home) and Bernardino Rodríguez (bases)
Scorer: Julio Franquiz

GAME THREE: OCTOBER 10, 1939, AT STADIUM LA TROPICAL

Homestead Grays	Pos	AB	R	H	O	A	E	Habana	Pos	AB	R	H	O	A	E
H. Kimbro	cf	4	0	0	1	0	0	A. Alvarez	rf	5	0	0	1	0	0
S. Bankhead	lf	4	1	2	2	0	0	P. Pages	cf	5	0	0	3	0	0
C. Jenkins	rf	4	1	1	2	0	0	G. Torres	1b	3	0	1	7	2	0
J. Gibson	c	3	0	0	5	2	0	S. Hernandez	c	4	0	1	6	0	0
W. Leonard	1b	5	0	2	13	0	0	S. Amaro	3b	2	0	1	0	1	1
W. Wells	ss	4	0	1	3	4	0	R. Ortiz	lf	2	0	0	4	0	1
F. Snow	3b	4	0	2	0	1	1	R. Heredia	2b	2	1	0	3	3	0
S. Hughes	2b	2	1	0	1	6	0	F. Valdés	ss	2	0	0	2	2	0
H. Cozart	p	4	1	0	0	0	0	T. de la Cruz	p	3	0	1	1	1	0
E. Walker	p	0	0	0	0	0	0	A. Ruiz	(x)	1	0	0	0	0	0
R. Partlow	p	0	0	0	0	1	0	M. Fortes	lf	0	0	0	0	0	0
A. Aragon	(xx)	1	0	0	0	0	0	Totals		30	1	4	27	9	2
Totals		34	4	8	27	14	1								

(x)—Out for R. Ortiz in eighth.
(xx)—Out for T. de la Cruz in ninth.

Homestead Grays	000	040	000–4
Habana	000	010	000–1

Runs batted in: S. Bankhead 2, W. Leonard 2, A. Alvarez
Sacrifice hits: S. Hughes 2, C. Jenkins
Double-plays: F. Valdés, R. Heredia to G. Torres; S. Hughes, W. Wells to W. Leonard; R. Partlow, J. Gibson to W. Leonard
Left on bases: Homestead Grays 10, Habana 10
Base on balls: T. de la Cruz 4, H. Cozart 6, R. Partlow 0, E. Walker 2
Strikeouts: T. de la Cruz 5, H. Cozart 2, R. Partlow 1, E. Walker 0
Hits: H. Cozart   3 in 7.1 (25 vb), E. Walker 0 in 0.2 (2 vb)
Winning pitcher: H. Cozart
Losing pitcher: T. de la Cruz
Time: 2 hours 10 minutes
Umpires: Raul Atan (home) and José M. Magrinat (bases)
Scorer: Julio Franquiz

GAME FOUR: OCTOBER 12, 1939, AT STADIUM LA TROPICAL

Homestead Grays	Pos	AB	R	H	O	A	E	Almendares	Pos	AB	R	H	O	A	E
H. Kimbro	cf	4	2	2	3	0	0	J.J. Vargas	cf	4	0	2	1	0	0
S. Bankhead	lf	5	0	0	1	0	0	F. Correa	2b	4	0	0	4	4	0
C. Jenkins	rf	2	2	1	0	0	0	R. Linares	1b	2	0	1	4	0	0
J. Gibson	c	4	0	2	1	0	0	M. Veitia	lf	4	0	0	2	0	0
W. Leonard	1b	3	0	0	13	0	0	C. Williams	ss	3	1	1	5	5	1
W. Wells	ss	5	0	3	5	5	0	A. Mirabal	rf	4	0	2	3	0	0

Homestead Grays	Pos	AB	R	H	O	A	E
F. Snow	3b	5	0	0	2	3	0
S. Hughes	2b	4	0	0	2	3	1
E. Walker	p	4	1	2	0	4	0
S. Owens	p	0	0	0	0	0	0
Totals		36	5	10	27	16	1

Almendares	Pos	AB	R	H	O	A	E
A. Rodríguez	3b	4	0	0	1	0	0
G. Valdivia	c	4	0	1	3	1	0
R. Monteagudo	p	0	0	0	0	0	0
F. Guerra	1b	3	0	1	4	0	0
R. Fernandez	p	1	1	0	0	0	0
Totals		33	2	8	27	10	1

Homestead Grays	002	003	000–5
Almendares	000	100	000–1

Runs batted in: S. Bankhead 2, J. Gibson 2, W. Leonard, A. Rodríguez
Three-base hits: C. Jenkins
Two-base hits: C. Williams, E. Walker
Sacrifice hits: W. Leonard, F. Correa
Stolen bases: C. Jenkins, H. Kimbro
Double-plays: W. Wells to W. Leonard
Left on bases: Homestead Grays 12, Almendares 11
Base on balls: R. Monteagudo 6, E. Walker 5, R. Fernandez 1, S. Owens 1
Strikeouts: R. Monteagudo 0, E. Walker 1, R. Fernandez 0, S. Owens 0
Winning pitcher: E. Walker
Losing pitcher: R. Monteagudo
Time: 1.50
Umpires: Amado Maestri (home) and Bernardino Rodríguez (bases)
Scorer: Julio Franquiz

GAME FIVE: OCTOBER 14, 1939, AT STADIUM LA TROPICAL

Homestead Grays	Pos	AB	R	H	O	A	E
H. Kimbro	cf	4	0	2	4	2	0
S. Bankhead	lf	3	0	0	0	0	0
C. Jenkins	rf	4	0	0	3	1	0
J. Gibson	c	4	1	2	3	0	0
W. Leonard	1b	4	0	1	8	0	0
W. Wells	ss	4	0	0	5	2	1
F. Snow	3b	4	0	1	2	4	1
S. Hughes	2b	3	1	2	2	3	1
R. Partlow	p	3	0	0	0	2	0
Totals		33	2	8	27	14	3

All-Stars	Pos	AB	R	H	O	A	E
J.J. Vargas	cf	4	0	0	3	0	0
L. Salazar	rf	4	0	2	2	0	0
S. Amaro	3b	4	1	0	2	1	1
M. Dihigo	2b	4	0	0	1	2	0
G. Torres	1b	3	0	2	5	0	0
S. Hernandez	c	4	0	0	4	0	0
A. Castano	lf	2	0	0	5	0	0
C. Williams	ss	2	0	0	5	1	0
R. Monteagudo	p	2	0	0	0	1	0
F. Guerra	(x)	1	0	0	0	0	0
Totals		31	1	4	27	5	1

(x)—Out for R. Monteagudo in ninth.

Homestead Grays	000	010	010–2
Estrellas Cubanas	000	100	000–1

Runs batted in: G. Torres, S. Bankhead, W. Leonard
Two-base hits: W. Leonard
Sacrifice hits: R. Partlow
Stolen bases: J. Gibson, G. Torres
Double-plays: C. Jenkins to H. Kimbro; H. Kimbro to W. Wells
Left on bases: Homestead Grays 6, Estrellas Cubanas 7
Base on balls: R. Partlow 4, R. Monteagudo 1
Strikeouts: R. Partlow 4, R. Monteagudo 3
Winning pitcher: R. Partlow
Losing pitcher: R. Monteagudo
Time: 1 hour 50 minutes
Umpires: Amado Maestri (home) and Bernardino Rodríguez (bases)
Scorer: Julio Franquiz

GAME SIX: OCTOBER 15, 1939, AT STADIUM LA TROPICAL

Homestead Grays	Pos	AB	C	H	O	A	E
H. Kimbro	cf	5	0	1	4	0	0
S. Bankhead	3b	3	2	2	1	3	1
C. Jenkins	rf	4	0	2	2	0	0
J. Gibson	c	4	0	2	4	0	0
W. Leonard	1b	4	0	0	11	0	0
N. Harris	lf	3	1	1	1	0	0
F. Snow	3b	4	1	0	0	5	0
S. Hughes	2b	4	1	3	4	5	1
B. Barbee	p	4	0	0	0	1	0
Totals		35	5	11	27	14	2

All-Stars	Pos	AB	C	H	O	A	E
J.J. Vargas	cf	4	0	0	4	0	0
L. Salazar	rf	3	0	0	1	1	0
S. Amaro	3b	4	0	0	0	0	1
S. Hernandez	c	4	0	2	4	2	2
G. Torres	1b	3	0	0	10	2	1
M. Dihigo	p	3	0	0	0	2	0
A. Castano	lf	3	0	1	1	0	0
C. Williams	ss	3	0	0	4	4	0
A. Rodríguez	2b	3	0	0	3	4	0
Totals		30	0	3	27	15	4

Homestead Grays	110	001	200–5
Estrellas Cubanas	000	000	000–0

Runs batted in: H. Kimbro, S. Bankhead, J. Gibson 2, S. Hughes
Three-base hits: S. Hughes
Two-base hits: S. Bankhead, J. Gibson, N. Harris
Sacrifice hits: J. Gibson, C. Jenkins, S. Bankhead
Stolen bases: H. Kimbro
Double-plays: G. Torres to S. Hernandez; C. Williams to S. Hughes to W. Leonard; L. Salazar to A. Rodríguez; S. Hughes to S. Bankhead to W. Leonard
Left on bases: Homestead Grays 8, Estrellas Cubanas 5
Bases on balls: M. Dihigo 2, B. Barbee 2
Strikeouts: M. Dihigo 4, B. Barbee 3
Winning pitcher: B. Barbee
Losing pitcher: M. Dihigo
Time: 2 hours, 4 minutes
Umpires: Raul Atan (home), José M. Magrinat (bases)
Scorer: Julio Franquiz

Final Statistics

Individual Pitching

Pitchers	J	JC	G	P	Pct	IP	C	H	BB	SO	PCP
Quincy "Bud" Barbee	2	1	1	0	1.000	13.0	3	7	4	3	2.30
Harry Cozart	1	0	1	0	1.000	7.1	1	4	6	2	1.36
Raymond Owens	2	1	1	0	1.000	10.0	4	12	2	2	3.88
Roy Parlow	3	1	2	0	1.000	15.0	2	10	7	5	1.33
Edsall Walker	2	1	1	0	1.000	8.2	1	8	7	1	1.14
Totals	10	4	6	0	1.000	54.0	11	41	26	13	2.04

Individual Batting

Players	Pos	J	AB	C	H	TB	2B	3B	HR	CI	BR	Pct
Samuel Bankead	ss,of	6	24	4	8	9	1	0	0	5	0	.333
Quincy "Bud" Barbee	p	2	6	1	1	1	0	0	0	0	0	.167
Harry Cozart	p	1	4	1	0	0	0	0	0	0	0	.000
Joshua Gibson	c	6	24	2	9	10	1	0	0	5	1	.375
Victor E. Harris	of	1	3	1	1	1	0	0	0	0	0	.333
Samuel Hughes	2b	6	21	7	7	10	1	1	0	1	1	.333
Clarence Jenkins	of	6	23	4	7	9	0	1	0	3	1	.304
Henry Kimbro	of	6	27	2	10	12	2	0	0	6	1	.370
Walter "Buck" Leonard	1b	6	24	1	6	8	2	0	0	8	0	.250

Players	Pos	J	AB	C	H	TB	2B	3B	HR	CI	BR	Pct
Raymond "Smoky" Owens	p	2	4	0	0	0	0	0	0	0	0	.000
Roy Partlow	p	3	5	0	1	1	0	0	0	0	0	.000
Felton Snow	3b	6	25	2	4	4	0	0	0	1	0	.160
Erdsall "Big" Walker	p	2	4	1	2	2	0	0	0	0	0	.500
Willie Wells	ss	5	20	0	6	6	0	0	0	0	0	.300
Totals		6	214	29	60	71	7	2	0	29	4	.280

Individual Fielding

Players	Pos	J	O	A	E	TL	Pct
Samuel Bankhead	of,ss	6	8	4	1	13	.923
Quincy "Bud" Barbee	p	2	0	1	0	1	1.000
Harry Cozart	p	1	0	0	0	0	.000
Joshua Gibson	c	6	18	4	0	22	1.000
Victor E. Harris	of	1	1	0	0	1	1.000
Samuel Hughes	2b	6	17	22	4	43	.907
Clarence Jenkins	of	6	12	2	0	14	1.000
Henry Kimbro	of	6	17	2	0	19	1.000
Walter "Buck" Leonard	1b	6	66	1	0	67	1.000
Raymond "Smoky" Owens	p	2	0	3	0	0	1.000
Roy Partlow	p	3	0	4	0	4	1.000
Felton Snow	3b	6	6	18	2	26	.923
Edsall "Big" Walker	p	2	0	4	0	4	1.000
Willie Wells	ss	5	17	18	2	37	.946
Totals		6	62	84	8	254	.969

Habana

Individual Pitching

Pitchers	J	JC	G	P	Pct	IP	C	H	W	K	PCP
Luis Tiant	1	0	0	1	.000	7.0	4	6	2	2	5.19
Manuel Fortes	1	0	0	0	.000	2.0	2	5	0	0	9.00
Tomas de la Cruz	1	1	0	1	.000	9.0	4	8	4	5	4.00
Totals	3	1	0	2	.000	18.0	10	19	6	7	5.00

Individual Batting

Players	Pos	J	AB	C	H	TB	2B	3B	HR	CI	BR	Pct
Avelino "Belito" Alvarez	rf	2	10	0	1	3	0	1	0	3	0	.100
Justo "Cando" López	cf	1	5	1	3	4	1	0	0	1	0	.600
Pedro Pages	ph,cf	2	6	1	0	0	0	0	0	0	0	.000
Gilberto Torres	1b	2	8	0	4	6	2	0	0	1	0	.500
Salvador Hernandez	c	2	7	0	1	1	0	0	0	0	0	.143
Santos Amaro	3b	2	6	0	2	2	0	0	0	0	0	.333
Roberto Ortiz	lf	2	6	0	0	0	0	0	0	0	0	.000
Ramon "Napoleon" Heredia	2b	2	5	1	2	2	0	0	0	0	0	.400
Fermin "Strike" Valdés	ss	2	6	2	2	2	0	0	0	0	0	.333
Angel Aragon	ph,c	2	3	0	1	1	0	0	0	0	0	.333
Luis Tiant	p	1	1	0	0	0	0	0	0	0	0	.000
Manuel Fortes	p,lf	1	1	0	0	0	0	0	0	0	0	.000
Antonio "Loco" Ruiz	ph	1	0	0	0	0	0	0	0	0	0	.000
Tomas de la Cruz	p	1	3	0	1	1	0	0	0	0	0	.000
Totals		2	68	5	16	21	3	1	0	5	0	.235

ALMENDARES

Individual Pitching

Pitchers	J	JC	G	P	Pct	IP	C	H	BB	SO	Pct
Silvino Ruiz	1	0	0	1	.000	6.0	6	9	0	2	9.00
Agapito Mayor	1	0	0	0	.000	3.0	0	3	1	1	0.00
Rene Monteagudo	1	0	0	1	.000	3.0	2	3	6	0	6.00
Rodolfo Fernandez	1	0	0	0	.000	6.0	3	7	1	0	4.50
Totals	4	0	0	2	.000	18.0	11	22	8	3	5.50

Individual Batting

Players	Pos	J	AB	C	H	TB	2B	3B	HR	CI	BR	Pct
José Julio "Huesito" Vargas	cf	2	7	0	2	2	0	0	0	0	0	.286
Francisco "Cuco" Correa	2b	2	7	0	0	0	0	0	0	0	0	.000
Chester Williams	ss	2	6	2	1	2	1	0	0	0	0	.167
Rogelio Linares	1b	2	6	1	3	5	2	0	0	1	0	.500
Manuel "Pototo" Veitia	rf	2	8	1	0	0	0	0	0	0	0	.000
Antonio "Pollo" Rodríguez	3b	2	7	1	2	2	0	0	0	1	0	.286
Antonio "Helio" Mirsbal	lf	2	8	0	3	3	0	0	0	1	0	.375
Fermin Guerra	c,1b	2	7	0	2	2	0	0	0	0	0	.286
Gilberto Valdivia	c	2	5	0	1	1	0	0	0	0	0	.200
Silvino Ruiz	p	1	2	0	0	0	0	0	0	0	0	.000
Agapito Mayor	p	1	0	0	0	0	0	0	0	0	0	.000
Rene Monteagudo	p	1	0	0	0	0	0	0	0	0	0	.000
Rodolfo Fernandez	p	1	1	0	0	0	0	0	0	0	0	.000
Totals		2	64	5	14	17	3	0	0	3	0	.219

ALL-STARS

Individual Pitching

Pitchers	J	C	G	P	Pct	IP	C	H	BB	SO	PCP
Rene Monteagudo	1	1	0	1	.000	9.0	2	8	1	3	2.00
Martin Dihigo	1	1	0	1	.000	9.0	5	11	2	4	5.00
Totals	2	2	0	2	.000	18.0	7	19	3	7	3.50

Individual Batting

Players	Pos	J	AB	C	H	TB	2B	3B	HR	CI	BR	Pct
José Julio Vargas	cf	8	0	0	0	0	0	0	0	0	0	.000
Lazaro Salazar	rf	2	7	0	2	2	0	0	0	0	0	.286
Santos Amaro	3b	2	8	1	0	0	0	0	0	0	0	.000
Martin Dihigo	2b,p	2	7	0	0	0	0	0	0	0	0	.000
Gilberto Torres	1b	2	6	0	2	2	0	0	0	1	1	.333
Salvador Hernandez	c	2	8	0	2	2	0	0	0	0	0	.000
Antonio Castano	lf	2	5	0	1	1	0	0	0	0	0	.200
Chester Williams	ss	2	5	0	0	0	0	0	0	0	0	.000
Antonio "Pollo" Rodríguez	2b	1	3	0	0	0	0	0	0	0	0	.000
Fermin Guerra	ph	1	1	0	0	0	0	0	0	0	0	.000
Rene Monteagudo	p	1	2	0	0	0	0	0	0	0	0	.000
Totals		2	61	1	7	7	0	0	0	1	0	.115

◆ 16 ◆
1945
New York Cubans

Before beginning the 1945–1946 championship, Alejandro Pompez's New York Cubans visited Cuba in October 1945 for a series of five games, among them a double-header on October 12.

In the first game of the double-header, the Cuban All-Star team crushed the visitors with a score of 11–5. They tied the second game at 1–1.

In the opening double-header game, Isidoro Leon was the victim of a four-run rally by the visitors, who bombarded him with seven hits and five runs in three innings. Rene Monteagudo took his place in an attempt to hold off further assault.

Opening for José Maria Fernandez's New York Cubans was "Gallego" Gutiérrez, who exploded in the second inning. Following him were Francisco "Cayuco" Martinez and then Juan "Bibi" Crespo, neither of whom had any success at containing the locals, who fought back with five hits from Mario Fajo and another three shots from Oscar Garmendia.

In the second contest, sugar-worker-turned-pitcher Pedro "Natilla" Jimenez battled against hurlers Oliver Ortiz and Luis Tiant (the elder), who both labored for New York.

Jimenez, who played that season for Indianapolis of the American Association, allowed one unearned run by Francisco "Cisco" Campos, due to an error by first baseman Virgilio Arteaga. Counted against Oliver Ortiz was one run batted in by Fermin Guerra in the first inning.

Fernando Díaz Pedroso was the star defender, playing short stop in both games.

Roster

Player	Position	Club
Cleveland "Chiflan" Clark	of	New York Cubans
Fernando "Bicho" Díaz Pedroso	2b	New York Cubans
Rogelio Linares	1b	New York Cubans
Rafael Noble	c	New York Cubans
Luis Tinat	p	New York Cubans
Raul Navarro	c	Cincinnati-Indianapolis Clowns
Armando Vazquez	1b	Cincinbnati-Indianapolis Clowns
Oliverio Ortiz	p	Washington Senators
Hector Arago	2b	Williamsport
Francisco "Cisco" Campos	lf	Portsmouth
Joaquin Gutiérrez	p	Chattanooga, Williamsport
Miguel Lastra	if	Buffalo
Antonio Ordenana	ss	Atlanta
Antonio "Pollo" Rodríguez	3b	Syracuse
Rafael Sangil	p	Portsmouth
F. Soler		
Juan "Bibi" Crespo	p	Mexican League
Pedro Díaz	c	Mexican League

Player	Position	Club
Francisco "Cayuco" Martinez	p	Mexican League
Jacinto "Battling Siki" Roque	of	Mexican League
Wilfredo Salas	p	Mexican League

Manager: José Maria Fernandez

ALL STARS

Roster

Fermin Guerra	c,of	Major Leagues
Rene Monteagudo	of	Major Leagues
Gilberto Torres	ss,of	Major Leagues
Julian Acosta	p	Milwaukee
Virginio Arteaga	1b	Minneapolis, Little Rock
Lazaro Bernal	of	Portsmouth
Oscar del Calvo	of,p	Portsmouth
Daniel Doy	ss	Newark, Binghamton, Kansas City
Mario Fajo	2b	Atlanta-Mobile, Newport News
Oscar Garmendia	of	Atlanta
Fermin Guerra	c,of	Washington
Manuel "Chino" Hidalgo	3b	Williamsport
Pedro Jimenez	p	Indianapolis
Isidoro Leon	p	Minneapolis, Washington
Gilberto Torres	1b,ss,of	Washington
Rogelio Valdés	c	Williamsport
Luis Zequeira	p	Beisbol juvenil

Manager: Fermin Guerra

Games Played

Date	Winning Club		Losing Club		Winning Pitcher	Losing Pitcher
Oct 10	New York Cubans	0	Al Stars	3	J. Acosta	L. Tiant
Oct 11	All Stars	7	New York Cubans	5	O. del Calvo	W. Salas
Oct 12	New York Cubans	5	All Stars	11	R. Monteagudo	F. Martinez
Oct 12	All Stars	1	New York Cubans	1	Tie-P. Jimenez-O. Ortiz	
Oct 13	New York Cubans	1	All Stars	2	L. Zequeira	W. Salas

Club Standings

Clubs	J	G	P	E	Pct	Managers
All Stars	5	4	0	1	1.000	Fermin Guerra
New York Cubans	5	0	4	1	.000	José Maria Fernandez
Totals	5	4	4	1	.000	

The Games

GAME ONE: WEDNESDAY, OCTOBER 10, 1945, IN STADIUM LA TROPICAL

New York Cubans	Pos	AB	C	H	O	A	E		All Stars	Pos	AB	C	H	O	A	E
A. Ordenana	ss	4	0	0	3	5	0		M. Hidalgo	3b	3	0	0	1	1	0
A. Rodríguez	3b	4	0	0	2	1	0		O. Garmendia	cf	4	0	1	4	0	0
R. Linares	1b	4	0	1	8	1	0		G. Torres	ss	1	1	1	0	1	1
C. Clark	cf	4	0	0	5	0	0		R. Monteagudo	rf	4	0	0	1	0	0
F. Díaz	2b	4	0	1	3	1	0		F. Guerra	c	2	0	1	2	1	0
J. Roque	cf	4	0	0	3	1	0		M. Fajo	2b	3	0	1	4	4	0
F. Campos	lf	2	0	1	0	0	0		V. Arteaga	1b	3	0	0	11	1	0

New York Cubans	Pos	AB	C	H	O	A	E
R. Noble	c	2	0	0	0	0	0
L. Tiant	p	0	0	0	0	2	0
R. Navarro	c	1	0	0	0	0	0
M. Lastra	(1)	1	0	0	0	0	0
F. Martinez	p	0	0	0	0	0	0
Totals		29	0	3	24	11	0

All Stars	Pos	AB	C	H	O	A	E
O. del Calvo	lf	3	1	1	1	0	0
J. Acosta	p	3	1	1	1	1	0
D. Doy	ss	2	0	1	1	0	0
R. Valdés	c	1	0	0	1	1	0
Totals		29	3	7	27	10	1

New York Cubans 000 000 000 : 0–3–0
All Stars 100 000 20x : 3–7–1

Runs batted in: O. Garmendia 2
Three-base hits: G. Torres
Sacrifice hits: L. Tiant, M. Hidalgo
Stolen bases: G. Torres (home), D. Doy
Left on base: New York Cubans 0, All Stars 4
Bases on balls: J. Acosta 3, L. Tiant 0, F. Martinez 1
Strikeouts: J. Acosta 1, L. Tiant 0, F. Martinez 0
Hits Allowed: L. Tiant 4 in 7.0 (25 ab, 1 run)
Winning Pitcher: J. Acosta
Losing Pitcher: L. Tiant
Time: 1 hour, 30 minutes
Umpires: J. Calderon (home) and B. Rodríguez (bases)

GAME TWO: THURSDAY, OCTOBER 11, 1945, AT STADIUM LA TROPICAL

All Stars	Pos	AB	C	H	O	A	E
M. Hidalgo	3b	4	2	2	1	6	0
V. Arteaga	1b	4	1	0	8	0	0
G. Torres	ss	3	1	1	1	1	0
R. Monteagudo	rf	2	1	0	3	0	0
O. Garmendia	cf	5	1	3	4	1	0
M. Fajo	2b	4	1	2	4	1	0
L. Bernal	lf	4	0	0	1	0	0
R. Valdés	c	4	0	0	5	2	1
O. Calvo	p	4	0	1	0	3	0
D. Doy	ss	2	0	1	0	0	0
Totals		36	7	10	27	16	1

New York Cubans	Pos	AB	C	H	O	A	E
F. Campos	lf	5	0	1	2	0	1
A. Rodríguez	3b	5	0	2	1	4	0
C. Clark	cf	3	2	0	1	0	1
R. Linares	1b	4	2	2	13	0	0
F. Díaz	ss	3	0	2	4	3	1
J. Roque	rf	4	0	1	2	1	0
H. Arago	2b	5	0	2	1	5	0
R. Noble	c	5	1	2	3	0	0
W. Salas	p	1	0	0	0	0	0
F. Martinez	p	0	0	0	0	0	0
P. Díaz	(1)	0	0	0	0	0	0
S. Gil	p	0	0	0	0	0	0
F. Soler	(2)	1	0	0	0	0	0
J. Gutiérrez	p	0	0	0	0	0	0
Totals		36	5	12	27	13	3

All Stars 000 005 110 : 7–10–1
New York Cubans 000 011 102 : 5–12–3

Runs batted in: A. Rodríguez, G. Torres, O. Garmendia 2, M. Fajo 2, H. Arago 2, D. Doy, P. Díaz, J. Roque
Home run: M. Fajo
Three-base hits: A. Rodríguez.
Two-base hits: O. Garmendia, G. Torres, D. Doy
Sacrifice hits: J. Roque, P. Díaz, W. Salas
Stolen bases: O. Garmendia
Double-plays: H. Arago to F. Díaz to R. Linares; O. Garmendia to R. Valdés
Left on base: All Stars 3, New York Cubans 12
Bases on balls: W. Salas 4, O.del Calvo 5, F. Martinez 0, S. Gil 0, J. Gutiérrez 1
Strikeouts: W. Salas 0, O.del Cavo 2, F. Martinez 1, S. Gil 0, J. Gutiérrez 0
Wild pitches: W. Salas 1, J. Gutiérrez 1
Hits Allowed: W. Salas 6 in 5.0 (19 ab); F. Martinez 1 in 1.0 (4 ab)
Winning pitcher: O. del Calvo
Losing pitcher: W. Salas

Time: 1 hour, 55 minutes
Umpires: R. Morales (home) and M. Puyans (bases)

GAME THREE: FRIDAY, OCTOBER 12, 1945, AT STADIUM LA TROPICAL

New York Cubans	Pos	AB	C	H	O	A	E
F. Campos	lf	4	1	0	1	0	0
A. Rodríguez	3b	4	0	2	1	0	0
F. Díaz	ss	5	0	2	2	3	0
C. Clark	cf	2	2	1	2	0	0
J. Roque	rf	4	1	2	3	0	0
H. Arago	2b	4	0	0	2	3	0
P. Díaz	c	4	1	1	2	0	0
J. Gutiérrez	p	0	0	0	0	1	0
F. Martinez	p	1	0	0	0	1	0
J. Crespo	p	1	0	0	0	1	0
Totals		33	5	9	24	14	0

All Stars	Pos	AB	C	H	O	A	E
M. Hidalgo	3b	5	1	1	2	2	0
V. Arteaga	1b	5	3	1	10	0	0
O. Garmendia	cf	5	2	3	2	0	0
M. Fajo	2b	5	2	5	7	4	1
D. Doy	ss	4	0	2	1	4	0
L. Bernal	lf	1	0	0	1	0	0
R. Valdés	c	5	0	1	1	0	0
I. Leon	p	0	0	0	1	0	0
O. del Calvo	rf	3	1	1	0	0	0
F. Guerra	lf	1	0	0	0	0	0
G. Torres	lf	2	0	0	1	0	0
Totals		37	11	15	27	12	1

New York Cubans	041	000	000 : 5–9–0
All Stars	201	024	20x : 11–15–1

Runs batted in: M. Fajo 3, P. Díaz 2, F. Campos, A. Rodríguez, J. Roque, D. Doy 2, F. Guerra, R. Valdés, O. Garmendia, G. Torres, R. Monteagudo 2
Three-base hits: M. Fajo, P. Díaz, C. Clark
Two-base hits: A. Rodríguez, M. Hidalgo, V. Arteaga
Sacrifice hits: D. Doy, F. Campos
Stolen bases: F. Campos 2, O. Garmendia, O.del Calvo
Double-plays: M. Fajo to V. Arteaga; J. Gutiérrez to F. Díaz to R. Linares; M. Fajo to D. Doy to V. Arteaga; M. Sajo (unassisted)
Left on base: New York Cubans 8, All Stars 11
Bases on balls: J. Gutiérrez 4, I. Leon 2, F. Martinez 3, R. Monteagudo 4, J. Crespo 1
Strikeouts: J. Gutiérrez 0, I. Leon 0, F. Martinez 1, R. Monteagudi 0, J. Crespo 1
Wild pitch: J. Crespo 1
Hits Allowed: J. Gutiérrez 3 in 2.0 (8 ab); I. Leon 7 in 3.0 (14 ab); F. Martinez 6 in 3.1 (15 ab)
Winning pitcher: R. Monteagudo
Losing pitcher: F. Martinez
Time: 2 hours, 15 minutes
Umpires: J. Calderon (home) and José M. Magrinat (bases)

GAME FOUR: FRIDAY, OCTOBER 12, 1945, AT STADIUM LA TROPICAL

All Stars	Pos	AB	C	H	O	A	E
D. Doy	3b	3	0	1	1	2	0
V. Arteaga	1b	3	1	1	12	2	1
G. Torres	ss	3	0	0	2	3	0
F. Guerra	c	4	0	2	4	0	0
O. Garmendia	cf	3	0	0	1	0	0
M. Fajo	2b	4	0	0	1	1	0
O. del Calvo	rf	4	0	0	4	0	0
L. Bernal	lf	2	0	0	1	0	0
P. Jimenez	p	3	0	0	1	4	1
Totals		29	1	4	27	12	2

New York Cubans	Pos	AB	C	H	O	A	E
F. Campos	lf	4	1	1	2	0	0
A. Rodríguez	3b	3	0	0	0	0	0
F. Díaz	ss	3	0	0	3	5	0
R. Linares	1b	4	0	0	12	0	0
C. Clark	cf	4	0	0	2	0	0
J. Roque	rf	3	0	0	3	0	0
H. Arago	2b	4	0	1	1	4	0
R. Navarro	c	0	0	0	0	0	0
O. Ortiz	p	1	0	0	0	2	0
L. Tiant	p	1	0	0	0	1	0
J. Crespo	(x)	1	0	0	0	0	0
P. Díaz	c	3	0	1	4	1	0
Totals		31	1	3	27	12	0

(x)—Out for L. Tiant in the ninth.

| All Stars | 100 | 000 | 000 : 1–4–2 |
| New York Cubans | 100 | 000 | 000 : 1–3–0 |

Runs batted in: F. Guerra
Two-base hits: H. Arago
Stolen bases: V. Arteaga, A. Rodríguez, D. Doy
Double-plays: H. Arago a F. Díaz a R. Linares; F. Díaz a R. Linares
Left on base: All Stars 7, New York Cubans 8
Bases on balls: P. Jimenez 5, O. Ortiz 6, L. Tiant 0
Strikeouts: P. Jimenez 3, O. Ortiz 1, L. Tiant 2
Hits Allowed: O. Ortiz 3 in 4.0 (14 ab)
Time: 1 hour, 40 minutes
Umpires: J. Calderon (home) and José M. Magrinat (bases)

GAME FIVE: SATURDAY, OCTOBER 13, 1945, AT STADIUM LA TROPICAL

New York Cubans	Pos	AB	C	H	O	A	E
E. Gavilan	ss	3	0	0	2	1	0
F. Campos	lf	4	0	2	5	0	0
C. Clark	cf	4	0	0	2	0	0
F. Díaz	rf	4	0	1	3	0	0
A. Vazquez	1b	4	0	2	8	0	0
H. Arago	2b	4	0	0	2	0	1
C. Orta	3b	3	0	0	0	5	0
P. Díaz	c	2	0	0	1	1	0
W. Salas	p	3	1	1	1	0	0
J. Roque	c	1	0	0	1	0	0
J. Terry	(x)	0	0	0	0	0	0
Totals		32	1	6	24	7	1

(x)— Ran for A. Vazquez in the ninth.

All Stars	Pos	AB	C	H	O	A	E
M. Hidalgo	3b	3	0	0	1	2	0
V. Arteaga	1b	4	0	0	8	0	0
O. Garmendia	cf	3	2	1	4	0	0
R. Monteagudo	rf	3	0	3	0	0	0
M. Fajo	2b	2	0	0	0	2	0
D. Doy	ss,2b	4	0	0	4	2	1
L. Bernal	lf	3	0	1	4	0	0
R. Valdés	c	2	0	1	2	0	0
L. Zequeira	p	3	0	0	0	0	0
G. Torres	ss	2	0	1	0	2	0
F. Guerra	c	1	0	0	4	1	0
Totals		30	2	7	27	9	1

| New York Cubans | 001 | 000 | 000 : 1–6–1 |
| All Stars | 100 | 100 | 00x : 2–7–1 |

Runs batted in: R. Monteagudo, M. Fajo
Two-base hits: F. Campos, R. Monteagudo, A. Vazquez
Stolen bases: G. Torres, M. Hidalgo
Double-plays: M. Fajo to D. Doy to V. Arteaga
Left on base: New York Cubans 5, All Stars 6
Bases on balls: L. Zequeira 1, W. Salas 2
Strikeouts: L. Zequeira 3, W. Salas 2
Dead ball: W. Salas 1 (O. Garmendia)
Winning pitcher L. Zequeira
Losing pitcher: W. Salas
Umpires: J. Calderon (home) and José M. Magrinat (bases)

Final Statistics

Individual Pitching

Pitchers	Club	J	JC	G	P	Pct	IP	C	H	BB	SS	PCP
L. Zequeira	AS	1	1	1	0	1.000	9.0	1	6	1	3	1.00
J. Acosta	AS	1	1	1	0	1.000	9.0	0	3	3	1	0.00
O. del Calvo	AS	1	1	1	0	1.000	9.0	5	12	5	2	5.00
R. Monteagudo	AS	1	0	1	0	1.000	.	.	.	.	.	....
L. Tiant	NYC	2	0	0	1	.000	.	.	.	.	.	....

Pitchers	Club	J	JC	G	P	Pct	IP	C	H	BB	SS	PCP
F. Martinez	NYC	1	0	0	1	.000	.	.	.	.	.	....
W. Salas	NYC	2	1	0	2	.000	.	.	.	.	.	....
P. Jimenez	AS	1	1	0	0	.000	9.0	1	3	5	3	1.00
O. Ortiz	NYC	1	0	0	0	.000	.	.	.	.	.	....

Individual Batting

Clubs	J	AB	C	H	2B	3B	HR	CI	SH	BR	Pct
All Stars	5	161	24	43	6	2	1	22	2	9	.267
New York Cubans	5	161	12	33	4	3	0	10	5	3	.205

Individual Fielding

Clubs	J	O	A	E	TL	Pct
New York Cubans	5	126	57	4	187	.979
All Stars	5	135	59	6	200	.970

New York Cubans

Individual Batting

Players	Pos	J	AB	C	H	2B	3B	HR	CI	SH	BR	Pct
A. Vazquez	1b	1	4	0	2	1	0	0	0	0	0	.500
F. Díaz	2b,rf	5	19	0	6	0	0	0	0	0	0	.315
R. Noble	c	2	7	1	2	0	0	0	0	0	0	.286
F. Campos	lf	5	19	2	5	1	0	0	2	1	0	.263
A. Rodríguez	3b	4	16	0	4	1	1	0	2	0	1	.250
R. Linares	1b	3	12	2	3	0	0	0	0	0	0	.250
W. Salas	p	2	4	1	1	0	0	0	0	1	0	.250
P. Díaz	c	4	9	1	2	0	1	0	3	1	0	.222
J. Roque	cf,c	5	16	1	3	0	0	0	2	1	0	.186
H. Arago	2b	4	17	0	3	1	0	0	2	0	0	.176
C. Clark	cf	5	17	4	1	0	1	0	0	0	0	.158
A. Ordenana	ss	1	4	0	0	0	0	0	0	0	0	.000
L. Tiant	p	2	1	0	0	0	0	0	0	1	0	.000
R. Navarro	c	2	1	0	0	0	0	0	0	0	0	.000
M. Lastra	x	1	1	0	0	0	0	0	0	0	0	.000
F. Martinez	p	2	1	0	0	0	0	0	0	0	0	.000
R. Sangil	p	1	0	0	0	0	0	0	0	0	0	.000
F. Soler	xx	1	1	0	0	0	0	0	0	0	0	.000
J. Gutiérrez	p	2	0	0	0	0	0	0	0	0	0	.000
J. Crespo	p	2	2	0	0	0	0	0	0	0	0	.000
O. Ortiz	p.	1	1	0	0	0	0	0	0	0	0	.000
E. Gavilan	ss	1	3	0	0	0	0	0	0	0	0	.000
C. Orta	3b	1	3	0	0	0	0	0	0	0	0	.000
J. Terry	xxx	1	0	0	0	0	0	0	0	0	0	.000
Totals		5	161	12	32	4	3	0	11	5	1	.199

All Stars

Individual Batting

Players	Pos	J	AB	C	H	2B	3B	HR	CI	SH	BR	Pct
M. Fajo	2b	4	16	3	8	0	1	0	4	0	0	.500
O. Garmendia	cf	5	20	5	8	2	0	0	5	0	1	.400
F. Guerra	c,lf	4	8	0	3	1	0	0	2	0	0	.375
D. Doy	ss,2b	5	15	0	5	1	0	0	3	1	2	.333
R. Monteagudo	rf	3	9	1	3	0	0	0	3	0	0	.333

Players	Pos	J	AB	C	H	2B	3B	HR	CI	SH	BR	Pct
J. Acosta	p	1	3	1	1	0	0	0	0	0	0	.333
G. Torres	ss,lf	5	11	2	3	1	2	0	2	0	3	.276
M. Hidalgo	3b	4	15	3	3	0	0	0	0	1	1	.200
O.del Calvo	p,lf	5	18	2	3	0	0	0	0	0	1	.167
R. Valdés	c	4	12	0	2	0	0	0	1	0	0	.167
V. Arteaga	1b	5	17	5	2	1	0	1	2	0	1	.115
L. Bernal	lf	4	10	0	1	0	0	0	0	0	0	.100
I. Leon	p	1	0	0	0	0	0	0	0	0	0	.000
P. Jimenez	p	1	3	0	0	0	0	0	0	0	0	.000
L. Zequeira	p	1	3	0	0	0	0	0	0	0	0	.000
Totals		5	161	22	42	6	3	1	22	2	9	.261

Non-Cuban players on the New York Cubans who did not make the trip:

c: Louis Louden

c: Ameal "Macon" Brooks

1b: Dave Thomas

2b: Gil Garrido (Panamanian)

3b: Jesse Cannady

ss: Horacio Martinez (Dominican)

if: Carlos Santiago (Puerto Rican)

of: Tom Parker

p: Dave Barnhill

p: Barney Morris

p: Carranza Howard

p: Johnny Taylor

p: Patricio Scantlebury (Panamanian)

p: Victor Greenidge (Panamanian)

p: Greene Farmer

p: Bill Anderson

Cuban players who did not participate in the series:

Martin Dihigo p,of

Ramon Heredia 3b

Orestes Minoso 3b

Javier Pérez 2b,of

Santos "Chago" Salazar ut

Epilogue

So concluded the visits of the black baseball teams belonging, until 1920, to the independent leagues, and later to the organized circuit called the Negro Major Leagues, such as the Negro National League (1920–1948), the Eastern Colored League (1923–1928), and the Negro American League (1937–1960). Other black baseball circuits of varying duration included the Southern Negro League (1920), American Negro League (1929), Negro Southern League (1926, 1932, 1945), and the East-West League (1932).

It should be emphasized, however, that so-called black baseball, like Cuban baseball, saw the beginnings of its organized form as early as 1886 with the creation of the Southern League of Colored Baseballists (ALCB), whose name changed in 1887 to the League of Colored Base Ball Players (LCBBP).

Little is known of these early years, but by 1870 a United States team called the Boston Resolutes was integrated with black ballplayers. Afterwards there was a surge in the number of black teams, with teams in Cleveland, St. Louis, Baltimore, Philadelphia, Brooklyn, New Orleans, New York, and others, but all had a short, troubled life.

The intense racial discrimination in the United States in that era was an impediment to progress in organized black baseball. But the visits of the Major League teams to Cuba, which received widespread publicity in the U.S., gave an opportunity to a team called the Cuban X-Giants, integrated only by black players from the United States, who spent several years traveling to Cuba and other countries. This trip gave African American players a way to demonstrate the skills and worth they could bring to baseball.

Although it took many years, the racial barriers in American baseball were broken with the arrival of John Roosevelt Robinson, the tremendously famous "Jackie" Robinson, who integrated the Major Leagues in 1947 wearing the uniform of the Brooklyn Dodgers. No longer in the United States would baseball players be discriminated against because of the color of their skin. In Cuba, however, and in other countries, that discrimination had not been seen since the year 1900.

Appendix A:
Batting Register
for the American Series

The register below includes only the statistics from American Series contests. Batting statistics for players competing in the Cuban League seasons of 1916, with the Chicago American Giants, and 1920–1921, with the Bacharach Giants, appear in appendices C and D, respectively.

Newton Allen

Year	Pos	G	AB	R	H	2B	3B	HR	SH	SB	AVG
1925	3b	8	30	2	8	0	1	0	0	0	.267

Todd Allen

Year	Pos	G	AB	R	H	2B	3B	HR	SH	SB	AVG
1915	3b,1b	17	57	12	23	4	1	0	1	6	.404

Toussaint Allen

Year	Pos	G	AB	R	H	2B	3B	HR	SH	SB	AVG
1920	1b	6	18	0	1	0	0	0	0	0	.056

Héctor Aragó

Year	Pos	G	AB	R	H	2B	3B	HR	RBI	SH	SB	AVG
1945	2b	4	17	0	3	1	0	0	2	0	0	.176

Samuel Bankhead

Year	Pos	G	AB	R	H	2B	3B	HR	SH	SB	AVG
1938	of	6	25	0	6	0	0	0	0	0	.240
1939	ss,of	6	24	4	8	1	0	0	5	0	.333
Totals		12	49	4	14	1	0	0	5	0	.286

Quincy "Bud" Barbee

Year	Pos	G	AB	R	H	2B	3B	HR	SH	SB	AVG
1939	p	2	6	1	1	0	0	0	0	0	.167

Charles Blackwell

Year	Pos	G	AB	R	H	2B	3B	HR	SH	SB	AVG
1920	lf	6	23	3	4	1	1	0	0	1	.174

James Booker

Year	Pos	G	AB	R	H	2B	3B	HR	SH	SB	AVG
1910	1b,lf	14	56	1	13	1	0	0	1	6	.232
1912	c,1b	10	28	2	7	1	0	0	1	0	.250
Totals		24	84	3	20	2	0	0	2	6	.238

Bill Bowman

Year	Pos	G	AB	R	H	2B	3B	HR	SH	SB	AVG
1904	p,f	3	10	3	1	0	0	0	2	0	.100

Emmett Bowman

Year	Pos	G	AB	R	H	2B	3B	HR	SH	SB	AVG
1906	2b,p	11	40	5	10	0	0	0	2	0	.250
1907	3b	10	40	6	10	0	0	0	0	4	.250
Totals		21	80	11	20	0	0	0	2	4	.250

Phil Bradley

Year	Pos	G	AB	R	H	2B	3B	HR	SH	SB	AVG
1908	c,rf	15	51	2	8	0	0	0	5	0	.157
1910	c,rf	8	25	1	4	0	0	0	2	0	.160
Totals		23	76	3	12	0	0	0	7	0	.158

Barney Brown

Year	Pos	G	AB	R	H	2B	3B	HR	SH	SB	AVG
1938	p,ph	5	5	1	1	0	0	0	0	0	.200

Raymond Brown

Year	Pos	G	AB	R	H	2B	3B	HR	SH	SB	AVG
1938	p,ph	4	8	0	0	0	0	0	0	0	.000

Harry Buckner

Year	Pos	G	AB	R	H	2B	3B	HR	SH	SB	AVG
1904	p,rf,3b	7	28	1	4	0	0	0	1	1	.143
1905	p	6	23	2	3	0	0	0	0	1	.130
1906	cf,p	11	44	6	9	1	0	0	1	5	.205
1908	p	9	22	4	4	1	0	0	0	0	.182
Totals		33	117	13	20	2	0	0	2	7	.171

Luis Bustamente

Year	Pos	G	AB	R	H	2B	3B	HR	SH	SB	AVG
1904	ss	2	8	2	3	0	0	0	0	3	.375
1906	ss	2	9	0	0	0	0	0	0	0	.000
Totals		4	17	2	3	0	0	0	0	3	.176

Francisco Campos

Year	Pos	G	AB	R	H	2B	3B	HR	RBI	SH	SB	AVG
1945	lf	5	19	2	5	1	0	0	2	1	0	.263

Matthew Carlisle

Year	Pos	G	AB	R	H	2B	3B	HR	SH	SB	AVG
1938	2b	6	18	0	2	0	0	0	1	0	.111

Charles "Kid" Carter

Year	Pos	G	AB	R	H	2B	3B	HR	SH	SB	AVG
1900	p				no statistics available						

Oscar Charleston

Year	Pos	G	AB	R	H	2B	3B	HR	SH	SB	AVG
1915	cf,p	19	69	7	12	1	0	0	1	2	.174
1920	cf	6	22	2	4	1	1	0	0	0	.182
1925	cf	3	11	1	3	2	0	0	0	0	.273
Totals		28	102	10	19	4	1	0	1	2	.186

C. Clark*

Year	Pos	G	AB	R	H	2B	3B	HR	RBI	SH	SB	AVG
1945	cf	5	17	4	1	0	1	0	0	0	0	.158

Dell Clark

Year	Pos	G	AB	R	H	2B	3B	HR	SH	SB	AVG
1914	2b,ss	14	38	2	5	0	0	0	3	1	.132

Morten Clark

Year	Pos	G	AB	R	H	2B	3B	HR	SH	SB	AVG
1915	ss	20	68	11	19	2	2	0	1	3	.279
1920	2b	6	23	0	4	0	0	0	1	1	.174
Totals		26	91	11	23	2	2	0	2	4	.253

Andy Cooper

Year	Pos	G	AB	R	H	2B	3B	HR	SH	SB	AVG
1925	p	1	3	0	1	0	0	0	0	0	.333

Harry Cozart

Year	Pos	G	AB	R	H	2B	3B	HR	SH	SB	AVG
1939	p	1	4	1	0	0	0	0	0	0	.000

Juan "Bibi" Crespo

Year	Pos	G	AB	R	H	2B	3B	HR	RBI	SH	SB	AVG
1945	p	2	2	0	0	0	0	0	0	0	0	.000

Leon Daniels

Year	Pos	G	AB	R	H	2B	3B	HR	SH	SB	AVG
1925	2b	4	11	1	5	0	0	0	0	0	.455

John Davis

Year	Pos	G	AB	R	H	2B	3B	HR	SH	SB	AVG
1907	p,rf,1b	10	30	3	5	2	1	0	1	1	.167

Elwood DeMoss

Year	Pos	G	AB	R	H	2B	3B	HR	SH	SB	AVG
1915	2b	20	72	19	24	1	1	0	2	10	.333

*Probably Chifian Cleveland Clark.

S.R. "Eddie" Dewitt

Year	Pos	G	AB	R	H	2B	3B	HR	SH	SB	AVG
1920	3b	6	21	2	1	0	0	0	0	0	.048

F. Díaz*

Year	Pos	G	AB	R	H	2B	3B	HR	RBI	SH	SB	AVG
1945	2b,rf	5	19	0	6	0	0	0	0	0	0	.315

Pedro Díaz

Year	Pos	G	AB	R	H	2B	3B	HR	RBI	SH	SB	AVG
1945	c	4	9	1	2	0	1	0	3	1	0	.222

William "Dizzy" Dismukes

Year	Pos	G	AB	R	H	2B	3B	HR	SH	SB	AVG
1914	p	6	14	1	0	0	0	0	1	0	.000

Charles Dougherty

Year	Pos	G	AB	R	H	2B	3B	HR	SH	SB	AVG
1910	p	6	15	0	5	0	0	0	1	0	.333

Thomas Dukes

Year	Pos	G	AB	R	H	2B	3B	HR	SH	SB	AVG
1938	c	1	4	0	1	0	1	0	1	0	.250

Ashby Dunbar

Year	Pos	G	AB	R	H	2B	3B	HR	SH	SB	AVG
1908	cf	16	60	8	14	3	1	0	0	3	.233

Frank Duncan

Year	Pos	G	AB	R	H	2B	3B	HR	SH	SB	AVG
1910	lf,1b	10	36	6	6	0	0	0	0	3	.167

Charles B. "Frank" Earle

Year	Pos	G	AB	R	H	2B	3B	HR	SH	SB	AVG
1907	2b,p,rf	9	29	8	12	0	0	1	3	4	.414
1908	p,rf,lf	15	51	8	9	2	0	0	2	1	.176
Totals		24	80	16	21	2	0	1	5	5	.263

Rafael Figarola

Year	Pos	G	AB	R	H	2B	3B	HR	SH	SB	AVG
1912	c	1	3	0	0	0	0	0	0	0	.000

Willis Pud Flournoy

Year	Pos	G	AB	R	H	2B	3B	HR	SH	SB	AVG
1920	p	2	2	1	0	0	0	0	0	0	.000

Joe Forbes

Year	Pos	G	AB	R	H	2B	3B	HR	SH	SB	AVG
1914	3b	11	32	1	3	0	0	0	1	0	.094

*Probably Fernando Diaz Pedroso, an infielder and outfielder whose stints in the Cuban League (1943–1945 and 1950–1957) sandwiched six seasons in the States, where he played for the New York Cubans.

Andrew "Rube" Foster

Year	Pos	G	AB	R	H	2B	3B	HR	SH	SB	AVG
1903	p,rf	7	28	0	1	0	0	0	0	0	.036
1905	p	6	25	2	5	1	0	0	0	0	.200
1910	p	5	13	1	2	1	0	0	1	0	.154
Totals		18	66	3	8	2	0	0	1	0	.121

William "Billy" Francis

Year	Pos	G	AB	R	H	2B	3B	HR	SH	SB	AVG
1912	3b	15	43	3	10	1	0	0	1	0	.233

Robert "Jude" Gans

Year	Pos	G	AB	R	H	2B	3B	HR	SH	SB	AVG
1908	p,rf	8	21	1	2	0	0	0	0	1	.095
1912	lf	12	39	3	9	0	2	0	1	2	.231
Totals		20	60	4	11	0	2	0	1	3	.183

Regino "Mamelo" García

Year	Pos	G	AB	R	H	2B	3B	HR	SH	SB	AVG
1906	c	2	9	1	4	0	0	0	0	0	.400

Alexander Gaston

Year	Pos	G	AB	R	H	2B	3B	HR	SH	SB	AVG
1925	C	2	7	0	1	1	0	0	0	1	.143

Bill Gatewood

Year	Pos	G	AB	R	H	2B	3B	HR	SH	SB	AVG
1906	rf,p	11	44	5	7	1	1	0	1	1	.159
1907	p,lf,1b	7	21	0	0	0	0	0	0	0	.000
Totals		18	65	5	7	1	1	0	1	1	.108

E. Gavilan*

Year	Pos	G	AB	R	H	2B	3B	HR	RBI	SH	SB	AVG
1945	ss	1	3	0	0	0	0	0	0	0	0	.000

Josh Gibson

Year	Pos	G	AB	R	H	2B	3B	HR	SH	SB	AVG
1938	c,1b	6	23	3	8	4	0	0	4	0	.347
1939	c	6	24	2	9	1	0	0	5	1	.375
Totals		12	47	5	17	5	0	0	9	1	.362

Luis "Chicho" González

Year	Pos	G	AB	R	H	2B	3B	HR	SH	SB	AVG
1907	rf	1	2	1	0	0	0	0	0	1	.000

Charles Grant

Year	Pos	G	AB	R	H	2B	3B	HR	SH	SB	AVG
1900	2b				no statistics available						
1903	2b	9	37	2	6	0	0	0	0	0	.108

*Identity uncertain. Jorge Figueredo (*Who's Who in Cuban Baseball, 1878–1961*) indicates that one Ray Gavilan, a pitcher, recorded two innings of work for Habana during the 1944–1945 Cuban League season.

LeRoy Grant

Year	Pos	G	AB	R	H	2B	3B	HR	SH	SB	AVG
1912	1b	13	39	5	8	1	0	0	4	1	.205

Peter "Ed" Green

Year	Pos	G	AB	R	H	2B	3B	HR	SH	SB	AVG
1914	p,rf	4	4	0	1	0	0	0	0	0	.250

Joaquín Gutiérrez

Year	Pos	G	AB	R	H	2B	3B	HR	RBI	SH	SB	AVG
1945	p	2	0	0	0	0	0	0	0	0	0	.000

Bill Handy

Year	Pos	G	AB	R	H	2B	3B	HR	SH	SB	AVG
1914	ss,2b	14	41	2	7	1	1	0	4	1	.171

E. Victor "Vic" Harris

Year	Pos	G	AB	R	H	2B	3B	HR	SH	SB	AVG
1938	of	6	20	2	4	0	0	0	1	0	.200
1939	of	1	3	1	1	0	0	0	0	0	.333
Totals		7	23	3	5	0	0	0	1	0	.217

Frank Harvey

Year	Pos	G	AB	R	H	2B	3B	HR	SH	SB	AVG
1914	p,rf	10	18	0	2	0	0	0	0	0	.111

Art Henderson

Year	Pos	G	AB	R	H	2B	3B	HR	SH	SB	AVG
1925	P	2	5	0	0	0	0	0	1	0	.000

Ricardo Hernández

Year	Pos	G	AB	R	H	2B	3B	HR	SH	SB	AVG
1908	2b	1	3	0	0	0	0	0	0	0	.000

John A. Hill

Year	Pos	G	AB	R	H	2B	3B	HR	SH	SB	AVG
1903	3b	9	34	1	6	0	0	0	0	0	.176
1905	ss	9	25	4	4	0	0	0	3	0	.160
1906	ss	9	30	1	3	0	0	0	5	0	.100
Totals		27	89	6	13	0	0	0	8	0	.146

J. Preston "Pete" Hill

Year	Pos	G	AB	R	H	2B	3B	HR	SH	SB	AVG
1903	cf	5	15	0	0	0	0	0	0	0	.000
1905	lf	9	37	7	13	0	1	0	1	4	.351
1906	cf	9	37	9	13	1	1	0	1	5	.351
1908	lf	16	56	9	15	1	1	0	3	2	.269
1910	cf	14	58	8	13	1	0	0	2	4	.224
Totals		53	203	33	54	3	3	0	7	15	.266

William "Billy" Holland

Year	Pos	G	AB	R	H	2B	3B	HR	SH	SB	AVG
1925	p	2	7	0	1	0	0	0	1	0	.143

Crush Holloway

Year	Pos	G	AB	R	H	2B	3B	HR	SH	SB	AVG
1925	rf,cf	8	33	4	11	0	1	0	2	0	.333

Samuel Hughes

Year	Pos	G	AB	R	H	2B	3B	HR	SH	SB	AVG
1939	2b	6	21	7	7	1	1	0	1	1	.333

Andrew Jackson

Year	Pos	G	AB	R	H	2B	3B	HR	SH	SB	AVG
1900	3b				no statistics available						

Norman Jackson

Year	Pos	G	AB	R	H	2B	3B	HR	SH	SB	AVG
1938	ss,pr	2	2	0	0	0	0	0	0	0	.000

William Jackson

Year	Pos	G	AB	R	H	2B	3B	HR	SH	SB	AVG
1900	cf				no statistics available						

Gus James

Year	Pos	G	AB	R	H	2B	3B	HR	SH	SB	AVG
1908	c,rf	8	26	1	3	0	0	0	0	0	.115

James C. Jeffries

Year	Pos	G	AB	R	H	2B	3B	HR	SH	SB	AVG
1915	p,rf	7	11	3	4	0	0	0	0	2	.364

Clarence Jenkins

Year	Pos	G	AB	R	H	2B	3B	HR	SH	SB	AVG
1939	of	6	23	4	7	0	1	0	3	1	.304

George Johnson

Year	Pos	G	AB	R	H	2B	3B	HR	SH	SB	AVG
1906	1b	11	36	7	12	0	3	0	3	3	.333

Grant Johnson

Year	Pos	G	AB	R	H	2B	3B	HR	SH	SB	AVG
1903	ss,lf	9	33	7	5	0	0	1	1	0	.152
1904	ss	7	32	4	6	0	0	0	1	1	.188
1908	ss	16	60	8	14	0	1	0	0	1	.233
1910	ss,2b	14	51	10	8	0	0	0	3	1	.157
Totals		46	176	29	33	0	1	1	5	3	.188

Louis Johnson

Year	Pos	G	AB	R	H	2B	3B	HR	SH	SB	AVG
1915	p	8	11	3	1	0	0	0	0	0	.091

Robert Jordan

Year	Pos	G	AB	R	H	2B	3B	HR	SH	SB	AVG
1900	cf				no statistics available						

Year	Pos	G	AB	R	H	2B	3B	HR	SH	SB	AVG
1903	ss,lf	9	39	3	4	0	0	0	0	0	.103
1904	cf	3	12	1	1	0	0	0	1	0	.083
Totals		12	51	4	5	0	0	0	1	0	.098

Dan Kennard

Year	Pos	G	AB	R	H	2B	3B	HR	SH	SB	AVG
1915	c	8	24	3	8	0	1	0	0	1	.333

Henry Kimbro

Year	Pos	G	AB	R	H	2B	3B	HR	SH	SB	AVG
1939	of	6	27	2	10	2	0	0	6	1	.370

Miguel Lastra

Year	Pos	G	AB	R	H	2B	3B	HR	RBI	SH	SB	AVG
1945	inf	1	1	0	0	0	0	0	0	0	0	.000

Walter "Buck" Leonard

Year	Pos	G	AB	R	H	2B	3B	HR	SH	SB	AVG
1938	1b	6	18	1	3	1	0	0	3	0	.167
1939	1b	6	24	1	6	2	0	0	8	0	.250
Totals		12	42	2	9	3	0	0	11	0	.214

Rogelio "Montecado" Linares

Year	Pos	G	AB	R	H	2B	3B	HR	RBI	SH	SB	AVG
1945	1b	3	12	2	3	0	0	0	0	0	0	.250

Bill Lindsay

Year	Pos	G	AB	R	H	2B	3B	HR	SH	SB	AVG
1910	p,rf	5	11	0	2	0	0	0	0	0	.182

John Henry "Pop" Lloyd

Year	Pos	G	AB	R	H	2B	3B	HR	SH	SB	AVG
1907	ss	10	40	7	11	2	0	0	0	0	.275
1910	ss	11	41	8	16	2	0	0	2	4	.390
1912	ss	13	46	13	17	1	1	0	0	8	.370
1925	1b	8	28	7	9	2	2	0	0	1	.321
Totals		42	155	35	52	7	3	0	2	13	.335

Richard "Dick" Lundy

Year	Pos	G	AB	R	H	2B	3B	HR	SH	SB	AVG
1920	ss	6	22	1	5	2	0	0	0	0	.227

James Lyons

Year	Pos	G	AB	R	H	2B	3B	HR	SH	SB	AVG
1915	rf,cf,1b,lf	20	78	11	23	0	1	0	3	8	.295

Raleigh "Biz" Mackey

Year	Pos	G	AB	R	H	2B	3B	HR	SH	SB	AVG
1925	c,rf	8	27	3	9	1	3	0	1	2	.333

Francisco "Cayuco" Martinez

Year	Pos	G	AB	R	H	2B	3B	HR	RBI	SH	SB	AVG
1945	p	2	1	0	0	0	0	0	0		0	0	.000

Dan McClellan

Year	Pos	G	AB	R	H	2B	3B	HR	SH	SB	AVG
1903	p,lf	6	24	2	2	0	0	0	0	0	.083
1904	p,lf	7	29	4	7	0	0	0	0	0	.241
1905	cf,p	9	33	5	6	1	0	0	2	1	.182
Totals		22	83	11	15	1	0	0	2	1	.181

Terris McDuffie

Year	Pos	G	AB	R	H	2B	3B	HR	SH	SB	AVG
1938	p	3	2	0	0	0	0	0	0	0	.000

Samuel Mongin

Year	Pos	G	AB	R	H	2B	3B	HR	SH	SB	AVG
1908	2b	16	56	3	13	1	0	0	1	3	.232

William "Diamond Bill" Monroe

Year	Pos	G	AB	R	H	2B	3B	HR	SH	SB	AVG
1908	3b	15	56	6	13	0	0	0	2	4	.232

Harry Moore

Year	Pos	G	AB	R	H	2B	3B	HR	SH	SB	AVG
1904	lf	7	27	3	7	0	0	0	0	0	.259
1905	3b	9	36	5	7	0	0	0	0	1	.194
1906	3b	11	42	6	9	0	0	0	0	3	.214
1912	cf	13	42	7	11	2	0	0	3	5	.262
Totals		40	147	21	34	2	0	0	3	9	.231

Raúl Navarro

Year	Pos	R	AB	R	H	2B	3B	HR	RBI	SH	SB	AVG
1945	c	2	1	0	0	0	0	0	0	0	0	.000

John Nelson

Year	Pos	G	AB	R	H	2B	3B	HR	SH	SB	AVG
1900	p,rf				no statistics available						

Rafael Noble

Year	Pos	G	AB	R	H	2B	3B	HR	RBI	SH	SB	AVG
1945	c	2	7	1	2	0	0	0	0	0	0	.286

Antonio "Mosquito" Ordeñana

Year	Pos	G	AB	R	H	2B	3B	HR	RBI	SH	SB	AVG
1945	ss	1	4	0	0	0	0	0	0	0	0	.000

C. Orta*

Year	Pos	G	AB	R	H	2B	3B	HR	RBI	SH	SB	AVG
1945	3b	1	3	0	0	0	0	0	0	0	0	.000

*Probably Pedro "Charolito" Orta.

Oliverio Ortiz

Year	Pos	G	AB	R	H	2B	3B	HR	RBI	SH	SB	AVG
1945	p	1	1	0	0	0	0	0	0	0	0	.000

Raymond "Smoky" Owens

Year	Pos	G	AB	R	H	2B	3B	HR	SH	SB	AVG
1939	p	2	4	0	0	0	0	0	0	0	.000

Parker

Year	Pos	G	AB	R	H	2B	3B	HR	SH	SB	AVG
1900	c,lf				no statistics available						

William Parks

Year	Pos	G	AB	R	H	2B	3B	HR	SH	SB	AVG
1914	1b,3b,rf	14	52	3	8	0	0	0	2	0	.154

Agustín Parpetti

Year	Pos	G	AB	R	H	2B	3B	HR	SH	SB	AVG
1908	1b	1	3	0	0	0	0	0	0	0	.000

Roy Partlow

Year	Pos	G	AB	R	H	2B	3B	HR	SH	SB	AVG
1938	p,ph	4	4	0	1	0	0	0	1	0	.250
1939	p	3	5	0	1	0	0	0	0	0	.000
Totals		7	9	0	2	0	0	0	1	0	.222

John B. Patterson

Year	Pos	G	AB	R	H	2B	3B	HR	SH	SB	AVG
1904	2b	7	31	3	6	1	0	0	2	2	.194

Andrew H. Payne

Year	Pos	G	AB	R	H	2B	3B	HR	SH	SB	AVG
1907	cf	10	34	2	5	2	1	0	1	1	.147
1910	lf	14	52	7	15	2	0	0	5	3	.288
Totals		24	86	9	20	4	1	0	6	4	.233

Bruce Petway

Year	Pos	G	AB	R	H	2B	3B	HR	SH	SB	AVG
1906	c	7	22	3	5	1	0	0	1	2	.227
1907	rf,1b	10	36	2	6	0	0	0	0	1	.167
1910	c,rf	14	41	3	4	1	0	0	3	2	.098
Totals		31	99	8	15	2	0	0	4	5	.151

Spottswood Poles

Year	Pos	G	AB	R	H	2B	3B	HR	SH	SB	AVG
1912	rf	13	48	4	14	0	0	0	1	6	.292
1914	cf	14	52	8	16	1	2	0	0	2	.308
Totals		27	100	12	30	1	2	0	1	8	.300

Russell Powell

Year	Pos	G	AB	R	H	2B	3B	HR	SH	SB	AVG
1915	c,3b,1b	20	72	7	15	2	0	0	1	1	.208

Wes Pryor

Year	Pos	G	AB	R	H	2B	3B	HR	SH	SB	AVG
1910	3b	14	47	5	11	1	0	0	1	4	.234

Richard "Cannonball" Redding

Year	Pos	G	AB	R	H	2B	3B	HR	SH	SB	AVG
1912	p	6	13	3	4	0	0	0	0	0	.308
1914	p,rf	10	23	2	4	1	0	0	0	0	.173
1915	p	13	21	5	6	0	0	0	4	2	.286
1920	p	4	11	0	0	0	0	0	0	0	.000
Totals	p	33	68	10	14	1	0	0	4	2	.206

James Robinson

Year	Pos	G	AB	R	H	2B	3B	HR	SH	SB	AVG
1900	p				no statistics available						

Antonio "Pollo" Rodríguez

Year	Pos	G	AB	R	H	2B	3B	HR	RBI	SH	SB	AVG
1945	3b	4	16	0	4	1	1	0	2	0	1	.250

Wilbur "Bullet" Rogan

Year	Pos	G	AB	R	H	2B	3B	HR	SH	SB	AVG
1925	p	5	5	2	2	0	0	0	0	0	.400

Julio Rojo

Year	Pos	G	AB	R	H	2B	3B	HR	SH	SB	AVG
1920	rf,c	6	23	0	4	1	0	0	0	1	.174

Jacinto "Battling Siki" Roque

Year	Pos	G	AB	R	H	2B	3B	HR	RBI	SH	SB	AVG
1945	cf,c	5	16	1	3	0	0	0	2	1	0	.186

Merven J. "Red" Ryan

Year	Pos	G	AB	R	H	2B	3B	HR	SH	SB	AVG
1920	p	5	6	2	1	0	0	0	0	0	.167
1925	p	2	6	1	1	0	0	0	0	0	.167
Totals		7	12	3	2	0	0	0	0	0	.167

Wilfredo Salas

Year	Pos	G	AB	R	H	2B	3B	HR	RBI	SH	SB	AVG
1945	p	2	4	1	1	0	0	0	0	1	0	.250

Rafael Sangil

Year	Pos	G	AB	R	H	2B	3B	HR	RBI	SH	SB	AVG
1945	p	1	0	0	0	0	0	0	0	0	0	.000

Louis Santop

Year	Pos	G	AB	R	H	2B	3B	HR	SH	SB	AVG
1912	c	7	20	1	4	0	0	0	0	0	.200
1914	c,1b	14	44	5	13	1	0	0	1	1	.265
1920	c,rf	6	21	3	4	0	0	0	0	0	.190
Totals		27	85	9	21	1	0	0	0	0	.247

George "Rabbit" Shively

Year	Pos	G	AB	R	H	2B	3B	HR	SH	SB	AVG
1915	lf,rf	20	82	15	17	0	1	0	1	5	.207

James Smith

Year	Pos	G	AB	R	H	2B	3B	HR	SH	SB	AVG
1904	3b	6	22	6	4	0	0	0	2	1	.182

Felton "Skipper" Snow

Year	Pos	G	AB	R	H	2B	3B	HR	SH	SB	AVG
1939	3b	6	25	2	4	0	0	0	1	0	.160

F. Soler*

Year	Pos	G	AB	R	H	2B	3B	HR	RBI	SH	SB	AVG
1945	ph	1	1	0	0	0	0	0	0	0	0	.000

Dangerfield Talbot

Year	Pos	G	AB	R	H	2B	3B	HR	SH	SB	AVG
1905	2b	9	36	2	5	1	0	0	0	1	.139

Ben Taylor

Year	Pos	G	AB	R	H	2B	3B	HR	SH	SB	AVG
1915	1b,p	20	79	8	30	6	1	0	1	7	.380

Charles Ishum "C.I." Taylor

Year	Pos	G	AB	R	H	2B	3B	HR	SH	SB	AVG
1915	rf	9	10	0	0	0	0	0	0	0	.000

J. Terry†

Year	Pos	G	AB	R	H	2B	3B	HR	RBI	SH	SB	AVG
1945	pr	1	0	0	0	0	0	0	0	0	0	.000

Clinton Thomas

Year	Pos	G	AB	R	H	2B	3B	HR	SH	SB	AVG
1925	lf,cf	8	27	4	9	2	1	0	2	2	.333

Jules Thomas

Year	Pos	G	AB	R	H	2B	3B	HR	SH	SB	AVG
1914	lf	14	52	3	8	2	1	0	0	3	.154

Louis Tiant

Year	Pos	G	AB	R	H	2B	3B	HR	RBI	SH	SB	AVG
1945	p	2	1	0	0	0	0	0	0	1	0	.000

Armando Vázquez

Year	Pos	G	AB	R	H	2B	3B	HR	RBI	SH	SB	AVG
1945	1b	1	4	0	2	1	0	0	0	0	0	.500

*No first name found.

†Possibly an aged John Terry, a middle infielder who played for the Indianapolis ABCs, Homestead Grays, Cincinnati Tigers, and Newark Dodgers from 1931–1936.

Edsall "Big" Walker

Year	Pos	G	AB	R	H	2B	3B	HR	SH	SB	AVG
1939	p	2	4	1	2	0	0	0	0	0	.500

Felix Wallace

Year	Pos	G	AB	R	H	2B	3B	HR	SH	SB	AVG
1907	1b,2b	3	7	2	2	0	0	0	1	0	.286

Frank Warfield

Year	Pos	G	AB	R	H	2B	3B	HR	SH	SB	AVG
1925	2b,lf	8	33	4	8	2	0	0	0	3	.242

William Webster

Year	Pos	G	AB	R	H	2B	3B	HR	SH	SB	AVG
1914	1b,c	14	51	6	11	3	0	0	3	7	.215

Willie Wells

Year	Pos	G	AB	R	H	2B	3B	HR	SH	SB	AVG
1938	3b,ss	6	22	1	6	1	0	0	1	0	.273
1939	ss	5	20	0	6	0	0	0	0	0	.300
Totals		11	42	1	12	1	0	0	1	0	.286

Solomon "Sol" White

Year	Pos	G	AB	R	H	2B	3B	HR	SH	SB	AVG
1900	ss				no statistics available						

Frank Wickware

Year	Pos	G	AB	R	H	2B	3B	HR	SH	SB	AVG
1910	p	4	12	1	4	0	0	0	0	0	.333
1912	p	6	13	0	1	0	0	0	0	0	.077
Totals		10	25	1	5	0	0	0	0	0	.200

Clarence Williams

Year	Pos	G	AB	R	H	2B	3B	HR	SH	SB	AVG
1900	c				no statistics available						
1903	c	9	31	3	4	0	0	0	0	0	.129
1904	c	7	23	3	6	0	0	0	1	1	.261
1905	c	9	29	3	4	0	0	0	0	1	.138
1906	c	7	17	3	2	0	0	0	1	0	.118
1907	c,1b	10	26	1	8	0	0	0	0	3	.307
Totals		42	126	13	24	0	0	0	2	5	.190

Harry Williams

Year	Pos	G	AB	R	H	2B	3B	HR	SH	SB	AVG
1938	3b	6	21	3	6	0	0	0	0	1	.286

Jim Williams

Year	Pos	G	AB	R	H	2B	3B	HR	SH	SB	AVG
1938	of	6	19	2	1	0	0	0	0	0	.053

Joseph "Cyclone" Williams

Year	Pos	G	AB	R	H	2B	3B	HR	SH	SB	AVG
1912	p	8	17	1	1	0	0	0	0	0	.059

Ed Wilson

Year	Pos	G	AB	R	H	2B	3B	HR	SH	SB	AVG
1900	1b					no statistics available					
1903	p,lf	6	21	1	4	0	0	0	0	1	.190

George Wilson

Year	Pos	G	AB	R	H	2B	3B	HR	SH	SB	AVG
1903	rf	3	11	1	1	0	0	0	0	0	.091

Ray Wilson

Year	Pos	G	AB	R	H	2B	3B	HR	SH	SB	AVG
1903	1b	9	29	0	7	0	0	0	0	0	.241
1904	1b	7	27	4	3	1	0	0	0	2	.111
1905	1b	9	37	2	7	1	0	0	1	0	.189
Totals		26	93	6	17	2	0	0	1	2	.183

Clarence Winston

Year	Pos	G	AB	R	H	2B	3B	HR	SH	SB	AVG
1905	cf	8	32	4	8	0	0	0	1	2	.250
1906	lf	11	40	9	13	0	1	0	2	6	.325
1907	lf	10	37	12	11	0	0	0	0	6	.297
Totals		29	109	25	32	0	1	0	3	14	.294

George C. Wright

Year	Pos	G	AB	R	H	2B	3B	HR	SH	SB	AVG
1912	2b	13	52	5	8	0	0	0	1	0	.154

Appendix B:
Pitching Register for
the American Series

Included below are the American Series records for all U.S. blackball pitchers, 1903–1945. Nieto found no box scores from 1900, the year of the inaugural series. The three pitchers that year — Kid Carter, John Nelson, and James Robinson — are not included in the appendix, as none pitched in subsequent series.

Statistics for the Cuban League seasons of 1916, with the Chicago American Giants, and 1920–1921, with the Bacharach Giants, appear in appendices C and D, respectively.

Quincy "Bud" Barbee

Year	G	GS	CG	P	Pct	IP	R	H	BB	SO	ERA
1939	2	1	1	0	1.000	13.0	3	7	4	3	2.30

Bill Bowman

Year	G	GS	CG	W	L	Pct	IP	R	H	BB	K	ERA
1904	2	2	2	1	1	.500	17.0	19	15	7	6	ND

Emmett Bowman

Year	G	GS	CG	W	L	Pct	IP	R	H	BB	K	ERA
1906	3	3	3	2	1	.667	27.0	12	18	15	13	ND

Barney Brown

Year	G	GS	CG	RA*	W	L	Pct	IP	AB	R	ER	H	W	K	ERA
1938	3	2	1	1	1	1	.500	13.1	50	5	5	11	2	5	3.38

Raymond Brown

Year	G	GS	GC	GR	W	L	Pct	IP	BF	R	ER	H	W	K	ERA
1938	3	2	1	1	1	0	1.000	19.1	62	2	2	9	10	8	0.93

Harry Buckner

Year	G	GS	CG	W	L	Pct	IP	R	H	BB	K	ERA
1904	3	3	3	2	1	.667	27.0	10	18	6	13	ND
1905	5	4	4	2	2	.500	37.0	16	4	10	23	ND
1906	4	4	4	2	2	.500	37.0	14	25	7	14	ND
1908	7	7	5	4	3	.571	56.2	16	33	16	16	2.54
Totals	19	18	16	10	8	.556	157.2	56	80	39	66	ND

*Relief Appearances

Oscar Charleston

Year	G	CG	W	L	Pct	IP	R	H	BB	K	ERA
1915	1	1	0	1	.000	8.0	10	12	5	2	11.25

Andy Cooper

Year	G	CG	W	L	T	Pct	IP	BF	R	H	BB	SO	ERA
1925	1	1	1	0	0	1.000	9.0	31	1	7	4	3	1.00

Harry Cozart

Year	G	CC	W	L	Pct	IP	R	H	BB	SO	ERA
1939	1	0	1	0	1.000	7.1	1	4	6	2	1.36

John Davis

Year	G	GS	CG	W	L	Pct	IP	R	H	BB	SO	HP	WP
1907	6	6	6	4	2	.667	53.0	11	31	15	14	0	0

William Dismukes

Year	G	GS	CG	W	L	Pct	IP	R	H	BB	K	ERA
1914	6	6	6	2	4	.333	48.1	19	37	16	16	3.56
1916	3	1	0	0	1	.000	15.1	25	24	11	7	14.67
Totals	9	7	6	2	5	.286	63.2	44	61	27	23	6.27

Charles Dougherty

Year	G	GS	CG	W	L	Pct	IP	R	H	BB	K	ERA
1910	4	4	4	1	2	.333	35.0	9	15	17	22	ND
Totals	4	4	4	1	2	.333	35.0	9	15	17	22	ND

Charles B. Earle

Year	G	GS	CG	W	L	Pct	IP	R	H	BB	SO	HP	WP
1907	1	1	1	1	0	1.000	8.0	2	1	2	1	0	0

Charles B. Earle

Year	G	GS	CG	W	L	Pct	IP	R	H	BB	K	HP	WP	ERA
1908	7	6	5	2	3	.400	50.2	21	35	18	18	1	0	3.73

Willis "Pud" Flournoy

Year	G	GS	CG	W	L	Pct	IP	R	H	BB	K	HP	ERA
1920	2	1	0	0	1	.000	7.2	7	7	11	2	0	8.21

Andrew Foster

Year	G	GS	CG	W	L	Pct	IP	R	H	BB	K	ERA
1903	4	3	3	1	2	.333	31.0	6	14	10	31	ND
1905	4	4	4	2	2	.500	34.0	13	25	6	12	ND
1910	4	3	3	3	1	.750	29.0	9	23	5	12	ND
1916	1	1	0	0	1	.000	3.0	5	5	1	0	15.00
Totals	13	11	10	6	6	.500	97.0	33	67	22	55	ND

Robert Gans

Year	G	GS	CG	W	L	Pct	IP	R	H	BB	K	HP	WP	ERA
1908	5	4	2	2	2	.500	30.1	11	25	11	11	1	0	3.26

William Gatewood

Year	G	GS	CG	W	L	Pct	IP	R	H	BB	K	ERA
1906	4	4	4	2	2	.500	34.2	19	27	9	16	ND

William Gatewood

Year	G	GS	CG	W	L	Pct	IP	R	H	BB	SO	HP	WP
1907	3	3	3	0	3	.000	26.1	20	23	15	7	1	1

Peter "Ed" Green

Year	G	GS	CG	W	L	Pct	IP	R	H	BB	K	ERA
1914	2	0	0	0	0	.000	5.0	5	5	1	0	9.00

Frank Harvey

Year	G	GS	CG	W	L	Pct	IP	R	H	BB	K	ERA
1914	3	2	0	0	2	.000	14.0	11	14	16	12	7.07

Art Henderson

Year	G	CG	W	L	T	Pct	IP	BF	R	H	BB	SO	ERA
1925	2	2	1	1	0	.500	17.0	60	7	10	6	8	3.71

William Holland

Year	G	CG	W	L	T	Pct	IP	BF	R	H	BB	SO	ERA
1925	2	2	2	0	0	1.000	18.0	69	8	17	3	9	4.00

James C. Jeffries

Year	G	GS	CG	W	L	Pct	IP	R	H	BB	K	ERA
1915	5	4	2	1	2	.333	30.1	18	28	19	7	5.34

Louis Johnson

Year	G	GS	CG	W	L	Pct	IP	R	H	BB	K	ERA
1915	9	6	3	1	3	.250	41.1	39	41	23	25	4.29

Bill Lindsay

Year	G	GS	CG	W	L	Pct	IP	R	H	BB	K	ERA
1910	3	3	3	1	2	.333	27.0	8	16	11	11	ND

F. Martinez

Year	G	CG	W	L	Pct	IP	R	H	BB	SO	ERA
1945	1	0	0	1	.000						

Daniel McClellan

Year	G	GS	CG	W	L	Pct	IP	R	H	BB	K	ERA
1904	2	2	2	2	0	1.000	18.0	7	16	3	12	ND

Daniel McClellan

Year	G	GS	CG	W	L	Pct	IP	R	H	BB	K	HP	ERA
1903	3	2	2	0	2	.000	18.0	14	19	3	7	X	ND
1904	2	2	2	2	0	1.000	18.0	7	16	3	12	X	ND
1905	1	1	0	0	1	.000	5.0	5	9	1	3	0	ND
Totals	6	5	4	2	3	.400	41.0	26	44	7	22	X	ND

Terris McDuffie

Year	G	GS	CG	GR	W	L	Pct	IP	AB	R	ER	H	BB	K	ERA
1938	3	1	0	2	0	1	.000	9.0	39	8	7	15	2	6	7.00

O. Ortiz

Year	G	CG	W	L	Pct	IP	R	H	BB	SO	ERA
1945	1	0	0	0	.000						

Raymond Owens

Year	G	CG	W	L	Pct	IP	R	H	BB	SO	ERA
1939	2	1	1	0	1.000	10.0	4	12	2	2	3.88

Roy Partlow

Year	G	GS	CG	GR	W	L	Pct	IP	AB	R	ER	H	BB	K	ERA
1938	3	1	0	2	0	2	.000	8.1	37	7	7	14	5	5	7.56
1939	3	1	X	X	2	0	1.000	15.0	XX	2	XX	10	7	5	ND
Totals	6	2	X	X	2	2	.500	23.1	XX	9	XX	24	12	10	ND

Richard Redding

Year	G	GS	CG	W	L	Pct	IP	R	H	BB	K	HP	ERA
1912	4	3	2	2	1	.667	23.2	15	28	9	9	–	ND
1914	8	6	6	2	3	.400	49.0	14	31	16	27	–	2.57
1915	12	8	7	6	5	.545	79.1	49	81	33	33	–	5.56
1920	3	3	3	0	2	.000	25.0	11	17	10	17	1	3.96
Totals	27	20	18	10	11	.476	176.3	89	157	79	86	–	ND

Wilbur Rogan

Year	G	CG	W	L	T	Pct	IP	BF	R	H	BB	SO	ERA
1925	1	1	1	0	0	1.000	9.0	32	0	8	3	3	0.00

Merven J. Ryan

Year	G	GS	CG	W	L	Pct	IP	R	H	BB	K	HP	ERA
1920	4	2	1	0	1	.000	19.0	4	12	6	5	0	1.89
1925	2	–	1	1	1	.500	15.0	17	25	3	5	–	–
Totals	6	4	3	1	2	.333	34.0	21	37	9	10	–	–

W. Salas

Year	G	CG	W	L	Pct	IP	R	H	BB	SO	ERA
1945	2	1	0	2	.000						

Benjamin Taylor

Year	G	GS	CG	W	L	Pct	IP	R	H	BB	K	ERA
1915	3	1	1	0	1	.000	12.0	7	10	3	4	5.25

L. Tiant

Year	G	CG	W	L	Pct	IP	R	H	BB	SO	ERA
1945	2	0	0	1	.000						

Edsall Walker

Year	G	CG	W	L	Pct	IP	R	H	BB	SO	ERA
1939	2	1	1	0	1.000	8.2	1	8	7	1	1.14

Frank Wickware

Year	G	GS	CG	W	L	Pct	IP	R	H	BB	K	ERA
1910	4	4	3	2	1	.667	31.0	15	31	13	11	ND
1912	6	5	3	2	3	.400	38.1	26	36	21	15	ND
1916	8	7	4	2	4	.333	50.1	31	44	24	26	5.54
Totals	18	16	10	6	8	.429	119.2	72	111	58	52	ND

Joseph Williams

Year	G	GS	CG	W	L	Pct	IP	R	H	BB	K	ERA
1912	7	5	4	1	4	.200	44.1	27	40	16	31	ND

Thomas Williams

Year	G	GS	CG	W	L	Pct	IP	R	H	BB	K	ERA
1916	8	6	6	3	3	.500	61.1	34	65	23	19	4.99

Appendix C:
1916 Chicago American Giants
in the Cuban League

There was no American Series in the fall of 1916, but in the spring of that year Rube Foster's Chicago American Giants played in the championship of the Cuban League of Professional Baseball. According to Jorge Figueredo, the Giants played as San Francisco, replacing the local team's roster with their own after San Francisco got off to a 1–21 start. The Americans played considerably better than the local team they replaced but ended, nevertheless, with more losses than wins (Bjarkman, *A History of Cuban Baseball, 1864–2006*, 117–118).

Roster

Player	Pos	Club
Jess Barbour	3b	Chicago American Giants
Harry Bauchman	2b	Chicago American Giants
John Clarkson Brazelton	c	Chicago American Giants
William Dismukes	p	Chicago American Giants
Frank Duncan	lf,rf	Chicago American Giants
Andrew Foster	p	Chicago American Giants
Robert Gans	cf,lf	Chicago American Giants
J. Preston Hill	rf,cf	Chicago American Giants
John Henry Lloyd	ss	Chicago American Giants
Tully McAdoo	1b	Chicago American Giants
Bruce Petway	c,1b,of	Chicago American Giants
Frank Wickware	p	Chicago American Giants
Tom Williams	p	Chicago American Giants

Manager: Andrew "Rube" Foster

Jess "Barber" Barbour started with the Philadelphia Giants in 1910 and also played with the Chicago American Giants.

Harry Bauchman started with the Chicago American Giants in 1915.

John Clarkson Brazelton began with the Chicago American Giants in 1916.

William "Dizzy" Dismukes started with the Philadelphia Giants in 1913. This right-handed pitcher played with the Lincoln Stars for a 1914 trip to Cuba and with the Chicago American Giants for this 1916 trip.

Frank Duncan played with the Philadelphia Giants (1909), Leland Giants and Chicago American Giants.

Andrew "Rube" Foster was the manager as well as a pitcher for this team. He started with the Chicago Union Giants in 1902 and also played with the Cuban X-Giants beginning in 1903.

Robert Edward "Jude" Gans started with the Brooklyn Royal Giants in 1908. He played with the Cuban Giants, Smart Set and Lincoln Giants.

J. Preston "Pete" Hill started in 1903 with the Philadelphia Giants.

John Henry Lloyd began his career as a twenty-year-old professional ball player, a catcher for the Macon Acmes, Georgia. He also played with the Cuban X Giants, Philadelphia Giants, Leland Giants and Lincoln Giants. The 1916 series was his fourth trip to Cuba.

Tully McAdoo started with the Topeka Giants (1907), then played for the Giants of Kansas City, Kansas, and the Saint Louis Giants. For this trip to Cuba he played with the Chicago American Giants.

Bruce Petway began with the Leland Giants in 1906. He also played with the Brooklyn Royal Giants and Philadelphia Giants.

Frank Wickware righthander with great speed, started with the Leland Giants in 1910. He also played with the Saint Louis Giants, Mohawk Giants and Lincoln Giants.

Thomas "Tom" Williams began his career with the Bacharach Giants. Later he played with the Chicago American Giants.

Games Played

Date	Winning Club		Losing Club		Winning Pitcher	Losing Pitcher
Feb 6	Habana	2	San Francisco	1	E. Palmero	T. Williamsxxxx
Feb 7	Almendares	16	San Francisco	8	A. Luque	F. Wickware
Feb 12	Habana	7	San Francisco	3	E. Palmero	W. Dismuke
Feb 14	Almendares	17	San Francisco	0	A. Luque	F. Wickware
Feb 17	San Francisco	3	Habana	1	T. Williams	E. Palmero
Feb 20	San Francisco	6	Almendares	6	Tie-F. Wickware/F. Campos	
Feb 21	Almendares	15	San Francisco	1	E. Pedroso	T. Wlliams
Feb 24	San Francisco	2	Habana	0	F. Wickware	E. Palmero
Feb 26	Almendares	8	San Francisco	2	F. Campos	A. Foster
Feb 28	San Francisco	14	Habana	3	T. Williams	P. Pareda
Mar 2	San Francisco	8	Almendares	1	F. Wickware	F. Campos
Mar 5	Almendares	5	San Francisco	4	A. Luque	T. Williams
Mar 6	Habana	1	San Francisco	0	J. Acosta	F. Wickware
Mar 11	San Francisco	4	Almendares	3	T. Williams	J. Mendez
Mar 12	Habana	10	San Francisco	4	P. Pareda	F. Wickware
(15)						

The American players abandoned the San Francisco club after March 12, and most of them returned to the United States. The scores above are for only the 15 games the American Giants played as San Francisco.

Club Standings

Pos	Club	G	W	L	T	Pct
1.	Almendares	8	5	2	1	.714
2.	Habana	7	4	3	0	.571
3.	San Francisco	15	5	9	1	.357
	Totals	30	14	14	2	.500

The Games

GAME ONE: FEBRUARY 6, 1916, AT ALMENDARES PARK

San Francisco	Pos	AB	R	H	O	A	E	Habana	Pos	AB	R	H	O	A	E
J. Barbour	3b	3	0	0	0	0	0	A. Marsans	1b,lf	3	1	0	3	0	0
J.P. Hill	rf	3	1	2	2	0	0	B. Acosta	lf,rf	4	1	1	1	0	0

San Francisco	Pos	AB	R	H	O	A	E		Habana	Pos	AB	R	H	O	A	E
F. Duncan	lf	3	0	1	3	0	0		J. Calvo	cf	4	0	1	1	0	0
J.H. Lloyd	ss	4	0	1	4	1	1		A. Aragon	3b	2	0	2	0	0	0
R. Gans	cf	3	0	0	1	0	0		E. González	2b	4	0	1	1	4	0
T. McAdoo	1b	3	0	1	10	0	0		T. Calvo	rf	2	0	0	0	0	0
H. Bauchman	2b	3	0	0	0	4	0		T. Romanach	ss	3	0	1	2	3	0
B. Petway	c	3	0	0	3	2	1		R. Torres	c,1b	3	0	1	13	0	0
T. Williams	p	3	0	0	1	4	0		E. Palmero	p	3	0	0	0	5	0
Totals		28	1	5	24	11	2		R. González	3b	1	0	0	2	2	0
									M.A. González	c	0	0	0	5	0	0
									Totals		29	2	7	27	14	0

San Francisco	000	100	000 — 1
Almendares	101	000	00x — 2

Three-base hits: T. Romanach
Double-plays: T. Romanach and R. Torres
Bases on balls: T. Williams 2, E. Palmero 3
Strikeouts: T. Williams 2, E. Palmero 9
Hit by pitcher: E. Palmero (2)
Winning pitcher: E. Palmero
Losing pitcher: T. Williams
Time: 2 hours 10 minutes
Umpires: Eustaquio Gutiérrez (home) and José M. Magrinat (bases)
Scorer: Hilario Franquiz

GAME TWO: FEBRUARY 7, 1916, AT ALMENDARES PARK

San Francisco	Pos	AB	R	H	O	A	E		Almendares	Pos	AB	R	H	O	A	E
J. Barbour	3b	4	0	4	3	2	3		F. Campos	2b	4	2	1	2	4	0
J.P. Hill	rf	5	2	3	1	0	0		M. Cueto	3b	5	2	2	3	2	0
F. Duncan	lf	4	2	3	2	0	0		G. González	c	3	2	2	11	1	0
J.H. Lloyd	ss	4	1	3	3	5	0		C. Torriente	cf	4	1	2	1	0	0
R. Gans	cf	5	1	3	0	1	0		R. Herrera	ss	4	2	1	3	0	0
T. McAdoo	1b	4	1	0	8	1	1		E. Pedroso	rf	5	2	3	1	1	1
H. Bauchman	2b	3	1	1	1	2	1		J. Mendez	lf	3	2	1	1	0	0
B. Petway	c	3	0	1	5	1	1		J. Rodríguez	1b	3	2	0	5	2	0
F. Wickware	p	0	0	0	0	0	0		A. Luque	p	3	1	1	0	4	0
W. Dismukes	p	4	0	0	0	1	0		H. Hidalgo	cf	0	0	0	0	0	0
J. Brazelton	c	1	0	0	1	2	1		T. Williams	(x)	1	0	0	0	0	0
Totals		34	16	13	27	14	1		Totals		40	8	19	24	15	7

(x)— Out for W. Dismukes in Ninth.

San Francisco	002	200	202 — 8
Almendares	166	000	03x — 16

Three-base hits: C. Torriente (2), A. Luque
Two-base hits: J. Barbour, R. Gans, J.P. Hill, J.H. Lloyd
Sacrifice hits: A. Luque, G. González
Stolen bases: R. Herrera (2), E. Pedroso (2), J. Rodríguez, J.H. Lloyd, R. Gans, G. González
Double-plays: F. Campos (no assist)
Bases on balls: F. Wickware 2, W. Dismukes 4, A. Luque 5
Strikeouts: F. Wickware 0, W. Dismukes 4, A. Luque 5
Hit by pitcher: A. Luque 1, F. Wickware 1, W. Dismukes 1
Hits allowed by pitchers: F. Wickware 4 in 1.1
Winning Pitcher: A. Luque
Losing Pitcher: F. Wickware
Time: 2 hours 25 minutes
Umpires: Eustaquio Gutiérrez (home) and José M. Magrinat (bases)
Scorer: Hilario Franquiz

GAME THREE: FEBRUARY 12, 1916, AT ALMENDARES PARK

Habana	Pos	AB	R	H	O	A	E	San Francisco	Pos	AB	R	H	O	A	E
A. Marsans	lf	5	1	3	0	1	1	J. Barbour	3b	4	0	0	1	2	0
B. Acosta	rf,cf	4	1	2	0	0	0	J.P. Hill	rf	3	0	1	0	0	0
J. Calvo	cf	4	1	1	2	1	0	F. Duncan	lf	2	1	0	1	0	0
M.A. González	c	5	1	3	6	3	0	J.H. Lloyd	ss	3	0	1	4	0	0
A. Aragon	3b	5	0	0	1	0	0	R. Gans	cf	3	0	1	4	0	0
E. González	2b	4	1	2	1	4	0	T. McAdoo	1b	4	0	1	11	0	1
T. Romanach	ss	3	1	2	4	3	0	H. Bauchman	2b	4	0	1	2	4	0
R. Torres	1b	3	0	0	12	0	0	B. Petway	c	2	0	1	4	1	0
E. Palmero	p	3	1	0	0	4	0	W. Dismukes	p	2	0	0	0	4	0
T. Calvo	rf	0	0	0	0	0	0	T. Williams	p	1	0	0	0	1	0
Totals		36	7	13	27	16	1	Totals		28	3	6	27	17	1

Habana	001	006	000 — 7
San Francisco	000	102	000 — 3

Two-base hits: E. González (2)
Sacrifice hits: R. Torres
Stolen bases: B. Petway
Double-plays: J.H. Lloyd, H. Bauchman and T. McAdoo (2); W. Dismukes, J.H. Lloyd and T. McAdoo; T. Romanach and R. Torres
Bases on balls: E. Palmero 5, W. Dismukes 2, T. Williams 1
Strikeouts: E. Palmero 5, W. Dismukes 3, T. Williams 1
Hit by pitcher: E. Palmero 1 (J. Williams)
Hits: W. Dismukes 8 in 5.1 innings
Winning pitcher: E. Palmero
Losing pitcher: W. Dismukes
Time: 2 hours 25 minutes
Umpires: Eustaquio Gutiérrez (home) and José M. Magrinat (bases)
Scorer: Hilario Franquiz

GAME FOUR: FEBRUARY 14, 1916, AT ALMENDARES PARK

Almendares	Pos	AB	R	H	O	A	E	San Francisco	Pos	AB	R	H	O	A	E
P. Chacon	ss	5	1	0	2	7	1	J. Barbour	3b	5	0	1	2	2	0
M. Cueto	3b	3	2	1	1	3	1	J.P. Hill	rf	3	0	1	0	0	1
G. González	c	4	2	2	3	0	0	F. Duncan	lf	4	0	0	1	1	2
C. Torriente	cf	4	2	1	1	0	0	J.H. Lloyd	ss	4	0	2	2	5	0
E. Pedroso	rf	4	3	3	0	1	0	R. Gans	cf	3	0	0	1	0	0
J. Mendez	lf	4	2	1	1	0	0	T. McAdoo	1b	3	0	0	14	0	0
A. Luque	p	2	0	0	0	1	0	H. Bauchman	2b	4	0	2	2	4	2
J. Rodríguez	1b	3	2	2	12	0	0	J. Brazelton	c	4	0	0	4	1	0
R. Herrera	2b	4	2	0	5	3	0	F. Wickware	p	2	0	1	0	1	1
F. Campos	p	2	1	1	0	2	0	W. Dismukes	p	2	0	0	0	3	1
Totals		37	17	12	27	17	2	Totals		34	0	7	27	17	7

Almendares	200	403	107 — 17
San Francisco	000	000	000 — 0

Two-base hits: J.P. Hill, F. Campos
Sacrifice hits: E. Pedroso, R. Herrera, J. Mendez (2)
Sacrifice fly: F. Campos
Stolen bases: G. González, J. Barbour, M. Cueto, E. Pedroso, J. Rodríguez, Herrera (2), J. Mendez
Bases on balls: F. Wickare 4, W. Dismukes 4, E. Pedroso 2, A. Luque 0
Strikeouts: F. Wickware 2, W. Dismukes 1, E. Pedroso 0, A. Luque 4
Hit by pitcher: F. Wickware 1
Hits: F. Wickware 5 in 5.2 innings; E. Pedroso 4 in 4.0 innings

Winning pitcher: A. Luque
Losing pitcher: F. Wickware
Time: 2 hours 30 minutes
Umpires: Eustaquio Gutiérrez (home) and José M. Magrinat (bases)
Scorer: Hilario Franquiz

GAME FIVE: FEBRUARY 17, 1916, AT ALMENDARES PARK

San Francisco	Pos	AB	R	H	O	A	E	Habana	Pos	AB	R	H	O	A	E
B. Petway	c	5	1	3	5	0	0	A. Marsans	lf,1b	4	1	1	1	0	0
J.P. Hill	rf	4	2	3	2	0	0	B. Acosta	rf	4	0	1	1	0	0
F. Duncan	lf	4	0	3	1	0	0	J. Calvo	cf	3	0	1	1	0	0
J.H. Lloyd	ss	4	0	1	2	2	1	M.A. González	c	4	0	0	2	1	0
R. Gans	cf	3	0	2	2	0	0	A. Aragon	3b	4	0	0	0	1	0
J. Barbour	3b	4	0	0	0	5	0	R. González	2b	4	0	0	2	2	0
T. McAdoo	1b	3	0	0	13	2	2	T. Romanach	ss	4	0	1	6	12	0
H. Bauchman	2b	3	0	0	2	5	1	R. Torres	1b	3	0	0	12	3	0
T. Williams	p	4	0	0	0	3	0	E. Palmero	p	2	0	0	0	2	0
								T. Calvo	rf	0	0	0	0	0	0
Totals		34	3	12	27	17	4	Totals		33	1	4	27	23	0

San Francisco   100   002   000 — 3
Habana   001   000   000 — 1

Two-base hits: R. Gans
Double-plays: T. Romanach to R. Torres (2); R. González to T. Romanach to R. Torres
Bases on balls: E. Palmero 3, T. Williams 1
Strikeouts: E. Palmero 1, T. Williams 2
Winning pitcher: T. Williams
Losing pitcher: E. Palmero
Time: 2 hours
Umpires: Eustaquio Gutiérrez (home) and José M. Magrinat (bases)
Scorer: Hilario Franquiz

GAME SIX: FEBRUARY 20, 1916, AT ALMENDARES PARK

San Francisco	Pos	AB	R	H	O	A	E	Almendares	Pos	AB	R	H	O	A	E
B. Petway	c	4	1	2	5	1	0	P. Chacon	ss	4	1	0	4	4	0
J.P. Hill	rf	4	0	0	0	0	0	M. Cueto	3b	5	3	3	3	0	0
F. Duncan	lf	4	0	1	0	0	0	G. González	c	3	1	2	7	0	0
J.H. Lloyd	ss	4	0	2	4	4	2	C. Torriente	cf	3	1	1	2	0	0
R. Gans	cf	3	1	1	4	0	0	J. Mendez	lf	5	0	0	3	0	0
J. Barbour	3b	5	2	2	0	2	0	R. Herrera	2b	5	0	3	0	5	0
T. McAdoo	1b	4	1	1	9	3	1	H. Hidalgo	rf	5	0	0	0	0	0
H. Bauchman	2b	5	0	0	7	3	0	J. Rodríguez	1b	5	0	1	9	1	0
F. Wickware	p	3	1	1	1	0	0	F. Campos	p	2	0	0	0	2	0
								E. Pedroso	p	1	0	0	0	3	0
								A. Luque	p	1	0	0	1	2	0
Totals		36	6	10	30	16	3	Totals		39	6	10	30	17	0

San Francisco   000   204   000   0 — 6
Almendares   103   010   100   0 — 6

Note: Game called on account of darkness
Three-base hits: C. Torriente
Two-base hits: F. Duncan
Sacrifice hits: J.P. Hill, G. González
Stolen bases: P. Chacon, R. Gans, M. Cueto, R. Herrera, J. Rodríguez, J. Barbour
Double-plays: H. Bauchman and T. McAdoo

Bases on balls: F. Campos 1, E. Pedroso 4, A. Luque 1, F. Wickware 3
Strikeouts: F. Campos 0, E. Pedroso 1, A. Luque 2, F. Wickware 1
Hit by pitcher: F. Campos 1
Hits: F. Campos 6 in 4.0 innings; E. Pedroso 5 in 2.1 innings
Time: 2 hours 30 minutes
Umpires: Eustaquio Gutiérrez (home) and José M. Magrinat (bases)
Scorer: Hilario Franquiz

GAME SEVEN: FEBRUARY 21, 1916, AT ALMENDARES PARK

Almendares	Pos	AB	R	H	O	A	E		San Francisco	Pos	AB	R	H	O	A	E
P. Chacon	ss	5	0	1	2	7	0		B. Petway	c	4	0	0	3	4	0
M. Cueto	3b	3	3	2	0	4	0		J.P. Hill	rf	2	1	1	4	1	0
G. González	c	3	3	2	0	1	1		F. Duncan	lf	4	0	2	2	1	0
C. Torriente	cf	2	3	1	1	0	1		J.H. Lloyd	ss	4	0	0	3	4	0
E. Pedroso	p	4	2	3	1	1	0		R. Gans	cf	3	0	0	2	0	0
R. Herrera	2b	5	1	3	2	6	0		J. Barbour	3b	3	0	0	1	4	0
J. Mendez	lf	5	1	1	2	0	0		T. McAdoo	1b	3	0	1	8	0	0
J. Rodríguez	1b	5	1	1	16	1	0		H. Bauchman	2b	3	0	0	3	2	0
H. Hidalgo	rf	5	1	3	2	0	0		T. Williams	p	3	0	0	0	2	0
D. Hernandez	c	0	0	0	1	0	0		Totals		29	1	4	27	18	0
F. Campos	cf	0	0	0	0	0	0									
Totals		37	15	17	27	18	2									

Almendares	000	203	028 — 15
San Francisco	100	000	000 — 1

Home run: C. Torriente
Two-base hits: F. Duncan, H. Hidalgo (2)
Sacrifice hits: M. Cueto, G. González
Stolen bases: J.P. Hill, C. Torriente, E. Pedroso, R. Herrera, J. Rodríguez
Double-plays: J.P. Hill, H. Bauchman and J. Barbour; R. Herrera, P. Chacon and J. Rodríguez;
 B. Petway and H. Bauchman; P. Chacon and J. Rodríguez
Bases on balls: T. Williams 6, E. Pedroso 2
Strikeouts: T. Williams 2, E. Pedroso 1
Hit by pitcher: T. Williams 1
Wild pitches: T. Williams 1
Balks: T. Williams 2
Winning pitcher: E. Pedroso
Losing pitcher: T. Williams
Time: 2 hours
Umpires: Eustaquio Gutiérrez (home) and José M. Magrinat (bases)
Scorer: Hilario Franquiz

GAME EIGHT: FEBRUARY 24, 1916, AT ALMENDARES PARK

Habana	Pos	AB	R	H	O	A	E		San Francisco	Pos	AB	R	H	O	A	E
A. Marsans	lf	3	0	1	0	0	0		B. Petway	c	2	0	0	2	1	0
J. Calvo	cf	3	0	0	1	0	0		J.P. Hill	rf	4	0	1	1	0	0
A. Aragon	3b	4	0	1	1	5	0		F. Duncan	lf	4	0	0	1	1	0
M.A. González	c	4	0	0	8	1	0		J.H. Lloyd	ss	3	0	1	1	3	1
E. González	2b	3	0	0	5	2	0		R. Gans	cf	2	1	0	1	0	0
T. Romanach	ss	3	0	0	2	0	1		J. Barbour	3b	2	1	0	3	1	0
R. Torres	1b	3	0	0	6	0	0		T. McAdoo	1b	3	0	1	10	0	0
T. Calvo	rf	2	0	0	0	0	0		H. Bauchman	2b	3	0	1	1	3	0
E. Palmero	p	2	0	0	0	2	0		F. Wickware	p	3	0	0	0	2	0
R. González	rf	1	0	0	1	0	0		Totals		26	2	4	27	11	1
Totals		28	0	2	24	10										

Habana	000	000	000 — 0
San Francisco	010	100	00x — 2

Three-base hits: A. Marsans
Stolen bases: A. Marsans (3), J. Calvo, R. Gans (2), H. Bauchman
Double-plays: A. Aragon, E. González and R. Torres; F. Duncan and B. Petway
Bases on balls: E. Palmero 4, F. Wickware 4
Strikeouts: E. Palmero 8, F. Wickware 7
Hit by pitcher: E. Palmero 1, F. Wickware 1
Winning pitcher: F. Wickware
Losing pitcher: E. Palmero
Time: 2 hours
Umpires: Eustaquio Gutiérrez (home) and José M. Magrinat (bases)
Scorer: Hilario Franquiz

The March 11, 1916, edition of the *Chicago Defender* included an account of Game Eight:

Wickware Bests Palmerio in a Pitching Duel

New York Giants Hurler Goes Down to Defeat in Great Battle — Duncan in His Usual Sensational Stunt

Havana, Cuba, March 10.—(Special)—The American Giants scored another victory over the Havana team when Wickware emerged the winner in a pitching duel with Palermo, the New York Giant twirler. Six hits were all that were collected in the game, the Giants getting four off Palermo and Wickware holding the islanders to two, one a three-base slam by Marsans. The latter had a good day on the paths, stealing three times from Petway. In the fourth inning Palermo struck out Lloyd, Hill and Duncan. Duncan made a sensational catch in the eight of Calvo's fly and threw Marsans, who was perched on third, out at the plate when he tried to score after the catch. Wickware was in trouble several times, but managed to wiggle out with the stellar support of his mates. These two defeats of the Havanas have shoved the Giants into second place and they are in grand form to give the Almendares a trimming. The latter team is the pride of the island and is the one that defeated the champion Athletics in 1910.

GAME NINE: FEBRUARY 26, 1916, AT ALMENDARES PARK

San Francisco	Pos	AB	R	H	O	A	E	Almendares	Pos	AB	R	H	O	A	E
B. Petway	c	5	2	2	3	1	0	P. Chacon	ss	3	0	1	4	2	0
J.P. Hill	cf	5	0	2	1	0	0	M. Cueto	3b	3	1	0	0	2	0
F. Duncan	rf	4	0	2	0	1	0	G. González	c	4	3	3	4	0	0
J.H. Lloyd	ss	5	0	2	4	9	1	C. Torriente	cf	3	1	2	5	0	0
R. Gans	lf	4	0	1	1	0	0	J. Mendez	lf	4	0	2	5	0	0
J. Barbour	3b	3	0	0	1	2	0	R. Herrera	2b	4	0	1	0	5	0
T. McAdoo	1b	4	0	0	14	0	0	F. Campos	p	4	0	0	0	0	0
H. Bauchman	2b	4	0	1	0	4	0	H. Hidalgo	cf	4	1	2	0	0	0
A. Foster	p	2	0	1	0	0	0	D. Hernandez	1b	3	2	1	9	2	1
F. Wickware	p	2	0	1	0	1	0	Totals		33	8	12	27	11	1
Totals		38	2	12	24	19	1								

San Francisco	100	000	001 — 2
Almendares	104	021	00x — 8

Two-base hits: C. Torriente, J. Mendez, B. Petway
Sacrifice hits: P. Chacon
Stolen bases: A. Foster, G. González, D. Hernandez, P. Chacon
Double-plays: H. Bauchman, J.H. Lloyd and T. McAdoo; P. Chacon and D. Hernandez
Bases on balls: A. Foster 3, F. Wickware 0, F. Campos 3
Strikeouts: A. Foster 0, F. Wickware 2, F. Campos 1
Balks: A. Foster 1
Winning Pitcher: F. Campos
Losing Pitcher: A. Foster

Time: 1 hour 50 minutes
Umpires: Eustaquio Gutiérrez (home) and José M. Magrinat (bases)
Scorer: Hilario Franquiz

GAME TEN: FEBRUARY 28, 1916, AT ALMENDARES PARK

San Francisco	Pos	AB	R	H	O	A	E
B. Petway	c	4	3	2	1	0	0
J.P. Hill	cf	3	2	1	1	0	0
F. Duncan	rf	5	0	0	0	0	0
J.H. Lloyd	ss	3	3	3	0	3	0
R. Gans	lf	4	2	1	4	1	0
J. Barbour	3b	4	1	1	3	2	0
T. McAdoo	1b	3	1	1	14	0	1
H. Bauchman	2b	5	0	0	4	3	0
T. Williams	p	5	2	1	0	3	0
Totals		36	14	10	27	14	1

Habana	Pos	AB	R	H	O	A	E
A. Marsans	1b,lf	3	0	0	3	1	0
B. Acosta	rf	0	0	0	2	0	0
J. Calvo	cf	4	0	1	6	0	0
E. González	2b	3	0	2	2	0	0
R. González	3b	4	0	1	1	1	0
T. Calvo	lf,rf	4	1	1	2	0	0
R. Torres	c,1b	4	1	1	8	0	2
T. Romanach	ss	4	0	0	2	10	0
P. Pareda	p	1	0	0	0	0	0
G. Ballesteros	rf	0	0	0	0	0	0
M.A. González	c	3	1	2	3	1	1
J. Acosta	p	3	0	0	0	1	0
Totals		33	3	8	27	14	

San Francisco	436	000	100 — 14
Habana	000	003	000 — 3

Two-base hits: J. Barbour
Sacrifice hits: J.P. Hill, J. Barbour, A. Marsans
Sacrifice fly: T. McAdoo
Stolen bases: J.H. Lloyd (3), R. Gans (3), J. Barbour (2), J. Williams, B. Petway, J.P. Hill (2), T. McAdoo
Double-plays: J.H. Lloyd, H. Bauchman and T. McAdoo
Bases on balls: P. Pareda 6, J. Acosta 1, T. Williams 1
Strikeouts: P. Pareda 1, J. Acosta 1, T. Williams 4
Hit by pitcher: J. Acosta 1, T. Williams 1
Passed balls: R. Torres 1, M.A. González 1
Hits: P. Pareda 7 in 3.0
Winning pitcher: T. Williams
Losing pitcher: P. Pareda
Time: 2 hours
Umpires: Eustaquio Gutiérrez (home) and José M. Magrinat (bases)
Scorer: Hilario Franquiz

A brief account of Game Six, which appeared in the March 11 issue of the Chicago Defender, follows:

American Giants Win

Take One-Sided Game from the Havana Reds—Williams Pitching Good Ball

Havana, Cuba, March 1 [illegible]—Special)—The American Giants defeated the Havana Reds in a one-sided game. They played the Cubans off their feet. Williams hurled good ball, having but one bad inning, this being the sixth, when five hits in a row, coupled with a base on balls and one error, netted them three runs. A lightning double play, Lloyd to Bauchman to McAdoo, ended the agony. Petway has come back into his own and is playing and hitting like he used to do twelve years ago.

GAME ELEVEN: MARCH 2, 1916, AT ALMENDARES PARK

Almendares	Pos	AB	R	H	O	A	E
P. Chacon	ss	4	0	1	3	1	1
M. Cueto	3b	4	0	0	3	3	1

San Francisco	Pos	AB	R	H	O	A	E
B. Petway	c	5	1	2	4	0	0
F. Duncan	cf	5	0	2	2	1	0

Almendares	Pos	AB	R	H	O	A	E
G. González	c	3	1	0	6	1	0
C. Torriente	cf	4	0	2	0	0	0
R. Herrera	2b	2	0	1	2	4	0
J. Mendez	lf	4	0	1	2	0	1
H. Hidalgo	rf	3	0	0	0	1	0
D. Hernandez	1b	3	0	0	8	0	0
F. Campos	p	2	0	1	0	2	0
E. Pedroso	p	1	0	1	0	1	0
Totals		31	1	6	24	13	3

(x)—Out for D. Hernandez in Ninth.

San Francisco	Pos	AB	R	H	O	A	E
J.H. Lloyd	ss	5	2	4	3	3	1
R.Gans	lf	4	2	2	2	0	0
J. Barbour	3b	5	1	3	2	2	0
T. McAdoo	1b	4	1	1	9	0	0
H. Bauchman	2b	4	1	2	0	1	1
J. Brazelton	c	2	0	0	5	0	0
F. Wickware	p	4	0	0	0	2	0
A. Luque	(x)	1	0	0	0	0	0
Totals		38	8	16	27	9	2

```
Almendares      000   001   000 — 1
San Francisco   200   003   12x — 8
```

Three-base hits: J.H. Lloyd, J. Barbour
Two-base hits: T. McAdoo
Sacrifice hits: M. Cueto, R. Herrera
Stolen bases: H. Bauchman (2), R. Herrera, H. Hidalgo, J. Barbour, G. González, R. Gans
Double-plays: M. Cueto and D. Hernandez; F. Duncan and Brazelton
Bases on balls: F. Campos 1, E. Pedroso 2, F. Wickware 6
Strikeouts: F. Campos 3, E. Pedroso 2, F. Wickware 4
Hits: F. Campos 8 in 5.0 innings
Winning pitcher: F. Wickware
Losing pitcher: F. Campos
Time: 1 hour 50 minutes
Umpires: Eustaquio Gutiérrez (home) and José M. Magrinat (bases)
Scorer: Hilario Franquiz

Game Twelve: March 5, 1916, at Almendares Park

Habana	Pos	AB	R	H	O	A	E
J. Rodes	lf	4	1	1	3	0	1
J. Calvo	cf	4	0	0	2	0	0
E. González	2b	3	0	1	1	2	0
R. González	3b	2	0	0	3	4	0
T. Romanach	ss	4	0	2	3	1	0
T. Calvo	rf	4	0	2	3	1	0
R. Torres	c	4	0	1	5	1	0
M. Perramon	1b	3	0	0	9	0	1
J. Acosta	p	3	0	0	0	3	0
Totals		31	1	7	27	11	2

San Francisco	Pos	AB	R	H	O	A	E
J. Barbour	3b	4	0	0	1	2	1
J.P. Hill	cf	4	0	0	2	1	0
F. Duncan	rf	4	0	0	1	0	0
J.H. Lloyd	ss	4	0	2	0	4	0
R. Gans	lf	4	0	1	2	0	0
T. McAdoo	1b	4	0	1	14	0	0
H. Bauchman	2b	4	0	2	1	2	0
J. Brazelton	c	3	0	0	6	2	0
F. Wickware	p	3	0	0	0	2	0
Totals		30	0	6	27	13	1

```
Habana          001   000   000 — 1
San Francisco   000   000   000 — 0
```

Sacrifice hits: E. González
Sacrifice flies: R. González
Stolen bases: J.Rodes, E. González, T. Calvo, H. Bauchman
Double-plays: Brazelton and T. McAdoo
Bases on balls: F. Wickware 5, J. Acosta 0
Strikeouts: F. Wickware 5, J. Acosta 4
Winning pitcher: J. Acosta
Losing pitcher: F. Wickware
Time: 1 hour 35 minutes
Umpires: Eustaquio Gutiérrez (home) and José M. Magrinat (bases)
Scorer: Hilario Franquiz

GAME THIRTEEN: MARCH 6, 1916, AT ALMENDARES PARK

San Francisco	Pos	AB	R	H	O	A	E	Almendares	Pos	AB	R	H	O	A	E
B. Petway	rf,c	4	1	1	4	1	0	P. Chacon	ss	4	0	0	4	1	0
F. Duncan	cf	4	0	2	1	0	0	M. Cueto	3b	4	1	3	0	6	0
J.H. Lloyd	ss	4	0	1	5	7	0	G. González	c	2	2	1	4	1	0
R. Gans	lf	4	1	0	1	0	0	C. Torriente	cf	4	2	2	2	0	0
J. Barbour	3b	4	1	2	2	1	2	R. Herrera	2b	4	0	1	0	4	0
T. McAdoo	1b	4	0	1	9	0	0	E. Pedroso	p,1b	3	0	2	8	4	0
H. Bauchman	2b	3	1	1	2	1	0	J. Mendez	lf	1	0	0	0	0	1
J. Brazelton	c	0	0	0	0	1	0	H. Hidalgo	rf	2	0	0	1	0	0
T. Williams	p	4	0	0	0	2	0	D. Hernandez	1b	2	0	0	8	0	0
J.P. Hill	rf	4	0	1	0	1	0	A. Luque	p	1	0	0	0	2	0
Totals		35	4	9	24	14	2	Totals		28	5	9	27	18	

San Francisco	002	002	000 — 4
Almendares	300	000	002 — 5

Note: One out when winning run scored in ninth
Sacrifice hits: G. González, J. Mendez
Stolen bases: M. Cueto, J. Barbour, R. Gans, T. McAdoo, H. Bauchman
Double-plays: P. Chacon and D. Hernandez; H. Bauchman and J.H. Lloyd
Bases on balls: E. Pedroso 1, A. Luque 1, T. Williams 0
Strikeouts: E. Pedroso 2, A. Luque 1, T. Williams 4
Hits: E. Pedroso 8 in 6.0 innings
Winning pitcher: A. Luque
Losing pitcher: T. Williams
Time: 2 hours
Umpires: Eustaquio Gutiérrez (home) and José M. Magrinat (bases)
Scorer: Hilario Franquiz

GAME FOURTEEN: MARCH 11, 1916, AT ALMENDARES PARK

Almendares	Pos	AB	R	H	O	A	E	San Francisco	Pos	AB	R	H	O	A	E
P. Chacon	ss	5	0	0	2	3	2	B. Petway	c	4	1	2	3	3	1
M. Cueto	3b	4	0	1	1	1	0	J.P. Hill	cf	3	0	1	3	0	0
G. González	c	4	0	1	9	1	0	F. Duncan	rf	3	1	2	0	0	0
C. Torriente	cf	3	1	1	2	1	0	J.H. Lloyd	ss	4	0	0	0	0	2
E. Pedroso	p	2	0	1	0	2	0	R. Gans	lf	3	0	1	5	0	0
R. Herrera	2b	2	0	0	2	3	0	T. McAdoo	1b	4	1	1	10	0	0
J. Mendez	lf,p	3	0	1	0	0	0	J. Barbour	3b	3	0	0	1	1	0
H. Hidalgo	rf	2	1	0	2	0	0	H. Bauchman	2b	3	1	0	1	3	0
D. Hernandez	c	4	1	1	4	0	0	T. Williams	p	2	0	0	0	3	0
F. Campos	p,lf	2	0	1	2	1	0	Totals		29	4	7	27	15	3
Totals		31	3	7	24	12									

Almendares	002	100	000 — 3
San Francisco	001	100	02x — 4

Sacrifice hits: J. Williams
Sacrifice fly: R. Herrera.
Stolen bases: J.P. Hill, D. Hernandez, J. Mendez
Double-plays: P. Chacon and G. González
Bases on balls: E. Pedroso 2, F. Campos 1, J. Mendez 0, T. Williams 4
Strikeouts: E. Pedroso 2, F. Campos 0, J. Mendez 0, T. Williams 3
Hit by pitcher: T. Williams 1
Passed balls: D. Hernandez
Hits: E. Pedroso 2 in 3.0 innings; F.Campos 2 in 4.0 innings
Winning pitcher: T. Williams

Losing pitcher: J. Mendez
Time: 2 hours
Umpires: Eustaquio Gutiérrez (home) and José M. Magrinat (bases)
Scorer: Hilario Franquiz

GAME FIFTEEN: MARCH 12, 1916, AT ALMENDARES PARK

San Francisco	Pos	AB	R	H	O	A	E	Habana	Pos	AB	R	H	O	A	E
B. Petway	1b	4	0	1	6	2	0	J. Rodes	lf	3	2	2	2	0	0
J.P. Hill	cf	4	0	3	3	0	0	J. Calvo	cf	3	1	1	3	0	0
F. Duncan	rf	4	0	1	1	0	0	E. González	2b	4	1	3	4	7	1
J.H. Lloyd	ss	4	1	1	4	1	0	R. González	3b	5	1	2	0	1	0
R. Gans	lf	3	1	2	2	0	0	T. Romanach	ss	5	1	1	2	5	0
J. Barbour	3b	4	0	1	3	1	0	T. Calvo	rf	3	1	1	2	0	0
H. Bauchman	2b	4	0	0	2	3	0	R. Torres	c	5	0	1	3	0	0
J. Brazelton	c	1	1	0	3	2	1	M. Perramon	1b	3	1	1	11	2	0
F. Wickware	p	0	0	0	0	1	0	P. Pareda	p	2	2	1	0	3	0
T. Williams	p	3	1	1	0	0	0	Totals		33	10	13	27	18	1
Totals		31	4	10	24	10	1								

San Francisco   002   000   101 — 4
Habana   320   111   02x — 10

Three-base hits: J. Rodes, J. Williams
Two-base hits: E. González, M. Perramon
Sacrifice hits: J. Rodes
Sacrifice fly: R. Gans
Stolen bases: T. Romanach, J.H. Lloyd
Double-plays: R. González, E. González and M. Perramon; T. Romanach, E. González and
    M. Perramon; J. Barbour (s.a); E. González, T. Romanach and M. Perramon
Bases on balls: F. Wickware 5, T. Williams 4, P. Pareda 2
Strikeouts: F. Wickware 1, T. Williams 1, P. Pareda 3
Wild pitches: P. Pareda 1
Hits: F. Wickware 2 in 1.1 innings
Passed balls: Brazelton (2)
Winning pitcher: P. Pareda
Losing pitcher: T. Williams
Time: 1 hour 50 minutes
Umpires: Eustaquio Gutiérrez (home) and José M. Magrinat (bases)
Scorer: Hilario Franquiz

Final Statistics

CHICAGO AMERICAN GIANTS—1916

Individual Pitching

Pitcher	G	GS	GC	W	L	Pct	IP	R	H	W	K	ERT
William Dismukes	3	1	0	0	1	.000	15.1	25	24	11	7	14.67
Andrew Foster	1	1	0	0	1	.000	3.0	5	5	1	0	15.00
Frank Wickware	8	7	4	2	4	.333	50.1	31	44	24	26	5.54
Thomas Williams	8	6	6	3	3	.500	61.1	34	65	23	19	4.99
Totals	16	15	10	5	9	.357	130.0	95	138	59	52	6.58

Individual Batting

Player	Pos	G	AB	R	H	TB	2b	3b	HR	SH	SB	Pct
Jess Barbour	3b	15	59	7	15	16	1	0	0	0	0	.254

Player	Pos	G	AB	R	H	TB	2b	3b	HR	SH	SB	Pct
Harry Bauchman	2b	15	47	4	11	12	1	0	0	–	5	.234
John C. Brazelton	c	6	10	1	1	1	0	0	0	0	0	.100
William Dismukes	p	3	8	0	0	0	0	0	0	0	0	.000
Frank Duncan	lf,rf	15	58	4	19	20	1	0	0	0	1	.327
Andrew Foster	p	1	2	0	1	1	0	0	0	0	0	.500
Robert Gans	cf,lf	15	50	9	15	16	1	0	0	8	1	.300
J. Preston Hill	rf,cf	14	51	8	20	22	2	0	0	0	1	.392
John Henry Lloyd	ss	15	60	9	24	25	1	0	0	6	1	.403
Tully McAdoo	1b	15	45	5	9	11	2	0	0	–	2	.191
Bruce Petway	c,1b,of	13	45	9	15	15	0	0	0	2	1	.333
Frank Wickware	p	9	14	1	3	3	0	0	0	0	0	.214
Thomas Williams	p	9	26	3	2	2	0	0	0	0	0	.077
Totals		15	475	60	135	144	9	0	0	16	10	.284

Individual Fielding

Player	Pos	G	O	A	E	Pct
Jess Barbour	3b	15	21	30	6	.895
Harry Bauchman	2b	15	28	42	5	.933
John C. Brazelton	c	6	19	8	2	.931
William Dismukes	p	3	0	8	1	.889
Frank Duncan	lf,rf	15	16	5	2	.913
Andrew Foster	p	1	0	0	0	.000
Robert Gans	cf,lf	15	32	3	0	1.000
J. Preston Hill	rf,cf	14	18	3	1	.955
John Henry Lloyd	ss	15	45	62	9	.920
Tully McAdoo	1b	15	153	6	6	.964
Bruce Petway	c,1b,of	13	55	18	3	.961
Frank Wickware	p	9	1	13	1	.933
Thomas Williams	p	9	1	20	0	1.000
Totals		15	389	218	36	.944

Appendix D:
1920–1921 Bacharach Giants
in the Cuban League

Roster

Player	Pos	Club
Toussaint Allen	1b	Hilldale
Charles Blackwell	lf	Hilldale
Oscar Charleston	cf	Indianapolis ABCs
Morten Clark	2b	Indianapolis ABCs
S.R. "Eddie" DeWith	3b	Indianapolis ABCs
Willis "Pud" Flournoy	p	Hilldale
Richard Lundy	ss	Bacharach Giants
Richard Redding	p	Bacharach Giants
Julio Rojo	rf, c	Bacharach Giants
Merven J. Ryan	p	Bacharach Giants
Louis Santop	c, rf	Hilldale

Toussaint "Tom" Allen started with the Havana Red Sox in 1914. He played with Hilldale, but for this trip to Cuba he played with the Bacharach Giants.

Charles Blackwell started with the Saint Louis Giants in 1916 and later played with the Saint Louis Stars, Birmingham Barons and Indianapolis ABCs. For this trip to Cuba he played with the Bacharach Giants.

Oscar Charleston a superstar blend of power and speed, started with the Indianoplis ABCs in 1915.

Morten "Specs" Clark started with the Indianapolis ABCS in 1910. He also played with the Baltimore Black Sox.

S.R. "Eddie" DeWitt started with the Dayton Giants (1910) and played with the Dayton Marcos and Indianapolis ABCs.

Willis "Pud" Flournoy started with Hilldale (1919) and played with the Brooklyn Royal Giants and Bacharach Giants.

Richard Lundy a shortstop with a wide range and a strong arm, began in 191 with the Bacharach Giants.

Richard "Cannonball Dick" Redding as his nickname suggests, was a pitcher noted for overpowering speed. This right-hander started with the Lincoln Giants in 1911. In 1912 he won 43 games and lost 12. He played with the Lincoln Stars, Indianapolis ABCs, Chicago American Giants, Brooklyn Royal Giants and Bacharach Giants.

Julio Rojo a Cuban, began in 1916 with the Cuban Stars and later played with the Havana Stars and Bacharach Giants.

Merven J. "Red" Ryan started with the Pittsburgh Stars of Buffalo (1916) and also played with the Brooklyn Royal Giants, Hilldale, Harrisburg Giants and Bacharach Giants.

Louis "Top" Santop was a lefthanded power hitter and skilled catcher. Beginning his career with the Fort Worth Wonders in 1909, he went on to play with the Oklahoma Monarchs, Philadelphia Giants, Lincoln Giants, Chicago American Giants, Lincoln Stars and, for this trip to Cuba, with the Bacharach Giants.

Games Played

Date	Winning Club		Losing Club		Winning Pitcher	Losing Pitcher
Dec 2	Bacharach	2	Almendares	2	- Tied -	
Dec 4	Habana	11	Bacharach	4	J. Acosta	R. Redding
Dec 6	Bacharach	4	Habana	3	M.J. Ryan	O. Tuero
Dec 9	Almendares	5	Bacharach	4	E. Palmero	R. Redding
Dec 12	Almendares	12	Bacharach	7	E. Palmero	P. Flournoy
Dec 13	Habana	5	Bacharach	2	W.C. Stewart	P. Flournoy
Dec 18	Bacharach	2	Almendares	1	M.J. Ryan	E. Palmero
Dec 23	Habana	9	Bacharach	8	O. Tuero	P. Flournoy
Dec 25	Bacharach	9	Almendares	5	M.J. Ryan	I. Fabre
Dec 30	Almendares	11	Bacharach	0	A. Luque	R. Redding
Jan 1	Bacharach	2	Habana	1	R. Redding	O. Tuero
Jan 3	Habana	4	Bacharach	0	J. Acosta	R. Redding
Jan 8	Almendares	7	Bacharach	4	J. Mendez	P. Flournoy
Jan 9	Habana	4	Bacharach	3	J. Acosta	R. Redding
Jan 10	Almendares	4	Bacharach	0	J. Hernandez	P. Flournoy
Jan 12	Almendares	11	Bacharach	0	A. Luque	R. Redding
Jan 13	Habana	2	Bacharach	0	J. Acosta	P. Flournoy
(17)						

Club Standings

(Bacharach Giants losses by forefeit are not included.)

Clubs	G	W	L	T	Pct
Habana	32	17	10	5	.630
Almendares	31	13	12	6	.520
Bacharach Giants	17	4	12	1	.250
Totals	80	34	34	12	.500

The Games

GAME ONE: THURSDAY, DECEMBER 2, 1920, AT ALMENDARES PARK

Bacharach	Pos	AB	R	H	O	A	E		Almendares	Pos	AB	R	H	O	A	E
M. Clark	2b	4	2	2	3	3	1		B. Portuondo	3b	4	0	1	1	0	0
S.R. Dewitt	3b	4	0	1	1	1	0		B. Baro	rf	4	0	0	0	0	0
O. Charleston	cf	4	0	3	2	1	0		B. Acosta	lf	3	1	1	3	0	0
L. Santop	rf	4	0	0	1	0	0		P. Chacon	ss	3	1	1	1	4	0
C. Blackwell	lf	2	0	0	1	0	0		C. Torriente	cf	3	0	2	3	1	0
R. Lundy	ss	2	0	0	3	2	1		R. Herrera	2b	3	0	1	1	3	0
J. Rojo	c	1	0	0	6	3	0		M. Guerra	1b	3	0	0	9	0	0
T. Allen	1b	3	0	1	7	0	0		E. Abreu	c	3	0	0	5	2	1
R. Redding	p	3	0	0	0	0	0		I. Fabre	p	2	0	0	1	3	0
Totals		27	2	8	24	9	2		E. Palmero	p	1	0	0	0	0	0
									Totals		29	2	7	24	14	1

| Bacharach Giants | 100 | 000 | 01 : 2 |
| Almendares | 100 | 100 | 00 : 2 |

Two-base hits: B. Acosta, P. Chacon, B. Portuondo, O. Charleston
Sacrifice hits: J. Rojo
Stolen bases: M. Clark (2), O. Charleston, R. Lundy
Bases on balls: R. Redding 5, I. Fabre 1, E. Palmero 0
Strikeouts: R. Redding 5, I. Fabre 1, E. Palmero 0
Time: 1 hour 50 minutes
Umpires: Alfredo Cabrera (home) and José M. Magrinat (bases)
Scorer: Hilario Franquiz

GAME TWO: SATURDAY, DECEMBER 4, 1920, AT ALMENDARES PARK

Habana	Pos	AB	R	H	O	A	E
M. Cueto	3b	4	2	3	2	0	0
J. Calvo	cf	6	0	3	1	0	0
G. Burns	lf	4	1	1	3	1	0
L. Doyle	2b	4	1	2	4	1	0
R. Almeida	rf	5	1	1	2	1	0
H.H. Ford	ss	5	2	2	3	3	1
J. Rodríguez	1b	4	1	0	4	0	0
R. Torres	c	5	0	1	7	0	0
J. Acosta	p	3	3	1	0	2	0
O. Rodríguez	3b	1	0	0	1	0	0
F. Hungo	2b	0	0	0	0	1	0
J. López	ss	0	0	0	0	0	0
M.A. González	1b	0	0	0	0	0	0
Totals		41	11	14	27	9	

Bacharach	Pos	AB	R	H	O	A	E
M. Clark	2b	4	0	2	2	1	1
S.R. Dewitt	3b	5	1	2	2	0	2
O. Charleston	cf	5	1	1	4	0	0
L. Santop	rf	5	1	3	2	0	0
C. Blackwell	lf	4	0	1	1	1	0
R. Lundy	ss	5	0	0	4	6	0
J. Rojo	c	4	0	2	3	2	0
T. Allen	1b	3	1	2	9	0	1
R. Redding	p	0	0	0	0	0	0
M.J. Ryan	p	4	0	0	0	3	0
Totals		39	4	13	27	13	4

| Habana | 700 | 020 | 200 : 11 |
| Bacharach Giants | 201 | 001 | 000 : 4 |

Three-base hits: J. Calvo
Two-base hits: L. Santop (2)
Stolen bases: J. Calvo
Double-plays: G. Burns and R. Torres
Bases on balls: J. Acosta 2, R. Redding 4, M.J. Ryan 2
Strikeouts: J. Acosta 3, R. Redding 1, M.J. Ryan 2
Hit by pitcher: J. Acosta 1 (D. Clark)
Winning pitcher: J. Acosta
Losing pitcher: R. Redding
Umpires: Alfredo Cabrera (home) and José M. Magrinat (bases)
Scorer: Julio Franquiz

GAME THREE: MONDAY, DECEMBER 6, 1920, AT ALMENDARES PARK

Bacharach	Pos	AB	R	H	O	A	E
M. Clark	2b	4	0	0	0	1	0
S.R. Dewitt	3b	5	0	2	1	2	0
O. Charleston	cf	3	1	2	2	1	0
L. Santop	c	4	0	2	5	0	1
C. Blackwell	lf	4	0	1	4	0	0
R. Lundy	ss	2	1	1	3	5	0
J. Rojo	c	3	1	1	2	0	0
T. Allen	1b	4	1	1	9	0	0
M.J. Ryan	p	4	0	1	1	1	1
Totals		31	4	11	27	10	2

Habana	Pos	AB	R	H	O	A	E
J. Rodríguez	ss,2b	4	0	1	0	2	0
J. Calvo	rf	4	0	0	0	0	0
M. Cueto	3b	3	1	1	1	2	0
R. Almeida	rf	4	1	1	1	0	0
H.H. Ford	ss	4	1	0	1	2	0
J. López	lf	1	0	1	1	0	0
O. Rodríguez	2b	0	0	0	0	0	1
R. Torres	c	3	0	0	7	5	0
0. Tuero	p	2	0	1	0	5	0
M.A. González	1b	3	0	1	10	2	0

Bacharach	Pos	AB	R	H	O	A	E	Habana	Pos	AB	R	H	O	A	E
								W.C. Stewart	p	1	0	0	0	0	0
								F. Hungo	(x)	1	0	0	0	0	0
								Totals		30	3	6	27	18	1

(x)—Out for W.C. Stewart in the ninth.

Bacharach Giants	021	000	100 : 4
Habana	000	003	000 : 3

Sacrifice hits: J. López, R. Lundy
Solen bases: O. Charleston, J. Rodríguez
Double-plays: R. Lundy and T. Allen; W.C. Stewart, M.A. González and R. Torres
Bases on balls: O. Tuero 3, W.C. Stewart 1, M.J. Ryan 7
Strikeouts: O. Tuero 3, W.C. Stewart 2, M.J. Ryan 3
Winning pitcher: M.J. Ryan
Losing pitcher: O. Tuero
Time: 2 hours
Umpires: Alfredo Cabrera (home) and José M. Magrinat (bases)
Scorer: Julio Franquiz

GAME FOUR: THURSDAY, DECEMBER 9, 1920, AT ALMENDARES PARK

Almendares	Pos	AB	R	H	O	A	E	Bacharach	Pos	AB	R	H	O	A	E
B. Portuondo	3b	3	0	0	1	0	0	M. Clark	rf,ss	4	0	1	4	2	3
R. Herrera	2b	4	3	0	0	1	0	S.R. Dewitt	3b	1	1	0	0	4	0
B. Acosta	lf	3	2	1	0	0	0	O. Charleston	cf	3	1	1	2	0	0
P. Chacon	ss	4	0	3	3	5	0	C. Blackwell	lf	3	1	1	2	0	0
C. Torriente	cf	4	0	1	3	0	1	R. Lundy	ss	0	0	0	0	0	1
J. Mendez	rf	4	0	0	0	0	0	J. Rojo	c	2	1	1	5	2	1
M. Guerra	1b	4	0	1	10	1	0	J. Teran	2b	2	0	1	1	5	1
E. Abreu	c	4	0	1	7	2	0	T. Allen	1b	4	0	1	10	0	0
E. Palmero	p	2	0	0	0	4	1	R. Redding	p	3	0	1	0	0	0
I. Fabre	p	0	0	0	0	0	0	L. Santop	rf	3	0	0	1	2	0
Totals		32	5	7	24	13	2	P. Cockrell	2b	0	0	0	0	0	0
								Totals		26	4	8	24	13	6

Almendares	200	010	20 : 5
Bacharach Giants	010	000	03 : 4

Two-base hits: M. Guerra
Sacrifice hits: J. Teran, S.R. Dewitt, L. Santop, J. Rojo
Stolen bases: E. Palmero, R. Herrera, P. Chacon, B. Acosta
Double-plays: P. Chacon and M. Guerra; E. Abreu and P. Chacon
Bases on balls: E. Palmero 4, I. Fabre 0, R. Redding 3
Strikeouts: E. Palmero 7, I. Fabre 0, R. Redding 5
Hit by pitcher: E. Palmero 1 (J. Hewitt) y R. Redding 1 (B. Portuondo)
Balks: E. Palmero
Passed balls: J. Rojo
Winning pitcher: E. Palmero
Losing pitcher: R. Redding
Time: 2 hours 10 minutes
Umpires: Alfredo Cabrera (home) and José M. Magrinat (bases)
Scorer: Julio Franquiz

GAME FIVE: SUNDAY, DECEMBER 12, 1920, AT ALMENDARES PARK

Bacharach	Pos	AB	R	H	O	A	E	Almendares	Pos	AB	R	H	O	A	E
M. Clark	rf	4	1	1	1	0	0	B. Portuondo	3b	6	1	3	0	4	1

Bacharach	Pos	AB	R	H	O	A	E
S.R. Dewitt	3b	4	2	1	0	2	1
O. Charleston	cf	2	1	2	4	0	0
L. Santop	c	4	0	1	6	0	0
C. Blackwell	lf	4	2	3	2	0	0
R. Lundy	ss	3	1	0	1	2	0
J. Teran	2b	4	0	2	2	1	0
T. Allen	1b	4	0	1	8	0	0
R. Redding	p	2	0	1	0	0	0
P. Flournoy	p	1	0	0	0	2	0
Totals		33	7	12	24	7	1

Almendares	Pos	AB	R	H	O	A	E
R. Herrera	2b	6	1	0	2	2	0
B. Acosta	lf	2	2	2	0	0	0
P. Chacon	ss	2	1	1	6	2	0
C. Torriente	cf	3	2	1	0	0	0
M. Guerra	1b	5	2	2	11	0	2
J. Mendez	rf	5	1	1	0	0	0
E. Abreu	c	4	1	2	7	3	2
E. Palmero	p	3	1	2	0	3	0
E. González	2b	0	0	0	1	1	0
M.J. Ryan	p	1	0	0	0	0	0
Totals		36	12	14	27	13	5

Bacharach Giants 500   011   000 : 7
Almendares   004   010   010 : 12

Three-base hits: M. Guerra
Sacrifice hits: E. Palmero, D. Clark, O. Charleston, R. Herrera, B. Acosta, C. Blackwell, J. Teran,
   E. Abreu, M. Guerra
Double-plays: P. Chacon, R. Herrera to M. Guerra; R. Lundy to J. Teran; E. Palmero, P. Chacon to M.
   Guerra; E. González to P. Chacon
Bases on balls: R. Redding 3, P. Flournoy 2, M.J. Ryan 2, E. Palmero 4
Strikeouts: R. Redding 2, P. Flournoy 0, M.J. Ryan 2, E. Palmero 5
Dead balls: P. Flournoy 2 (P. Chacon and C. Torriente)
Passed balls: E. Abreu 1, L. Santop 1
Winning Pitcher: E. Palmero
Losing Pitcher: P. Flournoy
Time: 2 hours 30 minutes
Arbitros: Alfredo Cabrera (home) and José M. Magrinat (bases)
Scorer: Julio Franquiz

GAME SIX: MONDAY, DECEMBER 13, 1920, AT ALMENDARES PARK

Habana	Pos	AB	R	H	O	A	E
B. Jimenez	2b	4	0	0	3	1	0
J. Calvo	cf	4	1	1	4	1	0
M. Cueto	3b	3	2	2	0	3	0
R. Almeida	rf	4	2	1	1	0	0
J. Rodríguez	1b	4	0	2	11	0	1
H.H. Ford	ss	2	0	0	2	1	0
J. López	lf	3	0	1	1	0	0
R. Torres	c	4	0	0	5	2	0
W.C. Stewart	p	3	0	0	0	3	0
Totals		31	5	7	27	11	1

Bacharach	Pos	AB	R	H	O	A	E
M. Clark	ss	4	0	2	5	2	1
S.R. Dewitt	3b	4	0	1	1	2	0
O. Charleston	cf	4	2	2	1	1	0
L. Santop	c	4	0	3	8	3	0
C. Blackwell	lf	3	0	1	2	0	0
A. Parpetti	1b	4	0	1	8	1	0
J. Teran	2b	4	0	0	1	2	0
P. Cockrell	rf	1	0	0	1	0	0
P. Flournoy	p	3	0	0	0	0	0
M.J. Ryan	rf	2	0	0	0	0	0
T. Allen	(x)	1	0	0	0	0	0
R. Redding	(xx)	1	0	0	0	0	0
Totals		35	2	10	27	17	1

(x)—Out for M.C. Ryan in ninth.
(xx)—Out for P. Flournoy in eighth.

Habana   300   000   020 : 5
Bacharach Giants 100   100   000 : 2

Three-base hits: J. Rodríguez (2)
Two-base hits: M. Cueto
Sacrifice hits: C. Blackwell
Stolen bases: O. Charleston, M. Cueto
Double-plays: A. Parpetti and L. Santop
Bases on balls: W.C. Stewart, P. Flournoy

Strikeouts: W.C. Stewart 5, P. Flournoy 6
Winning pitcher: W.C. Stewart
Losing pitcher: P. Flournoy
Time: 1 hour 38 minutes
Umpires: Alfredo Cabrera (home) and José M. Magrinat (bases)
Scorer: Hilario Franquiz

GAME SEVEN: SATURDAY, DECEMBER 18, 1920, AT ALMENDARES PARK

Almendares	Pos	AB	R	H	O	A	E		Bacharach	Pos	AB	R	H	O	A	E
B. Portuondo	3b	4	0	1	2	0	0		M. Clark	ss	4	0	2	2	3	0
R. Herrera	2b	4	0	0	5	1	0		S.R. Dewitt	3b	3	0	0	2	2	0
E. González	ss	4	0	1	2	2	0		O. Charleston	cf	4	0	1	4	0	0
C. Torriente	cf	4	1	0	0	0	0		L. Santop	c	4	0	1	4	0	0
M. Guerra	lf	4	0	0	3	0	0		C. Blackwell	lf	4	1	1	2	0	1
A. Luque	1b	3	0	0	8	0	1		A. Parpetti	1b	2	0	2	10	0	1
J. Mendez	rf	3	0	1	3	0	0		J. Teran	2b	3	1	1	2	1	0
E. Abreu	c	3	0	1	3	4	0		A. Casanas	rf	0	0	0	0	0	0
E. Palmero	p	3	0	0	0	6	0		M.J. Ryan	p	2	0	1	0	4	0
									P. Cockrell	rf	2	0	0	0	0	0
Totals		32	1	4	24	13	1		Totals		28	2	9	27	10	2

Almendares   010   000   000 — 1
Bacharach Giants 010   010   00x — 2

Three-base hits: C. Blackwell, L. Santop
Two-base hits: J. Mendez, J. Teran
Stolen bases: M. Clark, C. Torriente, J. Hewitt
Bases on balls: E. Palmero 3, M.J. Ryan 0
Strikeouts: E. Palmero 2, M.J. Ryan 1
Hit by pitcher: E. Palmero 1 (J. Hewitt)
Winning pitcher: M.J. Ryan
Losing pitcher: E. Palmero
Time: 1 hour 50 minutes
Umpires: Alfredo Cabrera (home) and José M. Magrinat (bases)
Scorer: Julio Franquiz

GAME EIGHT: MONDAY, DECEMBER 20, 1920, AT ALMENDARES PARK

Bacharach	Pos	AB	R	H	O	A	E		Habana	Pos	AB	R	H	O	A	E
M. Clark	ss	4	1	1	1	2	1		B. Jimenez	2b	3	1	0	2	2	2
S.R. Dewitt	3b	1	0	0	0	0	1		J. Calvo	cf	4	1	2	1	0	0
O. Charleston	cf	4	0	2	2	0	0		M. Cueto	3b	3	0	1	3	3	0
L. Santop	rf	3	1	2	0	0	0		R. Almeida	rf	2	0	0	1	0	0
C. Blackwell	lf	2	0	1	0	0	0		J. Rodríguez	1b	4	0	0	9	0	0
A. Parpetti	1b	4	0	1	11	0	0		J. López	lf	2	0	0	0	0	0
J. Teran	2b	4	0	0	0	5	0		H.H. Ford	ss	2	0	0	2	2	0
P. Cockrell	rf	4	0	0	2	0	0		R. Torres	c	3	0	0	4	2	0
R. Redding	p	2	1	2	0	6	0		O. Tuero	p	0	0	0	1	2	0
T. Allen	1b	0	0	0	3	0	0		M.A. González	1b	2	1	1	4	0	0
Totals		29	2	7	25	14	3		Totals		29	3	4	27	11	0

Bacharach Giants 000   020   000 — 2
Habana   000   200   001 — 3

Note: One out when winning run scored in ninth
Two-base hits: R. Redding
Sacrifice hits: R. Almeida, S.R. Dewitt, H.H. Ford
Stolen bases: M. Cueto, H.H. Ford, R. Almeida

Double-plays: M. Cueto, B. Jimenez and J. Rodríguez
Bases on balls: R. Redding 4, O. Tuero 4
Strikeouts: R. Redding 3, O. Tuero 2
Balks: O. Tuero
Passed balls: L. Santop 1
Winning pitcher: O. Tuero
Losing Pitcher: R. Redding
Time: 1 hour 50 minutes
Umpires: Alfredo Cabrera (home) and José M. Magrinat (bases)
Scorer: Hilario Franquiz

GAME NINE: THURSDAY, DECEMBER 23, 1920, AT ALMENDARES PARK

Habana	Pos	AB	R	H	O	A	E
B. Jimenez	2b	4	3	3	0	7	0
J. Rodríguez	3b	3	0	1	1	1	1
M. Cueto	cf	3	2	2	2	0	0
R. Almeida	rf	2	1	0	1	0	0
M.A. González	c	2	1	0	10	0	0
J. López	lf	2	0	1	0	0	0
H.H. Ford	ss	3	0	0	3	1	0
R. Torres	1b	3	0	0	4	0	0
O. Tuero	p	3	2	1	0	4	2
Totals		25	9	9	21	13	3

Bacharach	Pos	AB	R	H	O	A	E
M. Clark	ss	4	1	3	2	5	1
C. Blackwell	lf	4	1	2	2	0	0
O. Charleston	cf	4	2	1	0	0	0
L. Santop	rf	3	1	2	0	0	0
A. Parpetti	1b	4	0	1	10	0	1
M. Martinez	3b	3	0	0	1	2	0
F. Campos	2b	2	1	0	4	3	0
V. Rodríguez	c	4	1	1	2	3	0
P. Flournoy	p	1	0	0	0	3	0
P. Cockrell	p	2	1	0	0	1	0
Totals		31	8	10	21	17	2

Habana	301	212	0 — 9
Bacharach Giants	110	006	0 — 8

Home runs: B. Jimenez
Two-base hits: M. Cueto, L. Santop, O. Tuero, O. Charleston
Stolen bases: M. Cueto, A. Parpetti, B. Jimenez, L. Santop
Double-plays: B. Jimenez, H.H. Ford and M.A. González
Bases on balls: O. Tuero 4, P. Flournoy 2, P. Cockrell 1
Strikeouts: O. Tuero 4, P. Flournoy 1, P. Cockrell 0
Winning pitcher: O. Tuero
Losing pitcher: P. Flournoy
Umpires: Alfredo Cabrera (home) and José M. Magrinat (bases)
Scorer: Julio Franquiz

GAME TEN: SATURDAY, DECEMBER 25, 1920, AT ALMENDARES PARK

Bacharach	Pos	AB	R	H	O	A	E
S. Valdés	lf	4	1	0	3	0	0
P. Cockrell	cf	2	3	0	0	0	0
M. Clark	ss	4	1	2	1	1	0
M. Martinez	3b	4	1	2	2	1	0
A. Parpetti	1b	4	0	1	8	0	0
J. Arumiz	2b	3	1	0	1	1	1
F. Campos	rf	1	0	0	0	0	0
V. Rodríguez	c	4	1	1	11	0	0
M.J. Ryan	p	4	1	1	0	3	0
J. Teran	2b	1	0	1	0	0	0
J.A. Rodríguez	p	1	0	1	1	0	0
Totals		36	9	9	27	6	1

Almendares	Pos	AB	R	H	O	A	E
B. Portuondo	3b	3	1	0	3	2	0
R. González	2b	5	0	2	1	4	0
B. Acosta	lf	3	2	1	3	0	0
P. Chacon	ss	5	0	2	3	3	0
C. Torriente	cf	5	1	3	2	0	1
M. Guerra	1b	5	1	1	9	0	0
R. Herrera	rf	3	0	0	0	0	0
E. Abreu	c	4	0	0	6	1	0
I. Fabre	p	3	0	0	0	1	0
J. Mendez	(x)	1	0	0	0	0	0
J. Hernandez	p	1	0	0	0	0	0
Totals		37	5	10	27	11	1

(x) — Out for I. Fabre in seventh.

| Bacharach Giants | 000 | 170 | 001 — 9 |
| Almendares | 203 | 000 | 000 — 5 |

Home runs: C. Torriente
Three-base hits: M. Guerra
Two-base hits: P. Chacon, J. Teran
Sacrifice hits: M. Martinez
Stolen bases: B. Portuondo (2), B. Acosta, P. Cockrell, J. Hernandez
Double-plays: P. Chacon and M. Guerra; P. Chacon, R. González and M. Guerra
Bases on balls: M.J. Ryan 4, I. Fabre 5, J. Hernandez 2
Strikeouts: M.J. Ryan 9, I. Fabre 5, J. Hernandez 1
Hit by pitcher: I. Fabre 1 (A. Parpetti); M.C. Ryan 1 (R. Herrera)
Passed balls: V. Rodríguez 1
Winning pitcher: M.J. Ryan
Losing pitcher: I. Fabre
Time: 2 hours 10 minutes
Umpires: Alfredo Cabrera (home) and José M. Magrinat (bases)
Scorer: Julio Franquiz

GAME ELEVEN: SATURDAY, JANUARY 1, 1921, AT ALMENDARES PARK

Bacharach	*OS*	*AB*	*R*	*H*	*O*	*A*	*E*
S. Valdés	lf	3	0	0	0	0	0
M. Clark	ss	4	0	1	0	3	1
M. Martinez	3b	3	0	0	0	0	1
A. Parpetti	rf	3	0	0	3	0	0
T. Allen	1b	4	0	0	11	0	0
V. Rodríguez	c	4	0	1	10	0	0
J. Arumiz	2b	3	1	1	2	1	0
M. Clemente	cf	3	1	1	1	0	1
R. Redding	p	4	0	2	0	6	0
Totals		32	2	6	27	10	2

Habana	*Pos*	*AB*	*R*	*H*	*O*	*A*	*E*
B. Jimenez	2b	3	1	1	1	4	0
J. Rodríguez	3b	4	0	0	0	1	2
M. Cueto	3b	2	0	1	1	0	0
R. Almeida	rf	3	0	0	0	0	0
M.A. González	1b	4	0	0	16	0	0
J. López	lf	2	0	0	1	0	0
H.H. Ford	ss	3	0	0	3	1	0
R. Torres	c	4	0	0	5	1	0
O. Tuero	p	2	0	0	0	7	0
F. Hungo	(x)	1	0	0	0	0	0
W.C. Stewart	p	1	0	0	0	2	0
Totals		29	1	2	27	16	2

(x) — Out for O. Tuero in eighth.

| Bacharach Giants | 000 | 000 | 200 — 2 |
| Habana | 000 | 001 | 000 — 1 |

Three-base hits: B. Jimenez
Sacrifice hits: R. Almeida, M. Cueto, J. Arumiz
Stolen bases: B. Jimenez, J. López, J. Rodríguez
Double-plays: O. Tuero, H.H. Ford and M.A. González
Bases on balls: O. Tuero 4, W.C. Stewart 0, R. Redding 5
Strikeouts: O. Tuero 2, W.C. Stewart 0, R. Redding 9
Balks: Off R. Redding 1
Winning pitcher: R. Redding
Losing pitcher: O. Tuero
Umpires: Alfredo Cabrera (home) and José M. Magrinat (bases)
Scorer: Hilario Franquiz

GAME TWELVE: MONDAY, JANUARY 3, 1921, AT ALMENDARES PARK

Habana	*Pos*	*AB*	*R*	*H*	*O*	*A*	*E*
B. Jimenez	2b	3	3	1	5	2	0
J. Rodríguez	3b	5	0	3	0	4	0
M. Cueto	cf	4	0	1	1	0	0

Bacharach	*Pos*	*AB*	*R*	*H*	*O*	*A*	*E*
S. Valdés	lf	3	0	2	5	0	0
M. Clark	ss	4	0	2	2	2	1
M. Martinez	3b	4	0	0	0	2	0

Habana	Pos	AB	R	H	O	A	E
R. Almeida	rf	4	0	0	0	0	0
M.A. González	c	4	0	1	17	1	0
J. López	lf	4	0	2	0	0	0
H.H. Ford	ss	4	0	0	6	4	0
F. Hungo	1b	3	1	2	8	0	0
J. Acosta	p	3	0	0	0	2	0
O. Rodríguez	lf	0	0	0	0	0	0
Totals		34	4	10	27	13	0

Bacharach	Pos	AB	R	H	O	A	E
A. Parpetti	1b	4	0	1	10	1	0
J. Menocal	cf	4	0	0	8	0	1
V. Rodríguez	c	4	0	0	8	0	1
M. Clemente	rf	3	0	1	1	0	0
J. Arumiz	2b	3	0	1	0	3	2
R. Redding	p	3	0	1	1	5	0
Totals		31	0	8	27	13	4

Habana	101	100	001 — 4
Bacharach Giants	000	000	000 — 0

Two-base hits: F. Hungo
Sacrifice hits: R. Almeida, J. Acosta
Stolen bases: M. Cueto, S. Valdés
Double-plays: B. Jimenez, H.H. Ford and F. Hungo; J. Arumiz, D. Clark and A. Parpetti
Bases on balls: J. Acosta 2, R. Redding 4
Strikeouts: J. Acosta 5, R. Redding 3
Passed balls: M.A. Gonzále
Winning pitcher: J. Acosta
Losing pitcher: R. Redding
Umpires: Alfredo Cabrera (home) and José M. Magrinat (bases)
Scorer: Julio Franquiz

GAME THIRTEEN: SATURDAY, JANUARY 8, 1921, AT ALMENDARES PARK

Almendares	Pos	AB	R	H	O	A	E
B. Acosta	lf	4	1	2	1	0	0
E. González	2b	1	1	1	0	1	0
C. Torriente	cf	5	0	0	2	0	0
P. Chacon	ss	3	1	1	1	2	1
M. Guerra	1b	5	1	1	9	0	0
R. González	3b	2	0	2	2	1	1
R. Herrera	rf,2b	4	1	1	2	2	1
E. Abreu	c	2	1	0	7	0	0
J. Mendez	p	3	1	2	1	4	0
J. Hernandez	rf	3	0	1	2	0	0
I. Fabre	p	0	0	0	0	0	0
Totals		32	7	11	27	10	3

Bacharach	Pos	AB	R	H	O	A	E
S. Valdés	lf	4	1	1	4	0	0
M. Clark	ss	4	0	0	2	1	0
M. Martinez	3b	4	2	2	2	0	0
E. Pedroso	1b	4	0	1	6	0	2
V. Rodríguez	c	4	0	1	9	3	0
M. Clemente	rf	3	0	1	0	0	0
J. Menocal	cf	3	0	0	2	0	0
M.F. Villarin	2b	3	1	1	1	1	1
P. Flournoy	p	0	0	0	0	0	1
J. Arumiz	2b	1	0	0	0	0	0
J.A. Rodríguez	p	4	1	1	1	5	0
R. Redding	rf	1	0	0	0	0	0
Totals		35	4	8	27	10	4

Almendares	121	200	001 — 7
Bacharach Giants	003	010	000 — 4

Home runs: M. Guerra
Three-base hits: B. Acosta
Two-base hits: P. Chacon, M. Clemente
Sacrifice hits: R. Herrera, D. Clark y J. Hernandez
Stolen bases: P. Chacon, R. González (2), V. Rodríguez, S. Valdés
Double-plays: J.A. Rodríguez, V. Rodríguez and E. Pedroso
Bases on balls: P. Flournoy 2, J.A. Rodríguez 3, J. Mendez 1, I. Fabre 0
Strikeouts: P. Flournoy 0, J.A. Rodríguez 4, J. Mendez 4, I. Fabre 0
Hit by pitcher: J. Mendez 1 (M. Clemente); J.A. Rodríguez 2 (R. González, P. Chacon)
Passed balls: V. Rodríguez (2)
Winning pitcher: J. Mendez
Losing pitcher: P. Flournoy
Time: 2 hours 15 minutes
Umpires: Alfredo Cabrera (home) and José M. Magrinat (bases)
Scorer: Julio Franquiz

GAME FOURTEEN: SUNDAY, JANUARY 9, 1921, AT ALMENDARES PARK

Bacharach	Pos	AB	R	H	O	A	E
S. Valdés	lf	4	0	1	5	0	0
M. Clark	ss	4	2	1	2	3	1
M. Martinez	3b	3	1	0	2	3	0
E. Pedroso	1b	2	0	0	9	2	1
J.A. Rodríguez	rf	3	0	0	1	0	0
R. Redding	p	4	0	0	0	1	0
V. Rodríguez	c	4	0	2	7	1	0
J. Menocal	cf	4	0	1	2	0	1
M.F. Villarin	2b	3	0	0	4	2	0
Totals		31	3	5	32	12	3

Habana	Pos	AB	R	H	O	A	E
B. Jimenez	2b	5	1	1	2	4	0
H.H. Ford	ss	4	1	0	3	6	1
M. Cueto	lf	5	0	2	2	1	0
R. Almeida	rf	4	0	0	0	0	0
M.A. González	1b	4	1	0	15	3	1
J. López	lf	5	0	2	0	0	0
O. Rodríguez	3b	4	1	0	2	3	0
R. Torres	c	4	0	1	7	1	0
W.C. Stewart	p	1	0	0	2	5	0
F. Hungo	(x)	1	0	0	0	0	0
J. Acosta	p	0	0	0	0	1	0
Totals		37	4	6	33	24	2

(x)—Out for W.C. Stewart in ninth.

Bacharach Giants	000	100	002	00 — 3
Habana	200	100	000	01 — 4

Two outs when winning scored in eleventh inning
Two-base hits: M. Clark
Sacrifice hits: M.A. González, E. Pedroso, W.C. Stewart, R. Torres
Stolen bases: B. Jimenez, M. Cueto, D. Clark, O. Rodríguez, R. Almeida
Double-plays: H.H. Ford a B. Jimenez a M.A. González; W.C. Stewart a O. Rodríguez a M.A. González;
   M. Cueto a M.A. González; W.C. Stewart a H.H. Ford
Bases on balls: W.C. Stewart 7, J. Acosta 0, R. Redding 3
Strikeouts: W.C. Stewart 3, J. Acosta 1, R. Redding 4
Hit by pitcher: R. Redding 1 (W.C. Stewart)
Passed balls: V. Rodríguez (2)
Winning pitcher: J. Acosta
Losing pitcher: R. Redding
Umpires: Alfredo Cabrera (home) and José M. Magrinat (bases)
Scorer: Hilario Franquiz

GAME FIFTEEN: MONDAY, JANUARY 10, 1921, AT ALMENDARES PARK

Bacharach	Pos	AB	R	H	O	A	E
S. Valdés	lf	4	0	1	0	0	0
M. Clemente	3b	3	0	0	0	3	0
R. Redding	rf	4	0	2	0	0	0
E. Pedroso	1b	3	0	1	11	0	1
V. Rodríguez	c	3	0	0	6	3	0
J. Menocal	cf	3	0	0	0	0	0
J. Arumiz	2b	4	0	1	3	3	0
M.F. Villarin	ss	3	0	0	3	1	2
P. Flournoy	p	2	0	0	1	5	0
M. Martinez	(x)	1	0	0	0	0	0
T. Allen	(xx)	1	0	0	0	0	0
Totals		30	0	5	24	15	3

Almendares	Pos	AB	R	H	O	A	E
J. Mendez	rf	4	1	0	0	0	0
P. Palmero	lf	3	0	1	1	0	0
C. Torriente	cf	1	2	0	0	0	0
P. Chacon	ss	3	0	2	2	1	0
M. Guerra	1b	4	0	2	14	0	0
R. González	3b	1	0	0	2	6	0
R. Herrera	2b	3	0	0	1	4	0
E. Abreu	c	3	0	0	7	1	0
J. Hernandez	p	3	1	2	0	3	0
Totals		23	4	7	27	15	1

(x)—Out for J. Menocal in ninth.
(xx)—Out for M. Villarin in ninth.

Bacharach Giants	000	000	000 — 0
Almendares	100	030	00x — 4

Sacrifice hits: R. González
Stolen bases: S. Valdés, J. Mendez

Double-plays: P. Flournoy and E. Pedroso; J. Arumiz and E. Pedroso
Bases on balls: P. Flournoy 3, J. Hernandez 4
Strikeouts: P. Flournoy 5, J. Hernandez 5
Hit by pitcher: P. Flournoy 1 (C. Torriente)
Winning ptcher: J. Hernandez
Losing pitcher: P. Flournoy
Time: 2 hours
Umpires: Alfredo Cabrera (home) and José M. Magrinat (bases)
Scorer: Julio Franquiz

GAME SIXTEEN: WEDNESDAY, JANUARY 12, 1921, AT ALMENDARES PARK

Bacharach	Pos	AB	R	H	O	A	E		Almendares	Pos	AB	R	H	O	A	E
S. Valdés	lf	4	0	0	3	0	0		B. Portuondo	3b	2	0	0	1	1	0
M. Clemente	3b	4	0	2	0	3	0		E. González	2b	5	0	0	3	4	0
M. Clark	ss	4	0	2	1	1	2		C. Torriente	cf	4	3	3	1	0	0
R. Redding	p	4	0	0	1	1	1		P. Chacon	ss	3	2	1	2	4	0
E. Pedroso	1b	3	0	1	8	0	2		B. Acosta	lf	3	2	0	2	0	0
V. Rodríguez	c	3	0	0	7	0	1		M. Guerra	1b	4	2	3	12	0	0
J. Menocal	cf	3	0	1	3	0	0		E. Abreu	c	4	1	2	6	0	0
M.F. Villarin	2b	3	0	0	0	0	0		R. Herrera	rf	3	1	2	0	1	0
J. Arumiz	rf	1	0	1	1	0	0		A. Luque	p	4	0	0	0	4	0
P. Alonso	rf	1	0	0	0	0	0		R. González	3b	3	0	1	0	1	0
Totals		30	0	7	24	5	6		I. Fabre	lf	0	0	0	0	0	0
									J. Hernandez	cf	1	0	1	0	0	0
									Totals		36	11	13	27	15	0

Bacharach Giants	000	000	000 — 0
Almendares	630	100	10x — 11

Summary:
Three-base hits: C. Torriente (3), M. Guerra
Two-base hits: J. Hernandez
Sacrifice hits: P. Chacon
Double-plays: P. Chacon to E. González to M. Guerra; A. Luque, P. Chacon to M. Guerra
Bases on balls: R. Redding 2, A. Luque 1
Strikeouts: R. Redding 2, A. Luque 4
Passed balls: V. Rodríguez 1
Winning Pitcher: A. Luque
Losing Pitcher: R. Redding
Time: 1 hour 45 minutes
Umpires: Alfredo Cabrera (home) and José M. Magrinat (bases)
Scorer: Julio Franquiz

GAME SEVENTEEN: THURSDAY, JANUARY 13, 1921, AT ALMENDARES PARK

Habana	Pos	AB	R	H	O	A	E		Bacharach	Pos	AB	R	H	O	A	E
B. Jimenez	2b	4	0	0	3	3	0		S. Valdés	lf	2	0	0	1	0	0
J. Rodríguez	3b	4	0	2	0	0	0		M. Clemente	3b	4	0	2	2	3	0
M. Cueto	cf	3	0	0	2	0	0		R. Redding	rf	4	0	0	1	0	0
R. Almeida	rf	4	0	1	0	0	0		E. Pedroso	1b	3	0	1	8	0	0
M.A. González	1b	4	0	1	10	0	0		V. Rodríguez	c	3	0	0	5	0	0
J. López	lf	4	1	2	1	0	0		P. Alonso	cf	3	0	0	2	2	0
H.H. Ford	ss	4	1	2	3	5	0		J. Menocal	ss	2	0	0	6	2	0
R. Torres	c	4	0	0	8	1	0		M.F. Villarin	3b	3	0	0	2	1	0
W.C. Stewart	p	1	0	0	0	2	0		P. Flournoy	p	3	0	0	0	2	0
J. Acosta	p	0	0	0	0	2	0		Totals		27	0	3	27	10	0

Habana	Pos	AB	R	H	O	A	E		Bacharach	Pos	AB	R	H	O	A	E
O. Tuero	p	1	0	0	0	2	0									
Totals		33	2	8	27	17	0									

Habana		000	000	200 — 2
Bacharach Giants		000	000	000 — 0

Three-base hits: J. Rodríguez, H.H. Ford
Two-base hits: J. Rodríguez
Stolen Bases: J. López
Double-plays: W.C. Stewart to H.H. Ford to M.A. González; B. Jimenez to H.H. Ford to M.A. González
Bases on balls: P. Flournoy 1, W.C. Stewart 1, J. Acosta 1, O. Tuero 2
Strikeouts: P. Flournoy 5, W.C. Stewart 3, J. Acosta 0, O. Tuero 0
Hit by pitcher: P. Flournoy 1 (J. Acosta)
Winning pitcher: J. Acosta
Losing pitcher: P. Flournoy
Umpires: Alfredo Cabrera (home) and José M. Magrinat (bases)
Scorer: Julio Franquiz

FINAL STATISTICS
BACHARACH GIANTS—1920–1921

Individual Pitching

Pitcher	G	GS	GC	W	L	PC	IP	R	H	BB	SO	ERT
Phil Cockrell	1	0	0	0	0	.000						
Willis Pud Flournoy	6	5	2	0	6	.000						
Richard Redding	9	9	7	1	6	.143						
José A. Rodríguez	1	0	0	0	0	.000						
Merven J. Ryan	3	3	3	3	0	1.000						
Totals	20	17	12	4	12	.250						

Individual Batting

Player	Pos	G	AB	R	H	2b	3b	HR	SH	SB	Pct
Todd Allen	1b	9	25	2	6	0	0	0		0	.244
Charles Blackwell	lf	9	18	1	7	0	1	0		0	.389
Oscar Charleston	cf	9	39	9	16	2	0	0		6	.471
Morten Clark	2b,ss	15	60	8	21	1	0	0		4	.350
Phil Cockrell	p,rf	6	11	4	0	0	0	0		0	.000
S.R. "Eddie" Dewitt	3b	8	27	4	7	0	0	0		2	.253
Pud Flournoy	p	6	10	0	0	0	0	0		0	.000
Richard Lundy	ss	5	12	2	2	0	0	0		1	.167
Richard Redding	p,rf	13	35	1	9	1	0	0		0	.257
Julio Rojo	c	4	10	2	4	0	0	0		0	.400
Merven J. Ryan	p,rf	6	17	1	3	0	0	0		0	.176
Louis Santop	c,rf	9	35	1	13	3	1	0		2	.371
José Pio Alonso	rf,cf	2	4	0	0	0	0	0		0	.000
José Arumiz	2b	6	25	0	7	0	0	0		0	.280
Francisco Campos	2b,rf	2	3	1	0	0	0	0		0	.000
Abelardo Casanas	rf	1	0	0	0	0	0	0		0	.000
Mario Clemente	c,rf,3b	6	18	1	7	1	0	0		0	.389
Manelo Martinez	3b	7	22	4	4	0	0	0		0	.182
J. Menocal	cf,ss	5	16	0	2	0	0	0		0	.125
Agustin Parpetti	1b,rf	7	25	0	7	0	0	0		1	.280
Eustaquio Pedroso	1b	5	15	2	4	0	0	0		0	.267
José Ag. Rodríguez	p,rf	4	11	1	2	0	0	0		0	.182
Vicente Rodríguez	c	9	30	2	6	0	0	0		1	.200

Player	Pos	G	AB	R	H	2b	3b	HR	SH	SB	Pct
Julio Teran	2b	6	18	1	5	2	0	0		1	.278
Severino Valdés	lf	8	28	2	5	1	0	0		3	.179
M.F. Villarin	2b,3b,ss	5	13	0	1	0	0	0		0	.077
Totals		17	529	62	129	11	2	0		21	.243

Individual Fielding

Player	Pos	G		O	A	E		Pct
Todd Allen	1b	9		46	0	1		.979
Charles Blackwell	lf	9		16	1	1		.944
Oscar Charleston	cf	9		21	3	0		1.000
Morten Clark	2b,ss	15		27	30	13		.814
Phil Cockrell	p,rf	6		3	1	0		1.000
S.R. "Eddie" Dewitt	3b	8		7	9	4		.800
Pud Flournoy	p	6		1	12	1		.929
Richard Lundy	ss	5		11	15	3		.897
Richard Redding	p,rf	13		2	29	2		.939
Julio Rojo	c	4		11	7	1		.947
Merven J. Ryan	p,rf	6		1	11	1		.923
Louis Santop	c,rf	9		33	7	2		.952
José Pio Alonso	rf,cf	2		2	2	0		1.000
José Arumiz	2b	6		7	8	3		.833
Francisco Campos	2b,rf	2		4	3	0		1.000
Abelardo Casanas	rf	1		0	0	0		.000
Mario Clemente	c,rf,3b	6		4	9	1		.929
Manelo Martinez	3b	7		7	8	1		.938
J. Menocal	cf,ss	5		11	4	1		.938
Agustin Parpetti	1b,rf	7		55	3	2		.967
Eustaquio Pedroso	1b	5		42	2	6		.880
José Ag. Rodríguez	p,rf	4		3	5	0		1.000
Vicente Rodríguez	c	9		65	10	2		.974
Julio Teran	2b	6		6	14	1		.952
Severino Valdés	lf	8		21	0	0		1.000
M.F. Villarin	2b,3b,ss	5		8	6	3		.824
Totals		17	3	346	18	4	4	8	.929

Bibliography

Original List of Works

Degado, Gabino and Severo Nieto. *Béisbol Cubano (Récords y Estadísticas)*. Havana: Editorial Lex, 1955. 186 pages.

Nieto, Severo. *Atletismo: Juegos Deportivos Panamericanos 1951–1991*. Havana: Editorial Científico-Técnica, 1995.

Nieto Fernández, Severo. *Conrado Marrero: El Premier*. Havana: Editorial Científico-Técnica, 2000. 281 pages.

_____. *José Méndez: El Diamante Negro*. Havana: Editorial Científico-Técnica, 2004. 203 pages.

Additional Works Cited by Editors

Bjarkman, Peter C. *A History of Cuban Baseball, 1864–2006*. Jefferson, NC, and London: McFarland, 2007.

Boswell, Thomas. *How Life Imitates the World Series*. New York: Simon and Schuster, 1982.

Casas, Edel, Jorge Alfonso, and Alberto Pestana. *Viva y en juego [Alive and playing]*. Havana: Editorial Científico-Técnica, 1986.

Díez Muro, Raúl. *Historia del base ball profesional de Cuba: Libro official de la Liga del Base Ball Profesional Cubana*. 3rd edition. Havana: self-published, 1949.

González Echevarría, Roberto. *The Pride of Havana: A History of Cuban Baseball*. New York and London: Oxford University Press, 1999.

Jamail, Milton. *Full Count: Inside Cuban Baseball*. Carbondale and Edwardsville: Southern Illinois University Press, 2000.

Letusé La O, Rogelio Augusto. *Béisbol Términos y Anécdotas [Baseball Terms and Anecdotes]*. Havana: Editorial Científico-Técnica, 2003. 200 pages.

Martin, Eddy. *Memorias a los setenta y... [Memories at seventy and...]*. Havana: Editorial Si-Mar, S.A., 2004. 315 pages.

Santana Alonso, Alfredo. *Martín Dihigo — El Inmortal del Béisbol*. Havana: Editorial Científico-Técnica, 1997. 140 pages.

Welch, Matt. "Foul ball: How a communist dictatorship and a U.S. embargo has silenced a Cuban historian," in: *Reason-online* (an internet on-line magazine at www.reason.com), June 2002.

Player Index

This is an index to player rosters only. The reader may use it to locate each roster in which a player appears; further references to the player may be found wherever information about the same team in the same year appears in the book.

Acosta, Baldomero 156
Acosta, Julian 180
Allen, Newt 155
Allen, Todd 129
Allen, Toussaint 148, 218
Arago, Hector 179
Arteaga, Virginio 180

Bankhead, Samuel "Sammy" 164, 172
Barbee, Lamb "Bud" 172
Barbour, Jess 206
Bauchman, Harry 206
Bernal, Lazaro 180
Blackwell, Charles 148, 218
Booker, James 92, 104
Bowman, Bill 26
Bowman, Emmett 26, 45, 56
Bradley, Phil 78, 92
Brazelton, John Clarkson 206
Brown, Barney 164
Brown, Raymond 164
Buckner, Harry 26, 35, 45, 78
Bustamente, Luis 26, 45

Calvo, Oscar del 180
Campos, Francisco "Cisco" 179
Carlisle, Matthew 164
Carter, Charles "Kid" 11
Chacon, Pelayo 155
Charleston, Oscar 129, 148, 155, 218
Clark, Cleveland "Chiflan" 179
Clark, Dell 116
Clark, Morten 129, 148, 218
Cooper, Andy 155
Cozart, Haywood "Harry" 172
Crespo, Juan "Bibi" 179
Cueto, Manuel 156

Daniels, Leon 155
Davis, John 56
DeMoss, Elwood 129

DeWith, S.R. "Eddie" 148, 218
Díaz, Pedro 179
Dihigo, Martin 155
Dismukes, William 116, 206
Dougherty, Charles 92
Doy, Daniel 180
Dreke, Valentin 155
Dukes, Thomas 164
Dunbar, Ashby 78
Duncan, Frank 92, 206

Earle, Charles B. 56, 78

Fajo, Mario 180
Fernandez, José Maria 155, 180
Figarola, Rafael 104
Flournoy, Willis "Pud" 148, 218
Forbes, Joe 116
Foster, Andrew "Rube" 11, 15, 35, 92, 206
Francis, William 104

Gans, Robert 78, 104, 206
García, Regino 45
Garmendia, Oscar 180
Gaston, Alexander 155
Gatewood, Bill 45
Gibson, Joshua 164, 172
Grant, Charles 11, 15
Grant, LeRoy 104
Green, Peter "Ed" 116
Guerra, Fermin 180
Gutiérrez, Joaquin 179

Handy, William 116
Harris, Elander Victor "Vic" 164, 172
Harvey, Frank 116
Henderson, Art 155
Hernandez, Ricardo 78
Herrera, Ramon 155
Hidalgo, Manuel "Chino" 180
Hill, J. Preston "Pete" 15, 35, 45, 56, 78, 92, 206

233